D1742293

FULFILLING *the*
TRUST

50 Years of Shaping Muslim Religious Life in Singapore

FULFILLING *the*

TRUST

50 Years of Shaping Muslim Religious Life in Singapore

Edited by

Norshahril Saat

Majlis Ugama Islam Singapura
(Islamic Religious Council of Singapore)

NEW JERSEY · LONDON · SINGAPORE · BEIJING · SHANGHAI · HONG KONG · TAIPEI · CHENNAI · TOKYO

Published by

World Scientific Publishing Co. Pte. Ltd.

5 Toh Tuck Link, Singapore 596224

USA office: 27 Warren Street, Suite 401-402, Hackensack, NJ 07601

UK office: 57 Shelton Street, Covent Garden, London WC2H 9HE

National Library Board, Singapore Cataloguing in Publication Data
Name(s): Norshahril Saat, editor.
Title: Fulfilling the trust : 50 years of shaping Muslim religious life in Singapore /
    editor, Dr Norshahril Saat.
Description: Singapore : World Scientific Publishing Co Pte Ltd, [2018] |
    Includes bibliographical references and index.
Identifier(s): OCN 1040690673 | ISBN 978-981-32-7426-6
Subject(s): LCSH: Islamic Religious Council of Singapore | Muslims--Singapore. |
    Islam--Singapore.
Classification: DDC 297.65095957--dc23

British Library Cataloguing-in-Publication Data
A catalogue record for this book is available from the British Library.

Copyright © 2018 by Majlis Ugama Islam Singapura (MUIS)

All rights reserved.

For any available supplementary material, please visit
https://www.worldscientific.com/worldscibooks/10.1142/11099#t=suppl

Desk Editors: Karimah Samsudin and Rhaimie Wahap

Typeset by Stallion Press
Email: enquiries@stallionpress.com

Printed in Singapore

Contents

Acronyms ix

Foreword by Masagos Zulkifli Masagos
Mohamad, Minister for the Environment
and Water Resources and Minister-in-Charge
of Muslim Affairs xv

Foreword by Mohammad Alami Musa,
Muis President xix

Foreword by Abdul Razak Maricar,
Muis Chief Executive xxi

Foreword by Dr Mohamed Fatris Bakaram,
Mufti of Singapore xxv

Muis at 50: A Personal Reflection by
Dr Yaacob Ibrahim, Former Minister
for Communications and Information,
Minister-in-Charge of Muslim Affairs
and Minister-in-Charge of Cyber Security xxxi

Acknowledgements xlvii

Note on Translation, Spelling, and Other
Conventions xlix

Introduction: Towards a Socio-Historical
Analysis of Muis Policies 1
Norshahril Saat

Part 1 — Building Muis' Foundations   **13**

1   The Institutionalisation of Islam
in Singapore: The Administration
of Muslim Law Act and the Birth
of a 'Majlis Ugama'   15
Alfian Yasrif Kuchit

2   Institution Building and Community
Development : Dynamics of Muis' Dual
Identity   33
Azree Rahim and Yazid Mohamed Ali

**Part 2 — Shaping Religious Life
and Education**   **55**

3   Contextualisation and Modernisation:
Islamic Thought through *Fatwas* in
Singapore   57
Nazirudin Nasir

4   Developing Asatizah in Singapore
through the Asatizah Recognition Scheme   73
*Mohammad Hannan Hassan and
Irwan Mohd Hadi Shuhaimy*

5   Madrasah Education:
A Journey Towards Excellence   89
*Farah Mahamood Aljunied and
Zalman Putra Ahmad Ali*

6   Rethinking Islamic Education for
the Young   111
*Farah Mahamood Aljunied and
Mohamad Khidir Abdul Rahman*

Part 3 — Managing Assets and Services   **129**

7   Mosques in Singapore: Managing
Expectations and the Future Ahead   131
Mohamad Helmy Mohd Isa

8   Doing Things Differently: *Zakat* and
     Social Development in Singapore   149
     Zulfadhli Ghazali

9   Enhancing Community Assets:
     Sustaining the *Wakaf* Legacy   165
     Masagoes Muhammad Isyak

10   *Haj* Aspirations: A 'Hybrid' of Public
     and Private Models for Singapore   179
     Abdul Rahim Saleh

11   Managing Demand Growth for
     Halal Food   199
     Dewi Hartaty Suratty

12   Seeking the Meaning of Sacrifice:
     Evolution of *Korban* in Singapore   221
     Sakdun Sardi

**Part 4 — Beyond the Singapore Muslim
          Community**   **239**

13   International Networking: Bringing
     the World to Muis   241
     Asri Aziz

14   Spirit of Blessings to All: Muis'
     Contribution to Social Cohesion   255
     *Zalman Putra Ahmad Ali and
     Zainul Abidin Ibrahim*

Conclusion: Diversity and Disruption:
Charting New Pathways for the Future   275
Albakri Ahmad and Zalman Putra Ahmad Ali

Profile of Contributors   293

Glossary   303

Past & Present Images   309

Index   335

Acronyms

ADIL	—	Adult Islamic Learning
AEDP	—	Asatizah Executive Development Programme
AKV	—	Approved Korban Vendor
aLIVE	—	Learning Islamic Values Everyday
AMAL	—	Administration of Mosque and Leadership
AMED	—	Asia-Middle East Dialogue
AMLA	—	Administration of Muslim Law Act
AMTAS	—	Association of Muslim Travel Agents Singapore
ARB	—	Asatizah Recognition Board
ARS	—	Asatizah Recognition Scheme
AVA	—	Agri-Food and Veterinary Authority of Singapore
BE	—	Business Excellence
BOG	—	Board of Governors
CDC	—	Community Development Council
CDP	—	Curriculum Development Project
CE	—	Compulsory Education
CEDAW	—	The Convention on the Elimination of all Forms of Discrimination against Women
CIRES	—	Comprehensive Islamic Religious Education System
CPE	—	Continuous Professional Education
CPF	—	Central Provident Fund
CRISPR	—	Clustered Regularly Interspaced Short Palindromic Repeats

CSCP	— Civil Service Computerisation Programme
DVP	— Muis Distinguished Visitor Programme
EIC	— East India Company
EMA	— Emergency Medical Assistance
EMC	— Enhanced Mosque Cluster
EMS	— English, Mathematics and Science
EPS	— Empowerment Partnership Scheme
ESCAS	— Exporter Supply Chain Assurance System
FA	— Financial Assistance
FCO	— Foreign and Commonwealth Office
FDC	— Family Development Centre
GSA	— General Sales Agent
GSFTA	— Gulf Cooperation Council (GCC) — Singapore Free Trade Agreement
HACCP	— Hazard Analysis Critical Control Point
HalMQ	— Halal Quality Management System
HBI	— Himpunan Belia Islam (Muslim Youth Assembly)
HDB	— Housing Development Board
HFMD	— Hand, Foot and Mouth Disease
HOTA	— Human Organ Transplant Act
HPB	— Health Promotion Board
IBDP	— International Baccalaureate Diploma Programme
IRCC	— Inter-Racial and Religious Confidence Circles
IRO	— Inter-Religious Organisation
ISA	— Internal Security Act
ISO	— International Organisation for Standardisation
JBPM	— Joint Committee of Madrasah Education
JCM	— Joint Committee of Madrasah
JI	— Jemaah Islamiah
JKMS	— Singapore Mosques Korban Committee
JMS	— Joint Madrasah System
KBE	— Knowledge-Based Economy

M3YP	—	Muis 3-Year Plan
MA	—	Muis Academy
MAAP	—	Muis Asatizah Immersion/Attachment Programme
MABIMS	—	Unofficial Meeting of Religious Affairs Ministers of Brunei, Indonesia, Malaysia and Singapore
MAIK	—	Majlis Agama Islam Kelantan
MBF	—	Mosque Building Fund
MBMF	—	Mosque Building and Mendaki Fund
MCD	—	Ministry of Community Development
MCF	—	Master Content Framework
MEC	—	Mosque Executive Chairman
MMB	—	Mosque Management Board
MMC	—	Mosque Madrasah Convention
MMO	—	Malay/Muslim Organisation
MODS	—	Mosque Officer Development Scheme
MOE	—	Ministry of Education
MSF	—	Ministry of Social and Family Development
MUIS	—	Islamic Religious Council of Singapore
NIE	—	National Institute of Education
OAP	—	Overseas Attachment Programme
OIE	—	World Organisation for Animal Health
PEL	—	Professional Executive Leadership
PIENet	—	Private Islamic Education Network
PRC	—	Pilgrimage Review Committee
PRISM	—	Programme for RISEAP Members
PROMAS	—	Progress Fund Madrasah Assistance Scheme
PS21	—	Public Sector in the 21st Century
PSLE	—	Primary School Leaving Examination
PST	—	Public Sector Transformation
QTRS	—	Qur'an Teachers Recognition Scheme
REAP	—	Religious Education Advisory Panel
RED	—	Religious Education Department
REU	—	Religious Education Unit
RICAP	—	Religious Resilience, Inclusive, Contributive, Adaptive, Progressive

RISEAP	—	Regional Islamic Da'wah Council of Southeast Asia and the Pacific
RLAF	—	Rahmatan lil Alamin Foundation
ROMM	—	Registry of Muslim Marriages
RRG	—	Religious Rehabilitation Group
SBACC	—	Singapore Business Advisors and Consultants Council
SD	—	Social Development
SDO	—	Social Development Officer
SIES	—	Singapore Islamic Education System
SLO	—	Student Liaison Officer
SMI	—	Singapore Muslim Identity
SPAO	—	Singapore Pilgrims' Affairs Office
SQA	—	Singapore Quality Award
SSO	—	Social Service Office
TAP	—	Technical Advisory Panel
VWO	—	Volunteer Welfare Organisation
WITS	—	Work Improvement Teams

Forewords

Masagos Zulkifli Masagos Mohamad
Minister for the Environment and
Water Resources and Minister-in-Charge
of Muslim Affairs

The early years of Muis' establishment was a time of change for the Muslim community in Singapore. Singapore's rapid industrialisation and urbanisation transformed the way we lived, as individuals, as families, and as a community. Like other Singaporeans, members of the community moved out of the *kampungs* into the HDB estates and found new jobs in new industries. Old village mosques were replaced by new mosques in our heartlands. As with all change, not all were at ease. For some in the community, there was a sense of uncertainty and anxiety, especially in the early years of a new nation. In its formative years, how could Muis, a nascent body of just seven staff, fulfil its mission to look after the community's need for religious guidance and services?

Muis has since worked very hard over the years to earn the trust and confidence of the community. It has forged closer rapport with the community and strived to meet its evolving needs and aspirations. Today, Muis provides indispensable services, such as *haj* management, *halal* certification, *wakaf* management, and *zakat* collection. It has invested in raising the standards of religious education, and enhanced the access to quality Islamic learning for every Muslim, so that Muslims in Singapore can have a considerable understanding and practice of Islam attuned to the context of Singapore's modern, multi-racial, and multi-religious society and secular state.

Singapore's experience as a nation has been unique. Muis' journey has therefore been also one of continuous policy innovation and determined implementation, to balance the needs of a fast-developing country, a fast-changing society, and a Muslim community that holds dear faith and traditions. To cite an example, one of the most pivotal policies in the history of Muis and our community is the mosque building programme. Seeing the community struggle to raise funds for a new mosque in Toa Payoh, Founding Prime Minister Mr Lee Kuan Yew proposed that Muis set up the Mosque Building Fund (MBF), through which Muslims could contribute voluntarily and pool resources for mosque development. The setting up of the MBF was a masterstroke. Since its launch in 1975, the MBF has successfully funded the building of modern mosques that catered to the needs of the growing community.

A key part of Muis is the Office of the Mufti (OOM), which guides the community on religious issues. OOM has proactively provided guidance on difficult issues. One example was the inclusion of Muslims under the Human Organ Transplant Act (HOTA). Initially, many Muslims had reservations over the auto-inclusion provision applicable to all citizens. The Government understood these religious concerns and had agreed not to include Muslims under HOTA. Over time, Muslims saw how HOTA saved lives. After much deliberation, Mufti and the Fatwa Committee concluded that including Muslims under HOTA was consistent with Islam's principle to protect lives. Once the *fatwa* was updated, Muis conducted dialogues and briefings to clarify lingering misconceptions and concerns about the Act. The inclusion of Muslims under HOTA is a clear example of how religious leaders and *asatizah* have been guided by Islamic principles to shape religious beliefs and practices so that they suit our modern context.

Another sensitive issue for the community and the wider Singapore society is the effort to counter extremism. It is a great challenge facing Muslim communities worldwide. The 9/11 attacks in the US and the uncovering of Jemaah Islamiyah (JI) in Singapore have brought the frontline against radical ideologies into our midst. Muis and the Muslim community have taken a firm and united stand against terrorism. Working with the *asatizah* fraternity and community partners, Muis has taken steps to help inoculate the community against extremist and segregationist beliefs, while promoting efforts to strengthen social cohesion.

Muis' continuing work over the years has strengthened its position within the Singapore Muslim community. Other overseas Muslim communities have taken notice of Muis' efforts and achievements. Many have come to learn how Muis administers and shapes the religious life of Muslims in Singapore.

Muis is where it is today because of the efforts of its leaders — pioneers like Haji Ismail Abdul Aziz, Mr Mahmood Hj Yusof, Haji Buang Siraj, Haji Sanusi Mahmood, Haji Jamil Dzafir and Haji Musa Yusof who were followed by leaders in the 1980s and 1990s like Haji Ismail Mohd Said, Haji Ridzwan Dzafir, Haji Zainul Abidin Rasheed, Haji Maarof Salleh, Shaikh Syed Isa Semait, Haji Shafawi Ahmad, and Syed Haroon Aljunied. Their legacies were continued by Haji Mohammad Alami Musa, Haji Abdul Razak Maricar, and Mufti Dr Mohamed Fatris Bakaram. They were of course supported by many unsung heroes — Muis staff, the mosque leaders and volunteers, the madrasahs, our community organisations, and our Muslim community. I look forward to building on the work of my past predecessors, the late Mr Othman Wok, Dr Ahmad Mattar, Mr Abdullah Tarmugi, and Dr Yaacob Ibrahim, who worked tirelessly together with Muis to build a Muslim Community of Excellence.

This book is a testimony of the 50 years of hard work that has significantly shaped the religious life of Muslims in Singapore. Here in Singapore, the Muslim community has worked closely with the Government to develop and implement unique policies, so that Muslims live a rich and vibrant religious life, while actively participating in the social commons of a multi-racial and multi-religious society and secular state. Muis has been central in proving that there is no contradiction between being a good Muslim, and a good, contributing citizen of Singapore. The policies featured in this book tell the story of Muis and through this, the journey of our Muslim community. I am confident this book will serve as an inspiration for future generations to continue to strive for the best for the community and the nation.

Mohammad Alami Musa
Muis President

Muslim minority communities in many parts of the world are now facing a number of issues with regard to their relations with the secular state. The extent of their integration depends on the nature of the existing secular system and their willingness to adopt a give-and-take attitude in balancing their religious demands with the overarching secular norms of the state. In several instances, the state limits the role of religion in its affairs, due to historical reasons. Nevertheless, there are other societies where religion is recognised and valued within a more accommodative secular state.

Singapore is an example of a secular nation which upholds a strict state–religion separation and yet, at the same time, it constitutionally provides for the freedom of religious practice and recognises all religions equally. Any religious community is free to express their conscience in morally significant matters as long as social harmony is safeguarded and enhanced.

Although Singapore's context is different as it has been a part of the larger predominantly Muslim Malay-Indonesian world since the 12th century, there are still useful learning points that can be gained from the Singapore Muslim community's experience. Like other minority Muslim communities elsewhere, it is also grappling with evolving issues of collective identity and how to live its religious life harmoniously within the larger secular society that has a significant variety of other religious adherents. Muis, as the statutory body administering the religious affairs of Muslims in Singapore, is very much at the centre of this relationship in ensuring harmonious relations between the different stakeholders. Some of these relational dynamics are reflected throughout this book, such as how the government, Muis and the Muslim community have been working hard to achieve the best possible outcome in facilitating the community's practice of its religious life while ensuring social cohesion in general.

At a more conceptual level, Muis' concrete experience reflects the larger narrative of the positive relationship between a religious community and a secular state. Singapore's experience has demonstrated that a secular state can both be facilitative to religious life and, at the same time, maintain its neutrality towards religions in general. Similarly, from the Muslim community's perspective, Islam can thrive within the secular state without going against its teachings. In other words, both the state and the community can be mutually facilitative to achieve the best feasible outcome for all. Thus, lessons can be gleaned from this book by both governments and communities alike, if they are grappling with such challenges and genuinely seeking a consensual resolution.

For governments, it would be more constructive to consider adopting a more pragmatic approach in how it accommodates religious communities to forge a robust relationship and working towards the common good, instead of taking an approach which could inadvertently marginalise them. Similarly, for religious communities driven by their ideals to reform, a better option is to strive to be more inclusive and committed in working towards becoming an integral partner in developing society and building the nation.

Various episodes in the last 50 years of Muis' journey have shown that such an approach has been proven valuable. This requires a deep commitment towards forging trust with various stakeholders, underpinned by a shared vision towards a common higher ideal and secured through collaborative and co-creative platforms. I hope this book can contribute to becoming another significant starting point for further study and research in pursuing a more constructive role for religious communities to thrive in a secular state and plural society.

Abdul Razak Maricar
Muis Chief Executive

Muis is a unique institution. Formed three years after Singapore's independence, it had to find its way in the midst of the trials and tribulations of a young emerging nation determined to transform itself into a modern city-state. Muis had to grapple with different community's interests and needs while simultaneously become a key partner in nation-building together with the rest of the larger Singapore society. This community-nation nexus embracing multiple stakeholders has become an important hallmark of Muis' reality which defines Muis' uniqueness as an institution.

As a statutory board, Muis is subjected to the same rigorous governance requirements and standards like any other. However, unlike other statutory boards, its primary focus is to administer the socio-religious affairs of a particular community, that is the Muslim community. Nevertheless, this is done sensitively, always taking cognisance of the well-being of the nation. From seemingly trivial matters like the loudspeakers for call-to-prayer at mosques, to issues of life and death like the human organ transplant and exhumation, all were given due care and attention, not just to fulfil religious obligations but with deep consideration of Singapore's context. Given such a working environment, the impact of Muis' policies transcends the community and has ramifications at both the community and at the national levels. Thus, the process of decision-making within Muis has increasingly become more complex as it has to deal with the various stakeholders. In recent years, Muis has become an integral part of the Whole-of-Government (WOG) efforts in dealing with various complex issues.

The last 50 years have demonstrated the significant transformation Muis has undergone and the positive impact on various aspects of the community's religious life. I had the honour of being designated the first Chief Executive of Muis in 2013, an important milestone in Muis' history in its transformation into a public institution. Personally, it has been a challenging yet fulfilling experience, and I have gained tremendously in my own learning and development by being a part of the Muis' journey. I had to fill in the big shoes of past Muis leaders who overcame the odds to win the trust of the community while single-mindedly putting Muis and the community on the right course as both progress together with the rest of the nation.

As we came closer to marking the 50 years of Muis, we saw that this would be an excellent opportunity to look back and unearth those key moments of that journey, particularly the struggles and achievements of those who were involved in transforming Muis to what it is today. Thus, the idea to produce this book came into being with the primary focus to document the policy considerations and decision-making processes involved in the implementation of key Muis policies. Hopefully, the next generation can extract the learning points and guiding principles as useful insights for future policy deliberation. They can learn not only about the achievements but also, most importantly, the struggles in responding to the different issues and dilemmas. At the very least, they can understand why things have become the way they are, and this will spur them to imagine and build a better future for the community and nation.

I would like to thank Dr Norshahril Saat for his role as the editor of the book and, more significantly, his encouragement and support to the Muis project team and writers to reflect critically on their respective domains. I would like to also thank all Muis officers who have contributed to this book whether as members of the project team or as writers to the chapters. This wide pool of in-house writers from the various units comprising individuals from both genders and varying age groups, and diverse expertise from both the religious and non-religious domains is a concrete testimony of how Muis has developed since its early years starting out with only seven staff. It is also a reflection of the range of talent brought into Muis through systematic efforts to grow Muis' capabilities. The writers have contributed in uncovering the important learning points in the different domains of the community's religious life and framing the narrative for the future as Muis ascends to the next level. Through this book, it is our humble effort to expand Muis' institutional knowledge assets as a valuable contribution to the community's cultural and historical heritage which should be shared with others, locally and beyond.

Dr Mohamed Fatris Bakaram
Mufti of Singapore

For many years before Muis was established in 1968, the Muslim community received religious guidance from individual *ulama* and religious teachers (*asatizah*) within their respective social circles — in villages, mosques, madrasahs and Muslim organisations. Like in the rest of the Malay-Indonesian world, Islam in Singapore has been predominantly Sunni since the coming of Islam to the region in the 12th century. However, unlike other Malay states during the colonial period, Islam in Singapore was not under the custodianship of the Malay rulers. Thus, Singapore attracted many of the Muslim reformist intellectuals who came to settle in Singapore and transformed it into an intellectual hub for progressive religious thinking, as evident from the publication of the *Al-Imam* journal and the establishment of the Madrasah Al-Iqbal Al-Islamiyyah, both of which were early proponents of Islamic reformist thought. Although the impact of Islamic reformist thought was not as sustained as elsewhere, the impulse to promote progress within the community continued to permeate the nascent Muslim organisations like Jamiyah, PPIS, Pergas, Muhammadiyah, Perdaus and Pertapis.

Even before there was Muis, the community's religious elites have played a part in setting the tone and ensuring that the community remained rooted to its Singapore context. Many of them contributed in providing inputs to the substance of the Administation of Muslim Law Act (AMLA). Thus, when Muis was eventually established in 1968, several *asatizah* also served in various capacities through different committees. However, it took many years before Muis eventually gained credibility as the official Islamic religious authority in Singapore. This recognition would not have been achieved if it had been merely about administrative processes or organisational management. The main source of legitimacy primarily came from the substantive religious ideas and content espoused by Muis. This was not just a formalistic regurgitation of religious ideas from classical texts, but a serious effort by our past religious leaders who translated the religious principles they had imbued and applied them to the realities of modern Singapore. Individual *asatizah* like Shaikh Syed Isa Semait, Ustaz Syed Abdillah Aljufri, Ustaz Ahmad Sonhadji Mohammad, Ustaz Osman Jantan, Ustaz Muhammad Kamil Fadhlullah Suhaimi, Kiyai Ahmad Zuhri Mutammim, Ustaz Daud Ali, Ustaz Syed Ahmad Semait, and many others had collectively paved the way in shaping the community's religious thinking. Much of the credibility Muis has attained with respect to religious leadership is owed to these prominent individuals.

In many of the policies highlighted in this book, several of the *asatizah* have been involved in providing religious guidance which have shaped the tenor and practice of Islam in Singapore. These encompassed areas like mosque building, *zakat* collection and disbursement, *wakaf* development, and relations with other communities. Thus, the *asatizah* fraternity has always been embraced by Muis as a valuable resource, partner and enabler. The religious talent plays a significant role within Muis, not only in developing religious content but also in formulation of policies. Similarly, our key institutions like the Syariah Court, Registry of Muslim Marriages, mosques and madrasahs, are ably administered and led by religious talent. Nevertheless, this did not just emerge in a vacuum. It came from a deliberate plan to develop an integrated pipeline covering the learning in the madrasahs, support for religious graduates at tertiary level and eventually, capacity building of the *asatizah*. The development of expertise also came from the close interaction with other talent who come from various professional sectors whether within Muis or through the various platforms like the Muis Council, Mosque Management Boards as well as Madrasah Management

Committees. This synergistic interaction between individuals of variegated expertise has made the community dynamic and forward-looking.

This partnership with the *asatizah* fraternity will continue to remain integral as Muis moves into its next phase of development. The last 50 years as documented in this book have shown how this partnership has helped the community to constructively adapt to some of the severe disruptions arising from Singapore's rapid urbanisation and economic transformation at various junctures. With stronger support from the community, Muis will be in good stead to continue to be confidently proactive in responding to the emerging challenges.

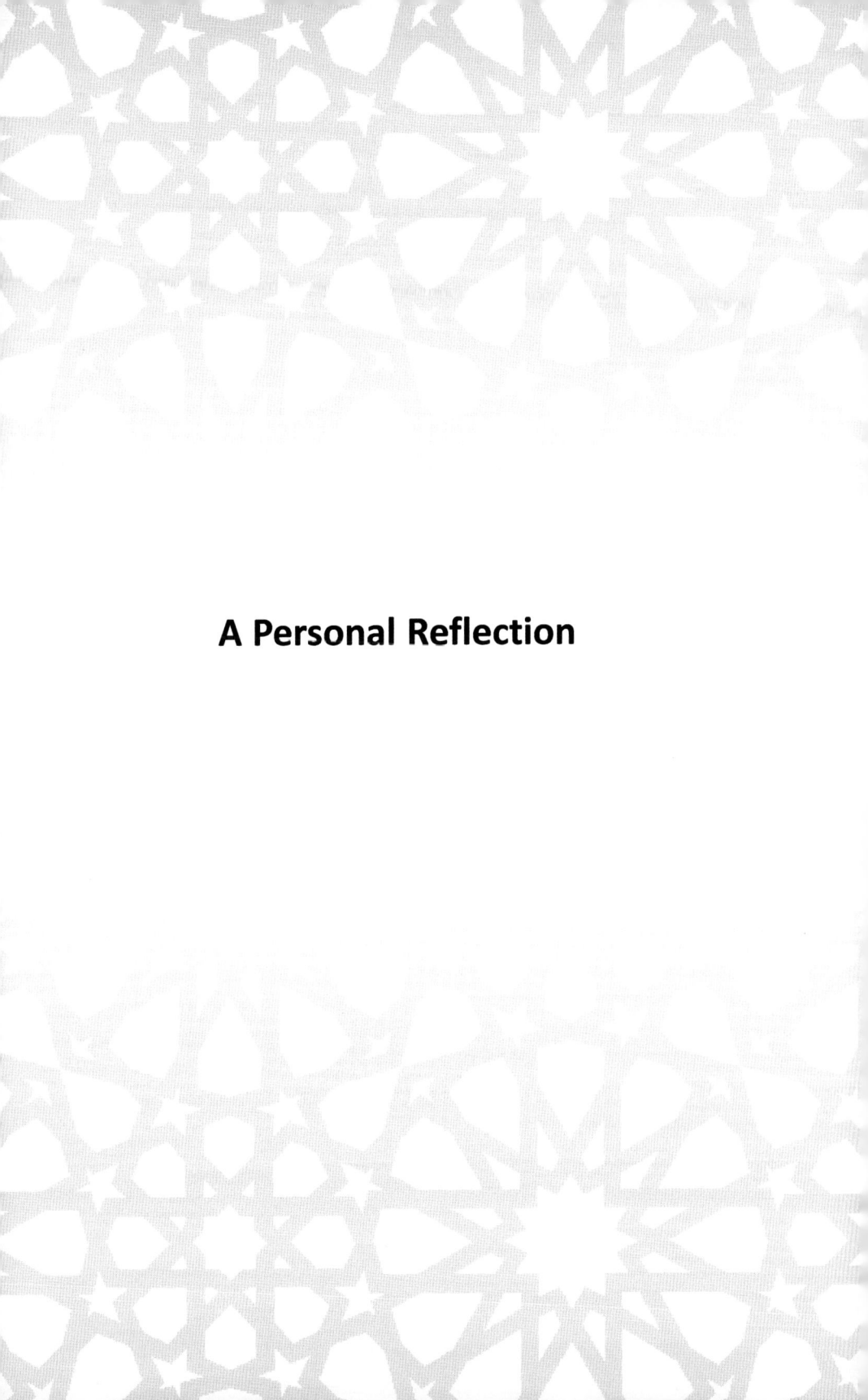

A Personal Reflection

Muis at 50: A Personal Reflection

Dr Yaacob Ibrahim
Former Minister for Communications and Information, Minister-in-Charge of Muslim Affairs and Minister-in-Charge of Cyber Security

Introduction — A Road Less Travelled

My association with the Islamic Religious Council of Singapore, better known by its Malay acronym, Muis (Majlis Ugama Islam Singapura), predates my entry into politics in 1997. In 1992, I was made a council member of Muis for a two-year term. I was given the opportunity to contribute at the highest statutory body governing the religious life of the Malay/Muslim community. It also gave me a better insight into the workings of Muis. When I became a member of Muis Council, I was given a copy of the Administration of Muslim Law Act (AMLA). That Muis was a statutory board formed and governed by an act of Parliament (AMLA) did not register in my mind or that of other members of the Council, as Muis was more generally seen as part of the community. I would spend my years as the Minister-in-charge of Muslim Affairs working to change this view and to ensure that Muis has the capabilities and professionalism associated with being a government agency and yet, in one of the instances when I presented a paper to amend AMLA, the late Mr Lee Kuan Yew reminded me that Muis must first and foremost represent the community. Herein lies the challenge of managing Muis — it is in fact a statutory body that has legal powers to act on certain matters but is more commonly regarded as a community organisation.

This interchangeable identity can perhaps be explained by the community's long history of efforts to create a central body administering Muslim religious life. The idea for such a body was mooted as far back as 1948 by representatives from various Muslim organisations.[1] Eventually, the idea was taken up by the government, with the Administration of Muslim Law Bill introduced and passed in Parliament. Today, Muis exercises oversight over almost all aspects of Muslim religious life in Singapore.[2]

In this introduction, I cannot do justice to the many twists and turns that Muis and the community had experienced in the last 50 years. Other chapters in this book will invariably fill in the details of this history. What I can offer here though, is my own personal reflection on the journey I have undertaken with Muis as well as a consideration of the challenges that lie ahead.

In my 16 years as Minister-in-charge of Muslim affairs, a constant theme that kept recurring in everything that Muis did and other Islamic

---

[1] Since colonial times, Muslims in Singapore, and as well as other states in Malaya had their own legal jurisdiction on issues relating to marriage, divorce and other matters. After the war, efforts were undertaken in various states in Malaya and Singapore to consolidate these into a central body. In 1948, representatives from various Singapore Muslim organisations suggested "either the formation of a central Muslim body or the strengthening of any existing organisation to become the mouthpiece of Singapore Muslims". The same idea for a central body resurfaced in October 1960 by four prominent Muslim groups, headed by Ahmad Mohamed Ibrahim, the first state advocate general in Singapore, who later played a major role in the introduction of systematic reforms to centralise the administration of Muslim affairs in Singapore. Subsequently, the Administration of Muslim Law Bill was introduced in the Legislative Assembly in 1960. A Select Committee was formed to hear representations on the bill. However, the bill was never further debated until it was first presented to parliament after independence on 13 December 1965. It was debated in parliament on 30 December 1965 and was subsequently sent to a Select Committee. All submissions of written representations to the Select Committee was to be in by 24th January 1966 but was extended till 31st March 1966. A total of 18 written representations were submitted and 14 representations were invited to present oral evidence to the committee. The bill was finally debated and passed in Parliament on 17 August 1966.

[2] AMLA empowers the government to form Muis, a statutory body, with the sole responsibility of administering all aspects of Muslim religious life in Singapore. AMLA also brought the Syariah Court and the Registry of Muslim Marriages (ROMM) under its purview. The Syariah Court predates AMLA while ROMM came into being in 1978.

institutions was the issue of trust. For me, Muis' key priority should be to respond to the changing socio-economic conditions of the Malay/Muslim community. The need for more prayer spaces, better information on *halal* outlets, and well-organised *haj* and *korban* exercises reflect a community growing in affluence and aspirations. Trust in Muis would be bolstered by its response to these new needs. I was also convinced that efforts to improve the level of professionalism and administrative capabilities of Muis would help to build confidence in its commitment to improving the community's religious life.

Yet many of the challenges and concerns that Muis has had to face have been linked to circumstances beyond the community's control. These challenges demanded that it steps beyond its traditional operational confines into areas such as interfaith engagement and dialogue. It had to tread carefully, lest some in the community might feel uncomfortable with these efforts. Muis also needed to do these because it wanted to assure the wider community of its place in Singapore society. Hence, it required that Muis balanced the sensitivities of the Muslim community and that of the wider national society when building bridges and trust between Muis and the Muslim community as well as between the Muslim community and the wider national society. In meeting these challenges, I faced my most difficult times as Minister-in-charge of Muslim Affairs, but I hoped I had made a lasting contribution to the state of our community with the opportunities presented to me.

Building Trust and Professionalism

As I mentioned earlier, the issue of trust keeps recurring throughout the history of Muis. There was much misperception and mistrust when AMLA was finally passed in Parliament on 7th August 1966. The bill was not without its detractors. A flavour of the mood at that time can be gleaned in the speeches by the four Malay People's Action Party (PAP) Members of Parliament (MPs) who supported the bill, including the then Minister Mr Othman Wok who moved the bill's third reading. There were concerns that the bill was meant to amend Muslim law rather than to administer it.[3] There were also concerns about the role and composition of the Council to

---

[3] The Minister and the MPs spoke to dispel this misperception. One MP even accused some in the community of misleading the community on this point.

be formed once the bill was passed[4] and the potential politicisation of the Council. Several MPs sought the Minister's assurance that only Muslims who were competent in Islamic law would be selected to sit in the Council.[5] The Minister assured that due consideration would be given to all applicants regardless of political affiliations, as the objective was to find suitably qualified persons to protect and promote the interest of the Muslim community.[6]

Despite the difficult beginnings, Muis' hard work and continued efforts to serve the community have helped to build trust and confidence. Its commitment to meeting new challenges and demands can be seen in its many new administrative and operational roles. In 1968, Muis focused its efforts largely on *zakat* and tithes collection and disbursement. In comparison, by 2018, Muis was involved in a wide range of activities including *zakat* collection, *halal* certification, *haj* operations, mosque management, *wakaf* management, full-time and part-time religious education, *fatwa* management, just to name a few.

Often Muis has to step in and take on new roles or fill the gaps to support the community's religious life. For example, when some *haj* pilgrims were stranded at the airport without an aircraft to take them to the holy land, Muis stepped in to resolve the issue. Even though a Pilgrimage Committee was formed by Muis in 1970, it did not play a regulatory role or had much oversight into the affairs of the pilgrims. Today, Muis plays a key role in regulating and managing pilgrim affairs every year. A more remarkable

---

[4] Some were concerned that the Council would take over functions which other groups had been undertaking such as *zakat* collection. The Minister was adamant that the current situation then where *zakat* was collected by organisations, individuals and political organisations, was not tenable. He opined that if *zakat* was collected centrally and properly accounted for, it would be a considerable sum of money that could be used to alleviate poverty among the Muslims. Another concern then was the management of Muslim charitable endowments or *wakaf*. Again those managing these assets would lose control to the Council. Clearly those with stakes in the community felt threatened by the existence of a Council managing all aspects of Muslim religious life. In fact, one PAP MP accused those opposed to the bill of being motivated by self-interest and not by a concern for the community.

[5] One MP even suggested that those in the opposition party (i.e., UMNO in this instance) who had the requisite qualifications could submit their applications to sit in the Council.

[6] He said that opposition parties should not be concerned as the government did not want to appoint those who will misuse religion for their own political interest. And he ended by saying that the opposition parties wanted to block the bill as it was brought to Parliament by a party that does not play the religious card. The ugly head of communal and racial politics was ever present and the Malay PAP MPs stood up to this with courage and conviction.

example is the building of new mosques. Before Muis was created, mosques and *suraus* in villages provided prayer spaces and fulfilled the religious needs of the community. After independence, with the advent of urbanisation, many villages and village amenities including mosques made way for new public housing estates. Then Prime Minister Lee Kuan Yew, recognising the community's difficulty in raising funds to build new mosques in public housing estates, suggested the setting up of a mosque building fund. In 1975, the Mosque Building Fund (MBF) was introduced in Parliament stipulating that every Muslim worker was to contribute 50 cents monthly to this fund. With the MBF, we have 27 new mosques in our public housing estates to date.

In 1981, the fund was also extended to include Yayasan Mendaki, a self-help group that supports the educational advancement of the Malay/Muslim community. The Mosque Building and Mendaki Fund (MBMF) was later extended to upkeep and upgrade existing mosques through the Mosque Upgrading Programme (MUP) and to support religious education in 2009. This expansion reflected the growing needs of the community. Over time, mosques needed not just a facelift but also structural improvements, such as lifts to cater to the elderly population, and larger prayer spaces to accommodate an increasing number of congregants. The use of MBMF for this purpose helps to alleviate the financial burden on the community in mosque-building and upgrading, as well as to support Mendaki's educational programmes and religious education.

Beyond expanding its range of activities, Muis' journey has also entailed a strengthening of both staff and governance structures. On 1st July 1968, Muis was formed with a President who chairs the Council comprising three members who were all male and seven full-time staff members managing the daily activities of Muis. Today, Muis has a staff strength of more than 200, with a governance structure similar to other statutory boards with a Chief Executive (CE) overseeing its day-to-day operations, and a President who chairs the Council, which also includes female members.

From the start, one of my missions as Minister was to ensure that Muis could live up to its expectations of professionalism as a statutory board. Towards that end, it was necessary not only to change the governance structure, but to ensure that Muis avail itself to the best talent in the Civil Service. I also paid special attention to the composition of the Council. We not only recruited capable and competent individuals but we ensured that they had varied skills, experiences, and viewpoints. Over time, with an infusion of a constant stream of talent, I am confident that Muis will become an even more effective organisation. No less important, I amended AMLA three times. Among other things, these amendments served to strengthen Muis' regulatory and operational functions in meeting the needs of the community. Every community needs its own institutions. They serve to meet the unique needs of that community. If well run, they can also help to forge a sense of solidarity. Pride in the institutions get embedded in defining that community. It becomes part of the community's identity.

Dialogue and Understanding

As a minority Muslim community in a multi-racial and plural society, we are always conscious of how others see us. Being part of the wider Singaporean society, we too play a role in strengthening the ties that bind us as a nation. If in the early years of its existence Muis had to build trust in the community, in the later years, Muis and the community had to confront issues relating to our religious life and its impact on the wider Singaporean society. There were intense discussions within and beyond the community about how our madrasah students can compete and integrate into the national society. The sensitive issue of *tudung* (headscarves) in schools flared up when some Muslim parents defied the school dress code. However, more recent developments would forever change the community and bring the issue of trust into the forefront of national discussion.

The events of 9/11 and subsequent responses from Muslims and non-Muslims would shape how I led Muis as Minister-in-charge of Muslim Affairs for the next 16 years. Acts of violence in the name of religion punctuated news in the global landscape. Within the region, we saw terrorists casting themselves as martyrs while conducting nihilistic acts of violence. Closer to home, self-radicalisation became a new buzzword when we discovered a terror group within our midst. As anxieties and fears of terrorism increased, everything about the Muslim community and its ritual practices became the subject of intense scrutiny by others. Our lifestyles, which include the donning of the *tudung* and the need for *halal* food, became points of contention in the larger discussion on the community's ability to integrate with the wider Singaporean society. While scholars and pundits pondered and analysed this emerging threat, Muis and I had the unenviable task of strengthening trust among the various communities. Against this backdrop,

I would admit that trust in Muis and myself as the Minister responsible for Muslim affairs, came under stress from within the community.

The issues of terrorism, self-radicalisation, and Islamophobia came head-to-head with the status of our religious institutions and the role of our religious leaders. Clearly, there were pressures for the community to do something immediately. I was in favour of a permanent response to the challenges based on evidence and analysis. My starting point was that there was nothing wrong with Islam and that we have taught a traditionalist and moderate interpretation of Islam for years. The ideas which had inspired those acts of violence had no roots in Islam. However, if some in Singapore and the region can be influenced by such ideas and events in faraway places, then clearly, deep reforms were needed in religious education. As such, I set out with Muis to make certain reforms to our religious education and the training of our religious elite to fit a modern age.

I began with our full-time madrasahs. Prior to 9/11 and the related events, there was a significant debate on madrasah and compulsory education in the late 1990s. Muis invariably had to step in into the management of our six full-time madrasahs. Even though AMLA empowers Muis to oversee religious schools and education, I was mindful that some of these schools predate Muis. Furthermore, as these were private schools with their own board of governors, Muis' role then was supporting these schools through some funding and streamlining curriculum and examinations. However, subsequent to the debate and arising from the need to meet the requirements of compulsory education, Muis stepped in and provided guidance and support to the six schools to meet this requirement. The Joint Madrasah System (JMS) was born to consolidate resources among three madrasahs, and strengthened co-ordination among all schools.

More importantly, it gave Muis a chance to shape madrasah education such that the graduates are familiar with Islam in the context of a multi-racial, secularly-governed nation. A whole series of reforms were undertaken by Muis including improving teachers' training, salaries, and governing structure for the schools. A standardised curriculum and diverse educational pathways for students were introduced. Non-religious subjects were introduced, especially at the primary levels. Madrasah students have continued to do well at both religious and non-religious subjects. Madrasahs have also been able to attract better qualified teachers. The net effect, among others, is the need for fresh funds. The MBMF was amended to allow Muis to tap into these funds for religious education. On balance, it was the right move.

In tandem with these changes, Muis and I also sought to make changes in the mosques which touch the lives of Muslims and have an important role to play in forging trust and cohesion with the wider national society. We revamped the part-time religious education system to move away from an examination-based system. Under the aLIVE programme, students are taught Islamic knowledge which are appropriate for their age and reflects their daily experiences. We also set up the Muis Academy so that the training of our mosque and other volunteers could be undertaken holistically. We wanted to professionalise the running of our mosques as we felt that our mosques are the direct interface between Muis and the community, and between the Muslim community and the wider national society. We wanted our mosques to offer better services to our community.

We also had to deal with the rise of Islamophobia. While not rampant here in Singapore, we needed to ensure that the wider national society accepted and trusted our community as being a part of the Singaporean family. Hence, we embarked on a whole series of efforts to build and strengthen trust among the communities. To formalise our involvement in interfaith work, we set up the Harmony Centre, within one of our larger mosques. It was designed as a small museum showcasing the best of what Islam can offer. It also offers a glimpse of the other faiths in Singapore. Our interfaith engagements and dialogues required that we look at ways of explaining our religious life to others and we consider the way others look at us. These were all new to us. We had to learn new skills of explaining Islam to non-Muslims and, at the same time, encourage our community to understand the faith of other communities.

One of the key stakeholders which needed special attention was our religious fraternity: the *asatizah*. Despite having an association to represent them, as a group, they are far from homogenous. While some of them are full-time employees at Muis, others worked as managers or full-time religious officers at mosques. Still, others are involved in the madrasahs or part-time religious programmes. As such, they have a widely felt impact and influence on our religious life. To ensure that the *asatizah* fraternity understood the context in which they are operating, Muis Academy launched several initiatives to engage and inform them of what it means to be a part of a modern, multi-racial, multi-religious, and secular nation. Today, our *asatizah* fraternity is actively involved in shaping our religious life. Some have taken upon themselves to engage young Muslims and other communities via social media. We launched the Asatizah Youth Network (AYN) comprising young *asatizah* trained in youth counselling. We wanted to create opportunities for young Muslims to engage young *asatizah* in safe spaces to discuss personal issues they might have. We could not have done all of the above if the *asatizah* fraternity did not have faith in Muis and myself, that we are doing what is right for our community

Apart from ensuring that Muslims can fulfil their religious obligation without difficulty in Singapore, Muis also took on the task of shaping the identity of the community. In response to a growing concern of an alternative narrative on how Muslims should live their lives in a modern world, Muis decided that it was timely to re-focus the community's mind on the values that have defined who we are. Hence, the Singapore Muslim Identity (SMI) project was launched in 2004. The re-assertion of what the community believes is important, given the resurgence of extremist, exclusivist, and divisive ideas among some in the Muslim world. Muis also undertook to register all *asatizah* who want to teach Islam locally. The Asatizah Recognition Scheme (ARS), led by Muis and Pergas, allows only those approved by the Asatizah Recognition Board to teach Islam in Singapore. It is meant to be inclusive. Those who do not qualify can either appeal against the disqualification, or upgrade their skills and competencies to meet the prescribed requirements. Underlying the ARS is a Code of Conduct which spells out the rules of behaviour and conduct. Among these is a specific rule to avoid denigrating other beliefs and faiths.

The SMI and ARS grew out of a period when the community wanted to reassure the wider Singaporean society of its adherence to values shared by all Singaporeans. As the threat of terrorism and radicalisation lingers on, trust building among Singaporeans has to be continued. Muis should reflect on how these efforts can be sustained and evolved into a community building effort. For example, the ARS could potentially be made part of continuing education for our *asatizah* within the Singapore Islamic College. In this way, the ARS is seen as something positive and useful for our community. Similarly, the SMI can be infused into our religious education curriculum, both in the part-time and full-time classes. In this way, all our efforts, largely in response to specific episodes in our community and globally, are not short-term but evolve into lasting community enhancements.

While we can take pride in how Muis has met many of these challenges, we need to guard against hubris. Today, Muis is often touted as a well-run statutory board and acclaimed internationally as an efficient model of Muslim administration, yet our work is far from over. In the next section, I will outline what I see as the challenges ahead for our community and what I believe Muis can do to meet these challenges.

Diversity and Sectarianism

Muis' underlying ethos of serving the community, of helping the underprivileged, of getting the community to come together in times of need, of strengthening our ties as a nation through interfaith dialogue and work, and of emphasising a community-centric approach in everything that it does have helped to shape a progressive outlook for generations of Muslims. However, this ethos could come undone if the challenges of diversity and sectarianism are not squarely addressed.

The phenomenon of diversity is not new in the community. In the early years of Muis' existence, the emergence of nascent organisations with their rigid interpretations of the religion, serves to remind us that diversity is ever present in our community's landscape and consciousness. Also, despite almost all Muslims in Singapore here being Sunnis, Muis has been able to integrate the small Shia community into the mainstream. For many years, Muis' corporate lawyer was from the Shia community that had settled in this region for several decades, so much so that they adopted the Malay language. Muis also has had to evolve with a community that is changing from single-income earner households to dual-income earners, and an increasing population of new converts and those born of mixed marriages. While these demographic changes lend themselves to manageable changes in how Muis operates and implements its programmes, the fundamental impact of diversity on how our community should be organised because of ideological differences at the theological level cannot be underestimated.

Too often, diversity is interpreted as a fragmenting force or unjustified heterodoxy giving rise to the knee-jerk reaction of imposing uniformity. Yet, any attempt to homogenise practices will come up against centuries-old traditions of diversity within Muslim civilisation itself. The fact that there are various schools of legal thought reflect the diversity of thinking among Muslim scholars. More importantly, much of the Muslim world accept this diversity. However, in recent years, fuelled by greater uncertainties and volatilities in the modern world, we are seeing a growing intolerance towards different groups, especially the Shias and the Sufis. Singapore is not insulated from such intolerance. We do see more Shia Malays. Furthermore, as their number grows, there is a likelihood for greater recognition. Inevitably, responses, negative or otherwise, will emerge from the dominant Sunni community. In this complex milieu of contesting ideas about how we should organise our religious life in Singapore, Muis has the unenviable task of ensuring that our community fabric remains cohesive.

Muis needs to ensure that its religious guidance helps to develop a healthy respect for others. Indian Muslim merchants came to Singapore long before independence and built mosques and other institutions. They are largely Hanafis, and their school of thought has persisted in modern Singapore. In fact, the Dawoodi Bohra community, an Indian Shia group, has been in Singapore for decades and have been accepted into mainstream Singapore. Hence, I hope that going forward, as a community, we will better accept Shias in our midst as we would for followers of other schools of thought. Perhaps, we will increasingly see that the Shia community will also inform and shape the evolving story of Muslims in Singapore. I see this as a positive development, as embracing such diversity will invariably enrich our religious life. It behoves Muis to seed this idea early in the life of the Muslim community. Beyond tolerance, we should build in our community a healthy curiosity of others. It is through the intermingling of ideas that fresh perspectives emerge. The corollary where Sunnis and Shias are intolerant of each other has led to the violence and killings seen in some Muslim countries. We must avoid this at all cost.

The lack of tolerance of diversity is usually borne out of narrow-mindedness and fear of the unknown. There is a belief that there can only be one way of doing things or organising society. If those who hold such views are given positions of power or, worse still, gain power over the community, then we are in danger of religious authoritarian rule. Many scholars have pointed out that religious authoritarian rule and military authoritarian rule are two of the most pernicious ways of organising society where violence and injustice are justified in the name of a narrow ideology. I do not think we are in danger of religious authoritarian rule here in Singapore. However, if we pander to certain segments of the community who see their views as definitive, then such thinking can lead to exclusivist and segregationist tendencies that can result in a fracturing of the community. Muis' role in this is very important. It must speak up against such tendencies so as to assure the majority of Muslims here that its role is to preserve the common good of the community. And that means Muis must create spaces for these various differences to co-exist healthily while preserving what is common to all groups. The five pillars of Islam, the various practices which have been adopted for centuries, including that of remembering the Prophet (peace be upon him) during his birthday and many other rituals that do not violate the key principles of Islam, should be preserved and defended by Muis in the face of absolutist authoritarian tendencies. I see this as the defining challenge of Muis in the years to come. Whether Muis becomes a religious authority that is inclusive by allowing many groups to co-exist or becomes conservative in its outlook and panders to special interest groups depends largely on its leadership. Hence, it is important that Muis is led by enlightened and broadminded individuals who understand that in this evolving milieu of ideas, there is a place for everyone as long as their positions are not at odds with the basic principles and humane ideals of Islam.

Beyond diversity in theological schools, Muis must contend with diversity in lifestyles and understanding of the faith. Such challenges are bound to happen as more Muslims are exposed to ideas from a variety of sources. Some Muslims, for example, while remaining faithful to the religion, see the need for greater flexibility in interpreting the Islamic laws of inheritance for circumstances that did not exist 14 centuries ago. Others may want a greater role for Muslim women in the religious life of the community. We can draw on a tradition of discussing diverse viewpoints in Islam in these situations. Our Fatwa Committee has taken on the task of conceptualising the religious rationale to allow for greater integration of civil law in some aspects of our religious life. Muis must proactively engage the thought leaders of our community in some of these thorny issues. A search for a middle ground that balances all points of view must continually be worked upon.

Role of Religion in the Modern World

In recent times, we have seen an increase in the rejection of the relevance of religion to modern life. In Europe, for example, religion is often seen as leading to decreased social mixing and a fragmented civic arena. Any outward symbol of belonging to a religious group is thus seen as an attempt at creating communities of exclusion and separation, exacerbating social distances between segments of society. We also find some who argue that any differences in consumer behaviour or leisure consumption are seen as a retreat from modernity and progress. These attacks rely on hyperbole and paranoia. Popular and news media exaggerate their reports on certain events, generalise and promote the idea that religion, at best, is not relevant to modernity and, at worst, amplifies irrational violence and delusional thinking. Critiques of religion are often reinforced by religious groups that ignore contemporary social problems, are adversarial towards outsiders, do not contribute to the larger national cultural sphere, and are overly dogmatic and rigid in their religious practices and interpretations.

However, religion has a potential role to play in fostering social cohesion through social morals. It has something to say about the need for community, good social cooperation, and the dangers of the unbridled pursuit of individual power, material interests, and desires. The civil rights movement in the US grew out of the concerns of religious groups about social justice and equality. Today, many social movements to help the poor and underprivileged are usually led by religious groups. That religion can inspire in their followers the desire to do good and make the world a better place is indeed a strong testament to the positive role of religion in society. The violence done in the name of religion that we see today is but one example of the misuse of ideas throughout human history — many other allegedly modern and objective ideas have also been similarly misused.

In Singapore, through the mutual efforts of the government and the various faith communities, religion has a place in civic society and in the conversations which ensued about how to organise society. We must cherish this. Yet the rise of over-simplified and phobic views of religion cannot be ignored. Muis will need to galvanise and work with other faith communities in Singapore to demonstrate the good that religion has done for Singapore. Beyond demonstrating good works in the name of religion, Muis could lead in the development of ideas that resonate and are in harmony with a modern, plural and multi religious society such as Singapore. The possibility that a minority community could play such a critical role in the positive development of religion should be defended and shared with other societies. Muis should develop experts who are familiar with religious thinking from the various traditions and develop intellectual arguments for the positive role of religions in modern societies. This will be a lasting contribution and a testimony to the role that Muslims can play in developing a better world.

One of the current efforts undertaken by Muis is the setting up of the Singapore Islamic College (SIC). I mooted this idea at the annual Hari Raya gathering in 2016 as I believed that the SIC will serve two key purposes. The first was to set the context. There was a concern then that our students coming back from Islamic universities overseas, especially from the Middle East, may not understand the local context in their teaching of the religion to others. Clearly, ideas taught by Islamic scholars in past centuries may not be meeting our needs and concerns since they are based on the situation and challenges faced by the scholars then. A classic example is the Qur'anic interpretation by the scholar Ibn Taymiyah, which reflects the acute concerns of the community which faced the Mongol invasion of the Muslim empire in the 13th century then. With the SIC, students who have spent their early years in local madrasahs can continue to study Islam in a local setting, allowing them to better appreciate local concerns and the role of Islam in managing those concerns.

A second purpose was my belief, which was not articulated then, that the SIC can be the vehicle through which we can work towards making our life experiences as Muslims and, more generally, as people of faith, more vibrant, meaningful, and relevant. In particular, I deeply believe that the SIC, if well-planned and executed, has the potential to nurture students who see Islam and religion in general, not as an ossified body of beliefs, rituals, and ceremonies that must be defended at all costs but as a living set of beliefs and practices that can adapt and change to different circumstances. While the SIC curriculum will ensure that the students have a deeper understanding of Islam, as they would in other universities, it must strive to develop critical thinking and inquiry among the students. The students can tap into and study a whole range of ideas and methodologies that can help them to better understand the human condition — including how societies are organised, how contemporary social and economic problems arise and may be addressed, and how our identities and behaviours are shaped by our culture and experiences. Courses in disciplines such psychology, sociology, economics, and social work should be offered to our students at the SIC.

Muis' role in shaping the SIC especially in its early days is very crucial. For those that argue that this undertaking is too idealistic, do be reminded that Islam and other religions have indeed adapted and changed over time without compromising their core beliefs. In Singapore, our own Fatwa Committee has made bold changes in their thinking on matters relating to the interplay between Islamic and civil laws. To those who want to take shortcuts by adopting wholesale models that are based on very different societies, with very different needs and concerns, Muis and its leaders must say no. They must have the breadth of vision and strength of character to reject these seemingly easier options and invest in long-term institutional building efforts. Colleges and universities take time to evolve to reach the desired level of excellence. There is no short cut to excellence. Muis must also guard against the SIC, and in fact other institutions under its charge, being captured by those who hold sectarian views and authoritarian thinking. The SIC is not an institution only for the Muslim community. It is a Singaporean institution that must reflect the best of what we as a country can offer to the evolving debate on the relevance and role of religion in the 21st century.

Conclusion — The Road Ahead

I began this essay with a personal journey and ended with some personal reflections. My journey has not ended. My association with Muis and the Muslim community is a lifetime's work. As an institution, Muis plays a very large role in the religious life of the community. The 50-year journey of Muis, and my own personal journey, have been about building trust, connecting communities, and weaving an interconnected network of ties and linkages among the various stakeholders here in Singapore. Muis and I are indebted to the thousands of volunteers, community leaders, religious leaders, and lay professionals who gave their trust and support to the work that we do. Going forward, Muis should tap on this well spring of support as our community faces the challenges ahead.

However, like any other agency, Muis must also be prepared to review its role and functions over time. The scope and breadth of what Muis offers to the community has grown over these past 50 years. A continuous expansion of functions is unsustainable simply because of the lack of resources and that such limited resources should be deployed to those areas which are more strategic, and see how it can empower other community players to take on some of its existing functions. For Muis to respond to challenges I have outlined above, it must develop new capabilities and embark on more strategic roles in guiding the community. Over time, I hope to see Muis accomplish more strategic work for the community and less operational functions.

Muis' journey over the last 50 years is a story worthy of a book capturing the key milestones, the policy responses to certain challenges, and key decisions that has made Muis into what it is today. However, the very idea of a Muis, an institution responsible for administering the religious life of a minority community within a multi-racial nation, was given short shrift 50 years ago. Then, authority was about to be transferred from many players in the religious life of the community to a new, untried and untested institution. Credit should be given to the early pioneers of Muis who sought not to abuse that authority but rather to use it to galvanise the community. Today, Muis is a lot more vigorous than it was 50 years ago. How it uses that vigour in the years to come, to deal with the challenges I outlined earlier, will define what will become of it in the next 50 years. Using that vigour wisely requires deep wisdom and understanding. Ultimately, it is not about the many programmes and institutions that we build that matters, it is about how we as a community see ourselves and our faith in the evolving story of modern Singapore.

Acknowledgements

2018 is a special year for Muis as it celebrates its 50th anniversary since its founding. To mark this special occasion, it has decided to publish this book, to capture important policy decisions and episodes affecting the Muslim community in Singapore. The book would not have seen the light of day without the hard work of the Editorial Team who supported me as the Editor in foundationally conceptualising the ideational tenor and tone of the policy narratives to be put forth, at both the level of individual chapters and the book as a whole, engaging the writers and publisher, thoroughly going through the manuscript and finally, putting everything together. I would like to thank Bohari Jaon, Zalman Putra Ahmad Ali, Yazid Mohamed Ali, Nurlaila Khalid and Farah Nurdiyanah Sanwari.

While the book's contributors are mainly Muis staff, who have the requisite expertise in their respective domains, the book would not have been possible without the research inputs and support from the following: Ahmad Aizat Rahmat, Khalid Shukur Bakri, Warintek Ismail, and Zaini Osman. I would like to thank all of them as well as others who have given their expert inputs through interviews for specific chapters. These would include Datin Dr Siti Zalikhah Mohd Noor who shared her insights on the administration of Muslim Law in British Malaya, Haji Abdul Halim Mohamed Amin and Haji Haffidz Abdul Hamid who contributed significantly to the *Haj* chapter through their inputs and suggestions.

Accounts from former and present Muis leaders are also crucial in capturing significant policy decisions Muis had embarked on over the years since its inception in 1968. I would like to express my gratitude to Haji Zainul Abidin Mohamed Rasheed (former Muis President), Haji Mohammad Alami Musa (current Muis President), Haji Maarof Salleh (former Muis President) and Haji Syed Haroon Aljunied (former Muis Secretary). Thank you for accepting the researchers' numerous requests for interviews.

I would like to thank former Minister-in-charge of Muslim Affairs, Dr Yaacob Ibrahim who first mooted the idea of producing this book and has kindly offered his personal reflections. I would like to also thank Chief Executive of Muis, Haji Abdul Razak Maricar, for entrusting me with the task of editing this book. Special thanks also to Deputy Chief Executives of Muis, Dr Albakri Ahmad and Esa Masood, and members of the Muis Directorate for their guidance, the Strategic Communications Strategic Unit (Muis) and the Singapore Press Holdings for their support in providing historical photos, Ministry of Communications and Information (MCI), and Ministry of Culture, Community and Youth (MCCY)'s Community Relations and Engagement Division (CRED) for their support and inputs.

Dr Norshahril Saat
June 2018

Note on Translation, Spelling and Other Conventions

Non-English terms, including Arabic and Malay terms, will be italicised throughout the book. However, the exceptions to this rule is the term madrasah, as the term is in the English dictionary with the same meaning. Although it is spelled in many different ways in English (madrassa, madrassah, madrasah etc.), we have kept the spelling of 'madrasah'. The spelling of *syariah* in Syariah Court is retained and not italicised as it is the name of the institution.

The plural forms of Arabic terms are mostly retained. The only exception is the term *ulama* (religious scholars). The term *ulama* in Arabic is the plural for *Alim*. However, in Malay usage, the term *ulama* refers to both singular and collective. Thus, *ulama* in this book refers to both singular and plural forms. The plural form of other Islamic terms will be indicated with an "s". Hence the plural for *fatwa* is *fatwas* and madrasah is madrasahs.

Direct quotes will be indicated with double open and close inverted commas ("...") and quotes within a quote with single open and close inverted commas ('...'). Quotes with more than three lines will be indented. Arab, Malay, and Indonesian authors are identified by their last name, not their first name. Hence, "Abu Bakar Hashim" will be cited as "Hashim", rather than "Abu Bakar", and "Abd al-Fattah Abu Ghuddah" will be cited as "Abu Ghuddah", rather than "Abd al-Fattah".

INTRODUCTION: TOWARDS A SOCIO-HISTORICAL ANALYSIS OF MUIS POLICIES

Norshahril Saat

Muslims in Singapore constitute about 15 percent of the country's population of five million people. Despite being a multi-ethnic and secular country, there are provisions in the Constitution which endorse institutions to oversee the administration of Islam, and no other religions in the country are accorded similar status. In 1968, the Singapore Parliament passed the Administration of Muslim Law Act (AMLA), which led to the formation of Muis (Islamic Religious Council of Singapore). The Act also institutionalises the position of the Mufti — an official religious scholar (*ulama*) whose role is to guide the religious community — and the formation of a *fatwa* committee, which is responsible for the passing of religious rulings. Muis also oversees the running of traditional Islamic institutions, such as *wakaf* (charities and endowments), *zakat* (tithe), and madrasahs (religious schools).

Although Muis' existence came into being after Singapore's independence in 1965, it had its roots during the British colonial period. Under the colonial government, the legal system in Singapore, particularly on criminal matters, mirrored the British model. It was only in the 1860s that the legal affairs of the Muslims came to the colonial administration's attention. In 1905, the British government established the Mohammedan and Hindu Endowment Board. Changes to Singapore's demography forced the Board to undergo evolution. With the growth of the Muslim population, due to natural increase and immigration from the region, the British government felt that the community's religious needs and identity must be represented. In 1915, the British created the Mohammedan Advisory Board and in 1947, the Muslim Advisory Board. Another significant creation occurred in 1958 with the establishment of the Syariah Court (National Library Board, 2013).

Before Muis was formed, the Muslim community relied mainly on village mosques or prayer spaces (*suraus*) for their religious needs. Wealthy philanthropists acquired lands in the form of *wakaf*, and established religious schools (madrasahs) and Qur'an classes to facilitate Islamic education for the community. Some of these madrasahs continue to exist to this day. Oral history interviews kept with the National Archives of Singapore provide anecdotal evidence on how Muslim parents prefer to send their children to the madrasahs or Qur'an classes close to their houses. For some parents, Qur'anic literacy, performance of religious rituals such as five daily prayers and fasting, and observing the Muslim diet, are essential traits of being good Muslims. In the past, there was no formal body to certify *halal* food (permissible in accordance to Islamic requirements), thus Muslims relied on a senior and respectable elderly Muslim living in the same village to slaughter animals and poultry in accordance with Islamic requirements. Similarly, there was no formal body to certify *imams* or to vet sermons to be delivered in mosques. The formation of Muis brought about better administration of Islam for Muslims in Singapore; clearer regulations, pronouncements, and guidance; and better quality religious elites. Muis also plays a part in facilitating change in the community, ensuring it is in-sync with modern realities, and understand Singapore's multi-racial setting.

Muis is a statutory board, which can be considered a quasi-state institution. It receives partial funding from the state, but most of its source of income comes from the community; through tithe collection, donations, and monthly contributions from the Mosque Building and Mendaki Fund (MBMF). The MBMF scheme refers to the fixed amount of money deducted from the salaries of Muslims in Singapore every month. The funds collected through this scheme endorsed by the Singapore government has led to the building of 27 mosques between 1977 and 2017. Since 1981, the funds are also partly used to subsidise Mendaki, a self-help group that looks into the educational upliftment of the Malay/Muslim community. More recently, the MBMF funds are used to help mosques upgrading and refurbishment, under the Mosque Upgrading Programme (MUP), which was launched in 2009.

The way Muis is financed is in a way unique. In some Islamic countries, particularly Muslim-dominant ones, religious institutions are formed by the government. At the end of the other spectrum, for countries where Muslims are the minority, religious institutions are autonomous of the state, functioning like NGOs. These NGO-like institutions articulate the interests of Muslims to their respective governments apart from helping build prayer spaces and Islamic schools.

Comparing to its counterparts in the region, Muis' role is similar to the Islamic religious councils and departments in Malaysia, though it does not have the powers of its Malaysian equivalent. Malaysia is a Muslim majority country, and its constitution indicates that Islam is a matter of the state's (Malaysia is a federal state), with the Malay Rulers being the Heads of Islam in their respective states. The Rulers appoint members of the religious councils and the Muftis. The religious councils issue *fatwa*s (legal opinions) which can be enforced if they are published in the state gazette. Muis *fatwa*s do not bestow such powers.

The way Islam is administered in Indonesia also differs from Singapore. Indonesia is a secular state, but it has a religious ministry which is headed by a Minister. The Ministry oversees the administration of six religions, including Islam. Yet, it is the NGOs that are active in the religious public sphere, and Indonesian Muslims are free to participate and become members in any of these groups. The two largest Muslim organisations in Indonesia are Nahdlatul Ulama (NU) and Muhammadiyah. The religious ministry does not issue any *fatwa*s, and members are free to follow religious rulings of their leaders of their respective organisations. In 1975, the Suharto government formed a quasi-state religious institution, Ulama Council of Indonesia (MUI). This institution receives partial funding from the state, but its *fatwa*s are not legally binding.

Objective of the Book

It is not in the interest of this book to trace Muis' history and function. Existing works, such as Anthony Green's *Honouring the Past, Shaping the Future: The Muis Story*; and Zuraidah Ibrahim's *Muslims in Singapore: A Shared Vision,* have covered these aspects extensively (Green, 2009; Ibrahim, 1994). This book also seeks to move away from discussing the technical aspects of Muis' work. For example, the book is not interested in the legal mechanisms underlying *fatwa* formulation, or the technicalities associated with the management of the Haj ritual. Rather, *Fulfilling the Trust: 50 Years of Shaping Muslim Religious Life in Singapore* traces the evolution of Muis' policies over the last 50 years since its founding in 1968. The chapters are written by domain experts currently serving in the various units in the institution. This book is by no means an attempt to glorify Muis' contributions or work. Conversely, I have urged all contributors to reflect critically about Muis policies, what it has achieved, and in what areas it can improve to serve the community better. While highlighting some of Muis' achievements, contributors are advised to ponder on the challenges their units have faced, including disagreements with the state, if any, and tensions with segments of the community who have differing views. For certain, there were instances where policy-makers had to make difficult decisions, and they did not have the luxury of satisfying all parties. Moreover, contributors are also requested to reflect on policies that can be improved in the years to come, as the community moves into the post-globalisation era commonly referred to as the "age of disruption". Muis policies have to be suited to the constantly changing context and needs.

This book showcases how policies are formulated within Muis, and how it engages different stakeholders. It primarily highlights the institution's policy thinking and considerations. Some of the chapters in the book clearly demonstrate that Muis has the autonomy to issue religious rulings and policies which, at times, contradict what the state had hoped for. Muis negotiates with three different actors when formulating policies. The first is the Muslim masses which, to begin with, is heterogeneous: there are the conservatives, the traditionalists, and the progressives. It is not the purpose here to evaluate which group represents the correct Islam or the wrong Islam, although it is important to note that the most vocal among them may not represent the community's vision of progress. In addition, the Muslim community in Singapore is also represented by various stakeholders and organisations that are not part of Muis. While Muis is an official body set up by the government, it is not the only body which can claim to represent the community. Other bodies include Pergas (Singapore Islamic Scholars and Religious Teachers Association), Jamiyah, Muhammadiyah, Association of Muslim Professionals (AMP), and Mendaki. Again, multiple claims to the religious authority is not a sign of weakness of the religious leadership, but a reality in the modern world. Different organisations have different values and different objectives, which may agree or disagree with the position undertaken by Muis.

The second stakeholder is the state, which upholds certain principles and values Muis cannot ignore. Since Singapore's independence in 1965, the country has been under the uninterrupted rule of the PAP (People's Action Party). The government upholds and cherishes the values of meritocracy, secularism, and multiculturalism, which no religious organisation, including Muis, can deviate from. Nevertheless, it would be inaccurate to claim that every of Muis' concurrence with the government is a sign of weakness or co-optation. The government of the day has to serve the interest of all citizens, regardless of race or religion. In fact, government policies must not be seen in binary terms: Islamic versus non-Islamic. Muis has to consider Muslims in Singapore as first and foremost citizens of a modern, secular, and democratic state. Hence, policies introduced by Muis has to be in line with the broad principles of the state and its values. Other values which the Singapore government promotes — democracy, strong family ties, equality, and justice — are also in line with Islamic principles. Over the years, Muis has had to grapple with policy changes affecting the government, such as the implementation of HOTA (Human Organ Transplant Act), the use of Central Provident Fund (CPF), and the Stop-at-Two family planning policy, which discouraged couples from having more than two children in the 1970s and 1980s. These government policies affect how Muslims understand their religion and require adjustments. For example, the changes to regulations above force Muslims to rethink about conception of the body, inheritance, and family values (which encourage more children).

The third stakeholder group is the non-Muslims. Although Muis is set up mainly to cater to the needs of the Muslim community, it cannot escape interacting and engaging the non-Muslims. Recent events that may indirectly cast negative spotlight on the Muslim community, such as religious extremism and radicalism, push Muis to play a more central role to debunk any form of inaccurate assumptions about the community. Muis has been at the forefront, together with the other Muslim organisations, in circumventing any unnecessary tensions in relation to 9/11, and the threats posed by Jemaah Islamiah (JI) and ISIS (Islamic State in Iraq and Syria). Muis also responded instantaneously whenever any member of the community is seen as promoting exclusivist ideas that destroy Singapore's religious harmony.

A study of the evolution of Muis policies should not only consider institutional analysis and key actors, but ideas. How the religious elites think also has an impact on the community's religious life. Here, it is important to understand the religious life of Malay society from pre-coloniah, colonial, and post-colonial period. This book is particularly interested in the events that occurred in the 1970s and beyond, as this period has been dubbed as the Islamic revivalism (or Islamic resurgence) period, which marked the increase in religiosity within the community. The phenomenon ushered in a new form of fundamentalist streak in Malay society which is anti-modern in nature; there are groups championing for a return to the Qur'an and Sunnah when they seek answers to modern problems. Rather than seeking the values from these text, some groups select verses from them, even quoting them out of context. There is a simplistic understanding of religion which shuns Western scientific knowledge as un-Islamic. It was during this period that some groups began to champion the compulsory wearing of the headscarf, the development of the madrasahs, piety of the political elites, and *halal* consumption; and these issues were unheard of previously. This book will see how Muis responded to this change in attitude of the Muslim masses resulting from the revivalist period.

How Muis functions today is also shaped by events in the 2000s, particularly 9/11; the discovery of terrorist cells in the region; and the presence of Jemaah Islamiah (JI) followers in Singapore. Security issues have placed the community under the spotlight and required a strong Muslim leadership to respond. It was during this period that there was a huge debate about what constitutes moderate Muslims. Muis contributed to this discourse by way of introducing the Singapore Muslim Identity (SMI). Much focus was also given to building interfaith understanding and dialogue, which led to the birth of the Harmony Centre. During this period, there was much attention given to madrasah education. The madrasah leaders reacted angrily to the initial proposal to make education compulsory (CE) in Singapore. Several stakeholders were concerned about the future of madrasahs, and whether the policy will lead to the eventual closure of decades-old religious schools. Again, questions were raised about Muis' leadership on these aspects.

Central Questions and Book Summary

The book has two central questions. First, why did Muis undertake certain policies even though they may be unpopular? Second, how did Muis overcome policy challenges and how were they remedied? In a way, the book argued that in order to understand Muis policies, one has to also understand the critical junctures, socio-historical context, diverse stakeholders, and elites' worldview that led to Muis to respond to issues and problems in a certain way. To be sure, every policy does not exist in a vacuum; for instance, as I have mentioned earlier, Muis' response to the government's values, Islamic revivalism of the 1970s, and 9/11. I have asked all contributors how policies can cater to present needs and circumstances, and how they will likely change in the years to come. The main objective of the book is to orientate readers to the unique role Muis plays in the mutual facilitation of community, state, and non-Muslim interests.

Fulfilling the Trust: 50 Years of Shaping Muslim Religious Life in Singapore is divided into 14 chapters. In Chapter 1, **Alfian Yasrif Kuchit** highlights the key milestones in the drafting of and subsequent revisions to AMLA in matters specifically relating to Muis. It makes the case for the importance of managing the practice of Islam in a complex multi-religious society. He argues that Muis' formation had its roots during the colonial era and was inspired by developments in the Malay Peninsula. Alfian also makes an interesting point on the development of a Majlis Agama (religious council) in the Malay Peninsula, which he claims, has its roots in the state of Kelantan. He then examines the inputs provided through parliamentary debates and Select Committee representations that were considered in the Administration of Muslim Law Bill.

This is followed by Chapter 2, which tackles the issue of institutional capacity building. In this chapter, **Azree Rahim** and **Yazid Mohamed Ali** study the efforts to strengthen institutional capabilities through innovation, benchmarking, and partnership with various public agencies and the private and non-profit sectors. It focuses on the professionalisation of Muis to improve its services and credibility. The chapter argues that Muis learns from the country's civil service standards in developing staff and leadership capabilities. It also explored corporatisation as a means to respond quickly to market changes. In Chapter 3, **Nazirudin Nasir** traces several transformations in the community's religious life through *fatwa* (Islamic legal rulings). The chapter highlights Muis' efforts to shape religious life through progressive and sound *fatwa* and religious guidance. It discusses the inherent tensions between state and religious elites, especially through the institutionalisation of religious guidance (through *fatwas*) and the negotiations by Muis with the Muslim community as it seeks to deliver what it sees as a progressive religious agenda. His chapter provides the debates surrounding organ donation (with the introduction of Human Organ Transplant Act, or HOTA) and inheritance (especially the Central Provident Fund, or CPF) scheme.

In Chapter 4, **Mohammad Hannan Hassan** and **Irwan Hadi Mohd Shuhaimy** discuss the role *asatizah* (religious teachers) play in shaping public discourse and religious life of the Malay/Muslim community. The chapter traces some of Muis' efforts to upgrade the *asatizah* through the Asatizah Recognition Scheme (ARS) which, in the past, was a voluntary accreditation scheme but was later made a mandatory one. The chapter also looks at the cooperation Muis has with other Islamic organisations, such as Pergas. This will be followed by chapters specific to education. In Chapter 5, **Farah Mahamood Aljunied** and **Zalman Putra Ahmad Ali** examine the transformation of madrasah education. It highlights some of the challenges as well as achievements of the madrasahs after the introduction of the Joint Madrasah System (JMS) in 2007. The chapter also notes some of the learning points from the whole Compulsory Education (CE) episode, and how Muis can play a mediating role in ensuring the madrasahs meet standards on par with the national schools, while allowing the madrasahs autonomy to develop their religious education and programs. The chapter also demonstrates how the madrasahs work closely with the religious leadership in maintaining a niche yet sustainable religious education relevant for the modern world. In Chapter 6, **Farah Mahamood Aljunied** and **Mohamad Khidir Abdul Rahman** analyse the challenges that Muis faced in its attempts to reform the curriculum and pedagogy for part-time mosque madrasahs. It highlights Muis' efforts to manage and communicate changes to stakeholders which later led to the introduction of the aLIVE programme.

The following set of chapters examines the key institutions supervised by Muis: they include mosques, *zakat, wakaf, haj, halal,* and *korban*. These chapters look at the services provided by Muis to the community. These institutions are key to the religious life of the Muslims as they represent the key rituals that define their religious identity. This part contains six chapters in all, each chapter focusing on the aspects mentioned. In Chapter 7, **Mohamad Helmy Mohd Isa** discusses the evolution of mosques against the backdrop of a changing national landscape. It highlights the movement towards increasing the capacity for mosques to provide services beyond solely providing prayer spaces, and the need for Muis to facilitate these changes. The chapter concludes by pondering how mosques need to consider developing a sustainable model to meet future divergent needs. *Zakat* is the subject of Chapter 8, and it is written by **Zulfadhli Ghazali.** It studies Muis' evolving policies in ensuring effective *zakat* disbursement, which promotes better self-reliance and facilitates upward social mobility. It discusses Muis' choice to connect the *zakat* disbursement system with the government's national safety net to ensure better outreach. In Chapter 9, **Masagoes Muhammad Isyak** explores how Muis manages the delicate issue of land endowments in Singapore. It also analyses Muis' considerations when choosing which *wakaf* to develop or renew, keeping in mind the unique and complex characteristic of each *wakaf*. The chapter highlights the processes put in place to ensure efficiency while maintaining stakeholders' emotional and familial ties to each *wakaf*. It also speaks about the challenges in managing *wakaf* in Singapore, especially when land is scarce and has to make way for housing and development needs.

The subject of *haj* is central to Chapter 10. In this chapter written by **Abdul Rahim Saleh**, the key considerations behind Muis' choice in adopting both the private and public models of *haj* is explored. It traces the historical challenges of Muis providing *haj* services amid a growing demand for quality services. Most importantly, the chapter looks at how Muis engaged private *haj* operators, and the Saudi government, and fulfilled community's expectations to ensure successful *haj* for Singaporean pilgrims every year.

In Chapter 11, **Dewi Hartaty Suratty** looks at how Muis has leveraged the growing momentum of the global *halal* market in order to provide quality *halal* certification in Singapore. It weighs the benefits and implications of centralising a *halal* certification body. The chapter examines how the amendment to AMLA in 1999 strengthened Muis' authority in *halal* certification. In Chapter 12, **Sakdun Sardi** explores the evolution of *korban* rituals in Singapore against the backdrop of an evolving national landscape.

It addresses the challenges of regulating the community's growing demand for *korban* ritual while at the same time maintaining quality standards of procedure. Interestingly, the chapter traces how *korban* rituals in Singapore underwent significant changes after 2011, when there was a debate regarding animal rights abuses in Indonesia, which was taken up by the Australian authorities.

The last part consists of two chapters which examine how Muis leverages global connections to serve local needs and how Muis contributes to national social cohesion. In Chapter 13, **Asri Aziz** traces the evolution of Muis' efforts at international relations, highlighting the structural challenges of limited resources, leadership, and the evolving focus of Muis' work. The chapter showcases how Muis developed ties with numerous organisations, institutions and officials from around the world, as it expands its scope beyond those originally defined by AMLA. In the last chapter, Chapter 14, **Zalman Putra Ahmad Ali** and **Zainul Abidin Ibrahim** highlight Muis' efforts to forge greater partnership and understanding both within the community and among non-Muslim groups. It discusses the importance of Muis' efforts in leading the discourse on interfaith relations rooted in the Islamic tradition. Moreover, it demonstrates how Muis' efforts lead to better social cohesion in Singapore.

The book concludes with a chapter by **Albakri Ahmad** and **Zalman Putra Ahmad Ali** which examines the possible future impact of Singapore's emerging challenges on the Muslim community, including Singapore's demographic transformation, a more contested political landscape, changing economic landscape, disruptions due to the digital revolution, and emergence of new social fault lines. Through these chapters, the book hopes that the community would be able to better appreciate the policy-making Muis has made over the years, and how they seek to serve the interests and needs of the community. Policy-making will evolve with time as the community's needs grow. The book serves as important learning points as the community braces itself for the opportunities and challenges in the next 50 years and beyond.

Dr Norshahril Saat
Editor
March 2018

References

Green, A. (2009) Honouring the Past, Shaping the Future: The Muis Story: 40 Years of Building a Singapore Muslim Community of Excellence. Singapore: Muis.

Ibrahim, Z. (1994). Muslims in Singapore: A Shared Vision. Singapore: Muis.

National Library Board Infopedia, "Majlis Ugama Islam Singapura." Retrieved from National Library Board website: http://eresources.nlb.gov.sg/infopedia/articles/SIP_1105_2011-09-27.html.

Part 1

Building Muis' Foundations

1

THE INSTITUTIONALISATION OF ISLAM IN SINGAPORE: THE ADMINISTRATION OF MUSLIM LAW ACT AND THE BIRTH OF A 'MAJLIS UGAMA'

Alfian Yasrif Kuchit

Introduction

When Singapore separated from Malaysia in 1965, the Republic made a pragmatic decision to retain the then State Constitution — albeit with some necessary changes — and to address the concerns of racial and religious minorities (Thio, 2009). As a multiracial and newly independent state, the government recognised that accommodating the special needs of racial and religious minorities was not only just but also important for its survival (Lee, 1967). Article 12 of the Constitution did not prohibit any provision regulating personal law and Article 153 directed Parliament to "make provision for *regulating Muslim religious affairs* and for *constituting a council to advise the President* in matters of the Muslim religion" (Constitution of the Republic of Singapore, 1965). It created the socio-political space for the institutionalisation of Islam in a Muslim-minority country.

In December 1965, four months after independence, the Administration of Muslim Law Bill was introduced at the first session of

Parliament[1]. Drafted by the Republic's first Attorney-General, Ahmad Mohamed Ibrahim, the Bill represented the culmination of efforts to modernise the administration of Muslim religious affairs and, by implication, Muslim law. The Bill was intended to "repeal and re-enact law relating to Muslims and to make provisions for regulating Muslim religious affairs and to constitute a Council to advice on matters relating to the Muslim" (Administration of Muslim Law Bill, 1965). The passing of the Act meant that, unlike other former British colonies with a minority Muslim population, Singapore would be the only one to have established an Islamic religious council embedded within the state structure.

This chapter investigates how an Islamic religious council like Muis became part of the domain of the modern state. What were the mechanisms of its incorporation, what was the trajectory that led to its establishment, what were the political and social structures that shaped the milieu, and who were the actors who drove this process? The chapter argues that the seeds for the institutionalisation of Islam via a council and its incorporation into a modern state germinated during the colonial encounter in the 19th and early 20th centuries. I begin with a historical narrative that locates this encounter within a place, time, and politics, and trace the various British instruments to regulate Muslim religious affairs. This will be followed by an examination of the concept of an Islamic religious council, which was first mooted in Kelantan, and later became the template for other Islamic religious councils in the region. The chapter will then trace the parliamentary debates and Select Committee representations on the Administration of Muslim Law Bill that led to the birth of an Islamic religious council in Singapore. By studying its origins, I conclude that the emergence of an Islamic religious council should be understood in the context of the socio-political history of its incorporation within the modern state; and it is in the humdrum details of institutionalisation and bureaucratisation that we see the development and

---

[1] Bills introduced in the first sitting of the Parliamentary session: Constitution (Amendment) Bill, Republic of Singapore Independence Bill, Interpretation Bill, Guardianship of Infants (Amendment) Bill, Probate and Administration (Amendment) Bill, Widows' and Orphans' Pension (Amendment) Bill, Property Tax (Amendment) Bill, Corporate Duty (Amendment) Bill, Stamp (Amendment) Bill, Estate Duty (Amendment) Bill, Income Tax (Amendment) Bill, Supply Bill, Supplementary Supply Bill, Singapore Asian Seamen's Club Incorporation (Amendment) Bill, Telecommunications Bill, Industrial Relations (Amendment) Bill, National Registration Bill, Administration of Muslim Law Bill, Destitute Persons Bill, People's Association (Amendment) Bill, and Singapore Army Bill.

transformation of Muslim religious affairs (as the later chapters in this book will show).

Legislation of Muslim Religious Affairs: Pre-Colonial to Independence

When Singapore was part of the Johor-Riau Sultanate during the 17th until the early 19th centuries, the religious functionaries appointed by the Sultan performed sacerdotal functions and provided religious advice for the palace (Borham, 2002). Like many Malay maritime polities in Southeast Asia, Islam and *adat* (customary law) formed the basis of social order in the Johor-Riau Sultanate, and the administration of Muslim religious affairs formed an important part of the symbolisation of legitimacy.

With the Treaty of 1824 signed by Sultan Hussein Shah and Temenggong Abdul Rahman of the Johor-Riau Sultanate to sell Singapore and the outer lying islands to the British East India Company (EIC), the Malay aristocracy could no longer exercise any formal authority though they continued to have a presence in Singapore.[2] The issuance of the second Charter of Justice in 1826 by King George IV meant that English law governed Singapore with due attention to the religions and customs of the native inhabitants (Phang, 1990). Since the EIC's imperatives were to extract economic surplus in the form of revenue and to maintain effective political control with minimal military involvement, it did not see the need to set up any institution to administer Muslim religious affairs specifically.

By the mid-19th century, the population in Singapore had grown substantially including that of the Muslim community.[3] Enticed by EIC's policies that enabled Singapore to become a thriving entrepôt, many came to Singapore in search of a better life. As a result, the local Muslim community not only

---

[2] However, by the late 19th century, the presence of the Malay aristocracy had considerably diminished. In January 1866, the then-Temenggong Abu Bakar (grandson of Temenggong Abdul Rahman) shifted his administrative capital from Telok Blangah, Singapore, to Tanjong Puteri, Johor. As for the then-Sultan Ali (son of Sultan Hussein Shah), he spent most of his time in Umbai, Malacca, where he was eventually buried in 1877.

[3] According to the census of the Straits Settlement of 1901, Singapore was the home (temporary or otherwise) of 23,060 Malays, 12,335 other natives of the archipelago, 1,508 Arabs, and about 600 Jawi Peranakan (the offspring of Indian Muslim and Malay unions). The total population of all races was 229,904, of whom 72 percent were Chinese.

became a minority, it also became more diverse in terms of ethnicities and schools of law (*mazhab*).

The administration of Muslim affairs only received attention after Singapore became a Crown Colony in 1867, which meant direct rule by the Colonial Office in London. Legislative powers of the Crown were delegated to the Legislative Council which had vast, unrestricted powers of legislation within the colony, similar to those exercised by the British Parliament. Laws passed by the Legislative Council were known as Ordinances. Executive power in the colony was exercised by the Governor — who represented the Crown — and the Executive Council. Nevertheless, the Crown retained the power to disallow any ordinance passed by the Legislative Council, to make peace and war, to create courts of justice, to be the instance of last appeal, to pardon offences, to coin money, to have allegiance, fealty and homage, and to impose taxes. It was also during this time that the British parliament vacillated between a Conservative-led government, which favoured an imperialist and expansionist policy under Benjamin Disraeli, and a Liberal-led government under William Gladstone, whose policies focused more on individual liberty while loosening political and economic restraints.

It was amid such political background that the Legislative Council made its first attempt to afford the Muslims in Singapore legal status in the administration of its affairs. In 1877,[4] a group of 143 influential Muslims submitted a petition to the Governor, F.D. Jervois for a religious functionary (Qadi) to be made registrar of Muslim marriages. They highlighted that it was important that a proper system of recording Muslim marriages and divorces be established. The then Attorney-General, Roland Braddell, drafted a Bill based on a Bengal Act (No. 1 of 1876) and highlighted that "Mohammedan inhabitants have been representing difficulties which arise in their community from the enforcement of the rules of English law to cases among them in which, owing to the different circumstances, customs and habits of the people, those rules are not merely inapplicable, but are in themselves inequitable" (Hickling, 1992: 137). According to Braddell, there was a need for the legislature to consider: (i) the effect of a Muslim marriage on the status and property of the wife; (ii) the impact of English law on Muslim

---

[4] The British Parliament at this time was controlled by the Conservative Party under Benjamin Disraeli. It was also in 1877 that he persuaded Queen Victoria to take the title "Empress of India".

intestacy; and (iii) the need to have properly constituted Qadis. There were apparently cases of Muslim families being cheated by unscrupulous individuals claiming to be Qadis but having taken the fee, did not turn up on the agreed wedding date. Introducing a law — to regulate the administration of Muslim marriages and divorces as well as Muslim law of property — was therefore beneficial to the community.

The Legislative Council was, however, wary of being involved in Muslim affairs. When asked by a member as to why the Legislative Council should not take a more a proactive role in having the Governor to appoint the Qadi, the Attorney General replied that the "British government was extremely unwilling and chary of interfering or appearing to interfere in the smallest degree with the religion of any of its subjects..." (The Legislative Council, 1880: 3). Nonetheless, the Legislative Council agreed with the petitioners on the need to regulate Muslim marriages and divorces and passed the Mohammedan Marriage Ordinance in 1880. It enabled the Governor to grant a license to a Muslim authorising him to register Muslim marriages and divorces (Mohammedan Marriage Ordinance, 1880). The Ordinance marked the beginning of British legislative intervention into the field of Muslim law. A British instrument (i.e. legislation by way of a statute) was now the key to plant the seeds of institutionalising the administration of Muslim religious affairs not only in Singapore but in the Malay Peninsula as well.[5]

The Ordinance also authorised the Governor to recognise Muslim religious functionaries known as the Qadi, who maintained the register of marriage, divorce, and revocation of divorce. Any Qadi recognised under the Ordinance shall have the authority that is necessary to decide upon questions relating to the status of marriage and divorce but cannot adjudicate in matters of matrimonial property unless the parties affected voluntarily accept the Qadi's adjudication. All the decisions, acts, and orders by the Qadis were open to revision by the Governor and may be ordered by him to be reversed, altered, or modified. For the first time, an

---

[5] The Perak State Council (headed by the British Resident to advise the Sultan on all matters except those concerning religion and custom) had passed laws on Muslim religious affairs by way of Orders in Council, e.g., the 1880 law prohibiting Qadis from accepting religious tithes (*zakat*); the 1881 ban on unauthorised display of flags in mosques; the 1885 law requiring Muslims to attend mosques for Friday prayers; and the 1885 law to provide for the voluntary registration of Muslim marriages.

Ordinance would provide a legal framework for the administration of Muslim religious affairs (Yegar, 1979).

Another legislation that governed Muslim religious affairs during the colonial period was that relating to Muslim endowments. In 1905, the colonial government introduced the Mohammedan and Hindu Endowment Ordinance, which established a Mohammedan and Hindu Endowment Board to administer and supervise Muslim and Hindu endowments. This Ordinance gave the Board power to require written accounts and answers to enquiries relating to any endowment or the property or income thereof to be rendered by the trustees or their agents or other persons having possession, custody, or control of any endowment. The Governor could also order such endowments be administered by the Board where it appeared to him that (a) an endowment has been mismanaged; or (b) there are no trustees appointed for the management of any endowment; or (c) that it would otherwise be to the advantage of any endowment that such endowment shall be administered by the Board (Ibrahim, 1965).

Unlike Muslim endowments, the issues of marriages and divorces impacted the Muslim community more. As such, several rounds of amendments were made to the Mohammedan Marriage Ordinance. If in 1880 the British colonial authorities were reticent in being involved in Muslim religious affairs, by the mid-20th century such reluctance fell away. The British colonial authorities slowly expanded the jurisdiction and powers of the Qadis. This was not surprising as similar expansion of powers and jurisdiction was taking place in the Malay States (Hussin, 2016). These states, by the early 20th century, had started to legislate Muslim religious affairs extensively. Most of these states began to make provisions for a special "Syariah Court", which administered Muslim marriage and divorce laws as well as "offences against religion", e.g., teaching religion without a *tauliah* (license), failure to fast during Ramadan or attend Friday prayers, and unlawful proximity (*khalwat*).

The idea of a Syariah Court also made its way to Singapore. In 1957, while under self-rule, the Singapore Legislative Assembly passed the Muslim Ordinance which established the Syariah Court. It had the jurisdiction to deal with cases in which the parties were Muslims, and involved disputes relating to Muslim marriages and divorces. It took over all the functions of the Qadis in adjudicating claims ancillary to a divorce, though the Qadis continued to have the power to register a divorce where both parties to a marriage have consented to the divorce. The Ordinance also established an Appeal Board to hear appeals against the decisions of the Qadi and the Syariah Court. In 1960, the Ordinance was amended to allow the orders of the Syariah Court to be enforced in the same manner as the orders of the Magistrate's Courts can be enforced, and extended the powers of the Syariah Court to deal with ancillary matters. It also marked the first time that polygamous marriage was regulated such that it may only be contracted if there was no lawful obstacle according to Muslim law to such marriages.

The Idea of an Islamic Religious Council

Apart from the Syariah Court, another institution that was rapidly being developed in the Malay States was the Majlis Agama. It was only a matter of time that the idea of a centralised Islamic authority would be mooted in Singapore. It was in Kota Bharu, Kelantan — about 700 kilometers north of Singapore — that the concept of an Islamic religious council had its beginnings. While a religious bureaucracy is not new in the Malay Peninsula,[6] none exercised powers and functions as extensive as that of the Majlis Agama Islam dan Isti'adat Melayu Kelantan (Council of Islamic Religion and Malay Custom, Kelantan, or MAIK). With the introduction of a British adviser taking charge of the state in 1910 and Sultan's authority unchallenged only in the area of Malay religion and custom, MAIK marked the Sultan's attempt to modernise the administration of Muslim affairs. The Sultan made it plain that the MAIK was an instrument to raise Kelantan "to a status consonant with that of other advanced states" (Roff, 2009: 203).

Like the other Malay states, Kelantan was caught up in processes of change not of its own choosing or direction, as colonial rule and the attendant political, social, and economic transformations impinged increasingly on public life, norms, and customs. British control had not only displaced traditional political and juridical institutions, but also failed to improve Kelantan's fortune or its people markedly. If Kelantan was to improve, then the Kelantanese had to do it themselves using the means available to them. The idea of a religious council, therefore, was the vehicle to re-assert the Sultan's authority and to modernise the state.

---

[6] For example, Johor's Department of Religious Affairs and Education (Jabatan Agama dan Pelajaran) which was set up in 1897.

MAIK — announced by the Sultan in December 1915 and established in 1916 by way of an Enactment[7] issued by the Kelantan State Council — formalised control over mosques and *suraus* (prayer houses) and their officers,[8] and was empowered to: (i) administer all matters relating to the practice and performance of Muslim law for the benefit of the state and its people;[9] (ii) prepare annual estimates of expenditure;[10] and (iii) submit annual reports to the State Council.[11] This was unprecedented as no other Malay states had similar division of powers where there was a central authority with relative autonomy and financial independence. *Fatwas* (religious opinions) were no longer issued on the authority of the Mufti but rather, was discussed in a committee and issued in MAIK's name. In consequence, institutionalised Islam became an important focus for the expression of residual Malay authority, primarily through MAIK and its bureaucracies, where the Sultan became the patron of the faith.

One striking feature is the composition of the members of MAIK. Of the 12 appointed by the Sultan, four were religious scholars (one of whom was Tok Kenali, known for his progressive views regarding the role of Islam in society), five civil servants (one of whom was a Singaporean who was the supervisor of schools in Kelantan),[12] two members of the aristocracy, and one businessman from Penang who owned properties in Kelantan.

Another striking feature was its concern for modernisation and progress of the state, as seen in its plans for education. MAIK established "Madrasah Muhammadi" (named after the Sultan) which incorporated three educational divisions: a Malay vernacular school, an English school, and a religious

---

[7] See *Undang-Undang bagi Anggota Majlis Ugama Islam dan Istiadat Melayu Kelantan*, No. 14 (1916).

[8] See section 24 of the Enactment, which stated that MAIK had to: "*mengaturkan segala perkara yang berkenaan dengan masjid-masjid dan surau serta pegawai-pegawainya*" (Mahmud, 2010: 29).

[9] See section 25 of the Enactment, which stated that MAIK had to "*menjaga, menasihat, mengatur, menfatwa, menzahir, menguat, melulus, menimbang, dan menjalankan segala perkara, perbuatan, tujuan dan perkataan yang berkenaan dengan ibadat dan lain-lainnya yang dibangsakan kepada syariat Muhammadiyyah bagi mendatangkan maslahat yang boleh menambahkan faedah kebajikan bagi negeri dan orang ramai.*" (Mahmud, 2010: 30).

[10] See section 26 of the Enactment (1916).

[11] See section 27 of the Enactment (1916).

[12] Mohd Ghazali Bin Arifin left Singapore in 1900. He was appointed head teacher of a government school in 1905. For his services to the state, he was awarded the title "Dato' Bentara Luar" in 1911.

school. When MAIK presented its plans to the Sultan, it explained that the purpose of the madrasah was to nurture religious scholars where graduates could then serve in the government or became teachers to teach in other schools throughout the state. Apart from the madrasah, MAIK also was involved in the translating and printing of books, producing textbooks and periodicals, and providing scholarships to students to study in Singapore and Perak.

Despite this, the establishment of the Majlis was not without criticism. There was apparent unhappiness with the zest in which MAIK prosecuted those who were lax in the collection and remittance of religious tithes (*zakat* and *fitrah*). There were also complaints about MAIK's expenditure. Some questioned MAIK's assumption of its right to issue *fatwa* for the state. The major question that consumed MAIK was the building of the state mosque at the expense of its progressive educational agenda. In 1919, the Sultan had expressed his desire for a mosque worthy of Kelantan, and asked the British adviser to procure plans of the mosques in Kuala Lumpur and Kuala Kangsar as well as those in Langkat and Deli in Sumatra. Unable to withstand the pressure, MAIK agreed to build a state mosque. The expenditure dedicated to building the state mosque caused MAIK's pioneering work in education to weaken.

This did not mean that MAIK's social impact was erased. It remained an agent of social change, using the institutions of Islam inspired by British bureaucratic forms, and continued to wield great power. Its extraordinary brief — both in its scope and depth — was exercised in a great variety of increasingly centralised ways and, in certain respects, an abiding insistence on self-determination, even if not always appreciated by elements of their own society. The idea of a religious council was soon to spread to other Malay States (Mackeen, 1969) and Singapore (*The Singapore Free Press*, 1948).[13]

The Omnibus Legislation — The Administration of Muslim Law

In 1952, the state of Selangor passed the Administration of Muslim Law Enactment (Hooker, 1984). An omnibus legislation that incorporated all

---

[13] The Singapore Free Press (1948) reported that "a committee to consider either the formation of a central Muslim body for Singapore, or of strengthening any existing organisation to become the mouthpiece of Singapore Muslims had been formed which consisted of 'prominent Muslim individuals' and 'delegates of Singapore Muslim organisations'" (p. 5).

previous piecemeal legislations relating to the institution of the Qadi and the Syariah Court, and legislated the establishment of a religious council (Majlis Ugama Islam dan Adat Istiadat Melayu) in Selangor. It was divided into 10 parts, with five parts relating specifically to the powers and functions of the Majlis. Those parts are as follows:

(i)   Part II dealt with the membership and proceedings of the Majlis. It also included the appointment of the Mufti and the Legal (*Fatwa*) Committee as well as the authorities to be followed, i.e., the Legal Committee "shall ordinarily follow the orthodox tenets of the Syafi'i sect (*sic*)" though if opposed to public interest may follow the tenets of "any of the three remaining sects";

(ii)   Part IV dealt with the establishment of a Fund known as *baitulmal* and powers of the Majlis to collect *zakat* and *fitrah*;

(iii) Part V empowered the Majlis to regulate mosques and the powers and duties of a *pegawai masjid* (mosque officer);

(iv)   Part VIII directed the Majlis to maintain a register of converts to the Muslim religion within the State; and

(v)   Part X dealt with general provisions that related to the protection of the Majlis, its members and employees and the power of the Sultan to make rules for the Majlis, Legal Committee, *pegawai masjid* and other officials.

After Selangor, many other states in Malaya followed suit and used the Selangor enactment to model their laws.[14] It was within this legal milieu that the State Advocate General (the government's top legal adviser) drafted the Administration of Muslim Law Bill. In December 1960, the Minister of Labour and Law, K.M. Byrne, moved the Bill in Singapore's Legislative Assembly for a Second Reading. The bill's purpose was to "follow the consolidation of the legislation relating to the administration of Muslim law in the States of the Federation of Malaya" (1960: Col. 912). It provided for the "establishment of a Majlis Ugama Islam to advise the Yang di-Pertuan Negara (Singapore's Head of State) on matters relating to the Muslim religion" (1960: Col. 912). As such, the Bill empowered the Head of State to appoint a

---

[14] *Administration of Islamic Law Enactment 1955* (Terengganu); *Administration of Islamic Law Enactment 1956* (Pahang); *Administration of Islamic Law Enactment 1959* (Malacca); *Administration of Islamic Law Enactment 1959* (Penang).

President of the Majlis, a Mufti, not more than two Muslim members of the Legislative Assembly, and not less than 10 members to constitute the Majlis. It also empowered the Majlis to deal with trusts intended for Muslim religious and charitable purposes, and to collect *zakat* and *fitrah*. Since 1915, Singapore had an advisory board made up of Muslim religious scholars and professionals to advise the colonial authorities on Muslim religious affairs but its power was limited.[15] The bill, therefore, was aimed at "re-organising the administration of the Muslim law and Muslim religion" (Administration of Muslim Law Bill, 1960) and having a central Islamic authority to replace the advisory board and the Muslim Endowment Board.

In the Legislative Assembly, Abdul Hamid Jumat (Member of Parliament for Geylang Serai) raised the issue of competence whether "Islamic laws can be enacted to govern Muslims in their way of life" in a country where there was no state religion (1960: Col. 915). He was also concerned how the Majlis would determine the *zakat* and whether those eligible for *zakat* would have their public assistance by the Social Welfare Department withdrawn. In response, Parliamentary Secretary of National Development, Yaacob Mohamed stated that the bill was in consonant with the state constitution which protects and safeguards Muslims. It was "promulgated on the advice of many religious experts" and had "received the blessings of the Muslim Advisory Board" (1960: Col. 918). On the issue of *zakat*, both the determination and distribution of *zakat* would be based on established principles and there should be no controversy arising as the Mufti would be able to give his ruling.

Recognising that the bill went beyond any previous measures to regulate Muslim religious affairs, the Law Minister committed it to a Select Committee, where the public could give written representations by 21 January 1961.[16]

---

[15] The Mohammedan Advisory Board (later known as Muslim Advisory Board in 1947) was constituted administratively and not by statute.

[16] In light of several requests by the public, the Select Committee had to extend the deadline to 26 April 1961, and by this time, it was already almost at the end of the current legislative session to allow the Committee to bring their consideration of the Bill to a satisfactory conclusion. The Committee then recommended that should a similar Bill be introduced in the next Session, and should it be committed to a Select Committee, that the 1961 Select Committee report be referred to that Select Committee for consideration.

In general, the representations during the 1961 Select Committee supported the Bill though proposed tweaks. Some felt that the Majlis should be given more powers and responsibilities, especially in relation to *wakaf*. Those who supported the Bill were nevertheless concerned how the Majlis would enforce *zakat*, and sought assurances that the law would not be enforced until there is "complete equality and justice" (Select Committee on the Administration of Muslim Law Bill, 1961: A8). There were also concerns regarding who would be appointed a member of the Majlis. As for those who opposed the Bill, the main plank of their argument was that it was unacceptable for a secular government to enact laws to control, regulate, and administer Islam. Even if the Bill would have to be put in storage for the moment, the idea of a Majlis was seeded in the mind of the public. The only question was the range of powers that the Majlis should have.

In September 1963, Singapore, Sabah, and Sarawak joined the Federation of Malaysia. As these states did not have a Malay sultan, under the Federal Constitution of Malaysia, Muslim religious affairs therefore had to come under the purview of the Yang di-Pertuan Agong (Malaysia's Head of State). The same State Advocate General who drafted the earlier Bill had to prepare a new Bill to incorporate the change. Before the Bill's introduction in the Legislative Assembly, the Muslim Advisory Board had sought to obtain inputs from Muslim organisations like the Muslimin Trust Fund Association, Singapore Muslim League, and Overseas Pakistani League.[17] Had it not been for the Separation on 9 August 1965, this Bill would have been placed before the Legislative Assembly. The Majlis Ugama's birth was to be via an Act passed by Parliament of an independent country rather than an Enactment passed by a state legislature in the Federation of Malaysia.

Even with the passage of time, the structure and the statutory language of the legislation that Selangor Legislative Assembly passed in 1952 remained deeply influential when the Administration of Muslim Law Bill (it was similarly divided into 10 parts, with five parts on the power and duties of the Majlis) was considered in Parliament. By then, the State Advocate General, who became the Attorney General of independent Singapore, would have

---

[17] However, some organisations complained that they were initially not consulted. See, "Muhammadiyah adu Majlis" (1964).

had a lot of experience in dealing with the various feedback and criticisms made against the Bill.

At the 1966 Select Committee, the Bill received 18 written representations, with 14 giving oral evidence.[18] Some highlighted similar concerns raised during the 1961 Select Committee. They were concerned on the extent of state power to enforce religious laws and sought assurances that there be no prosecution for non-payment of *zakat* and *fitrah*. As Muslims in Singapore already paid income tax, to impose the *zakat* on them would be a form of double taxation. While they understood that the Majlis would require funding, they suggested that part of the income tax be used to satisfy *zakat* obligations and be channelled to the Majlis. Another suggestion was that the government provide the necessary funding instead of the Majlis relying on *baitulmal* and *zakat*. The representors recognised that without strong financial support, the Majlis would not be able to accomplish much.

Another issue that the representors highlighted was the socio-economic status of the Malays, even though this issue was beyond the remit of the Select Committee. With the Separation still fresh in their minds, there was a tone of urgency in the expectation that the Majlis be an instrument to help raise the living standards of the Malays and Muslims in general.

Apart from these concerns, who would constitute the Majlis became the subject of intense discussions. Some suggested that the members of the Majlis should be elected rather than nominated, and others suggested that more members from Muslim societies were to be included in the Majlis. Others expressed hope that the Majlis ensured that there be sufficient representation. The powers of the Majlis over mosques and *wakaf* also occupied the minds of these representors. They worried that there was a possibility that the Majlis would abuse their powers if *wakaf* were vested in the Majlis, especially since the Majlis had the power to remove mosque or *wakaf* trustees where "it would be otherwise to the advantage of the mosque or *wakaf*" (1966: A21). Many also highlighted the need to ensure that there were adequate religious scholars (*ulama*) to sit in the Majlis and Legal (*Fatwa*) Committee.

---

[18] Organisations like the All-Malaya Muslim Missionary Society, Muslimin Trust Fund Association, Muslim Welfare Association, United Malays National Organisation, Jama'at Ahmadiyyah, South Indian Jamiathul Ulama as well as concerned individuals represented diverse interests.

One clause that received particular attention related to conducting a religious lecture in Singapore.[19] The representors argued that the requirement for written permission from the Majlis to conduct a religious lecture was a curious one, as it required Muslim non-residents of Singapore and Malaysia to seek written permission, whereas non-Muslims who were residents did not need to do so. Furthermore, other faith groups in Singapore did not have similar provisions. To the credit of the Select Committee, they removed this clause. They incorporated proposals to strengthen the governance of the Majlis and ensured that the proposed legislation would enable the Majlis to carry out its functions effectively.[20] They also took suggestions to strengthen Muslim family law,[21] so as to ensure that stronger support for Muslim women caught in an unjust marriage, and withstood pressure to remove progressive clauses.[22] On 20 May 1966, the Committee completed its deliberation and resolved to submit its report to Parliament.

During the Third Reading of the Administration of Muslim Law Bill on 17 August 1966, the then Minister for Culture and Social Affairs, Mr. Othman bin Wok, highlighted that "no political influence will be made to bear on [the Majlis]. All that the Government is interested in is to see that the affairs of the Muslims in Singapore are entrusted to a wise, forward-looking and stable organisation" (1966: Col. 241). He reiterated that the Majlis will not be used for any personal, sectional, or political purposes, and gave assurance that the Majlis' sole purpose is to serve the interests of Muslims in Singapore. On the

---

[19] The clause stated: "No person who is not ordinarily resident in Singapore or Malaysia shall give any lecture or talk dealing with the Muslim religion at any place to which the public or a class of the public have access, unless he has obtained the written permission of the Majlis" (1966: B46).

[20] The powers of the Majlis over mosques and *wakaf* remained intact despite misgivings by some representors over the Majlis' powers.

[21] Section 49 of AMLA on *fasakh* allows a wife to apply for a divorce if the husband has failed to provide for her maintenance for a period of three months. The original clause had stated "a period of one year". The same section also allows a wife to apply for a divorce if the husband has been sentenced to imprisonment for a period of three years or upwards, and such sentence has become final. The original clause had stated "a period of 7 years". The Select Committee also left out clauses that relate to "*nushuz*" (recalcitrancy) in divorce proceedings.

[22] Section 51(3) of AMLA allows the Syariah Court to make an order against the ex-husband to pay the ex-wife who has ceased to be entitled to an order of maintenance under Muslim law further sums of money if just and proper to do so. Some representors opined that the power of the Syariah Court to order further sums of money was not in accordance with Muslim law.

issue of *zakat* and *fitrah*, he pointed out that a centralised *zakat* collection and distribution system would enable help to be given more effectively to the poor and needy.

While the Bill was passed in 1966, the Act only came into effect in 1968. This was because some time was needed to find suitable candidates to fill the Majlis' top three positions, i.e., the President, Mufti, and Secretary (*The Straits Times*, 1967).

Conclusion

The establishment of an Islamic religious council in Kelantan emerged as a response to the colonial encounter. While coming under the Sultan's authority, it was nevertheless a component of a modern state bureaucracy in a colonial outpost. The unprecedented move of setting up an Islamic religious council involved reconstituting and re-embedding traditional structures into a new and different epistemological mould. Its establishment was not without its critics, even as its purpose — as announced by the Sultan — was to modernise the state and raise its status consonant with the other advanced nations.

While the idea of setting up an Islamic religious council was later adopted in other states in the Malay Peninsula, there was ambivalence and, to some extent, resistance towards the authority and powers of a Majlis Ugama in Singapore. It was not an easy passage, as it took about six years before a bill was finally passed (with the merger with and separation from Malaysia during the intervening years). It was the diligence, humility, and patience of the drafter — having done several versions of the bill during these six years — who played a major role in ensuring its safe passage.

Several Select Committee reports illustrate the articulation and contestation of ideas that characterise the heterogeneity of the Muslim community. The representors were divided by doctrinal differences, political affiliations, cultural practices, intellectual orientations, and several other factors. Even so, such divides would have also been shaped by the social milieu and colonial encounter, which was a complex socio-historical process. It is not surprising, therefore, that many of the themes and concerns raised by the representors still resonate till today, due to the irreversible impact and outcome of colonialisation. Thus, if one were to study the Islamic religious council in Singapore, a structural–historical examination of its development becomes important. The later chapters in this book will give concrete examples of this, in particular, how the Majlis had to adapt creatively throughout the years in coming to terms with modernisation and modernity.

References

Administration of Muslim Law Act, Rev. ed. Cap 3 (1966) Singapore.

Administration of Muslim Law Bill (1960) Singapore.

Administration of Muslim Law Bill (1965) Singapore.

Berita Harian (1964, June 4). Muhammadiyah adu Majlis Islam Singapura ketepikan badan2 lain. *Berita Harian*, p. 3.

Borham, A.J. (2002) Pentadbiran undang-undang Islam negeri Johor (pp. 64–76) Johor: Malaysia: Universiti Teknologi Malaysia.

Bryne, K.M. Singapore Legislative Assembly Report (Administration of Muslim Law Bill), 29 December 1960.

Constitution of the Republic of Singapore (1965) Singapore.

Hickling, R.H. (1992) The influence of Islam on Singapore law. In *Essays in Singapore law* (p. 137) Selangor, Malaysia: Pelanduk Publications.

Hooker, M.B. (1984) Islamic law in South-east Asia (p. 144) Oxford, UK: Oxford University Press.

Hussin, I.R. (2016) The politics of Islamic law: Local elites, colonial authority, and the making of the Muslim state (pp. 82–89) Chicago, Illinois: The University of Chicago Press.

Ibrahim, A.M. (1965) The legal status of the Muslims in Singapore (p. 41) Singapore: Malayan Law Journal.

Jumat, A.J. Singapore Legislative Assembly Report (Administration of Muslim Law Bill), 29 December 1960.

Lee, K.Y. (1967) *Speech at the opening ceremony of the congregation of Buddhists from Asia*. Retrieved from the National Archives of Singapore website: http://www.nas.gov.sg/archivesonline/data/pdfdoc/lky19670104

Mackeen, A.M.M. (1969) Contemporary Islamic legal organization in Malaya (p. 39) New Haven, Connecticut: Yale University.

Mohammedan Marriage Ordinance 1880 (Singapore) s. 2.

Mahmud, A.R. (2010) MAIK: Peranannya dalam bidang keagamaan, persekolahan, dan penerbitan di Kelantan sehingga 1990 (pp. 29–30) Kuala Lumpur, Malaysia: Dewan Bahasa dan Pustaka.

Mohamed, Y. Singapore Legislative Assembly Report (Administration of Muslim Law Bill), 29 December 1960.

Phang, A. (1990) The development of Singapore law: Historical and socio-legal perspectives (pp. 38–40) Singapore: Butterworths.

Report of the Select Committee on the Administration of Muslim Law Bill, Parl. 2 (1961, 3 May).

Report of the Select Committee on the Administration of Muslim Law Bill, Parl. 3 (1966, 31 May).

Roff, W.R. (2009) The origin and early years of the Majlis Agama Kelantan. In *Studies on Islam and society in Southeast Asia* (p 203) Singapore: NUS Press.

The Legislative Council, 6th July (1880, July 12) *Straits Times Overland Journal*, p. 3.

The Singapore Free Press (1948, January 26). Muslims Form Committee. *The Singapore Free Press*, p. 5.

The Straits Times (1967, December 23). No Suitable Men for 3 Top Posts. *The Straits Times*, p. 4.

Thio, L. (2009) The passage of a generation: Revisiting the report of the 1966 constitutional commission. In Thio, L. and Tan, Y.L. (Eds.) *Evolution of a revolution: Forty years of the Singapore constitution* (pp. 7–8). New York, NY: Routledge-Cavendish.

Undang-undang bagi Anggota Majlis Ugama Islam dan Istiadat Melayu Kelantan, No. 14 (1916), Kelantan.

Wok, O. Singapore Parliament Report (Administration of Muslim Law Bill), 17 August 1966.

Yegar, M. (1979) Islam and Islamic Institutions in British Malaya: Policies and implementation (pp. 94–109) Jerusalem, Israel: The Magnes Press.

2

INSTITUTION BUILDING
AND COMMUNITY
DEVELOPMENT : DYNAMICS
OF MUIS' DUAL IDENTITY
*Azree Rahim and
Yazid Mohamed Ali*

Introduction

In 2000, when the Singapore government made primary school education compulsory through the Compulsory Education (CE) Act, madrasahs in Singapore were brought to the forefront of public discussions. In his National Day Rally that same year, Prime Minister Goh Chok Tong shared his concerns that madrasah students may not be equipped to thrive in the New Economy given the nature of the madrasah curriculum which gives greater focus on religious subjects. With this new act, all madrasah students are required to sit for the Primary School Leaving Examinations (PSLE)[1] and all madrasahs had to ensure that their students meet a minimum performance benchmark in order for the madrasah to be allowed to continue taking in primary level students in future.[2] This led to anxieties within

---

[1] The PSLE is a national examination in Singapore that is administered by the Ministry of Education and taken by all students near the end of their sixth year in primary school before they move on to secondary school.

[2] The benchmark set by Ministry of Education (MOE) is pegged at the average PSLE aggregate score of Malay pupils in the six lowest performing national primary schools who take four Standard-level subjects.

the Muslim community about the future of the madrasahs and religious graduates. Many in the community feared that this will result in the closing of madrasahs.

Muis was at the centre of this debate. As a statutory board overseeing the madrasah sector, its statutory function was to ensure the compliance to the CE Act. At the same time, as the religious authority overseeing the community's religious life, its expected duty is also to ensure the continued existence and sustainability of key religious institutions in the community. This underscores the challenge in the duality of Muis' identity as both a statutory board and a community organisation. As a statutory board, it is apprised of the rationale behind the strict stipulations and expectations of a statutory board. Yet, at the same time, it is also partisan to some of the community's anxieties regarding the sustainability of its key religious institutions.[3]

This chapter will begin with an appreciation of the challenges faced by Muis in its initial years. These challenges which included a lack of expertise, governance, and systems to properly operate as a statutory board were compounded by the general climate of distrust towards Muis in a post-independence context. It will then examine how Muis adapted capability building approaches from the civil service, including leadership and people development, strengthening governance and corporatisation, to address these challenges. The chapter will then highlight key policy lessons drawn from the experience implementing these initiatives while having to deal with the dual identity which at times, has raised the distrust and dissatisfaction of the community. The chapter concludes by explaining Muis' efforts to mitigate these concerns through sustaining stakeholder engagement, leveraging superior administration, promoting shared ownership, and capability building of key partners.

Expectations on the Singapore Public Service

Singapore's model of governance is seen as a benchmark in many parts of the world. Key to this exemplary governance model is the quality of the country's public service which is renowned for its integrity, forward-thinking leadership, efficiency, and service quality. Transparency International ranked

---

[3] A more detailed narrative of the CE issue and Muis efforts to address government and community concerns can be found in Chapter 5.

Singapore the seventh least corrupt nation in the world out of 176 countries studied in their 2016 Corruptions Perceptions Index (Transparency International, 2017). Singapore ranked third in the 2017 Global Competitiveness Report by the World Economic Forum (WEF, 2017). According to the World Bank's Government Effectiveness Index, Singapore was ranked highest in 2015, and has consistently ranked highly against other nations (World Bank, 2015). The best practices of agencies such as the Inland Revenue Authority of Singapore, Singapore Customs, the Public Utilities Board, the Singapore Prisons Service, and the Housing Development Board have been cited at many international best practice conferences and journals.

However, this was not the situation when Singapore first started as a nation in 1965. Back then, given the many challenges faced by the fledgling nation, Singapore's political leadership made it their key priority to develop not only a competent and efficient civil service but also one which could anticipate and adapt to future challenges. In fact, Neo and Chen (2007) argue that the current standing of Singapore's public service could be attributed to the implementation of dynamic governance: when policy-makers think ahead to perceive changes in the environment; think again to reflect on what they are currently doing; and think across to learn from others and continually incorporate the new perceptions, reflections, and knowledge into their beliefs, rules, policies, and structures to enable them to adapt to environmental change. Similarly, to thrive through its challenging operating environment especially in its early years, Muis deliberately and inadvertently developed dynamic capabilities which can be defined as "the capacity of an organisation to purposefully create, extend or modify its resource base" (Hellfat *et al.*, 2007).

The Case for Institutional Capability Building

Lack of Trust and Expertise

In its early years, among the key issues faced by Muis were a lack of trust from the Muslim community and limited administrative expertise in running a statutory board. This lack of trust stemmed from the community's perception of Muis as primarily a government body which may put the interest of the government first at the community's expense. In fact, prior to the implementation of AMLA, among the key concerns raised included the possibility of political influence over Muis (*The Straits Times*, 1966). Such distrust was further exacerbated by Muis' perceived inaction in the early

1970s, when mosques were being demolished because of the government's urban redevelopment plan.

At the time of its inception in 1968, Muis had seven staff and a president serving in a part-time capacity (Green, 2009). Subsequently, as Muis' work scope grew due to the community's increasing religious needs (at times, expanding into areas not originally provided for by AMLA), the need to grow expertise within Muis became critical. The new areas of work included mosque building, *haj*, and *halal* administration. Along with the need for expertise for this expanded scope, there was also a need for a good leadership succession plan for the apex positions in Muis.

Lack of Governance and Systems

One of earliest issues facing Muis was the management of *zakat* and *fitrah*. Prior to the implementation of AMLA, the payment of *zakat* had been left to individual awareness and local initiative or informal action. With the inception of Muis, *zakat* collection needed to be centralised. However, there was no central database of Muslim households at that time, which made it difficult to know who were eligible to pay and receive *zakat* and *fitrah* (Green 2009).

In the area of *haj* administration, Muis was asked to intervene in 1975 when some pilgrims were left stranded at the local airport. In this case, the position of Muis as Singapore's *haj* authority was progressively determined by external demands. The next critical turning point came in 1984, when the Saudi authorities made the decision to appoint an authority in each country to be responsible for the country's pilgrims. With the increasing number of pilgrims and the imposition of the fixed pilgrim quota by the Saudi authority, Muis would have to devise schemes to determine the *haj* quota allocation.

Yet another example of Muis' expanded work scope in the early days came in 1978 when drinks company, Yeo Hiap Seng wanted to export its products to the Middle East. The importing country required a halal certificate from the Islamic authority in Singapore, and Muis seemed the logical authority to provide this service.

From the 1980s, with the advent of modern mosques funded by the MBMF, the community began to see new possibilities in the role of mosques, which also led to concerns on mosque governance. Issues raised through mainstream media ranged from the mismanagement of mosque funds (*Berita Harian*, 1981), a dearth of visionary mosque leadership, the practicality of mosque design, and the possibility of providing more services to neighbouring communities (*Berita Harian*, 1978). Likewise, the lack of proper maintenance of *wakaf* properties also became a prominent issue in the late 1980s.

Developing Dynamic Capabilities

In attempting to address the above challenges, Muis embarked on several broad strategies to enhance organisational capability. These strategies can be broadly categorised into leadership and people development, strengthening governance, and lastly, corporatisation.

Leadership and People Development

A key component of organisational capability is leadership and staff development. Muis' leadership structure is enshrined in AMLA. The President of Muis and Mufti are positions appointed by the President of Singapore. The appointment of the Chief Executive requires approval from the Minister-in-charge of Muslim Affairs. Besides ensuring only qualified, competent individuals can helm Muis' key leadership positions, this system results in a stable and organised succession planning process.

Beyond the apex, it is critical to ensure that the other positions in Muis are filled by the best candidates. In this regard, being a statutory board allows Muis to adopt the Civil Service human resource management system and make necessary adjustments to suit Muis' context. This includes drawing inspiration from the Singapore government's administrative service and public sector leadership programmes. With competitive compensation and benefits package coupled with various development schemes in place, Muis has been able to attract good talent to join the organisation. More importantly, Muis has managed to attract a good blend of staff from diverse backgrounds, including the private and public sectors, as well as, from religious and non-religious backgrounds. Over the years, in tandem with the community's growing socio-religious needs, the leadership team played a key role in attracting professionals into the Muis council and workforce. From just a single secretariat of not more than 25 staff in its first 10 years, Muis now has a staff strength of more than 200, with 77 percent of Muis staff holding at least a bachelor's degree, while 31 percent of staff have post-graduate qualifications. Muis workforce possesses a wide spectrum of expertise ranging from Islamic theology, jurisprudence, humanities, business, engineering, computer science, accountancy, finance, and media. However, what is noteworthy here is the organisational ability to bring this expertise together in addressing the community's challenges. Often, policy discussions are held involving staff from diverse backgrounds so to as to benefit from multiple perspectives.

As part of the public service, Muis staff attend courses conducted by the Civil Service College. These programmes not only train the officers to develop competencies in public administration from a world-class civil service, but more importantly, it provides a platform for them to network with civil servants from other agencies, enabling them to discover areas for strategic collaboration. Several officers had also been able to go on secondments to other ministries and statutory boards, and participate in inter-agency initiatives, further honing their skills as public officers.

This combination of good career development opportunities and competitive remuneration packages, together with a unique opportunity to impact the socio-religious life of the community helps Muis to maintain a high level of employee engagement. Indeed, long-serving staff have often shared that their passion to serve in Muis stems from an innate sense of mission. This high level of staff engagement is validated by higher than average employee engagement scores when compared to the rest of the civil service (Towers Watson, 2015).[4]

Muis relies on strong religious institutions to shape the socio-religious life of the community. In this regard, it has invested substantially in the development of mosque and madrasah leaders. For the mosque sector, the introduction of the Mosque Executive Chairman (MEC) Scheme in 2005 was a key milestone in the development of mosque capabilities while facilitating alignment to Muis strategic plans and policies.[5] As a full-salaried mosque chairman, the MEC plays a critical role in overseeing mosque governance and improving the quality of mosque programmes. Key mosque programmes supervised by

---

[4] Muis Employee Engagement Index Score of 83 percent is five percent higher than the Public Sector Norm (78 percent). The survey is conducted every three years by Towers Watson using the same instrument used by other public sector agencies.

[5] See Chapter 7 for the full discussion on Muis efforts to professionalise the mosque sector.

the MECs include Islamic education, youth and social development, as well as the disbursement of Financial Assistance to *zakat* recipients. As part of efforts to strengthen mosque governance, MECs play an active role in ensuring compliance to human resource, financial, and administrative regulations for good governance. MECs also pave the way for mosques to adopt *Rahmatan Lil-Alamin* initiatives, as well as better programme planning and volunteer management.[6]

Besides the MEC scheme for full-time mosque chairmen, mosque leaders attend the intensive Administration of Mosque and Leadership (AMAL) programme, which covers strategic planning, financial, human resource, and change management. On the other hand, mosque staff take part in the Mosque Officer Development Scheme (MODS), which offers role specific training such as programme management, youth development, and management of financial assistance.

The madrasah sector has also benefitted from Muis sponsorship of developmental programmes. Madrasah principals and heads of department are given the opportunity to participate in the Leadership in Education and the Management Leadership programmes run by the National Institute of Education (NIE). Madrasah teachers are also sponsored to attend the customised Specialist Diploma in Education offered by the same institution. This exposure to the kinds of training enjoyed by their counterparts in the civil service and national schools help the madrasah teachers keep abreast of the latest developments in the education sector.

In summary, the development of leadership and people systems in Muis, mosque and madrasah sectors owe much to Muis' position as a statutory board as well as its ability to adapt good practices from the public sector.

---

[6] *Rahmatan Lil-Alamin (RLA)* is translated into English as 'Blessings to All'. Muis has been collaborating closely with the mosque fraternity to promote the ethos of *Rahmatan Lil Alamin* (RLA) or blessings to all which is an integral part of the Muis vision to *develop a gracious Muslim community of Excellence that inspires and radiates blessing to all*. It started with the formation of the RLA Mosque Committee (RLAMC) by a group of chairmen of all the six mosque clusters in Singapore in 2005 (following the outpouring of compassion from the Singaporean Muslim Community for victims of the 2004 Aceh Tsunami). The Committee is tasked with exploring projects and initiatives to promote the ethos of *Rahmatan Lil Alamin* within and beyond the community. In 2009, this effort was given a boost through the setting up of the RLA Foundation (RLAF) by Muis, to institutionalise the promotion of the RLA ethos within the Singaporean Muslim Community.

Strengthening Governance

The second organisational capability building strategy employed by Muis is strengthening governance for improved organisational performance and greater stakeholder satisfaction. This broad strategy is implemented through the following efforts: leveraging technology, institutionalising continuous improvement, consultative strategic planning, benchmarking, and sector remodelling. The following segments will elaborate on how Muis has achieved this.

Leveraging Technology for Improved Productivity

Muis gradually adopted three government initiatives to improve overall governance and its management of key processes. The first was the Civil Service Computerisation Programme (CSCP) which started in the early 1980s. The CSCP began with the creation of the National Computer Board in 1980, which provided strategic leadership focusing on computerisation of basic functions and the development of IT professionals to increase productivity in government agencies. Like their counterparts in the civil service, Muis staff were provided with personal computers, and they were trained to use them to improve overall office productivity. With the widespread adoption of the internet in the late 1990s, Muis also began to promote the use of IT in mosques by facilitating the setting up of mosque websites, e-mail accounts, and local area networks for mosque offices. Since its humble beginnings in 1994, the Information Systems Strategic Unit in Muis currently maintains 30 applications and databases serving the entire range of Muis services. Significantly, Muis now maintains a database of *zakat* payers, which enables it to reach out to existing and potential *zakat* payers effectively — thereby overcoming the challenge it faced in its early years of not having records of Muslim households.

An example of how Muis has leveraged technology to improve governance and productivity was the implementation of the Mosque Shared Services. Up till the early 2000s, the management and auditing of mosques accounts had been a long outstanding problem, with lack of discipline and expertise being the key challenge. In the late 2000s, after a dedicated and intensive two-year effort spearheaded by the Mosque Strategic Unit with help from volunteer auditors, the audit of mosque accounts was completed. To ensure that the discipline was sustained, Muis formed the Mosque Shared

Services to deploy a common mosque financial system for the sector to facilitate execution and auditing of mosque financial transactions. This has greatly improved the accuracy and transparency of mosque financial transactions, which is critical in maintaining the trust and confidence of the community.

Institutionalising Continuous Improvement

The second key public sector initiative adopted by Muis was the PS21 (Public Service of the 21st Century) movement launched in 1995 to instil a sense of urgency for change in the public sector so that it would be prepared for an uncertain and unpredictable future. PS21 was a holistic approach of engaging all levels of the public sector for organisational change, which involved anticipating, welcoming, and executing change. PS21 built upon earlier efforts in productivity improvement. Tools such as Work Improvement Teams (WITS) and staff suggestion schemes were implemented across the public service to empower staff at all levels to make improvements to their working environment and work processes. Likewise, Muis staff at all levels were trained in basic WITS techniques, like the fish-bone diagrams, pareto charts, and process mapping, and participated in annual public sector wide WITS conventions. These conventions provided opportunities for Muis staff to share their process improvement efforts while learning from the WITS projects of other agencies.

Consultative Strategic Planning

With an expanding work scope, it was critical for Muis to have an effective strategic planning process. The first semblance of strategic planning started in 1995, when the first Muis mission and vision were developed. Then, Muis engaged external consultants to work on the plan. Muis' first 3-year plan (M3YP) was developed in 2004, under the leadership of President Haji Mohammad Alami Musa, who was seconded from the Public Utilities Board (PUB). His team expanded on the vision of a "Community of Excellence"and set a bold aspiration for Muis to become one of the better statutory boards.

Beginning with an intensive environmental scanning exercise involving a wide pool of stakeholder groups at the start of the planning cycle, Muis tracks organisational performance through quarterly reporting platforms.

Its annual workplan seminar allows Muis to report organisational achievements and share highlights for the coming year while seeking inputs from its stakeholders.

Beyond the workplan seminar, inputs are gathered via regular satisfaction surveys and focused group discussions for different stakeholder groups. Insights are fed back to annual plans, which are adjusted to accommodate changes in the operating environment. This focus on keeping stakeholders constantly informed and involved in its work is key towards keeping Muis responsive to their needs contributing to increased community trust in Muis.

The rigour of the public policy process expected of any Ministry or government agency applies to Muis as well. Issues are thought through deeply and with much consideration. Important decisions are documented in policy papers, which go through multiple layers of approvals before being tabled either at Council or Minister level meetings. Such discipline forces policy-makers and planners to factor in different — at times opposing — interests and confront trade-offs to achieve the best possible outcomes.

To further benefit from the expertise of the wider community, Muis also appoints volunteers comprising professionals from various fields to helm or sit in decision-making bodies such as the Fitrah Committee, the Pilgrimage Committee, and the Audit Committee. Muis is also subjected to statutory audits, and must submit its annual reports and accounts to the parliament.

Benchmarking

The third organisational initiative which Muis adopted to benchmark itself against public sector best practices was the adoption of the Singapore Quality Award (SQA) Business Excellence (BE) Framework.[7] In 2004, in line with its organisational goal to be "One of the Better Statutory Boards", Muis set up a dedicated Organisational Excellence Strategic Unit to drive service quality and business excellence efforts throughout the organisation. Service

---

[7] The SQA BE Framework is an organisational assessment tool used to evaluate organisational performance across seven categories—Leadership, Customers, People, Processes, Strategy, Knowledge, and Results. The Framework is based on the Malcolm Baldridge model from the US and is maintained by SPRING Singapore.

standards comparable to public sector agencies were established at key stakeholder touch points, and customer satisfaction surveys were conducted annually by front line units. A Quality Service Manager hotline and a dedicated call centre was established in 2009. These initiatives helped to bring about a significant improvement in customer satisfaction from 65 percent in 2012 to 88 percent in 2015 (Black Box, 2016). Its holistic approach to organisational excellence is reflected by its attainment of the Singapore Quality Class Star Certification in 2015, and its re-certification of the People Developer Standards, Singapore Service Class and Singapore Innovation Class.

Sector Remodelling

Recognising that its ability to shape the community's religious life is also dependent on the effectiveness of its key partner institutions, i.e., the mosque and madrasah, Muis also embarked on two strategic initiatives to remodel the mosque and madrasah sectors. These two initiatives are the Enhanced Mosque Cluster (EMC)[8] and the Joint Madrasah System (JMS).

One of the key Muis functions impacted by the EMC deployment was the disbursement of financial assistance to *zakat* recipients. The EMC effectively decentralised the disbursement function to 29 designated lead mosques around the island, which were empowered to disburse financial assistance to *zakat* recipients in their neighbourhoods. This increased accessibility of financial assistance coupled with higher amounts of *zakat* collected resulted in a 116 percent increase in the average number of monthly *zakat* beneficiaries from 2,940 in 2007, to 6,363 in 2017. The assistance provided by these designated lead mosques goes beyond cash handouts and food vouchers, and also extends to connecting the families in need to the national assistance network.

---

[8] Under the EMC, a team of Muis officers headed by a General Manager is deployed to each mosque cluster to undertake the following roles:

(i) To assist mosques to empower and support *zakat* recipients more effectively and holistically through collaborations with national and community agencies as well as providing them with Islamic learning programmes; and

(ii) To empower, support and facilitate mosque leaders and staff to enhance the capabilities of the mosques in areas of corporate governance, capacity-building and also improve efficiency through pooling of resources, collaborations and joint events.

Beyond facilitating the disbursement of financial assistance, the EMCs have also contributed greatly to outreach efforts to increase participation in structured Islamic Education among the young — a key strategic imperative for Muis. Enrolment into aLIVE[9] classes had increased from 11,610 in 2007 to 21,000 in 2018.

By far, Muis' greatest investment in the madrasah sector was the formation of the JMS in partnership with Madrasah Al-Irsyad (renamed as Madrasah Irsyad Zuhri Al-Islamiah in 2015), Madrasah Aljunied and Madrasah Al-Arabiah in 2008.[10] This initiative paved the way for greater specialisation of madrasah student pathways while reaping economies of scale in madrasah administration. The specialisation of each madrasah within JMS enables a more optimal allocation of teaching and administrative resources. In addition, the secondment of experienced educators as principals for Madrasah Al-Irsyad and Madrasah Al-Arabiah, and the injection of significant funding from Muis have also greatly improved overall madrasah administration and allowed the school staff to focus on their main responsibilities as educators while mitigating concerns on the madrasahs long term financial sustainability.[11]

Corporatisation

Another initiative which Muis adapted from the civil service was corporatisation. Up till the 1980s, *wakaf* management had been under-prioritised compared to other Muis work areas. Many *wakaf* properties were not properly maintained, generating minimal or no income for their intended beneficiaries. In the late 1990s, tapping on the prevailing public service thinking of that time, Muis began studying the feasibility of corporatising their property management

---

[9] aLIVE is a part-time Islamic Education curriculum initiated by Muis in 2004 which provides religious education to young Muslims aged five to 20. The primary objective of these age-specific programmes is to impart religious education which is relevant and applicable to contemporary times to young Muslims today.

[10] Within the JMS, Madrasah Al-Irsyad acts as the primary level feeder school for both Madrasah Aljunied and Madrasah Al-Arabiah which offer secondary level education. Madrasah students more inclined to specialise in religious studies are channeled to Madrasah Aljunied while those inclined to study academic subjects in a religious environment are channeled to study in Madrasah Al-Arabiah. This arrangement leverages the strengths of each madrasah while allowing clear specialisation pathways for madrasah students.

[11] The current principals of both Madrasah Al-Irsyad and Madrasah Al-Arabiah were former vice-principals of national schools at the primary and secondary levels respectively.

function. The incorporation of Warees Investments Pte Ltd in 2002 spurred the transformation of *wakaf* and mosques, achieving better revenues and increasing the value of assets. The inception of Warees allowed specialised real estate development and investment capabilities to be built within the Muis group at a scale and speed which might not have been possible within a statutory board setup. Notable success stories resulting from this strategic move included the completion of Wakaf Bencoolen, marked as a landmark innovative mixed development project. The former Bencoolen Mosque was redeveloped and now incorporated a three-storey commercial space and a 12-storey service apartment tower managed by The Ascott Limited.[12]

In summary, Muis had leveraged greatly its position as a statutory board to adapt civil service practices in building up its organisational capability to deal with the challenges it faced in its early years as a new statutory board with limited staff, expertise, and systems.

Trade-offs and Challenges

The dual role of Muis as both a statutory board and an authority overseeing the community's religious life, as well as the above capability-building initiatives has given rise to some trade-offs and criticisms.

A perennial issue which often arises especially when certain government policies are perceived to be unfavourable to the religious aspirations of the Muslim community is the independence of Muis religious leadership. This normally surfaces when *fatwa* decisions change over time — an example is the *fatwa* on organ donation.[13] The often-heard phrase then was that Muis had gone "liberal" and diluted the teachings of Islam to toe the government's line. A similar example was the CE issue highlighted at the beginning of this chapter when Muis was not seen to be doing enough to assist the madrasah community in advocating their concerns to the relevant ministry.

---

[12] The value of the *wakaf* appreciated from SGD800,000 to more than SGD71 million in under 10 years. Wakaf Bencoolen also won a Regional Award in 2006 for the category Regional Continuing Contribution to Islamic Finance at the Sheikh Mohammed Bin Rashid Al Makhtoum Islamic Finance Awards for its Islamic *Sukuk* financing model.

[13] See Chapter 3 on *Contextualisation and Modernisation: Islamic Thought through Fatwas in Singapore*, for a fuller discussion on the issues concerning Muis *fatwa* on organ donation.

Moreover, an inevitable concern as a result of Muis capability building efforts is the capability gap between Muis and the Malay/Muslim organisations. The perception of a professional and well-resourced Muis, and its ability to dynamically adapt its scope of work to address the community's needs has already given rise to the idea of Muis being a "one-stop-shop" for all issues deemed religious by the Muslim community, even when some of these issues are beyond Muis jurisdiction as a statutory board. For example, some Malay/Muslim organisations have often voiced their preference for Muis to undertake the coordination of social service assistance within the sector, especially since the EMCs are already disbursing financial assistance and are well connected to both government social service agencies in their vicinities. If left unchecked, this unhealthy trend will lead to a weaker civil society which in turn will cripple Muis' ability to achieve its mission — *to work with the community in developing a profound religious life and dynamic institutions.*

Another concern often raised is that the increased governance and efficiency of Muis and its key sectors (mosques and madrasah) comes at the expense of autonomy and bottom-up innovation, which is so critical in optimising the human social capital within the volunteer community. Such bureaucratisation also tends to decrease the voluntary and altruistic intent so vital in the provision of socio-religious services. For example, despite increased accessibility of financial assistance via the 29 designated lead mosques around the island, there have been complaints on the lack of empathy or poor service for *zakat* recipients on the part of mosque officers. There have also been reports that financial assistance was relatively easier to come by from other religious groups when compared to that from Muis or mosques.

Balancing Roles and Addressing Criticisms

In addressing the above challenges, Muis adopts a long-term orientation and holistic approach which can be broadly categorised as follows: sustained stakeholder engagement; leveraging superior administration for positive long-term results; promoting shared creation and ownership; and facilitating capability development of key partners.

As described above, among the most often-heard criticism of Muis' dual role is the independence of its religious leadership. Arguably, the credibility of its religious leadership is also dependent on its ability to command the respect of the local *asatizah* fraternity, which in turn commands the respect of the

Muslim community. Recognising this relationship, Muis has made *asatizah* engagement and development a priority over the years. Since the inception of the first Muis 3-year plan (M3YP) in 2004, the Asatizah Network Strategic Unit and, subsequently, Muis Academy has played a key role in sensitising the *asatizah* fraternity with the realities of exercising religious leadership in the context of a religious minority within a modern society and secular state. Various platforms including the Asatizah Executive Development programme, the annual Muis Seminar (for students pursuing tertiary religious education overseas), the Muis Asatizah Attachment programme, and regular roundtable discussions and conferences with renowned international religious scholars are conducted, with the key aim of developing the intellectual and religious leadership capabilities of the *asatizah* by enabling them to critically analyse and discuss solutions to emerging issues impacting the community's socio-religious life. In addition, before the release of important *fatwa* which have major impact on the Muslim community, Muis holds extensive consultations with the *asatizah* fraternity so that they fully appreciate the thinking behind the *fatwa* decision-making, which often takes into account multiple and inter-disciplinary perspectives. In general, this developmental and consultative approach in *asatizah* engagement has garnered encouraging responses from the *asatizah* fraternity.[14] *Asatizah* are now more confident in publishing their personal opinions in mainstream and social media on potentially controversial religious issues with sound and credible arguments. While some may remain openly critical of Muis' stand on certain issues, others are more receptive, which reflect the progress on Muis' efforts to produce a more informed and progressive religious leadership. In turn, such leadership will develop a more sophisticated religious community with a more profound understanding and practice of Islam in Singapore's unique context.

Complementing sustained stakeholder engagement with the mosque and madrasah sectors, Muis chose to leverage its superior administration to produce positive long-term results for these sectors. For the mosque sector, Muis had chosen to take a long-term and holistic improvement approach with clearly defined focus areas and outcomes. The focus on people, programmes, systems, and infrastructure was executed with strong administrative nous.

---

[14] In a public perception survey conducted in 2012, 69 percent of respondents acknowledged that Muis plays an important role in facilitating the development of *asatizah* and religious teachers. In another poll conducted in the same year, 90 percent of *asatizah* (aged 29 and below) acknowledged that the engagements have made them aware and confident in dealing with contemporary issues and 87 percent found that knowledge of the modern sciences is necessary.

Customised training for mosque staff and leaders was supplemented with development of sound governance practices and driven by clear strategies derived through extensive consultation with key stakeholder groups. The deployment of the MECs and the implementation of the EMC greatly facilitated the execution of strategies derived through the various mosque conventions. This has resulted in generally high stakeholder satisfaction as indicated by results from the Mosque Perception Survey (Muis, 2015). [15] These results validate the effectiveness of the convention strategies, which are further revised based on any areas of improvements uncovered through the survey. This result-oriented approach has enabled Muis to remain focused on the big picture while still keeping track of stakeholder concerns.

For the madrasah sector, Muis focused on a defined consolidation strategy (JMS) with clear focus areas and long-term outcomes for each madrasah. The emphasis on teacher training, curriculum enhancement, and an improved student experience is guided by a clear intent to consolidate and enable specialisation of student pathways, thereby reducing student attrition rates. This focus has reaped some early rewards. The modern curriculum of Madrasah Al-Irsyad has attracted attention from Thailand, Malaysia, Indonesia and as far as the United States, and spawned the setup of Madrasah Al-Irsyad-inspired schools. Seventy-five percent of survey respondents indicated that Muis provides the right direction for madrasah education (Black Box, 2016). In addition, the increased participation of students from madrasahs in national competitions in the academic and sports arena (Liew, 2010) has also gained much media attention.[16]

Muis had also continued to seek greater government assistance to the madrasah to help better prepare students and teachers for national examinations. The positive reports of madrasah performance have arguably played an important role in the eventual decision by the government to provide more support for madrasah education in the form of Edusave grants for madrasah students and, later, additional grants for teacher salary top-ups and student awards.[17] In particular, the government's latter contribution was

---

[15] The last survey conducted in 2014 by Nexus Link Pte Ltd on 1,000 respondents sought to measure mosques' effectiveness in meeting the expectations and needs of the Muslim community in relation to its services and administration. The findings indicated an engagement index of 84 percent which reflected the community's positive experience and perception of mosque services.

[16] See Simangoon (2015) and Diman (2016).

[17] See Afifah (2015) and Heng (2013).

also matched by Muis' additional grants to madrasah teachers teaching religious subjects. The government's open assistance to the madrasah here is unprecedented, and reflects its acknowledgement of the madrasahs' significance to the community's religious life which also contributes to a cohesive Singaporean society. On the other hand, the recent stable performances of madrasah students especially for the Primary School Leaving Examinations (PSLE)[18] had also raised some voices within the community on the need for the madrasah to be continually subjected to the PSLE benchmark given the government's acknowledgement of the madrasahs main role, i.e. the development of future religious leaders.

Relating to the issue of decreased autonomy for the mosque and madrasah sectors, Muis strives to ensure that in developing and implementing plans for the mosque and madrasah sectors, the relevant stakeholder groups were constantly engaged to promote co-creation and ensure the co-ownership of outcomes. Decision-making and planning platforms were established with adequate representations from key stakeholder groups. For the mosque sector, the mosque convention held every five years is a key platform for the mosque community to collectively review progress and chart future directions. In between the mosque conventions, mosque council meetings are held bi-annually to update on the progress of mosque convention strategies, and bring up any strategic issues requiring attention.

For the madrasah sector, quarterly meetings involving madrasah leaders and chaired by Muis ensured that issues affecting the madrasahs are discussed thoroughly. Likewise, the formation of the Board of Governors for the JMS greatly facilitated the coordination and alignment required for the three madrasahs to work in unison, especially in the formative stages of the partnership. In addition to these platforms Muis also works closely with JMS madrasah teachers in curriculum development and teacher training. These consultative approaches give ample space for the ground to voice out and discuss ideas while promoting co-creation and co-ownership of desired outcomes.

In relation to concerns on the increasing capability gap between Muis and Malay/Muslim organisations, the preceding paragraphs have also shown

---

[18] The percentage of madrasah students eligible for the Express Stream at Secondary level has improved from 39 percent in 2011 to 66 percent in 2017.

how Muis had extended its capability building efforts to the leadership and staff of two key institutions under its purview — mosque and madrasahs. The *asatizah* fraternity has also benefitted from Muis' development and engagement efforts, and these benefits may trickle down to organisations managed by or employing these *asatizah* beyond the mosque and madrasahs. Muis has also seconded staff to helm senior positions at the Registry of Muslim Marriages (ROMM) and the Syariah Court. Beyond manpower, Muis also funds selected socio-religious programmes run by Malay/Muslim organisations such as Darul Arqam, Pergas, Club Heal, Tabung Amal Aidilftri, as well as APKIM and PEACE (partners in the Empowerment Partnership Scheme).[19]

What the Future Holds

Muis' continued success depends on the level of trust it can generate from both the government and the community. Thus far, based on indicators such as stakeholder perception surveys,[20] the community's level of trust in Muis is favourable. There is also a positive co-relation of increasing income streams with this high trust.[21]

At the national level, the community's progressive religious life shaped by Muis religious and administrative leadership has been acknowledged by DPM Tharman Shanmugaratnam:

> We are not a model that any other society can or would want to simply repli-
> cate. But other nations do take note of our progress and innovations, just as we
> learn from their experiences. There is interest in what we do in various areas
> of public policy and administration. There is also growing interest in the ways
> in which we have developed social harmony. The inspiring efforts of our

---

[19] The Empowerment Partnership Scheme was launched by Muis in 2004 as a targeted effort to provide *zakat* beneficiaries with more holistic assistance in achieving self-reliance.

[20] The findings from Muis' last Public Perception Survey in 2016, showed that 83 percent of 1,030 respondents polled indicated their Trust in Muis for developing the Muslim community and for disbursing *zakat;* 73 percent felt that Muis was effective in advising the government in relation to the community's religious life while 77 percent indicated that Muis provides guidance in Islamic practices; and 78 percent felt that Muis adequately supports children from needy Muslim families.

[21] The inflow of community funds to Muis through key revenue streams such as *wakaf, zakat,* and *baitulmal* has grown in recent years. The total revenue has gone up from $75.7 million in 2013 to $95 million in 2016.

Muslim community in this regard are I am sure being noticed and discussed. (Shanmugaratnam, 2017).

With increasing stakeholder expectations, a more diverse society, and a rapidly changing inter-connected environment, trust-building will continue to be a key priority for Muis, both at the community and national level, as it strives to perform its dual role effectively. Indeed, the growing emphasis on building "a trusted public service that connects and works with citizens" is a key thrust of the government's Public Sector Transformation (PST) movement, which seeks to improve trust with greater citizen involvement in policy-making and co-creation of public services.[22]

Going forward, Muis will need to intensify its efforts to involve and work closely with existing and new partners to generate solutions to achieve its strategic goals. This is important in view of the current landscape where the Muslim community has become increasingly active and concerned about socio-religious issues and has shown higher expectation to be engaged and consulted. Thus, collaboration and co-creation will characterise Muis' approach in delivering and executing policies and programmes. In addition, the outcomes from Muis initiatives are also likely to have a positive impact at the national level. Dynamic socio-religious institutions and an inspiring Singaporean Muslim community will contribute towards religious harmony, a pillar of social stability. This leads to confidence in the country which then spurs further growth and development.

Another critical success factor for Muis is the capability of its key partners and civil society in general. To avoid or minimise over-dependence on Muis for all issues deemed religious, Muis' key partners, including Malay/Muslim organisations, may need to consider alternative levers for additional resources. For example, rather than focusing just on the needs of the Malay/Muslim community, would they be willing to consider extending their services to the larger Singaporean society, thereby increasing their accessibility to greater government and non-Muslim support and funding? This approach of mainstreaming services offered by MMOs may also contribute towards trust-building at the national level.

---

[22] See Ong (2016). The PST, launched in 2012, builds on the forward thinking and change readiness ethos of PS21 with a greater focus on inter-agency collaboration, citizen-centric policies and strengthening trust with citizens through more community partnerships.

Muis started its capability development journey in 1968 with a significant trust deficit with the community. While this deficit has shrunk significantly since then, trust building via collaboration and co-creation will remain a key priority in its continuing effort to realise its vision of "A Community of Excellence which Inspires and Radiates Blessings to All".

References

Ariffin, A. (2015, August 23). NDR 2015. Govt to help strengthen teaching of secular subjects in madrasahs. *ChannelNewsAsia*. Retrieved from http://www. channel newsasia.com/news/singapore/ndr-2015-govt-to-help-strengthen-teaching-of-secular-subjects-in-8225066.

Berita Harian (1981, January 5). Masjid perlukan satu system kewangan, harta yang baik. *Berita Harian*.

Berita Harian (1978, September 11). Masjid-masjid moden perlu penuhi fungsi sbg pusat pembentukan masyarakat. *Berita Harian*.

Black Box (2016). Muis Public Perception Survey.

Diman, H. (2016, August 8). Al-Arabiah raih pingat perak dalam pertandingan mema-nah. *Berita Harian*. Retrieved from http://www.beritaharian.sg/setempat/al-arabiah-raih-pingat-perak-dalam-pertandingan-memanah.

Green, A. (2009). Honouring the Past, Shaping the Future. The Muis Story: 40 Years of Building a Singapore Muslim Community of Excellence.

Heng, J. (2013, August 18). NDR 2013: Edusave extended to include madrasah students. *Straits Times*. Retrieved from www.straitstimes.com/singapore/ndr-2013-edusave-extended-to-include-*madrasah*-students.

Helfat, C.E., Finkelstein, S., Mitchell, W., Peteraf, M.A., Singh, H., Teece, D.J. and Winter, S.G. (2007). *Dynamic Capabilities: Understanding Strategic Change in Organizations*. London: Blackwell.

Liew, B. (2010, August 22). Bittersweet Day for Singapore's fourth medallist. *Urbanwire*. Retrieved from https://www.theurbanwire.com/2010/08/bittersweet-day-for-singaporea'%e2%80%99s-fourth-medallist/

Neo, B.S. and Chen, G. (2007). *Dynamic Governance: Embedding Culture, Capabilities and Change in Singapore*. Singapore: World Scientific.

Nexus Link (2014). Mosque Perception Survey.

Norimitsu, O. (2009, April 22). In Singapore, a More Progressive Islamic Education. *The New York Times*. Retrieved from https://www.nytimes.com/2009/04/23/world/asia/23singapore.html.

Ong, P. (2016, August 5). Catalysing Change in the Public Service. *Singapore Public Service Blog*. Retrieved from http://www.psd.gov.sg/blog/article/catalysing_change_in_the_public_service.

Simangoon, N. D. (2015, December 6). Pelajar madrasah julang tempat pertama per-aduan teknologi digital universiti Australia. *Berita Mediacorp*. Retrieved from https://berita.mediacorp.sg/mobilem/singapore/pelajar-*madrasah*-julang/2321670.html.

Shanmugaratnam, T. (2017, February 11). DPM Tharman Shanmugaratnam at the Conference on *Fatwa* in Contemporary Societies organised by MUIS. Retrieved from http://www.pmo.gov.sg/newsroom/dpm-tharman-shanmugaratnam-conference-*fatwa*-contemporary-societies-organised-Muis

The Straits Times (1966, August 18). Muslim Law Bill is passed in Parliament. *The Straits Times*, p. 18. Towers Watson (2015). Muis Employee Engagement Survey.

Transparency International (2016). Corruption Perceptions Index 2016. Retrieved from https://www.transparency.org/news/feature/corruption_perceptions_index_2016.

World Bank (2016). Government Effectiveness Index. Retrieved from https://www.theglobleconomy.com/rankings/wb_government_effectiveness.

World Economic Forum (2017). Global Competitiveness Report 2017-2018. Retrieved from https://www.weforum.org/reports/the-global-competitiveness-report-2017–2018.

Part 2

Shaping Religious Life and Education

3

CONTEXTUALISATION AND MODERNISATION: ISLAMIC THOUGHT THROUGH *FATWAS* IN SINGAPORE

Nazirudin Nasir

Issues of jurisprudence and law feature prominently in the corpus of Muslim religious works and in cultures of religious life. They document the diverse ways in which communities, under the guidance of jurists and scholars, negotiate the demands of lived realities and adherence to God's sacred law. Collectively, these issues and the debates around them provide insights into the development of Muslim communities, especially because of the relationship between socio-political realities and interpretations of sacred law.

A key tool of jurisprudence that sheds light on these negotiations is Muslim judicial *responsa* known as *fatwas*, or religious rulings, issued by a mufti (juristconsult) on points of Muslim law. In contemporary times where state and religion interact in complex ways, *fatwas* have evolved into more advanced forms beyond simply a response by a jurist to questions. Some *fatwas* have become official positions issued by state-appointed bodies, rather than opinions of individuals. In such a context, *fatwas* mediate between state and community. By examining points of Muslim law discussed from a *fatwa* perspective, and the rationale and justification provided in *fatwa* positions, as well as the concomitant responses and reactions to these *fatwa*s in society, we can discern the state of, and transformations within a community's religious life.

In the case of Singapore, *fatwa*s are centrally administered through Muis, a statutory board established through the Administration of Muslim Law Act. The *fatwa* institution, together with the religious leadership that administers it, operates in a secular political environment with the aim of guiding a minority Muslim community in its religious life. Inevitably, the *fatwa* institution, in responding to new issues and proposing novel solutions that may run against traditional Muslim ideas and teachings, has to overcome issues of credibility and representativeness. This is particularly evident where the receptivity of the community towards *fatwa*s is studied alongside the *fatwa*s themselves.

Fatwa Tradition in Islam

The practice of *fatwa*s by qualified jurists has a long and diverse tradition in Islam. The body of classical *fatwa* literature points to two main sources of *fatwa*s: individual jurists to whom questions on points of Muslim law were posed (Masud, Messick, and Powers, 1996) and muftis appointed by rulers or governments. The latter form was a common practice, especially during the Ottoman rule, and became more widespread with the formation of Muslim nation states (Zubaida, 2005). In more recent times, regional and international *fatwa* bodies were formed to encourage exchange of ideas and build consensus on issues commonly faced by different Muslim communities (Dien, 2004).

*Fatwa*s can serve a very basic function: to educate Muslims on religious laws — the permissible and prohibited acts in Islam. Most questions put forth by Muslims relate to fundamental Islamic teachings. However, as life transforms, and societies undergo change, issues with no precedent in the Islamic legal corpus have arisen. In this instance, the process of *fatwa* making, especially when it seeks to facilitate the religious life of Muslims in a new context, attests to the recognition in Islam that change is inevitable and must be dealt with appropriately. This suitability and adaptability of Islam to changed contexts and environments through the instrument of *ijtihad* (and by extension, *fatwa* making) have long been discussed. The continued development of Islamic law is well-noted, as a contemporary jurist describes:

> The small circle of innovative scholars of jurisprudence, small though their numbers may be, constitutes a guarantee that Islamic jurisprudence will go on progressing to the point at which it becomes linked anew with the objectives of Islamic Law and their supporting evidence, and comes to be applied in Muslim courts and lands (al-Raysuni, 2006).

For Muslim jurists and muftis, *ijtihad* has functioned as a key tool that permits a reasoned engagement with sacred texts while recognising that a change in environment and context may positively condition the interpretation of Muslim law. Through *ijtihad*, the teachings of Islam resist ossification which will only hinder progress and development of Muslim societies. Accordingly, jurists and muftis trained in the interpretation of sacred texts endeavour to offer new readings as part of seeking solutions and adapting the teachings of Islam to new conditions and environments.

Fatwa Institution in Singapore

As noted above, jurists who served as muftis were either state-appointed (as in the case of the Ottoman era) or independent. In the 20th century, many Muslim nations formed national *fatwa* councils comprising jurists and experts to discuss *fatwa*-related matters. Singapore was no exception. The formation of Muis through the enactment of the Administration of Muslim Law Act (AMLA) in 1966 paved the way for the formation of a Legal Committee within Muis tasked to issue official religious rulings. The need for such a committee to interpret religious law follows the role of Muis to administer the religious affairs of the Muslim community, given the emerging contextual needs faced by the community, the anticipated lack of precedent in Islamic jurisprudence, or when they relate to national policies. The formation of a Legal Committee under AMLA automatically differentiates the nature of *fatwas* issued in Singapore from its traditional variants mentioned above. For example, Muis' *fatwas* have been considered in the court of law as valid interpretations of Muslim law such as on the creation of *wakaf* properties and estate matters (Abbas, 2012).

More critically, the nature of the socio-religious life of any community has a profound impact on the type of *fatwa* issues. Over the course of almost half a century of its existence, the Legal Committee has had to address new questions or provide new answers to old questions as part of a review and re-evaluation warranted in new contexts. Consider the rapid scientific and technological advancements in a city such as Singapore, which situate Muslims at the centre of ethical and religious dilemmas given traditional religious injunctions that may conflict with a modern way of life. In areas such as scientific progress, medical advancements, and financial innovation, Muslims in Singapore could avail themselves to new instruments and technologies which would improve the quality of life, yet at the same time, encounter traditional rulings that require reinterpretation. An example is the determination of prayer times and the beginning and end of lunar months, which is an important aspect of the ritual practice in Islam. In view of Singapore's technological prowess and its emphasis on mathematical and scientific education, it is only natural that Singapore relies on accurate data on astronomical phenomena. In the Islamic case, the *hisab* method (astronomical calculations) can be used to determine prayer times and the lunar months, as opposed to physical observation of astronomical phenomena. For some Muslims, *hisab* as the default method conflicts with prophetic guidance.

Likewise, Singapore's position as one of the world's most important financial hubs means that the level of affluence and ownership of complex assets is likely to be higher than in other parts of the world. New and more complex financial instruments are thus a common feature in Singapore's wealth and financial landscape. Add to this the impact of modernity on society and family structures. Given these conditions, should and could, Muslims rely only on traditional forms of wealth transfers and instruments? These apparent conflicts can be unsettling to Muslims who rely heavily on religion as a stabilising force in their lives amid change and uncertainty in other domains of life. This stability is perceived through the immutability of God's laws as manifested in the life of the Prophet. In this vein, the prophetic injunction for Muslims to begin and end fasting in Ramadan when the crescent moon is *sighted* meant that astronomical calculations should not replace a physical sighting. For such individuals, relying on *hisab* alone is seen as a violation of God's immutable laws and an innovation that must be rejected.

In addition, the complexity and multi-dimensional nature of contemporary issues warrants new approaches as well as jurisprudential frameworks in interpreting religious texts. While the concept of *ijtihad* inspires and permits change and reform, it has usually operated within established frameworks and parameters in classical Islamic thought. Thus, it may not be able to yield creative responses for the purposes of adequately addressing complex new questions. For example, the conditions for its use as defined in classical works limits its scope of implementation to a specific juristic tradition or school. A case in point is the influential legal maxim that "certainty cannot be overridden by doubt" (*al-yaqin la yuzal bi al-syak*). In discussions on biomedical advancements, this maxim is often invoked to guard against speculative scientific methods and technologies (i.e., whose outcomes cannot be ascertained and therefore, reach a level of certainty). However, by definition, scientific research and experiment rests on the premise of doubt and speculation in the pursuit of new discoveries. To what extent then is this maxim relevant in discussing new scientific findings? This may matter less in a society that does not thrive on scientific progress, but becomes more pertinent in the Singapore context, as it actively encourages and invests heavily in scientific research.

More importantly, the responses of the Muslim community to these issues in our context have a greater and more pressing socio-political consequence — is Islam compatible with a modern and secular state such as Singapore? Put differently, will the Muslim religious life be an encumbrance to the progress of the rest of society? In relating this to the classical conditions of *ijtihad* and *fatwa* making, an important fact that needs to be considered is that the operative environments of past scholars and jurists are markedly different from contemporary life, especially after the institutionalisation of the nation state system and the importance given to the freedoms and rights of individuals.

In most cases, when a state or institution seeks its own unique solutions for its own problems, and in the process, departs from a mainstream or established ruling, it risks losing credibility. Additionally, the need for stability amidst constant and intense change, may also result in a resistance to any form of re-interpretation of religious laws. Differences in the contexts of Muslim communities around the world, while important for the purposes of interpreting and contextualising religious laws, are rarely considered by the Muslim laity due to the sense of a universal nature of Islamic teachings. This problem is now perpetuated by the circulation of views and ideas from all parts of the world on the Internet and social media. Singapore has an added challenge. Given that it is not ruled by a Muslim government, any reluctance to adhere to local *fatwas* and religious views can conveniently be reasoned by the perceived lack of credibility of the religious authority which is affiliated with a non-Muslim government.

In this context, *fatwas* signify more than just a form of religious guidance to the community. The process of *fatwa* making, and engagements with the Muslim community on new *fatwas*, show how religious laws are continuously re-interpreted to respond to the changing circumstances of lived experiences. In the case of Singapore, the *fatwa* institution contributes towards charting the direction for the community's religious life. To this end, the *fatwas* are derived with the Singapore context in mind, and thus may diverge from positions from *fatwa* bodies abroad. As discussed above, when the *fatwa* institution introduces fresh readings of Muslim law that seek to transform religious attitudes towards progressiveness, it must be supported by an updated religious education that addresses the non-immutable aspects of Islam as well as directs the community towards the values and spirit of Islam rather than its form. These currents of religious life can be seen in various issues which the *fatwa* institution has dealt with in its 40-years history. The following briefly discusses two areas, namely organ transplantation and inheritance, in which religious laws interplay with various other socio-political circumstances.

Organ Donation

The *fatwa* positions on the subject of organ donation and transplantation over a period of three decades dealt with various aspects, such as the sanctity of the human body, the act of donating one's organs as well as issues of public interest. It must be noted that juristic opinions on the subject, as seen from positions issued by international *fatwa* bodies, have also largely evolved from one of prohibition to permissibility (Ministry of Health Malaysia, 2011). In the context of Singapore, the issue was not just about the act of donating and harvesting organs but included other relevant points of Muslim law, such as presumed consent or permission for donation through the Human Organ Transplant Act (HOTA). While its primary consideration was how to read and reinterpret religious texts, the Fatwa Committee had to factor in the state of medical advancement, the extent to which the situation of organ failure was dire in the Muslim community, and public readiness to accept organs harvested from a cadaveric donor. These were critical in interpreting afresh religious injunctions and principles of jurisprudence such as emergency (*darura*) and public interest (*maslaha*). Its aim was to ensure that the Muslim community remained confident and participated fully in national life without compromising religious principles. However, central to the discussion was the broader implication of non-participation in a national scheme. When the *fatwa* prohibited organ donation, it automatically excluded Muslims from contributing to the national pool of organ donors — the exclusion of Muslims here had a deeper significance to Muslim participation, in this case, a lack thereof, in contributing towards the common good.

At the heart of its thinking is a fundamental theological issue: who has the right over the human body, especially after death, and how should the sanctity of the human body be understood in Islam where medical procedures on the cadaver are concerned. It followed from this that the issue of *maslaha* and *darura* were not primary considerations for many Muslims in the first instance, as the worry over what happens to the corpse if it is dissected for transplantation became the main preoccupation. In this sense, the concern that held Muslims back from becoming organ donors had little to do with the desire to or lack thereof help but rather, if the act was religiously permissible. In fact, the earliest *fatwa* discussions on the matter in the early 1970s reflected this sentiment. While the Fatwa Committee generally recognised the need for, and benefits of, medical research, there was unease in challenging the theological nature of the issue: God's absolute right over human beings, as this understanding is rooted in scripture. In this regard, the understanding that only God can do with our bodies what He wishes informed the position of the Committee. There were no considerations of the severity of the medical situation. This had led to the *fatwa* in 1973 which forbade all forms of organ transplantation. In essence, the Committee argued that the sanctity of the human body as entrusted to man by God must be protected, and the risks in transplant operations supersede potential benefits. For the Committee, the benefits of organ transplantation at the time were not widely known and were thus perceived as speculative (*dzanni*). For example, it was not public knowledge in the 1970s that the transplants of liver and lung were generally successful. There was thus no need for a review of the juristic position on organ transplantation (Watson and Dark, 2012) . What this meant was that the assumption that harm may result from such procedures was not convincingly challenged.

However, there were some voices in the Muslim community which argued for the permissibility of some transplants such as cornea and kidney, on the basis of the objectives and spirit of Islam, as opposed to its form and literal interpretations adopted by the Committee. In particular, a prominent local scholar Professor Syed Hussein Alatas, publicly challenged the Committee's interpretations in a series of articles published in the local paper *Berita Harian* in 1973, arguing that the Committee's views demonstrated "a lack of understanding of contemporary sciences, a lack of respect for the intellect, a narrow interpretation of the Qur'an and Prophetic traditions, and a confused reasoning" (Alatas, 2015). Alatas reasoned that organ donation is a form of charitable act permitted by Islam and is supported by its religious texts. Compared to such views, the Committee's position then was rather conservative. Given the nascent nature of the Fatwa Committee (these debates took place less than 10 years after its formation), it reflected a sense of caution and there was no appetite to differ from the positions of other *fatwa* bodies which prohibited organ donation.[1] The Committee maintained its position, and engaged the likes of Professor Alatas in the public realm.

It should also be noted that the Muslim community, however, was not alone in their rejection of organ donation. The Abrahamic religions (Judaism, Christianity, and Islam), which place special emphasis on sacred texts as source of law, had a common teaching on the resurrection of the whole body and prohibition of self-mutilation, although there were alternative Christian views that the act of donating an organ is consistent with the Christian values of humanitarianism and love for one's neighbour (Howard, 2005). However, no church prohibited donating or receiving organs, and the public discourse about the procedure in Singapore was generally supportive *(The Straits Times,* 1975; *The Straits Times,* 1986; *The Straits Times*, 2003).

It was only in 1985 that the Committee reviewed its *fatwa* and decided to permit organ transplantation on the basis of *darura*. The sharp increase in

---

[1] At the time, there were already *fatwas* which permitted organ donation, such as in Egypt, and some *fatwa* bodies in Malaysia. However, most jurists held a more cautious view of prohibition, whilst many others allowed it only under extenuating circumstances.

the number of people afflicted with kidney problems then requiring organ transplants may have been an impetus to the review, but this *fatwa* came on the heels of a *fatwa* issued by the International Islamic Fiqh Academy in Mecca. The Academy was influential in the Muslim world as it comprised international scholars and jurists, and consequently, its positions symbolised a consensus (*ijma'*), which is a source of law in Muslim jurisprudence.

The community's awareness on the new position was not particularly poignant until in 1994 when a local organisation, Jamiyah, organised an international seminar to discuss the subject of organ donation. The Fatwa Committee was represented by the Mufti and other international scholars including those from Brunei and Saudi Arabia attended the conference. As the need for organ transplants increased because of an increasingly acute medical situation, the juristic discussion moved towards considering less threatening but serious circumstances. Further, new organs for donation were considered, including cornea. The Committee then issued a *fatwa* to permit cornea donation, which was a considerable shift in *fatwa* thinking, as in this case, permissibility of a medical procedure was no longer limited to emergencies and life and death situations. In this instance, the basic needs of human beings, known as *hajjiyyat* in Islamic jurisprudence, (such as improving eyesight) was given the same level of consideration as a *darura*, in line with the legal maxim that "necessity may take the form of exigency". It also considers the objectives of law, and places emphasis on the importance of balancing between different types of harms, i.e., leaving the patient blind or using donated corneas from a deceased person.

The Fatwa Committee had also stressed that organ transplant is a form of treatment that is accepted by religion, and does not constitute a procedure that violates the sanctity of the deceased. The shift away from established norms such as the fundamental importance of the sanctity of the human body is paradigmatic, in that it prioritises the values and spirit of Islam in interpreting its laws over predefined structures and forms. This *fatwa* thus opened new pathways in the Fatwa Committee's assessment of subsequent issues on organ transplants.

However, the proposed participation of Muslims in HOTA presented the Fatwa Committee with two major new challenges from the religious perspective. First is that the scheme works on the basis of presumed consent, a concept that is alien to Islamic law. Second is that the scheme would place a majority number of Muslims as potential organ donors so long as they do not opt out from the scheme. The move to include Muslims under HOTA therefore was not simply about a change in religious law but was one that had a broader policy significance in the context of a multi-religious Singapore. As noted earlier, could Muslims participate fully, alongside others, in contributing towards the common good by becoming organ donors? To continue to be excluded from the scheme, therefore, had a more serious implication: that Islam resists change in a modern and progressive nation. The Committee thus needed to consider what could overcome these concerns.

To address these, the Committee considered anew the severity of organ failure case in Singapore. As a result of the exclusion of Muslims from HOTA, they were placed on a lower priority for receiving donated organs. Yet, the burden faced by kidney patients is very taxing; the cost of weekly kidney dialysis is exorbitant while many lose their jobs because of the need for dialysis treatment (Thye and Lee, 1998). Under the opt-in scheme, relatively few Muslims had signed up to be organ donors. In the decade between 1997 and 2007, the number of Muslims as a percentage of the total number of patients on dialysis jumped from 15 percent to 25 percent (Lin, 2008; Thye and Lee, 1998). The number of Muslim kidney patients who required dialysis was thus disproportionate to the number of Muslims in Singapore.

When the proposal to amend HOTA to include Muslims emerged in the early 2000s, (*Berita Harian*, 2003; *Berita Harian*, 2004; *Berita Harian*, 2007) the Muslim reaction was largely positive, and the idea had substantial support from the Muslim grassroots. However, HOTA had also resuscitated old debates on the subject. Concerns on organ donation generally stemming from theological grounds were heard from some quarters within the Muslim community. Those who felt strongly against the proposed move were invited to public dialogue sessions organised by the Ministry of Health, Muis, and People's Association (*Berita Harian*, 2007). Many valuable feedback and ideas were raised and subsequently implemented, including ensuring no delay to the funeral rites and burial because of HOTA procedures and the need to clarify on the definition on death (as HOTA relies on 'brain death' as the point of death). Government agencies worked together to find solutions and address these concerns. For example, all hospitals ensured that they have the adequate facilities for the washing of the deceased according to Muslim rites, should this step be needed to expedite the funeral process.

As a result of the amendment to include Muslims under HOTA, the number of successful transplants among the Malay/Muslim community almost doubled in 2008 compared to the preceding year, making up 19 percent of all organ transplants in Singapore (*Today*, 2009). From the perspective of Muslim jurisprudence, the Fatwa Committee found a balance between protecting life and preserving the sanctity of the deceased, by adopting the *maqasid* approach.

There are emerging areas in biomedicine which will continue to present opportunities to update and refresh Islamic thought. For example, the Committee, together with the Office of the Mufti, has actively given its views on various consultations by the Bioethics Advisory Committee on a range of issues.[2] In general, the religious positions have been supportive of new technologies for therapeutic purposes. Yet, much more can be expected in the horizon, some of which may fundamentally challenge religious principles and theological concepts. For example, some breakthroughs have been achieved in gene editing technology, such as Clustered Regularly Interspaced Short Palindromic Repeats (CRISPR), which has raised ethical concerns about genetic manipulation, or more popularly known as the "playing God" and "designer babies" debate. The Committee will thus need to deepen its grasp of these issues and move away from legalistic pronouncements towards ethical formulations. In doing so, it will have to work more closely than ever with scientists and ethicists to understand the full scale of the implications of these technologies (both benefits and possible dangers) while recognising the extent of its influence on public debates.

Inheritance

Another major area of Muslim life in which *fatwa*s have evolved is estate matters and inheritance. The issue of inheritance in Islamic jurisprudence has predominantly been informed by classical Muslim law developed in the various schools (*mazhabs*). These, in turn, were guided by Qur'anic teachings

---

[2] These include Human Stem Cell Research (2001), Human Tissue Research (2002), Genetic Testing and Research (2005), Personal Information in Biomedical Research (2007), and Human-Animal Combinations in Stem Cell Research (2010). Whilst this chapter is in print, the Fatwa Committee is providing its inputs on another BAC consultation on Mitochondrial Genome Replacement Technology (MGRT).

(such as on specific shares in inheritance under the Muslim law on inheritance or *faraidh*) as well as the injunctions of the Prophet Muhammad s.a.w. such as the restriction on wills (to not exceed one-third of the estate and only to non-beneficiaries). In the course of the development of jurisprudence on this subject in the form of *fiqh* writings as well as *fatwa* formulation, jurists presented details of these principles without necessarily revisiting them in light of new circumstances. For example, there is not as much discussion on the objectives and spirit of these laws as there is on their technical specificities. The focus has often been on ensuring how the specific apportioning of the estate can be achieved.

This clearly presented a problem where socio-economic conditions as well as societal structures, especially with regards to family life, undergo change. In particular, the nature of families (both immediate and extended), including its support structures and financial interdependence in modern societies, is very different from a traditional kinship structure in early Islam. To what extent then, could and should this affect the interpretation of law on matters of inheritance?

Add to this the introduction of new mechanisms by the state as well as financial schemes which offer individuals more options and greater control over the way they distribute their assets, especially after death. In the context of Singapore, these include the various schemes under the Central Provident Fund (such as nominations), insurance schemes, and trusts. Undoubtedly, Muslims wanted religious guidance on these and had put forth questions to the Fatwa Committee.

The early responses by the Committee showed that it simply followed established principles of inheritance as well as traditional definitions of estate as documented in classical legal corpus. In 1971, the Committee held that CPF monies formed part of a deceased's estate and were thus subjected to *faraidh*. Thus, although an individual may have expressed an intention to apportion the CPF monies differently by choosing his/her own beneficiaries and the quantum for each, the Committee did not consider this as valid ways of transferring the monies to the named beneficiaries. Rather, nominees were considered as trustees who were required to return the monies back to the rightful beneficiaries under *faraidh*.

However, there were various problems with this ruling, not least in that it did not reflect a more comprehensive understanding of the nature of CPF monies. By comparing CPF with normal asset types as defined under traditional Muslim law, the Committee only saw *faraidh* as the rule that applied in these cases. However, the implementation of this ruling could conflict with the objectives and spirit of Muslim law. Generally, CPF monies constitute one of the key savings of employed individuals but are restricted in its use. The main objective of the CPF monies to serve as a retirement plan also meant that they could be fully enjoyed only at a later stage in one's life. Should the owner die, the CPF monies could substantially support the deceased's dependants.

Thus, *faraidh* which seeks to ensure that one's dependants are well-supported, will not necessarily be effective if CPF monies are distributed to beneficiaries who are not normally involved in the maintenance of the deceased's family. The review of the CPF nomination *fatwa* in 2010 points to this: "... [with] the amendments to the CPF Act...contributors will no longer receive a substantive amount which would enable him/her to spend on his/her dependents" (Majlis Ugama Islam Singapura, 2010).

Apart from this recognition by the Committee, it also had to address the issue of nomination as an instrument of transfer of wealth, as its previous *fatwa* did not recognise nomination as a valid form of transfer. In its 2010 *fatwa*, it states:

> The nomination system is a contemporary form of property distribution not found in the writings and scholarly works of the scholars of the past. However, it is permitted as it is considered as a new form of *hibah*. It is also able to pre-serve the spirit of *faraidh* — in ensuring the welfare of one's dependents (Majlis Ugama Islam Singapura, 2010).

The approach of reinterpreting traditional forms of wealth transfer could also be seen in the issue of joint-ownership of properties (*fatwa* of 2008 on joint-tenancy agreement). As an outcome, these more recent *fatwas* have brought the practice of Muslim law in greater alignment with civil law provisions on assets and estate matters. This will benefit the Muslim public, as it reduces the conflict between two sets of laws and as well as confusion that has beset many in terms of the implications on their assets after death. However, many more challenges remain. For example, the *fatwas* do not recognise existing instruments such as joint-tenancy contracts (as practised under civil law) as valid unless a separate Islamic contract such as *hibah ruqbah* (*ruqbah* — gift) or *nuzriah* (vow made to give one's wealth, either in full or part, to another party before death) supports it. There is a dichotomy between "civil law" and "Islamic law" that seems to be maintained, yet, what separates the two seems more the form than the spirit and substance. In addition, as the Singaporean society progresses further, more complex issues on estate matters can be anticipated: new kinds of assets, instruments of wealth transfer, as well as gender differentiation in inheritance (through *faraidh*) in spite of changing gender roles in society.

Conclusion

The *fatwa* institution is one of many significant pillars of religious life in the context of a modern and secular state. Its role to interpret religious laws in context puts it at the foremost position in ensuring the compatibility of religious life with lived realities and conditions. Although the *fatwa* institution has responded positively to issues such as organ donation and inheritance, the pace of change globally in many aspects of modern life will require the institution to be more proactive and intensify its efforts to build institutional capabilities in dealing with emerging challenges. Advancements in the biomedical sciences alone have opened up new ethical questions and rendered existing guidelines and principles inadequate. As the case of organ donation has shown, the Fatwa Committee opted for a more conservative view in the early stages, which reflected its cautionary stance against an aggressive push for a more progressive interpretation of Islam. The extent to which the *fatwa* institution balances between caution and progress needs to be carefully deliberated moving forward.

What is clear is that the Muslim public will be in constant need of *fatwa*s as guidance to navigate the changing circumstances of life. At the same time, *fatwa*s have the potential to influence and steer the religious life of the community. This aim may not be achieved without the community's support and acceptance of the moral authority of the institution. For some Muslims who suspect the interference of state in religious affairs, the affiliation of the *fatwa* institution with the state becomes inherently problematic and automatically undermines its credibility. The *fatwa* institution in Singapore, through its review of *fatwa*s and public education initiatives, has shown that it did not take the issue of moral authority for granted. Instead, it seeks to disabuse this perception through education and engagement, and by providing credible solutions to the challenges that Muslims encounter in the modern world.

References

Abbas, A.N. (2012). Islamic Legal System in Singapore. *Pacific Rim Law & Policy Journal*, 21(1), pp. 163–187. Retrieved from http://digital.law.washington.edu/dspace-law/bitstream/handle/1773.1/1097/21prplj163.pdf?sequence=1.

Alatas, S. H. (2015). *Biarkan Butar Sekitar Perbahasan Ilmiah Derma Korneu Mutu.* Kuala Lumpur: Dewan Bahasa dan Pustaka.

al-Raysuni, A. (2006). *Imam al-Shatibi's Theory of the Higher Objectives and Intents of Islamic Law.* Kuala Lumpur: Islamic Book Trust.

Berita Harian. (2003, February 18). Peserta forum syor Muslim disertakan dalam HOTA. *Berita Harian.*

Berita Harian. (2004, January 9). Ramai Muslim tak keberatan diserta dalam HOTA. *Berita Harian.*

Berita Harian. (2007, August 21). Masyarakat alu-alu rancangan pemerintah pinda HOTA. *Berita Harian.*

Dien, M. I. (2004). *Islamic Law: From Historical Foundations to Contemporary Practice.* Edinburgh: Edinburgh University Press.

Howard, B. A. (2005). What the Bible Says about Organ Transplants. *Journal of Christian Nursing, 15.*

Lin, C. H. (2008). *Seventh Report of the Singapore Renal Registry 2007/2008.* Singapore: Singapore Health Promotion Board.

Masud, M. K., Messick, B., and Powers, D. S. (1996). Muftis, *Fatwas*, and Islamic Legal Interpretation. In M. K. Masud, B. Messick, & D. S. Powers, *Islamic Legal Interpretation: Muftis and their Fatwas* (pp. 3–32). Cambridge, Massachusetts: Harvard University Press.

Ministry of Health Malaysia. (2011). *Organ Transplantation from the Islamic Perspective.* Malaysia: Ministry of Health Malaysia.

The Straits Times. (1975, September 8). Donate Kidney Calls to Church Members. *The Straits Times.*

The Straits Times. (1986, July 12). Confused by Priest. *The Straits Times.*

The Straits Times. (2003, July 23). Last week's focus: Do other countries have laws like HOTA? *The Straits Times.*

Thye, W. K. and Lee, G. S. (1998). *First report of the Singapore Renal Registry 1997.* Singapore: Singapore Renal Registry.

Watson, C. and Dark, J. (2012). Organ transplantation: historical perspective and current practice. *British Journal of Anaesthesia, 108.*

Zubaida, S. (2005). *Law and Power in the Islamic World.* London: I.B.Tauris.

4

DEVELOPING ASATIZAH IN SINGAPORE THROUGH THE ASATIZAH RECOGNITION SCHEME

Mohammad Hannan Hassan and Irwan Hadi Mohd Shuhaimy

Introduction

Religious figures, such as the late Syed Abdillah Aljufri or Sheikh Muhammad Fadhlullah As-Suhaimi, had contributed immensely to the religious life of the Muslim community and society in Singapore. They inspired the *asatizah* and shaped their aspirations and purpose in the community. Yet the hopeful tone of those aspirations contrasted starkly with the realities which the *asatizah* faced during the transitional years of post-independence Singapore. As the country transitioned into rapid modernisation, many *asatizah* recalled the challenges they faced in fulfilling their aspirations in the midst of scarce developmental and career opportunities.

The first segment of this chapter will examine the impetus and challenges of *asatizah* development as well as the role of Muis and its many community partners in assisting the *asatizah* in accessing educational, professional or developmental opportunities. Due to institutional and financial constraints, the role that Muis played in this regard was limited in its initial years of establishment. This chapter will also show how *asatizah* developmental aspirations evolved beyond simply seeking the betterment of their socio-economic standing but also encompass the development of a progressive and contextual teaching of Islam so that the Muslim community can better respond to new challenges. Here, the chapter will explore the planning, programmes, and regulatory structures that have been initiated to support this objective, including the introduction of an accreditation scheme for the *asatizah* known as the Asatizah Recognition Scheme (ARS). From this exploration, various criticisms with regards to Muis' management of the *asatizah* will be highlighted. One such criticism is the limits to the *asatizah*'s agency and autonomy resulting from Muis' central management of *asatizah* development and regulation of professional ethics. This chapter will conclude by considering these criticisms within the unique context of religious life in Singapore.

Challenges Faced in Post-Independence Singapore

During the transitional years of post-independence Singapore, the socio-economic situation of the *asatizah* was in need of serious attention. Socio-economic stability was a primary concern for the *asatizah* after the separation from Malaysia in 1965. *Asatizah* struggled to survive economically, often relying solely on income from teaching in madrasahs. Significant number of *asatizah* were already leaving Singapore for better opportunities in Malaysia and Brunei. Morever, training opportunities for the *asatizah* were also limited. During this period, some *asatizah* attested to facing multiple challenges in accessing educational opportunities abroad. For example, Syed Abdillah Aljufri recounted that he was unable to pursue his studies overseas due to financial constraints and limited availability of scholarships or financial grants (Pergas and LBKM, 2013). Pasuni Maulan, former Registrar of Muslim Marriages, and a well-respected figure in the religious community, also shared that he missed the opportunity to pursue his post-graduate studies in a university in North Carolina in the US due to similar reasons.

While other well-known figures such as former Mufti of Singapore, Shaikh Syed Isa Semait, were privileged enough to be given the opportunity to pursue what his contemporaries were unable to, the path to such educational opportunities was filled with challenges. Shaikh Syed Isa Semait's struggle to complete his studies at Al-Azhar University is described in his biography *Keeping the Faith* (Hussain, 2012). Shaikh Syed Isa Semait recollected the challenges he encountered while pursuing his studies in 1961. Together with his peers, Hassan Salim and Mashor Awi, they struggled to cover their sea passage to

Cairo. They had to seek assistance from the Muslim Advisory Board and the Asia Foundation to cover their sea fare. This highlighted the lack of financial support available for *asatizah* to access further educational opportunities.

Organisations that were overseeing the development of the *asatizah* fraternity also faced some constraints. Shaikh Syed Isa Semait shared that Muis, in its early years, struggled to offer financial assistance to students pursuing Islamic Studies. It had to cope with its internal incapacities and limitations. Before 1978, there were just two departments within Muis looking into finance and administration, with fewer than 12 members, who were mainly clerical staff. Therefore, resources were stretched thin and had to be prioritised, leaving little for Muis to provide proper developmental and educational opportunities for *asatizah*. In fact, similar constraints were also faced by other community organisations such as Pergas and LBKM.

Despite financial constraints, the earlier generation of *asatizah* was still able to make a significant mark in the history of the community's religious life. For example, although Syed Abdillah Aljufri did not pursue overseas studies, he was still able to contribute significantly to the development of the community's religious life.[1] Even as the stories of these individuals continue to spur *asatizah*'s aspirations and hopes as the proceeding segments of this chapter will highlight, the contingencies and contemporary context of religious life in Singapore necessitated additional support for the *asatizah* in order for them to contribute significantly to the community and society at large, emulating the way of those early luminaries.

The Role of Muis and Community Partners in the Early Years

Speaking during the Committee of Supply debate in Parliament in 1973, and in response to the question by Member of Parliament (Geylang Serai) Mr Rahmat Kenap, Mr Othman Wok argued that Muis was not prepared to take over the administration of the madrasahs to which Mr Rahmat Kenap reportedly expressed his displeasure and fear for the loss of quality religious leadership filling the needs of mosques and Islamic education in the future (*Berita Harian*, 1973). This highlighted the general anxieties with regards to

---

[1] Syed Abdillah Aljufri's most significant contribution and work include writings and engagements with various segments of the community within and beyond the Muslim community (Pergas and LBKM, 2013).

the *asatizah* fraternity, which many felt that some form of institutional support for *asatizah* development was necessary.

In its early years, Muis' role in the development and uplifting of *asatizah*'s professional standing was limited to the development of *asatizah* in the madrasahs. The provisions under the Administration of Muslim Law Bill did not, in the beginning, include the development and management of *asatizah* as part of Muis' legally binding regulatory task. Muis' legal right to regulate religious teachers (Select Committee on the Administration of Muslim Law Bill, 1966: A28) was limited to the provision of AMLA in 1966 which stated that Muis had the power to forbid the employment of any religious teachers at "any private religious school" in the event that the said individual failed to pass "a test conducted by a Board appointed by [Muis]" (Select Committee on the Administration of Muslim Law Bill, 1966: A28). This power, however, does not extend to the larger pool of *asatizah* beyond the private religious schools. This accounted for the non-interventionist approach with respect to the development and management of the larger fraternity of *asatizah* beyond the madrasahs.

However, Muis' role in the professional development of *asatizah* in the madrasah expanded when there were calls by community leaders for the latter's developmental needs to be further enhanced. In September 1971, at the inaugural meeting of the new Muis Council, the then Minister for Social Welfare and the Minister-in-charge of Muslim Affairs, Mr Othman Wok, expressed his hope that the new Council would bring significant changes to the Muslim community, including areas touching on the administration of the madrasahs and its curriculum, and finance (*Berita Harian*, 1971). In late 1986, the Religious Education Department of Mendaki, chaired by Mr Sidek Saniff, submitted a list of recommendations that included, among others: the formation of a Religious Education Unit in Muis; the upgrading of the salary of *asatizah;* and the formation of an advisory board on religious education which would advise Muis on the appointment and training of the *asatizah* (*Berita Harian*, 1986).

The further strengthening of religious education in Muis through the formation of the Religious Education Department (RED) in 1993 signalled a serious effort to support madrasahs and, by extension, the *asatizah* and the growing demands of a formal religious education sector which required the expansion of *asatizah* professional development. At a meeting with more than 100 *asatizah* on 16

November 1985 held by the Mendaki's Religious Education Department chaired by Mr Sidek Saniff, also the Parliamentary Secretary of Trade and Commerce, *asatizah* supported the plan to develop a Religious Education Unit in Muis to upgrade and support the development of madrasahs and *asatizah*. Mr Sidek Saniff reportedly said that this unit would assume the responsibility pertaining to (the strengthening of) Islamic education; and that this responsibility was not just a religious one, but also a national imperative (*Berita Harian*, 1985).[2] In late 1986, Mendaki's Religious Education Department submitted its report recommending the formation of a Religious Education Unit (REU) in Muis to implement sections 81 and 82 of AMLA pertaining to religious education. Subsequently, the REU started in late 1987, with a Director, Assistant Director, and an Executive Officer. Later in 1993, this unit was upgraded to become a Religious Education Department (RED) staffed by a Director, an Assistant Director, two Executives, and two Administrative officers. This was followed by a plan to upgrade and professionalise *asatizah* which later translated into a series of developmental programmes.

The policy experience in setting up the REU in the pursuit of developing *asatizah* at madrasahs highlighted the importance of working with civil society to actualise the goals of upgrading the madrasahs and the *asatizah*. When the first plan to upgrade and professionalise *asatizah* was conceived after the formation of REU, a Joint Committee of Madrasah Education (Jawatankuasa Bersama Pendidikan Madrasah — JBPM) was formed in 1993, comprising members of Pergas and Mendaki as well as some senior education officers from the Ministry of Education (MOE). Muis chaired and provided secretariat support to the committee. This inter-sectorial collaboration was to oversee the review of the madrasah curriculum, finance, programmes, and most importantly, *asatizah* development.[3] The formation of the REU, and later the RED, highlighted the importance of the symbiotic relationship between Muis, Mendaki, Perdaus, the *asatizah* fraternity and Pergas. Nonetheless, the focus of those developmental initiatives for *asatizah* was primarily to help upgrade and professionalise the

---

[2] The call to form a Religious Education Unit was a way to implement sections 81/82 of the Administration of Muslim Law Act (AMLA) pertaining to religious education. Earlier, the community had also expressed strong support for the formation of a Religious Education Unit in Muis, see "Pendidikan Islam: Masyarakat Sokong Penubuhan Unit Penyelaras," *Berita Harian*, 30 October 1985: 3.

[3] In addition to the JBPM, the Curriculum Development Committee (CDC) was set up in 1995 to review and develop an integrated curriculum for full-time and part-time madrasahs, as well as plan for *asatizah* development.

training of the *asatizah* in the madrasahs so that they could improve their teaching. It was also meant to address the perennial problem of *asatizah's* low salary in the madrasahs as opposed to the larger fraternity of *asatizah* beyond the madrasahs.

Nonetheless, matters pertaining to the welfare, professional development, and conduct of the larger fraternity of *asatizah* beyond the madrasahs was still being supported by and dealt with mainly by the Singapore Islamic Scholars and Religious Teachers Assocation (Pergas). Established in 1958, Pergas is an organisation that has since tried to bring all *asatizah* under its membership and, in the process, cater to the needs, welfare, and development of its member *asatizah*. While Pergas was in a position to sanction its members on matters pertaining to their development and conduct, not all *asatizah* were registered as members of Pergas. This meant that there was a larger pool of *asatizah* who still remained beyond the reach of both Muis and Pergas.

Asatizah Development Today

As the community progressed and as its socio-religious needs became more complex and pressing, the developmental and professionalisation needs of the *asatizah* further evolved. The 9/11 incident in 2001 in New York and subsequently, the thwarted plan of the Jemaah Islamiah (JI) cells in Singapore in December of the same year had undoubtedly raised the urgency and importance to work with local religious leaders to address the challenges of extremism and radicalism in Singapore. It provided an impetus to develop the capacity within the *asatizah* to be able to address the challenge of religious radicalism through proper religious guidance for the Muslim masses. In other words, the agenda of developing the *asatizah* has evolved from just helping to enhance their socio-economic standing to a bigger purpose of enabling the *asatizah* to serve a specific objective which would impact the community and nation.

By this agenda, *asatizah* play a key role and an important stakeholder to build a Community of Excellence for the Singapore Muslim community. The concept of the Community of Excellence was developed by Muis as part of its vision and mission for the community. Here, excellence signifies strong values and practices that are founded on ethical and moral principles, and exemplify the idea of beauty and humanity, and a Muslim community that is religiously profound. Excellence also refers to common goodness, one that contributes to nation-building and shared humanity and, and a community that is socially progressive. Through consultations with various sectors of the community, especially the *asatizah*, the 10 desired attributes of a Singapore Muslim Community of Excellence were envisioned and articulated through the Singapore Muslim Identity (SMI). These attributes were further elucidated and recorded in a document also known as the *Risalah for Building a Singapore Muslim Community of Excellence*. The SMI was essentially co-created by Muis, the Muslim community, and the *asatizah*. In his acceptance speech for Anugerah Jauhari in 2015, Muis President, Haji Mohammad Alami Musa, expressed his honour in developing the SMI along with the *asatizah* within and outside of Muis, therefore underscoring the importance of *asatizah's* initiative in their own development as well as the Muslim community.

To realise this vision, it was important to create initiatives which contribute to the socialisation of a contextualised and progressive Islamic teachings. To this end, two units were created in Muis to oversee the fulfilment of this new strategic thrust in Muis' work, namely Asatizah Network and Muis Academy (MA), in 2004 and 2006 respectively. The former was tasked to mainstream *asatizah* by providing impactful leadership within and beyond the Singapore Muslim community; while MA was tasked to develop capacity-building programmes for the Muslim community, and the religious leaders. Through both units, Muis was able to deliver signature programme for the *asatizah*. For instance, the introduction of the Student Resource and Development Secretariat (SRDS) in 2004 was to provide overseas students pursuing Islamic Studies with comprehensive support programmes, and help them to remain connected to the context of religious life in Singapore. Another example was the baseline training for all *asatizah* under the Asatizah Executive Development Programme (AEDP) inaugurated in 2007, jointly developed by Muis and Pergas, and conducted by MA. The aim of these programmes was to orientate all *asatizah* to the socio-religious realities of a multi-racial and multi-religious Singapore and inculcate in them the value of continuous personal and professional development. Over the years, the programmes offered by MA were further intensified to engage *asatizah* at a deeper level of discussion with focus on methodologies and framework formulation. This included a three-day AEDP workshop, a one-month Asatizah Overseas Attachment Programme (OAP), a six-month Asatizah Immersion/Attachment Programme (MAAP), roundtable discussions, and *asatizah* masterclasses and quarterly seminars.

These development plans also required the backing of a regulatory framework that enabled all *asatizah* to be touched by these developmental initiatives. As mentioned earlier, while Muis and its partners such as Pergas had delivered initiatives to develop and oversee the welfare of the *asatizah*, many still remained beyond the reach of those initiatives. The introduction of an accreditation scheme known as the Asatizah Recognition Scheme (ARS) enabled Muis and its partners to ensure that those developmental initiatives were able to reach all *asatizah*.

The ARS was introduced with the primary intent of enhancing the professional standing and development of *asatizah*, in addition to addressing the concerns among the *asatizah* and the public regarding unqualified religious teachers teaching Islam.[4] Further, it would also serve the needs of the Muslim public to have a reference point for them to be able to engage the services of accredited *asatizah* for various religious needs. Under the ARS, Muis formed an independent board of senior *asatizah* who would evaluate and grant the recognition to *asatizah* and subsequently register them as accredited *asatizah*. To support the ARB, Pergas was appointed as the Secretariat to administer the scheme. Muis provided the necessary funding to ARB and its Secretariat to ensure it met its objectives and served its function.

The ARS as an accreditation scheme placed Muis in a better position to develop a greater pool of *asatizah* beyond the madrasah sector. This is especially so with the introduction of the Enhanced Asatizah Recognition Scheme in 2012 which made it compulsory for all *asatizah* to fulfil training hours known as the Continuous Professional Education (CPE) for ARS recognition renewal. Most of the programmes under CPE were developed by MA. Muis, together with Pergas, ARB and the ARS Secretariat, adopted an open and inclusive approach to enable all *asatizah* to participate in its programmes. Taking cognisant of the different background and educational attainment level of *asatizah*, Muis worked closely with the ARS Secretariat to offer a wide range of courses, taking a multi-disciplinary approach to further develop their knowledge and skills, not just in the religious sciences but also in the other disciplines so that they could perform their functions effectively. A case in point was the Asatizah Executive Development Programme (AEDP) that remained to be the foundation programme for *asatizah*. AEDP has evolved over time to meet the changing needs and new challenges. Thus far,

---

[4] The idea of accrediting *asatizah* was mooted by Pergas in the mid-1990s following a series of perverse and unqualified *asatizah* displaying unethical behaviour or promoting deviant teachings. This matter was debated at Pergas' Annual General Meeting in 1997, where members urged that the matter was seriously considered.

more than 1,000 *asatizah* have attended the AEDP.[5] Courses that offered content and discussions through a multi-disciplinary lens had also gained traction and appreciation from the *asatizah* fraternity. These courses include the History of Islam in Southeast Asia, Islamic Intellectual and Educational Traditions in the Malay World, Islam, Law and Society, Introduction to Sociology of Religion, Introduction to Philosophy, Introduction to Interfaith, Islamic Finance and *Wakaf*, Islamic Ethics, and Islam and Gender.

Community's Readiness for Mandatory ARS

Although the implementation of the ARS was non-mandatory in the beginning, some segments of the *asatizah* fraternity have voiced their preference for such an accreditation scheme to be mandatory for all *asatizah* as early as its conception. Yet, the ARS was introduced on a non-mandatory basis for three main reasons which became serious considerations for Muis and its partners upon the introduction of the mandatory ARS in 2017. Firstly, the expressed apprehension by some sectors of the community highlighted their lack of readiness to have a statutory body regulate or determine who is allowed to teach or what is allowed to be taught and learnt. Secondly, there were also apprehension within the *asatizah* fraternity that a mandatory ARS will stifle the autonomy of the *asatizah* to determine his or her own teaching style and content, as well as their independent voices as religious teachers. The apprehension of the *asatizah* and the community highlighted an important challenge when it came to the implementation of any modern institutional mechanism within the religious domain. Similar to the experience of centralising institutions such as *zakat* or mosques under a statutory board, the community was expected to be uncomfortable with such

---

[5] AEDP's primary intent was to provide an overarching view of the Singapore unique context within a global reality and contemporary challenges faced by the *asatizah* in discharging their responsibilities to develop a resilient, inclusive, contributive, adaptive, and progressive Muslim community. This intent remained as the foundational idea for AEDP, notwithstanding the variations to the content to meet evolving needs and challenges. AEDP 3.0 aims to equip the *asatizah* with the knowledge and competency necessary to understand and evaluate global and geopolitical developments. It hoped to instil values that are founded on an appreciation of Singapore's unique context that influence the policy-making process in Singapore. It is equally important for the *asatizah* to appreciate diversity and organic reality of today and in turn, play their role to help the community thrive in a plural world. AEDP 3.0 includes two modules: Global Challenges and Local Uniqueness: Think Global, Act Local; and Diversity in Islamic Thought and Traditions. This is then followed by a dialogue with the Mufti of Singapore.

a move. This was due to the fact that traditionally, such religious institutions fell within the private domain of an individual's personal or community life where the state or any state-linked entities neither existed nor played a role. Any move to centralise the management of such traditional religious institutions was expected to be met with discomfort if not suspicion.

Therefore, from a policy-making perspective, when the mandatory ARS was eventually introduced between 2016 and 2017, Muis recognised the need to properly socialise the notion of a mandatory accreditation scheme to both the *asatizah* fraternity and the Muslim community at large. Having studied the legal framework for the administration of the mandatory scheme, and consulted the senior religious leaders, Muis organised a series of engagements and consultations with *asatizah* who were already registered under the ARS and Qur'anic Teachers Recognition Scheme (QTRS).[6] More than 1,700 *asatizah* attended six engagement sessions at various locations island wide. Led by members of the ARB and representatives of Pergas, and facilitated by Muis, these sessions were intended to share the initial concept of the mandatory ARS as well as allow further suggestions on how it could be improved. An overwhelming majority of *asatizah* who attended, supported the mandatory ARS (more than 99 percent agreed that the mandatory ARS was important). The administrative and legal concerns raised above were addressed at these consultation sessions.

Various concerns were raised by the *asatizah* fraternity during these engagement sessions. Some were concerned over Pergas' purportedly diminishing role with the introduction of a mandatory scheme, yet, Pergas leaders themselves assuaged the worry. They acknowledged that the scheme would further enhance Pergas' role as it continued to play a key role in the implementation. It would continue to have a permanent representation in the ARB. The ARS Secretariat under Pergas would be further augmented. Muis had invariably acknowledged and highlighted the key role Pergas would play as its partner in the administration of the ARS. This was

---

[6] The Qur'anic Teachers Recognition Scheme (QTRS) was a sub-list for the Qur'anic teachers. They are not necessarily and strictly "*asatizah*" by the definition above but are teaching children and adults the reading of the Qur'an. In addition, they are also approved to teach basic Islamic teachings and practices. Under the mandatory scheme, both lists, namely the ARS and QTRS, were merged into a single ARS list with two tiers. Tier One refers to the earlier ARS list with three categories: Fellow, Graduate, and Associate. The student category is subsumed under the Associate, while Tier Two comprises the Qur'anic Teachers.

reiterated again after the implementation of the mandatory ARS in 2017. In the foreseeable future, Pergas would continue to remain an important partner as an organisation representing religious scholars and teachers, and its role in founding the idea of the scheme.

Some *asatizah* were also concerned over the legal repercussions of not meeting ARS requirements under the mandatory ARS. With regards to this, the *asatizah* and the community were assured that AMLA is adequately provided for in administering the scheme. *Asatizah* would be given ample time to transfer to the mandatory scheme when it was introduced in 1 January 2017. The *asatizah* and the Qur'anic teachers were given a three-month grace period to register. For those who did not meet the minimum academic qualification, a grace period of three-years was granted to enable them to upgrade themselves. They would be granted a provisional recognition allowing them to continue to teach and perform their roles as well as attend the numerous developmental programmes under the CPE. These measures would help the *asatizah* and the community to move to the new mandatory scheme. The scheme is important in order to protect the credibility and professionalism of the *asatizah* fraternity, and safeguard the community against wrong teachings and non-contextualised understanding of Islam. Abdul Razak Maricar, the Chief Executive of Muis, reiterated the point in December 2016 before the introduction of the mandatory scheme. He asserted that "there is a need to present contextualised teaching and guard against extreme and exclusive teachings, and of course, problematic teachers", and that this will give "some assurance to the community that they will get reliable and appropriate religious guidance, only from recognised *asatizah*" (Chua, 2016). To protect the credibility and professionalism of the *asatizah*, and the interest of the community, a code of ethics was also introduced.

The third reason why the ARS was first introduced on a non-mandatory basis, was the lack of legal and administrative infrastructure at the onset of the ARS that did not enable Muis or Pergas to properly administer the scheme. In other words, any overseeing regulatory body will not have the legal backing to enforce or definitively revoke the right of an *asatizah* to teach at any religious institution if he or she does not fulfil the necessary requirements such as the mandatory training. Before Muis could regulate, there had to be a proper agency or body that oversees the overall development of the *asatizah*. Otherwise, making the scheme mandatory would be inoperable.

Thus, when the mandatory ARS was being conceptualised, Muis recognised the importance of working with the partners to put in place the necessary legal and institutional framework to properly administer the ARS. To this end, Muis had worked with Pergas and the larger *asatizah* fraternity to produce a code of ethics for the *asatizah*. This code of ethics was developed and included as part of the schedule under the Administration of Muslim Law (Muslim Religious Schools).

ARS CODE OF ETHICS

1. An *Asatizah* or a Qur'anic teacher —

   (a) must adhere to the moderate teachings of Islam;

   (b) must exhibit a sound grasp of religious knowledge while being mindful of contextual considerations in the interpretation of religious teachings;

   (c) must always act in ways that retain the trust and confidence of the Muslim community of Singapore towards religious teachers, and that does not bring the profession into disrepute;

   (d) must recognise that there are diverse opinions and schools of thought in Islam, and may choose to adopt and teach any of these so long as this is not likely to be prejudicial to the maintenance of harmony between different religious or racial groups or to cause public disorder;

   (e) must be guided in matters of religious doctrine by the rulings of the Legal Committee.

2. An *Asatizah* or Qur'anic teacher must not —

   (a) state that any opinion concerning Islam or any practice of Islam is deviant or unacceptable unless the Legal Committee has pronounced it to be so in a ruling;

   (b) do anything that directly or indirectly denigrates any racial or religious group, or that is likely to be prejudicial to the maintenance of harmony between different religious or racial groups or to cause public disorder; or

   (c) advocate any idea that is likely to encourage extremism and violence, whether directly or indirectly.

The concerns of the *asatizah* fraternity and the larger community with regards to the code of ethics is similar, but to a larger degree, to their discomfort with the ARS even since it was non-mandatory. Their concerns were mainly with regards to the potential curtailing of the independent voices of the *asatizah* as religious teachers which they felt was crucial for religious guidance and religious education itself.

While the concerns were valid, it had to be asserted that the ARS was first and foremost a regulatory structure that was meant to support the development of *asatizah* as a sector, and ensure that the reach of these developmental programmes and initiatives remained extensive. In addition to that, it was also meant to professionalise the *asatizah* sector. Hence, it was only natural to have a baseline set of parameters that members of the fraternity would need to abide by. Therefore, taking into consideration the existence of diverse orientations within the fraternity, the ARS Code of Ethics was drafted on the basis that, while diversity is celebrated and encouraged, it must not transgress basic religious and civic values. These include not preaching hatred, violence, and not promoting strife or enmity, and the need for *asatizah* to maintain professional integrity which is demanded of one who assumes the role of a religious teacher.

The ARS Code of Ethics was not developed in a vacuum. The ARS has been in operation for more than a decade, and in its administration and review of any ethical misconduct prior to it being made mandatory, the ARB had relied upon religious and civic moral values which were not expressly written. Hence, what the ARS Code of Ethics sought to achieve was to crystallise those values and parameters, and set them out transparently in a proper document for *asatizah* registered under the ARS to refer to and not to be able to feign ignorance. This was especially pivotal in light of the scheme being made mandatory and therein for certain penalties to be sanctioned. Beyond the tacit norms within the *asatizah* sector, the ARS Code of Ethics was also based on values and principles drawn from established documents drafted by both local and regional scholars. Among the main documents included the Charter of Moderation instituted in Pergas' book entitled *Moderation in Islam*, which was also the product of its inaugural Convention of Religious Scholars held in 2004. Another important guiding document was the internationally endorsed Amman Declaration. Both documents touch on intra and interfaith relations.

It needs to be highlighted that, in the implementation of the mandatory ARS, penalties only serve as deterrence and they will only be the last resort, failing all other remedial measures. This is because Muis believes in rehabilitation and providing second chances as much as possible. Even in unfortunate cases of rejection of ARS application or cancellation of any current ARS registration, *asatizah* would have recourse to appeal to the Minister-in-charge of Muslim Affairs.[7] On the matter of the Minister-in-charge of Muslim Affairs being the final arbiter, concerns had been raised on the limitations of such an arrangement, especially on appeal matters relating to religious doctrine. This had been perceived as yet another attempt to "diminish" the role of senior religious leadership which formed the previous ARS Appeal Panel. Taking this into consideration, an advisory panel consisting of senior religious scholars, such as the Mufti, had been instituted by Muis to facilitate the Minister in his consideration of appeals, especially on religious matters requiring expert views, particularly on doctrinal and interpretational matters. This would enhance the credibility of the decisions and bolster the decision-making process through robust grounds of decisions that consider religious viewpoints. For other matters relating to non-compliance with requirements, criminal offences, ethical misconduct, and other non-religious or doctrinal matters, the Minister may decide without referring it to the appeal advisory board. This is yet another example of how the mandatory ARS was developed based on inputs and feedback from the fraternity and its partners.

Conclusion: Further Centralisation of Religious Life?

The experience of implementing the ARS and later, the mandatory ARS, had highlighted pain points that were similar to the experience of implementing policies and modern institutionalising mechanisms in other areas within the religious domain, such as with *zakat* and mosques. At the core of this concern lies a debate that remains central to any discussion regarding state policies and its role in religion. Should the state play a bigger role in regulating religious life or should it play a minimal role? As religions in modern secular states are regarded as a component of one's private life, it is deemed as inappropriate for the state, via any form, to regulate the details of one's private life and decisions. This is a natural and understandable predisposition, and it remains to be a common challenge to much of Muis' policy-making experience. While this is so, it is worthwhile to conclude this chapter with some thoughts on what future policy-makers may begin considering when it

---

[7] This is provided by section 87(8) of AMLA.

comes to the religious life of the community in the future and the role of *asatizah* therein.

While the exigencies of the current climate of religious exclusivism and religious self-radicalisation have escalated the need to regulate and accredit the *asatizah*, the complexity of this climate is not likely to recede and may, in fact, be further exacerbated by global drivers in the coming years. One must consider if the state and its agencies possess all the necessary resources to create structures to enforce regulation in such a complex climate. Perhaps, policy-makers within and beyond Muis must begin conversations with all segments of the larger national population, including civil society, on the possibility of co-creating effective upstream measures to tackle these challenges. In the process, perhaps this initiative can help create solutions that is more grounds up and therefore less reliant on state enforcement.

References

Berita Harian. (1985, November 17). *Guru agama setuju penubuhan unit pendidikan Islam. Berita Harian.* Retrieved from NewspaperSG.

Berita Harian. (1986, November 17). *Reaksi Terhadap Laporan Jabatan Pendidikan Yayasan Mendaki. Berita Harian.* Retrieved from NewspaperSG.

Berita Harian (1971, September 14). *Masa'alah Sekolah2 Ugama: Peranan Baru Majlis Ugama Islam Singapura. Berita Harian.* Retrieved from NewspaperSG.

Berita Harian. (1973, March 15). *Muis Belum Sanggup Ambilalih Madrasah2 di S'pura. Berita Harian.* Retrieved from NewspaperSG.

Chua, A. (2016, December 29). Islamic religious teachers must be registered with Muis from January 2017. *Today Online.* Retrieved from https://www.todayonline.com/singapore/islamic-religious-teachers-have-2020-gain-necessary-qualification-muis.

Duriat, N. (1980, November 26). *Badan jaga kebajikan guru ugama disarankan.* Singapore: Berita Harian.

Hussain, S.Z. (2012). *Keeping the Faith: Syed Isa Semait Mufti of Singapore 1971–2010.* Singapore: Straits Times Press.

Pergas and LBKM. (2013). *Obor Ummah: Jejak Tokoh Agama Islam di Singapura.* Singapore: Pergas and LBKM.

Select Committee on the Administration of Muslim Law Bill. (1966). Report of the Select Committee on the Administration of Muslim Law Bill. Singapore: Parliament of Singapore.

5

MADRASAH EDUCATION: A JOURNEY TOWARDS EXCELLENCE

Farah Mahamood Aljunied and Zalman Putra Ahmad Ali

Introduction

In the 1980s and 1990s, it was common to read about stories of madrasahs beset with problems and the bleak employment future of madrasah graduates. In his 1999 National Day Rally Malay speech, then Prime Minister Goh Chok Tong said:

> Presently, there are 4,000 Malay/Muslim children in several full-time madrasahs. Out of that, many have dropped out every year. A large segment did not complete tertiary education. Thus, I am concerned that many of these children will not be equipped to face the new economic environment. I am more concerned that based on the figures for the last three years, about 65 percent of our madrasah students end their education before completing Secondary Four. The level of drop-outs is too high. Students who have dropped out will face bleak employment opportunities. What is the opportunity and future hope for these children?

> (National Archives of Singapore, 1999)

In the following year, the proposal for education to be made compulsory was announced. This led to a divide within the community on whether Compulsory Education (CE) would be good for the madrasahs. For the stakeholders who felt that it could lead to the closure of madrasahs, the reaction was negative. Eventually, the Government offered a solution through a legislation enacted in 2000, which exempted madrasah students from compulsory attendance in national schools. Since the implementation of the Compulsory Education (CE) Act in 2003, the six madrasahs have taken various steps which led to significant changes in the sector.

Two decades later, stories about madrasahs presented a stark contrast. During the 2013 National Day Rally, Prime Minister Lee Hsien Loong announced the introduction of Edusave for madrasahs (*The Straits Times*, 2013). Two years later, Prime Minister Lee announced the government's support in raising the standards of English, Mathematics, and Science subjects of madrasahs (Ariffin, 2015). Both developments are testament to how the madrasahs have attained greater recognition by the government, and represent important milestones in the progress of madrasahs' journey towards excellence. The madrasahs have evolved to play a more central and important role in shaping the community's religious life in the context of a more volatile and complex environment. Madrasahs would need to sustain its good progress by raising the quality of learning and teaching in order to better prepare madrasah graduates for the future.

Today, three madrasahs have come under a common system to allow for specialisation and focus on specific curriculum/school levels, resulting in better optimisation of resources. Established in 2007, the system referred to as the Joint Madrasah System (JMS) consists of Madrasah Al-Irsyad, the primary school feeder to Madrasah Aljunied and Madrasah Al-Arabiah, with the former focusing on religious studies up to Pre-U level for eventual entry into Al-Azhar University, and the latter offering secondary education for both Express and Normal Academic streams, with a niche in Science and terminating at the GCE 'O' Level. The remaining non-JMS madrasahs — Madrasah Alsagoff Al-Arabiah, Madrasah Al-Ma'arif Al-Islamiah, and Madrasah Wak Tanjong Al-Islamiah — continue to offer primary education up to Pre-U level, with almost equal weightage in both the religious and academic subjects like English, Mathematics, Science, and the Humanities such as Geography. Since 2008, the four madrasahs are required under CE to clear the PSLE benchmark in order for them to continue taking in new enrolment. For the last few years, all four madrasahs offering primary education have successfully scored above the PSLE benchmark. [1]

This chapter will first highlight the fundamental challenges faced by the madrasahs which have hampered the madrasah sector's ability to operate optimally and the corresponding successive attempts to address these gaps. It then examines how the introduction of CE impacted ongoing efforts for Muis and the madrasahs to progress towards a more integrated policy to improve the sector holistically through the formation of JMS, as well as other measures. Important lessons can be drawn from that process, particularly how Muis played a balancing act by driving the changes in the sector, while at the same time, ensuring that madrasahs maintain a certain level of autonomy to preserve its valued heritage and legacy. This has succeeded in first, clearing the initial obstacle of meeting the PSLE benchmark, and second, progressing towards a higher standard of educational institution which provides excellent religious and secular education to produce future religious elites and functionaries. The chapter concludes by exploring the possible future trajectory of the madrasahs.

The Evolution of Singapore Madrasahs

Madrasahs are full-time Islamic religious schools with the aim of developing religious scholars, educators, and functionaries for the Muslim community. The six full-time madrasahs that remain today have their own unique identity, vision, and focus. Each of them has been in existence before Singapore's independence, and some established early in the 20th century.

---

[1] The four madrasahs include Madrasah Al-Irsyad Al-Islamiah, Madrasah Wak Tanjong Al-Islamiah, Madrasah Al-Ma'arif Al-Islamiah and Madrasah Alsagoff Al-Arabiah. Madrasah Aljunied and Madrasah Al-Arabiah ceased taking in Primary 1 students by 2008 with the start of JMS. Under the Compulsory Education (CE) Act, the six full-time madrasahs are required to meet a minimum PSLE benchmark at least twice in each three-year assessment period from 2008 onwards, in order to continue to admit new Primary 1 pupils. For madrasahs, the benchmark is pegged at the average PSLE aggregate score of Malay students taking four standard-level subjects in the six lowest-performing mainstream schools, ranked according to the performance of Malay students taking four standard-level subjects in the PSLE that year.

At the turn of the 20th century, the earliest madrasahs established were Madrasah As-Sibyan (established in 1905) and Madrasah Al-Iqbal Al-Islamiyyah (established in 1908). The latter was founded by Syed Sheikh Ahmad Al-Hadi, a prominent Muslim reformist, and adopted an infusion of modern curriculum, which included subjects like English, Geography, History, and Mathematics. However, both madrasahs did not last very long after their establishment and are no longer in existence today. In the following decades, Madrasah Alsagoff (established in 1912) and Madrasah Aljunied (established in 1927) were established by Arab philanthropists in order to meet the increasing demands for formal education, especially for the large number of Arabs and Muslims who settled in Singapore. At that time, the general philosophy was to provide Muslim children with an opportunity for education. Madrasah Aljunied later gained prominence for its good standard of Arabic in the region. Many students from the region studied at Madrasah Aljunied have graduated to eventually become prominent religious leaders.

In 1936, the first madrasah that admitted girls, Madrasah Al-Ma'arif, was established. Its founder, Sheikh Muhammad Fadhlullah Suhaimi, was a strong advocate of education for girls. In addition, academic subjects were immediately included in its curriculum. Around the same period, Madrasah Al-Arabiah Al-Islamiah was also established in 1937 by Sheikh Omar Bamadhaj at Hillside Drive, under the management of the Haji Mohd Yusoff Mosque (Madrasah Al-Arabiah Al-Islamiah, 2016). It went under its own management in the 1950s as a school offering religious studies. However, after it was destroyed in a fire in 1980, Muhammadiyah Association took over the running of the madrasah.

Madrasah Al-Irsyad and Madrasah Wak Tanjong were only established in subsequent decades in the 1940s and 1950s. By the time of Madrasah Wak Tanjong's establishment in 1958, Singapore attained self-government the following year. During this period, the number of madrasahs doubled and continued to increase in enrolment in the 1960s. This was particularly so during the period of the merger between Singapore and Malaysia (1963–1965), with the highest number reaching 28 Muslim schools in 1962 (Aljunied and Hussein, 2005). However, this was short-lived. Madrasahs were severely impacted after Singapore's independence when the nation went on its relentless path of rapid industrialisation. The growing importance of the state-resourced national schools as producers of Singapore's future workforce resulted in a reduced parental preference for the madrasahs and their eventually receding from the mainstream.

During the immediate years after the establishment of Muis in 1968, madrasahs continued to remain autonomous and ran its own curriculum with varying emphasis in the teaching of religious and academic subjects. Despite having the powers under the Administration of Muslim Law Act (AMLA) to control the conduct of the madrasah, Muis was unable to initiate any serious intervention (*Berita Harian*, 1973). Firstly, due to its lack of resources and expertise, Muis opted to prioritise other areas which required immediate attention, such as streamlining *zakat* and *fitrah* collection, and building stronger links with the community which was still not fully aware of Muis' role and functions. Secondly, the madrasahs strongly resisted any external attempts to impose standardisation, as they preferred to safeguard and maintain their own unique histories, institutional cultures, and aspirations.

Even without Muis' support, madrasahs decided to pursue their own reforms responding to the changing economic conditions. In 1966, for example, the curriculum at Madrasah Aljunied began to include academic subjects, and in 1971, Madrasah Al-Ma'arif became the first to prepare its students for the GCE 'O' and 'A' Level examinations as private candidates (Chee, 2006). However, the lack of standardisation in the syllabi and curricula across the madrasahs was a problem for the students. Thus, initial inroads into the sector were made by Muis, with the establishment of a sub-committee for religious school syllabi standardisation, which culminated with a standardised madrasah primary education syllabus by 1977 (*Berita Harian*, 1977). The effort resulted in some benefits for both students and teachers; however, it did not fundamentally address some of the more pressing concerns arising from Singapore's rapidly changing economic and educational landscape.

Juggling Dual Objectives

Madrasahs entered the 1980s without being able to keep up with the pace of change. The gap between madrasahs and the much better-resourced mainstream schools began to widen. Many madrasahs were closed due to falling enrolment, and the madrasahs generally declined in popularity. By 1982, the number of full-time madrasahs had dwindled significantly. Meanwhile, madrasahs' reputation also declined as they increasingly became the destination for weaker students who dropped out of the national schools.

Thus, calls were made by the Muslim political and community leaders to strengthen the learning of English, Mathematics, and Science, so that more parents would be willing to put their children in the madrasahs and reverse the enrolment decline (*Berita Harian*, 1982). While the intent was good (since it was important for the madrasahs to remain relevant and attractive), this caused the problems faced by the madrasahs to persist further (Abdul Rahman, 2006). It reinforced and formalised the dual objectives of madrasah education, which meant that madrasahs were no longer just to produce future religious scholars and teachers, but to prepare the madrasah graduates for the job market in other non-religious professions.

Without the necessary fundamental changes with respect to rethinking on the curriculum content and methods of instruction, injection of financial, manpower and infrastructural resources, and building of teacher capabilities, the expansion in curriculum by incorporating the academic subjects caused further deterioration to the madrasahs' quality of teaching and learning. This was represented by the teachers' lack of qualification and training in pedagogy, high teacher turnover due to low salaries and career prospects, and the heavy student workload. The poor outcome is evident from the low educational performance, with very few achieving tertiary level Islamic education and high dropout rates. Employment prospects of madrasah graduates were limited, with many eventually not pursuing religious fields and instead, finding employment in low-level jobs. In sum, this reflected how the entire madrasah system was not operating at the optimal level at that time.

The constant narrative that madrasah education offers Muslim students the best of both types of knowledge eventually helped to boost demand for places in madrasahs. This was also fuelled by the growing Islamic revivalism in the 1980s (Abu Bakar, 2006). The overall effect caused madrasah enrolment to increase again, particularly among female students. In 1985, 95 percent of madrasah students were female (Chee, 2006). By the 1990s, the demand for madrasah education was at its peak. Student enrolment had more than doubled, with all the six surviving madrasahs having record enrolments. However, the downside was that it portrayed an inaccurate picture to parents and the larger Muslim community, that the madrasah could provide a more comprehensive education than the national schools. Parents began to view madrasah not just as an institution for the development of future religious elites but as an institution with the Islamic ambience which offers a balance of Islamic and secular education (Abdul Rahman,

2006). This was further buttressed by a strong belief that madrasah education could inculcate a strong religious foundation which could be a safeguard against the corrupting influences of modern society. This is unlike in the national schools where the students are perceived to be more vulnerable to such influences.

In reality, the growth had put more pressure on madrasahs' limited resources at the expense of quality education which was already not in a good stead. This was also exacerbated by the fact that the government did not provide any financial assistance, such as the Edusave scheme,[2] school fees subsidies and school development grants, which mainstream schools enjoy, as the madrasahs are private educational institutions. The lack of resources immensely impeded madrasahs' progress due to their inability to attract and retain good teachers because of low salaries and inadequate facilities such as laboratories, libraries, computer facilities, and suitable premises.

Support from Mendaki and Muis

The first major effort to help alleviate the problems came through Mendaki after its formation in 1982.[3] Following from the Mendaki Educational Congress that year when the issues on madrasahs were raised, Mendaki set up a committee on religious education, consisting of representatives from Muslim organisations to establish a framework and guidelines to improve

---

[2] The Edusave scheme was launched by the Singapore government in 1993 with the aim of maximising opportunities for Singaporean students in MOE-funded schools (e.g., government and government-aided schools, and government-funded independent and special education schools) by providing resources for school enrichment activities in support of their holistic development and to encourage students to excel in both academic and non-academic areas. Since 2014, eligibility to receive Edusave contribution has been extended to all Singaporean children aged seven to 16, including those not studying in MOE-funded schools. The annual contribution per student is $200 at Primary level and $240 at Secondary level. Additionally, Edusave is also offered in the form of annual grants, awards and scholarships to deserving students.

[3] Yayasan Mendaki (Council for the Development of Singapore Malay/Muslim community) is a pioneer self-help group formed in 1982 dedicated to empowering the community through excellence in education, in the context of a multiracial and multi-religious Singapore. In 2002, Mendaki streamlined its focus along four key areas: Education, Youth, Family and Employability. Mendaki's programmes largely target the bottom 30 percent of the Malay/Muslim population and are therefore, highly subsidised. They are mostly preventive and developmental programmes providing early assistance to the beneficiaries. The programmes are designed to supplement or complement national initiatives.

religious education and coordinate improvement efforts (*Berita Harian*, 1982). Part of Mendaki's early efforts also arose from its preparation for the enforcement of Sections 81 and 82 of AMLA, which had conferred Muis power and authority over the administration of the madrasah in 1966 when the Act was first introduced. However, it was only in 1989 that Muis eventually set up its own Religious Education Unit (Hashim, 1989). With this, the Religious Education Department of Mendaki ceased to function, although the Mendaki Religious Advisory Committee remained in existence. The active entry of Muis onto the scene in 1989 ushered in a period of rapid development for madrasah education as a whole.

On 1 March 1990, Muis was able to enforce its powers to control the registration and management of religious schools and to approve curricula. Priority was placed first on the standardisation of curriculum in full-time madrasah. An Islamic Education Advisory Board, chaired by the Mufti of Singapore, was appointed by Muis on 15 September 1990 to steer the standardisation process (*Berita Harian*, 1990).

In 1991, Muis began to provide annual capitation grants to all full-time madrasahs (*Berita Harian*, 1991). Despite Muis' provision of financial aid to the madrasahs, there was still a shortage of funds. Thus, a stronger injection of funds eventually came in the form of the Dana Madrasah (Madrasah Fund) launched on 15 October 1994 (*The Straits Times*, 1994). The fund aims to help madrasahs achieve higher educational standards through the provision of students' annual capitation and resources grant. It also made possible top-up allowances for *asatizah* to supplement their income which, at the time, were far below the norm of national school teachers. The funding sources for Dana Madrasah were primarily from the Giro donations of the Muslim public and, in recent years, they have been supplemented by *zakat* funds.

Notwithstanding Muis' and Mendaki's efforts, the madrasahs also took it upon themselves to make the necessary changes to adjust to the changing educational landscape. For example, Madrasah Aljunied revamped its syllabus in 1989 to facilitate their students' admission into Al-Azhar University after pre-university. It also rebuilt the school with better facilities, which was completed in 2000. Similarly, for Madrasah Al-Ma'arif and Madrasah Wak Tanjong, they embarked on rebuilding their respective schools to be equipped with modern facilities. Madrasah Al-Irsyad was remodelled in the early 1990s to allow for better balance in its curriculum with respect to academic and religious subjects. In the late 1990s, further changes were made to the madrasah curriculum to incorporate initiatives from the Ministry of Education, such as the introduction of information technology (IT) in schools and the infusion of national education (Chee, 2006).

Despite the efforts, improvements were still piecemeal and did not holistically address the challenges faced by the madrasah. The overall system remained below optimal level with educational outcomes which were less than desirable. By the end of 1990s, the low success rate yet high demand for places in the madrasahs raised concerns among government leaders on the madrasah education's impact on national integration and nation-building. At the same time, the nation was also on the brink of another economic transition, which triggered further concerns of future employability of Singaporeans.

Impact of Compulsory Education(CE)

In 1999, Prime Minister Goh Chok Tong announced a proposal to introduce compulsory education in Singapore (*The Straits Times*, 1999). This move came within the context of Singapore's transition towards a knowledge-based economy (KBE). This brought new concerns on the future employability of all Singaporeans, particularly those who were more vulnerable, such as dropouts and school leavers. Compulsory education would serve to ensure all children will be in school and be equipped with the relevant knowledge and skills which would make them employable in the new KBE.

Madrasahs became the focus of the Singapore government's concern because of the upsurge in enrolment while, at the same time, there was a rather high attrition rate among students. The concern was that madrasah students would not receive quality education necessary for good jobs and would not be able to integrate well into the social and economic system. The proposed CE policy drew a mixed but intense response from different segments of the community. Muis viewed the proposal as an opportunity to strengthen the madrasah sector and developed initial plans catering to various models based on different configurations of CE implementation.

Muis suggested two alternative plans. The first plan adopted the scenario that all madrasahs are included in the proposed compulsory education system. In this scenario, Muis will implement its revised national madrasah education curriculum in all madrasahs and subjects will continue to be taught in an Islamic ambience. For the second plan, where the scenario is that compulsory education can only be introduced only in national schools, Muis proposed the setting up of a government-aided primary school run by Muis or a board appointed by Muis. The school will teach the national curriculum and will be open to students of different races (Osman, 2000).

Muis' approach to the CE proposal was supported by some segments of the community. However, the madrasahs and Pergas took an opposite view and stated their disagreement with the proposal, fearing that this would lead to the eventual closure of madrasahs, if madrasahs lose their feeder students from primary madrasahs (Osman, 2000).

Madrasahs were not supportive of Muis' plans, as they felt that Muis was not being adequately transparent in acting in their interests (Tan, 2001). This led to them forming the Joint Committee of Madrasah (JCM) to work out their own collective response to the CE proposal. Pergas advocated very strongly for the madrasahs' cause and through their online platform, Cyber Ummah, was able to galvanise strong community support (Tan, 2006). A significant segment of the community applauded Pergas' action as a bold move, made necessary by what appeared as inaction on the part of the Malay political and community leaders, including Muis.

Fortunately, the whole episode achieved a conciliatory closure when Mr Goh Chok Tong announced that madrasah schools could be exempted from compulsory national schooling, on the condition that they prepared their primary students for the Primary School Leaving Examination (PSLE). The students must meet the minimum passing standard, failing which, the particular madrasah would not be allowed to offer primary classes. The annual full-time madrasah Primary 1 intake for Singapore Citizens is also capped at 400 (Ministry of Education, 2000). Mr Goh emphasised that the compulsory education policy was not intended to close down the madrasahs and that the government was willing to support one madrasah from primary to secondary level. This brought much relief to the madrasahs and the community, and facilitated efforts to focus on improving the madrasah system.

Post-CE Efforts

By 2003, CE was implemented, and the first cohort of madrasah students would sit for the PSLE in 2008. In the years leading to the PSLE in 2008, various measures were put in place to ensure that the madrasahs could meet the PSLE benchmark. Muis set aside S$700,000 and collaborated with Mendaki to help all six madrasahs prepare their pupils for the PSLE in 2008 through the enrichment of English, Mathematics, and Science subjects, as well as remedial programmes and capacity-building of teachers (National Archives of Singapore, 2007).

To build capacity of teachers, madrasah teachers were sent on full or partial sponsorship for the Diploma in Education Course offered by Edith Cowan University, various courses offered by the National Institute of Education (NIE), and the Specialist Diploma in Teaching collaboratively offered by Muis Academy and NIE. Experienced primary level teachers from national schools were also seconded to madrasahs under the Teacher Mentor scheme, to guide and coach madrasah teachers in their teaching skills.

Muis also launched the Curriculum Development Project (CDP) in 2001 to introduce a more flexible and relevant religious curriculum. The seven-year project produced syllabi, textbooks, and materials for 10 years of education from Primary 1 to Secondary 4. Today, the curriculum developed under the CDP is still being used at Madrasah Irsyad and Madrasah Al-Ma'arif at the primary level.

Notwithstanding the importance of the above measures, a major overhaul which proved to be pivotal was the consolidation of three madrasahs which allowed for specialisation under one system known as the Joint Madrasah System (JMS) in 2009. Madrasah Irsyad by then was under Muis' management. The challenge was to persuade Madrasah Aljunied and Al-Arabiah to be part of the JMS. The positive outcome was achieved as the two madrasahs recognised the challenge of meeting the PSLE benchmark which might risk compromising the quality of education if they insisted on keeping their primary madrasahs. Furthermore, it was not financially viable and trial PSLE scores had shown that it was difficult to meet the PSLE benchmark. It was not the case for the remaining three madrasahs, which preferred to remain on their own as they were confident of running on their own and still meeting the PSLE benchmark. As anticipated, Madrasah Aljunied and Madrasah

Arabiah did not meet the PSLE benchmark in 2008, which validated the decision to cease primary education in the two madrasahs, to allow them to focus on secondary and pre-university level madrasahs. Nevertheless, Madrasah Irsyad, Madrasah Alsagoff, and Madrasah Al-Maa'rif performed well at their first PSLE in 2008 and cleared the benchmark. However, Madrasah Wak Tanjong failed to clear the benchmark, and eventually had to stop taking in Primary 1 students for three years from 2012.

Remodelling the *Madrasahs*

The initial phase of JMS formation focused largely on addressing the madrasahs' management systems and organisations and the urgent need to address the issue of madrasah PSLE performance. Once those were in place, Muis initiated a more rigorous review of its policies in running JMS in 2010, which covered areas such as the educational philosophy, desired outcomes, curriculum, and pedagogy, as well as financial model for sustainability. The intended outcome was to develop a more holistic and integrated policy for the madrasah which would fundamentally address and rationalise the purpose and substance of madrasah education. Muis initiated a series of internal consultations through sharing sessions with the respective madrasah Board of Governors (BOG), JMS teachers, students and madrasah alumni, consulted experts, and studied relevant local and overseas educational models, which involved visits to selected educational institutions in Singapore, Indonesia, Turkey, and the United Kingdom. A survey was also conducted to find out the aspirations of JMS madrasah students and their parents.[4]

At the end of the review process, Muis reaffirmed that it was necessary for the full-time madrasahs to serve dual objectives with different levels of emphasis between the two. It recognised that the primary objective of madrasah education is to provide the requisite education to produce a core of religious leaders and functionaries to serve the Singapore Muslim community's socio-religious needs. A lesser secondary objective is to provide academic education within an Islamic environment for parents who choose this pathway with the intent that their children would eventually enter the mainstream job market. By providing a holistic and realistic

---

[4] Respondents of the 2008 JMS Survey included Primary 6 and Secondary 3 to 5 students, as well as parents of Primary 1 and 6 students (Muis, 2008).

educational experience, it would not only allow students to navigate the mainstream educational and professional markets, but also to support the Islamic studies curriculum. The academic curriculum is thus not seen as an alternative to the Islamic studies curriculum but one that complements each other.

This rationalisation has informed the design of the JMS educational pathways. Being the feeder school, Madrasah Irsyad would prepare the students with foundational knowledge in both the Islamic sciences and the national curriculum. As the feeder school to Madrasah Aljunied, it has to enhance the teaching of Arabic so that students who enter Madrasah Aljunied would have the necessary language capabilities for a deeper Islamic and Arabic learning at the secondary level and onwards. Madrasah Aljunied would remain as the pathway towards a specialisation in the Islamic sciences, with eventual entry into Al-Azhar University or other tertiary Islamic universities. Madrasah Al-Arabiah also had to make adjustments by not offering a full slew of Islamic subjects but instead focusing on the academic subjects. Besides the ambience of a madrasah, exposure to Islamic studies would be limited to a focused module with lesser learning hours and to be delivered in English. This would provide madrasah students with more options after their primary education. Those with clear plans to pursue the Islamic studies pathway and have proven themselves able to take on the heavier workload could opt for Madrasah Aljunied. Those who prefer to eventually undertake a national post-secondary education in other fields would be better off studying in Madrasah Al-Arabiah while still being able to observe their Islamic religious obligations. This specialisation has allowed better optimisation of teacher deployment and teaching resources. Students could also be streamed according to their ability and preference.

Unlike certain points in the past when madrasahs became the destination for weaker students, this has reversed with madrasahs having the opportunity to select the better students through the Primary 1 aptitude entrance tests. This was necessary because of the limited spaces in the madrasah due to the 400 Primary 1 enrolment quota imposed as part of CE. Only students who are assessed to be able to cope with the heavy workload of madrasah education would be accepted. Throughout the primary school education, students who are found to be unable to cope with the load and pace of learning or have other learning disabilities would be channelled to national schools where they could receive better support. This was among the reasons why PSLE performance improved because only the more academically able students remained within the system. After the PSLE, another decision point is when madrasah students would decide whether to remain or opt for learning in the national school system. Some madrasah high PSLE achievers have opted to continue in more renowned national schools such as Raffles Institution or Victoria School. This convenient transfer to the national schools at various points meant that madrasahs are not isolated from the broader national education system.[5] Annually, less than 10 percent of the Madrasah Primary 1 cohort left the madrasah before Secondary 1 for the national schools.

Other than the educational pathways, a more important question would be what kind of religious leaders the community would wish to produce for the future. The revised curriculum has to provide a learning experience which not only exposes the students to specific disciplines, but makes connections across disciplines and encourages students to apply the knowledge critically. To achieve this, a different type of curriculum would be required but without having to compromise eligibility for entry into Al-Azhar University. The traditional Al-Azhar curriculum was enhanced by categorising the existing 17 Al-Azhar subjects into six subject groupings which would facilitate a more age-appropriate, integrated, and inter-disciplinary learning of the Islamic sciences. A new secondary-level subject called "Islam and Society" was introduced as the overarching inter-disciplinary subject taught in English to address contemporary and emerging issues related to learning about and living Islam in a modern society.[6] It is offered throughout the secondary level, with a focus on building up the necessary writing, research, analysis, and communication skills in the first four years of secondary education. These changes to the curriculum would provide the foundational knowledge and skills to prepare future religious leaders who are equipped to deal with emerging challenges and provide sound guidance.

---

[5] Based on Muis' data, less than 10 percent of the cohort leave the madrasah system after PSLE, while about 70 percent do so after 'O' Levels. Among the latter group, about 40 percent go on to polytechnics, four percent to junior colleges, and six percent to Institutes of Technical Education. The remaining either re-take their 'O' Level examinations as private candidates or enrol in other private institutions.

[6] Strands or themes to be featured include: Ethics, Banking and Finance, Globalisation, World Cultures and Religions, Inter- and Intra-faith issues, Gender, Poverty, Human Rights, Climate Change, and others.

Another major change was the adoption of the International Baccalaureate Diploma Programme (IBDP) framework (Davie, 2013).[7] This was meant for a segment of students who prefer to take an alternative route to the purely Al-Azhar entry route. After studying the experiences of local schools that have implemented the IBDP, it was assessed that the programme would meet the madrasahs' objectives. The key strength of the IBDP framework is that it facilitates the integration of academic and religious learning, as well as the infusion of philosophy and values into academic learning. As the IBDP offers Arabic and World Religions modules, Al-Azhar subjects could be woven into the IB framework and mitigate the subject loading for students. Students under the IB track would undergo a through-train programme (i.e. without sitting for the 'O' Level examinations) and take IB subjects at Years 5 and 6, in addition to four other Al-Azhar curriculum subjects. With an IB diploma, it would provide students with more tertiary options beyond Al-Azhar University and other traditional Islamic universities.

Financial Sustainability

The changes initiated would require further injection of funds. In order to ensure regular financial resourcing, the Mosque Building and Mendaki Fund (MBMF) was adjusted to channel some funds to the madrasahs and a new funding stream was created known as the Wakaf Ilmu.[8] These new streams of community funding would complement existing streams like *zakat*, Dana Madrasah, and fundraising by the madrasahs. Another source of funds would be the actual fees borne by parents.

The madrasahs' dual objectives would also inform the principles of funding. The emphasis on the full-time madrasahs' primary role of producing core religious leaders and functionaries would mean that higher community co-funding quantum for the madrasah offering the Islamic studies specialisation. Parents would have to bear the higher proportion of cost-sharing through higher fees for madrasahs which are not specialising in

---

[7] The IBDP was projected to be implemented by 2019.

[8] Wakaf Ilmu is a new Muslim endowment created by Muis beginning with a capital sum of S$3 million for the benefit of Islamic education. It was created initially through consecrating shares of the beneficial income of Muslim estates which would otherwise form part of the *baitul-mal* or General Fund. The creation of *wakaf* would pave the way for more Muslims to come forward to do "planned giving" to build up the capital of the *wakaf*. (*AsiaOne*, 2012)

Islamic studies, as the madrasah is essentially offering a similar academic education similar to what is offered in national schools, except it is delivered within an Islamic environment. Ideally, it has to be treated similarly to that of any school offering premium private education. Nevertheless, a minimum level of community cost-sharing is justified as graduates from these madrasahs could still contribute to the community or religious sector in other non-religious capacities like social workers, and counsellors. With higher fees, parents are generally encouraged to send their children to the national schools if they prefer academic education for their children. Nevertheless, Muis had made provisions from *zakat* funds through Progress Fund Madrasah Assistance Scheme (PROMAS) to continue to support madrasah students from low-income families who require financial assistance, such as bursaries and scholarships for top students.[9] This would help parents to plan ahead in deciding the best option for their children.

Balancing Change and Preserving of Legacy and Heritage

The significant changes that have been successfully achieved in the madrasah sector were made possible because Muis was able get the support from the madrasahs. This was facilitated by Muis' deep appreciation of madrasahs' concerns through the many years of interaction. A key consideration is the madrasahs' strong value of their respective historical legacy and heritage. Thus, Muis was very aware that attempts at standardisation of the madrasah sector could result in the loss of individual madrasahs' legacy and heritage. This would homogenise the sector and ultimately, diminish the rich diversity that has existed for many years. For example, Madrasah Aljunied's curriculum has been deeply aligned to Al-Azhar University's requirements, and this has facilitated entry of successive cohorts into the university and built the largest pool of the community's religious elite including several key religious luminaries. Thus, special care and attention had been given to ensure that the curriculum remained aligned despite the changes introduced.

---

[9] PROMAS (Progress Fund Madrasah Assistance Scheme) provides financial assistance for students from less privileged families who are studying in the six full-time madrasahs. Eligible families with a per capita income of not more than S$500 are eligible to fee subsidies of at least S$540. Depending on the needs of the families, PROMAS also provide other non-fee assistance such as financial assistance for books, uniform, meals, and transport expenses of up to S$1770. PROMAS awards recognise academic excellence among needy students of the six full-time madrasahs (Muis, 2018).

Unlike Madrasah Aljunied, Madrasah Al-Arabiah, and Madrasah Al-Irsyad had shorter histories and were not too fixed on particular models of education. Thus, over the years, both madrasahs had more laxity and flexibility to experiment with various models of learning under different leadership. Nevertheless, for Madrasah Al-Arabiah, having been under Muhammadiyah's care since the 1980s meant that it has adopted the specific orientation of the parent organisation which may differ from the traditionalist orientation of Madrasah Al-Irsyad and Madrasah Aljunied. Thus, in negotiating for Madrasah Al-Arabiah's inclusion, Muis was sensitive in not imposing any changes which might run against any acceptable teachings within Muhammadiyah's religious milieu, particularly within the Islamic Studies content in Madrasah Al-Arabiah's curriculum. Additionally, the respective madrasahs could nominate their preferred representatives to be part of the madrasah BOG. This was also a way to ensure that their interests were heard and could be addressed. From the onset, Muis was very clear that it had to work within those parameters in order to gain the full trust of the various parties involved. Subsequently, Muis was able to deploy its officers to work closely with the madrasah leadership and staff without any major problems. This had made the transformations within JMS operationally possible.

Although trust is relatively higher in recent years, it was possibly at its lowest during the CE episode, as seen from the formation of the Joint Committee of Madrasah (JCM). The JCM's hostility towards Muis continued even after the episode, albeit to a lesser degree when the madrasahs, with the exception of Al-Irsyad, opted not to adopt the curriculum developed by Muis under the CDP. Over the years, through better rapport-building and support for the madrasahs, relations have improved. Nevertheless, for some of the madrasahs, the trust deficit has not significantly diminished. By the time of the offer to be part of the JMS, three of the madrasahs declined to be part of the JMS, as they did not see any value in being part of it especially when they felt that they could sustain on their own. It was fortunate that Muis was able to regain the trust with Madrasah Aljunied and Madrasah Al-Arabiah which allowed to make the collaboration happen. This was despite an earlier unsuccessful attempt for Madrasah Al-Irsyad to be the feeder to Madrasah Aljunied. Those teething issues were subsequently addressed, which have allowed the later attempt to be successful.

Muis has to contend with having the JMS madrasahs and the three other autonomously run madrasahs. The positive side of this is that the community has the options to choose. However, it has created the unwanted differentiation of JMS and non-JMS madrasahs. In the aftermath of the JMS formation, there were concerns that the non-JMS madrasahs are discriminated as much of the resources will be channelled towards the JMS madrasahs. While it was true that Muis gave more attention initially to the JMS madrasahs, it has ensured that support was given to all the six madrasahs, particularly in the area of teacher training. Muis remained committed to strengthen the entire sector and not only the JMS. It has offered to work closely with the remaining non-JMS madrasahs without sacrificing their legacy.

Conclusion: Future of Madrasahs

The JMS madrasahs have shown good progress in raising the quality of education. The popularity of madrasahs has increased after a slight period of decline during the immediate years after the CE was introduced in 2003.[10] Unlike in the 1990s when the enrolment increase did not correspond with injection of resources, the post-CE enrolment increase is better managed because of the 400 Primary 1 enrolment quota. The multiple relatively steady streams of community funding and more reasonable fees have allowed madrasahs to be better resourced to meet the current educational demands. This is further aided by the government's support through the Edusave, the waiver of examination fees, and more recently, the support for the teaching of EMS subjects. With more resources, JMS madrasahs are able to adjust their teachers' salaries upwards, though there is still a big gap compared to the salaries of national school teachers. With a better pay package, the madrasahs have been able to attract experienced NIE-trained national school teachers to undertake key positions, which helped to raise the educational standards even further. This would translate into better educational performance and put madrasahs in better stead going into the future.

Nevertheless, the success of the madrasahs and the continuously evolving national educational landscape would also bring new dynamics and expectations, which require Muis to constantly make the necessary adjustments, particularly in how it manages the remaining madrasahs. The recent announcement on a possible plan to establish a local Islamic college

---

[10] Between 2003 and 2010, a general downward trend was observed in the number of madrasah applications. In 2003, the number of applications was 654 and by 2010, the number of applications was 401.

would have significant impact on the madrasah students' future educational pathways and options (Philomin, 2016).[11] With the college, it would ensure that madrasah graduates could be more seamlessly absorbed into the local job market, whether within or outside the religious sector. This may require madrasahs to rethink or reframe their current alignment to overseas institutions like Al-Azhar University. Madrasahs may be expected to make adjustments upstream to facilitate the students' entry into the new college. With a more complete ecology from primary to tertiary, the entire religious sector would also be optimally transformed so that it can be more effective in positively shaping the community's religious life.

References

Abdul Rahman, N. A. (2006). The Aims of Madrasah Education in Singapore: Problems and Perceptions. In Noor Aisha Abdul Rahman and A. E. Lai (Eds.), *Secularism and Spirituality—Seeking Integrated Knowledge and Success in Madrasah Education in Singapore* (pp. 58–92). Singapore: Marshall Cavendish.

Abu Bakar, M. (2006). Between State Interests and Citizen Rights: Whither the Madrasah? In Noor Aisha Abdul Rahman and A. E. Lai (eds.), *Secularism and Spirituality—Seeking Integrated Knowledge and Success in Madrasah Education in Singapore* (pp. 29–57). Singapore: Marshall Cavendish.

Aljunied, S. M. K. (2011). The 'other' Muhammadiyah movement: Singapore 1958–2008. *Journal of Southeast Asian Studies*, 42(2), pp. 281–302.

Aljunied, S. M. K. and Hussein, D. I. (2005). Estranged from the Ideal Past: Historical Evolution of Madrassahs in Singapore. *Journal of Muslim Minority Affairs*, 25(2), pp. 249–260.

Ariffin, A. (2015, August 23). NDR 2015: Govt to help strengthen teaching of secular subjects in madrasahs. Channel News Asia. Retrieved from: http://www.channelnewsasia.com/news/singapore/ndr-2015-govt-to-help-strengthenteaching-of-secular-subjects-in-8225066.

AsiaOne (2012, March 8). New Muslim endowment fund for Islamic education. AsiaOne. Retrieved from: http://www.asiaone.com/News/Latest%2BNews/Singapore/Story/A1Story20120308-332397.html.

Berita Harian (1982, March 13). Didikan agama: Mendaki bentuk jk. *Berita Harian*. Retrieved from NewspaperSG.

---

[11] In 2016, Minister for Communications and Information and Minister-in-charge of Muslim Affairs, Dr Yaacob Ibrahim raised the possibility of setting up an Islamic college in Singapore to train a new generation of religious teachers who understand Singapore's multi-racial and multi-religious context. The college is expected to be established within the next five years (Philomin, 2016).

Berita Harian (1999, February 20). Kaedah baru Muis bantu madrasah. *Berita Harian*. Retrieved from NewspaperSG.

Berita Harian (1973, March 15). Muis belum sanggup ambil alih madrasah-madrasah di Singapura. *Berita Harian*. Retrieved from NewspaperSG.

Berita Harian (1990, September 16). Muis bentuk lembaga penasihat pendidikan Islam. *Berita Harian*. Retrieved from NewspaperSG.

Berita Harian (1974, December 16). Muis berusaha menyusun sukatan pelajaran sekolah-sekolah agama. *Berita Harian*. Retrieved from NewspaperSG.

Berita Harian (1977, January 23). Sukatan pelajaran ugama rendah: MUIS siapkan. *Berita Harian*. Retrieved from NewspaperSG.

Berita Harian (1982, December 27). Syor tingkat taraf pendidikan Islamiah. *Berita Harian*. Retrieved from NewspaperSG.

Chee, M.F. (2006). The Historical Evolution of Madrasah in Singapore. In Noor Aisha Abdul Rahman and A.E. Lai (eds.), *Secularism and Spirituality — Seeking Integrated Knowledge and Success in Madrasah Education in Singapore* (pp. 6–28). Singapore: Marshall Cavendish.

Davie, S. (2013, January 15). Two madrasahs offer students new curriculum and pathways, including IB prog. *The Straits Times*. Retrieved from http://www.straitstimes.com/singapore/two-madrasahs-offer-students-new-curriculu-mand-pathways-including-ib-prog.

Hashim, A. B. (1989). The Madrasahs in Singapore — Past, Present and Future. *Fajar Islam — Journal of Muslim Issues in Singapore*, 2: 27–35.

History of Madrasah Al-Arabiah Al-Islamiah (2016). Retrieved from Madrasah Al-Arabiah Al-Islamiah website: http://mai.sg/history.

Islamic Religious Council of Singapore (Muis). (2008). Joint Madrasah System Survey 2008. Unpublished document.

Islamic Religious Council of Singapore (Muis) (2018, February 18). Madrasahs— Student Life. Retrieved from Muis website: http://www.muis.gov.sg/madrasah/About/Student-Life.

Ministry of Education (2000). Report of the Committee on Compulsory Education in Singapore. Retrieved from: https://www.moe.gov.sg/docs/default-source/doc-ument/initiatives/compulsory-education/files/ce-report.pdf.

National Archives of Singapore (1999, August 22). National Day Rally Address by Prime Minister Goh Chok Tong 1999, Speech in Malay on 22 August 1999. Retrieved from: http://www.nas.gov.sg/archivesonline/data/pdfdoc/1999NDRmalayspeech.pdf.

National Archives of Singapore (2007, October 26). Speech by Dr Yaacob Ibrahim, Minister for the Environment and Water Resources and Minister-in-charge of Muslim Affairs, At the Hari Raya Get-Together, 26 October 2007, 8.00 pm at the Istana. Retrieved from: http://www.nas.gov.sg/archivesonline/speeches/viewhtml?filename=20071026963.htm.

Osman, A. (2000, April 19). Ways to enable Islamic schools to co-exist. *The Straits Times*. Retrieved from NewspaperSG.

Osman A. (2000, April 21). At odds over madrasahs' future. *The Straits Times*. Retrieved from NewspaperSG.

Philomin, L. (2016, July 15). Singapore to consider having an Islamic college: Dr Yaacob. *Today*. Retrieved from: http://www.todayonline.com/singapore/singapore-consider-having-islamic-college-dr-yaacob.

Tan, T. K. (2001). Social Capital and State-Civil Society Relations in Singapore. IPS Working Papers No. 9. Retrieved from: http://lkyspp2.nus.edu.sg/ips/wp-content/uploads/sites/2/2013/06/wp9.pdf.

Tan, T.K. (2006). Knowledge Has Many Colours: The Public Policy Management of Madrasah Education. In Noor Aisha Abdul Rahman and A. E. Lai (eds.) *Secularism and Spirituality—Seeking Integrated Knowledge and Success in Madrasah Education in Singapore* (pp. 150–165). Singapore: Marshall Cavendish.

The Straits Times (1999, October 14). Government may make schooling compulsory. *The Straits Times*. Retrieved from NewspaperSG.

The Straits Times (1994, April 16). Muis to raise salaries for Madrasah teachers. *The Straits Times*. Retrieved from NewspaperSG.

The Straits Times (2013, August 18). NDR 2013: Edusave extended to include madrasah students. *The Straits Times*. Retrieved from http://www.straitstimes.com/singapore/ndr-2013-edusave-extended-to-include-madrasah-students.

6

RETHINKING ISLAMIC EDUCATION FOR THE YOUNG

Farah Mahamood Aljunied and Mohamad Khidir Abdul Rahman

Introduction

The educational landscape in Singapore has undergone several phases of transformation to suit the needs of its changing national demography. Islamic education is not immune to these changes, particularly in the demography of students. This is especially true for part-time Islamic education: the structured religious education (madrasahs) made available through mosques or private Islamic education centres for students attending national schools. Since part-time madrasahs are catered to students attending full-time national schools, the learning experience in national schools shapes students' expectations. National schools are becoming increasingly competitive, which limit the students' ability to dedicate time for Islamic education. At the same time, national schools' pedagogic approach was moving away from rote learning and incorporating different strategies, which altered students learning styles. Religious teachers in part-time madrasah then reported concerns over the dwindling rate of attendance while parents reported students' unwillingness to attend classes because they found them dull (*Berita Harian*, 1998). On top of the structural and systemic issues within mosque madrasahs, these challenges compelled Muis' Religious Education Department to holistically review the Islamic education sector.

This chapter will trace Muis' attempts at remedying the abovementioned. Muis embarked on an in-depth study to understand parents', teachers', and students' perspectives on part-time mosque madrasahs. Their inputs later led to the design and implementation of a new approach to Islamic education through the aLIVE programme. The programme relooks at the content and structure of mosque madrasahs, and incorporates pedagogies that are appropriate for each group of students from ages five to twenty. The holistic revamp of mosque madrasahs is centred on the main objective of part-time Islamic education: "to develop righteous (*soleh/solehah*) children who are God-consciousness (*taqwa*), good character (*akhlaq*), and are knowledgeable in Islam" (Muis, 2007: 21) and develop practising Muslims capable of articulating their knowledge on Islam.

However, the implementation of any educational reform is dependent on the receptivity of multiple players to the reform strategies and their aims; the players include teachers, parents, and educationists from private Islamic institutions. It requires a collective understanding and agreement of the objective, and an underlying philosophy of the reform through active engagement in the initiation phase. While many young parents and youths welcomed the change and felt that it was timely, there were teachers, parents, and Islamic education providers who were not immediately convinced of the reform strategies, questioning their purpose. Many were concerned that the changes might dilute the learning and understanding of the religion. Others felt that the changes could lead to the failure, if not the end, of credible and authentic religious learning. Through a thorough study of the new curriculum and the varied perspectives towards Islamic education, this chapter argues that part-time Islamic education should be understood within the context of a changing globalised world.

Background of Part-time Islamic Education in Singapore

Supplementary Islamic learning in Singapore has its roots in the villages and mosques. Muslims in the area would gather and listen to lectures held by a religious teacher or a prominent member of the village. As Singapore's urban landscape evolved, these villages were removed to develop Housing

Development Board (HDB) apartments, and Islamic learning became more interspersed. In the early days of the HDB flats, weekly Islamic lessons or lectures would be held either in the void decks of HDB blocks or in homes, where religious teachers (*asatizah*) would give sermons to a group of learners, young and old alike. Religious classes and sermons would also be held in Malay/Muslim Organisations (MMOs) such as Pergas, Pertapis, Jamiyah, or Perdaus. Non-Malay speaking Muslims tended to attend religious classes held in Tamil in Indian-Muslim associations and mosques.

By the 1980s, more mosques were built in various neighbourhoods, with classrooms and learning spaces for younger students to attend supplementary Islamic education. While some mosques and MMOs provided structured weekly Islamic education classes, the syllabus used was separate and not standardised across ages. It was only in 1992 that Muis developed a standardised primary-school level syllabus (for students aged 6 to 12-years-old) and final-year examinations for all part-time Islamic education centres, including mosques, MMOs, and private centres. The objective was to inculcate young Muslims with foundational Islamic knowledge through five main subjects: Creed (*tauhid*), Moral Education (*akhlaq*), Islamic Jurisprudence (*fiqh*), History (*sirah*), Arabic language, and Qur'anic Literacy.

In 1995, this syllabus was reviewed and repackaged into a modular format to meet the needs of students who had missed the earlier levels of the mosque madrasahs. It was well-received and was used by not only the mosque madrasahs but also by the private Islamic education centres. Islamic education providers also participated in the Joint Primary 6 mosque madrasah examinations that were conducted at the end of the six-year programme. However, since 1995, there had not been any major changes to the syllabus, and there was no syllabus developed for teenagers and youths. It was in 2000 when developments both in Singapore and among students' learning signalled a need to review the syllabus.

Challenges to the Relevance of Islamic Education Programmes at Mosques

The impetus for Muis to study the effectiveness of all mosque madrasahs was rooted firstly in various instances of students' poor response to weekly lessons. Teachers and school administrators highlighted to Muis that students' attendance would dwindle over the semester, especially during the examination periods in national schools. Parents too were concerned that those who were enrolled into these part-time mosque madrasahs were not motivated to attend classes for various reasons (*Berita Harian*, 1998; 2002).

A major issue that signalled the need for a review was the structural limitations of the current system. The syllabus for youths beyond the primary level has yet to be standardised across all part-time Islamic mosque madrasahs. This meant that centres providing Islamic education programmes prepared preschool and secondary level curriculum separately, resulting in variations and a lack of continuity between primary and secondary levels. Moreover, not all centres catered for all age groups, which made the progression from one level to another inconvenient and, at times, not possible. Students were thus not sure where they could continue their education once they had completed their secondary-level programme. The problem is further exacerbated by the fact that not all students in the class were of the same age group — differences in learning progress, and a difficulty in engaging students of different ages, thus resulted in students dropping out of school or not attending at all.

The education sector in Singapore was also undergoing some major transformations that would deeply impact student learning and receptivity towards Islamic education. As part of the effort to prepare the next generation for a globalised nation and a knowledge-based economy, national schools were becoming increasingly more competitive, with more examinations and co-curricular activities taking up more of students' time. The style of teaching was also being revamped to be more dynamic and engaging for students, emphasising student participation. This insight was significant as it informed policy-makers and curriculum developers that simply creating a standardised syllabus for teenagers in secondary school with traditional subjects was insufficient. To deliver quality and effective Islamic education, both content and pedagogy needed to be reviewed.

Review of Mosque Madrasahs

The review of the part-time Islamic education sector began in 2000. Muis formed the Comprehensive Islamic Religious Education System (CIRES) committee to study and review both the full-time and part-time Islamic education sectors. Following that, the Religious Education Advisory Panel (REAP) was formed in 2003. This panel conducted research, interviews, and focus group discussions to assess the needs of the part-time Islamic education sector, the changing social and educational landscape, and the areas that required improvements. The result of these studies, interviews, and discussions pointed to a few core areas of concern that demanded a relook at how the part-time Islamic education sector had to be revamped.

The study found that part of the reason mosque madrasah lessons did not appeal to students was because the content was not tailored to students' specific age groups, and not relevant to their everyday lives. For example, primary school students aged six to twelve were taught rituals that were neither mandatory nor relevant to their spiritual and daily needs, such as the prayer for the dead (*solat jenazah*) and cleansing rituals for childbirth and menstruation. Such examples revealed a disconnect between what was taught in class and the cognitive and moral abilities of the child of a particular age, causing the child to feel overwhelmed at times.

The findings also highlighted that the lecture-based style of teaching for young students also tended be inappropriate for younger students from the ages six to sixteen. While some Islamic educational institutions welcomed student participation and discussion, classes were mostly structured with teachers as active transmitters of knowledge and with students passively memorising theories for examinations. Such an approach was more didactic, lacked activities, and was not appealing or interesting enough to pique students' attention. Relative to the style of learning in national schools, where the "Teach Less, Learn More" movement compelled teachers to structure lessons with more group work, inquiry, and participation, traditional learning styles of rote memorisation and lecture-based lessons were considered dull (Muis, 2003). While such a methodology may be useful for older students who have the capacity for theory-based specialisation, younger students evidently require a different approach.

Interestingly, the use of Malay as the medium of instruction was a significant factor in reducing students' motivation towards attending mosque madrasah classes. Generally, Islamic education programmes in mosques are conducted in Malay as most religious teachers were trained in Malay and Arabic, and they were also used to delivering lessons in Malay. However, Malay-medium education in mainstream national schools had phased out and English-language education dominated mainstream national schools. Students were thus increasingly inclined towards learning and communicating in English. The study highlighted that students preferred to learn about Islam in English, which was rarely available, if at all. Furthermore, Islamic education needed to be accessible to non-Malay speaking Muslims, a demography that was growing due to a general growth in population, conversion of faith, or mixed marriages. Mosque madrasahs thus had to consider rethinking Malay as the only medium of instruction for Islamic educational programmes in mosques if they were to be accessible to a changing demography of students.

A practical issue that proved a hindrance to students' consistent attendance is their inability to juggle both national school and mosque madrasah lessons. Students were expected to attend two to three hours of mosque madrasah classes twice a week, or over three hours during the weekends. Since the structure of Islamic education programmes is mirrored after the national school system, students are expected to prepare for two different types of homework, tests, and exams. Many were unable to manage the pressure, especially since the workload and expectations in national schools were increasing. One student mentioned that he would be 45 minutes to an hour late as he was tired over the weekend (Marranci, 2009). With the introduction of single-session schools,[1] it became even more challenging for students, especially secondary-level students, to attend classes regularly. Some would skip classes and exams as they were too tired (Muis, 2003). This finding was significant as it showed that effective learning through an engaging curriculum would be futile if students are physically unable to attend lessons. This signalled a need to rethink the timing and duration of mosque madrasah classes.

The Singapore Islamic Education System

The above findings pointed to the need for Muis to revamp the current mosque madrasah and develop a new Islamic education system. In 2004, Muis developed the Singapore Islamic Education System (SIES), which entailed a revamp of part-time mosque madrasahs. Under this system, a new part-time Islamic education programme was produced: Learning Islamic Values Everyday (aLIVE). The new aLIVE programme drastically changed the content, pedagogy, and assessment methods in an attempt to make lessons more engaging, interactive, and relevant for students. The process of producing an educationally and religiously sound education system began firstly with setting a clear objective of part-time Islamic education, and then studying various methodologies from other education systems. The new curriculum was then validated and supported by a panel of education specialists.

---

[1] National schools in Singapore were held in two sessions for primary and secondary-level students: morning sessions from 7:30am to 1:00pm, and afternoon sessions from 1:00pm to 6:30pm.

The aLIVE curriculum is designed with the goal of inculcating relevant Islamic knowledge, moral values, and practices to youths (Mosque Madrasah Convention, 2007). In essence, its primary aim is not necessarily to develop students' academic capabilities in Islamic education, but to equip students with practical and applicable knowledge on Islam. With the objective of meaningful and relevant Islamic education in mind, curriculum developers studied not only Islamic educational models within the region and overseas such as the Dawud Tauhidi model from the US, but also different educational models from the UK and Australia (Australian Association for Early Childhood), as well as other character-building programmes. A key element in these models is that each age group has distinct needs in terms of content and pedagogy. The subsequent approaches are thus shaped by the needs of students in four age groups: "Kids" (5 to 8-year-olds), "Tweens" (9 to 12-year-olds), "Teens" (13 to 16-year-olds), and "Youths" (17 to 20-year-olds).

A distinct feature of the aLIVE curriculum is its thematic approach to subjects, integrating traditional Islamic subjects into broad themes that are relevant to each group of students' daily life. For example, under the broad theme of "Physical Care", students in the "Teens 1" programme would internalise elements from traditional subjects such as *fiqh* through learning cleansing rituals (*taharah*), e.g., mandatory ritual purifications (*ghusl*), and other hygienic practices. The theme links these rituals with the importance of being neat and presentable[2] while, at the same time, addressing the issue of vanity among teenagers. These are further supported and affirmed by *hadiths* and verses of the Qur'an. Aside from learning about rituals, the theme "Physical Care" also teaches *aqidah* by touching on the discussion of refraining from self-harm, eating healthy, and having a healthy body image — concerns that many teenagers have. It reminds students of having faith in Allah and that He has created humankind in the best of forms, thereby encouraging students to be confident with the way they look. Thematic and integrated learning is thus able to connect various aspects of students' daily activities and concerns to the spiritual and religious principles, encouraging them to stay engaged to and fully appreciate spiritual learning.[3]

---

[2] Qur'an, 95: 4.

[3] As the programme is designed for students to finish within 14 years, certain lessons are repeated in the form of a spiral curriculum. Basic knowledge such as *solat* are repeated in various parts of the programme in different intensity and focusing on different skillsets.

The aLIVE programme utilises a range of pedagogical approaches that are tailored to the needs of each age group. Curriculum developers studied early childhood learning models[4] and found that a play curriculum, with an emphasis on experiential and hands-on learning, is the best approach for kids. For "Tweens", this experiential learning could range from the use of new media, project work, field trips, and also role-play, to make lessons more meaningful, interactive, and engaging. The "Teens" curriculum is unique because it encourages students to explore a deeper sense of spirituality and identity through a more discursive lesson structure, with an emphasis on inquiry and criticality. The role of the teacher as a skilled facilitator of discussions is thus especially crucial here. The shift in approach is distinct — students are expected to actively participate and engage in making meaning of their personal spiritual development. With this foundational knowledge in place, the "Youth" curriculum, developed later on in 2008, undertook a different andragogical approach to learning, focusing on specialisation and an in-depth study of theories behind specific religious subjects.

The new pedagogical approach also features a change in the medium of instruction from Malay to English. This change was significant as it meant that all teaching and learning materials had to be developed in English and delivered in the same language, or bilingually where appropriate. Before aLIVE was implemented, mosque madrasah classes were delivered solely in Malay.[5] Books used in the Primary level[6] and the Primary 6 exams that Muis organised[7] were written in Malay, and teachers were trained and expected to teach in Malay. Despite the challenges, incorporating English in lessons is important in not only ensuring that students are able to learn Islamic education in their preferred language, but also in ensuring accessibility to non-Malay Muslim students.

Another significant departure from the initial Islamic education programme is the exclusion of examinations at the end of the semester. This served to firstly reframe students' perspective on Islamic education, and to also alleviate

---

[4] For references on early childhood learning pedagogy models utilised, see Muis (2008).

[5] Some books used in lessons were in Jawi Scripture, before that was phased out in the 1990s.

[6] *Sukatan Pelajaran Untuk Madrasah Masjid Sistem Modul Darjah I Hingga Darjah VI* (Muis, 1997) was a set of documents that compiled the syllabus of subjects that were taught in the part-time madrasah at the mosque. The subjects were *Tauhid* and *Feqeh*, *Akhlak* and *Sirah*, and *Bahasa Arab*.

[7] The Primary 6 Examinations ceased in 2008.

students' workload. Part of the objective of mosque madrasahs is that students internalise the beliefs and practices of living as a Muslim every day. This could not be assessed solely through theoretical examinations in which students memorise information from a textbook and sit for written examinations. The new programme introduced different approaches to assessing students' Islamic knowledge, e.g., class quizzes, inquiry, and discussion, and continuous observation of students' practices and skills during class. Beyond the classroom, parents are encouraged to observe students' understanding and practice of Islamic knowledge at home. Without the pressure of studying for written examinations in both mosque madrasah and national schools, students could reframe their perspective on Islamic education, viewing it not as just as another subject to ace, but as a way of life to be practised daily.

Lastly, to address the structural limitations of the preceding programme, in which students found themselves unable to juggle between national schools and mosque madrasahs, the timing and duration of aLIVE classes were adjusted. Students under the aLIVE programme had two options to complete a year of Islamic education: either in Academic Year or Holiday format. In the former, lessons are typically delivered during a three-hour class every week, usually over the weekends, a one-hour difference from the initial two-hour classes held twice a week. The Holiday programme catered to students who are too busy to attend during the academic year, offering classes during the holidays and in more than one delivery format. This flexibility in timing, in addition to the removal of written assessments, is aimed at both taking the pressure off of students to perform and to rethink the notion that Islamic education needs to be assessed with academic performance.

Critiques of the aLIVE Programme

The revamp of the structure and content of part-time Islamic education caused serious concerns among parents, teachers, and other private Islamic education providers. Although there were stakeholders who were supportive of the new curriculum, some were not keen on the new approach. The main issues brought up were, firstly, the perceived inauthenticity and dilution of Islamic education through the content and pedagogy, and secondly, the structural challenges of the implementation of the programme.

The concern some parents and teachers had with the content of the aLIVE programme stemmed from firstly, the absence of traditional subjects under the thematic and integrated curriculum, and secondly, the removal of formal and written assessments. Under the integrated values-based curriculum, parents were unable to locate traditional subjects such as *fardhu 'ain* and Qur'anic literacy under the themes.[8] Parents highlighted that the aLIVE programme was "too secular and too basic" (Marranci, 2009), especially when compared to the previous mosque madrasah, some of which they attended as youths. They cited the lack of memorisation as a big issue, as students reportedly had not memorised specific rituals, Islamic history, and names of prophets, all of which were considered important aspects of Islamic education. Without standardised written examinations, parents were also unable to measure the effectiveness of students' learning.

While there were private Islamic education providers who were keen on embarking on the curriculum, some shared the above view that the new curriculum had deviated from traditional Islamic learning and tradition. Teachers and curriculum providers in private Islamic education centres found that although the new syllabus was relevant to younger students, a certain academic rigour had to be in place to meet the needs of students who had the desire to learn the background and theory of Islamic subjects in-depth. This includes the use of rote memorisation, especially for subjects such as Qur'anic literacy, Islamic history, and *aqidah* and *fiqh*, and the use of written examinations to assess the depth of students' knowledge.

The most important aspect to the implementation of an education programme is the receptivity and readiness of teachers to deliver lessons — the initial stages of the aLIVE programme revealed structural challenges in teacher readiness. The transition from Malay to English was a challenge for some teachers. In 2004, the majority of teachers who had served in mosque madrasahs for more than five years were mostly 30-year-olds and above. Teaching Islam in English was challenging, as teachers were either not fluent in the language or did not know the right terminologies to use. Most, especially those teaching at the "Tweens" or "Teens" level (aged eight and above), were unable to respond to students effectively. For Malay-speaking parents, the language remains close to their hearts and they would want to retain its use in teaching their children Islam, even if they are aware that

---

[8] *Fardhu 'ain* is the acquisition of knowledge that is considered as an individual obligation that every Muslim must undertake, as opposed to knowledge of *fardhu kifayah* which is considered as a collective responsibility, that is, the obligation to acquire certain knowledge is fulfilled if a section of the community fulfils it.

children learn better in a language that they are more proficient in, in this case English (Abu Bakar, 2011).

The above responses to the aLIVE programme revealed insights that were useful to its continuous development. Yet, a key element for curriculum developers to consider is whether the new approach is truly cognitively effective and spiritually meaningful for students. As part of the process of the first phase of implementation for aLIVE, Muis conducted evaluation exercises, both by internal staff (e.g., school principals, curriculum designers) and education specialists who studied students' and parents' responses to the "Kids" aLIVE and "Teens" aLIVE programmes in 2009.[9] These were conducted through focus group discussions with parents and students, classroom observations, and analyses of textbooks and the curriculum framework.[10]

Review Areas (for Validation)		Key Research Questions
A. Content	• Overall programme design • Islamic education and religious content	• Is aLIVE's approach to integrate the different conventional subjects into themes justified? • Is the religious content of aLIVE rooted and anchored to Islamic traditions? • Has aLIVE in any way "diluted" the religious content at mosque madrasahs?
B. Pedagogy	• Appropriateness of the teaching methodology and pedagogical approaches employed (e.g. in relation to the developmental needs of the participants)	• Is aLIVE delivered in an age-appropriate manner? • Is the activity-based approach of aLIVE really effective in teaching Islamic values? • Are the assessment tools employed by aLIVE suitable?
C. Achievement of Desired Outcomes	• Effectiveness of programme implementation with respect to the design	• Has aLIVE achieved its objectives of making Islamic education relevant to the students?

[9] For list of specialists, refer to Annex A.

[10] See Chew (2014) for a case study of a *Teens* aLIVE classroom setting.

Overall, reviewers validated the programme's conceptual design, and affirmed that the religious content of aLIVE is sufficient to meet the basic Islamic learning needs of students at the respective levels, given the context of a weekly programme. In validating aLIVE's interdisciplinary, thematic, and interactive design, Professor Sidek Baba and Dr Johdi Salleh commented that the curriculum content covers the basic tenets of Islam adequately. This view is echoed by Sheikh Ali Abdul Baqi, Secretary-General of the Islamic Research Academy of the Al-Azhar University. Based on the "Teens" aLIVE research conducted by Dr Gabriele Marranci, the programme has been found to be comprehensive and its content facilitates a deeper understanding of the Islamic creed and practice.

However, while the interactive pedagogy used in teaching "Teens" aLIVE has been effective in engaging students, reviewers found that much about the delivery could be improved. There were, firstly, instances of mismatch of activities with the target students, as some activities were not suitable for the age group. Furthermore, not all teachers were well-equipped with the proper training to efficiently deliver and facilitate lessons. For example, many would use the teacher manual as a script instead of treating it as a reference. The development of suitable curriculum activities and the continued training of teachers, who are critical to the delivery of effective Islamic learning, were key to the delivery of the programme.

The contrast between specialists' assessment of the programme and the above stakeholders' view that it is a 'dilution' of Islamic education may stem from: i) a difference in conception of 'authentic' Islamic education; ii) a disjuncture in expectations on the objective and structure of part-time Islamic education; and iii) the lack of engagements between parents and aLIVE administrators. The response to and assessments of the aLIVE programme have thus highlighted the need to further develop two key areas: i) teachers' development and ii) stronger parental involvement in students' learning.

The anxiety in using what is considered new pedagogic approaches in madrasahs may stem from the perceived novelty of an approach that deviates from the traditional teacher-centric method that focuses on memorisation and recitation. Indeed, teacher-centred pedagogies and rote memorisation techniques have long been privileged in madrasahs and Islamic institutions. Yet, student-centred pedagogies have, in fact, always been in Islamic educational traditions — problem-solving as a teaching tool for Islamic jurists, discussions to strengthen students' understanding of lessons, and dialogue techniques are just some of the ways Islamic thinkers and *imams* have taught Islamic education (Tan and Abbas, 2009). The concept of an organised learning institution only came about much later in Baghdad, and was not the method employed by the Prophet with his companions. Similarly, the Prophet himself had used various teaching methods to teach Islam to his companions, and many a times were very experiential and in thought provoking ways (Abu Ghuddah, 2003). Islamic history and the traditions of the Prophet have proven that Islamic teaching strategies have always evolved based on the needs and conventions of the people at the time.

Additionally, the persistent view that the aLIVE programme's content "dilutes" authentic Islamic education may stem from a disjuncture in expectations on the objective and structure of part-time Islamic education. In the initial curriculum, the pedagogy, examination formats, and language were all mirrored after full-time madrasahs. Given that such an approach is consistent with that of religious institutions in the region, parents and teachers may consider it the *right* form of Islamic education, and thus appropriate for part-time madrasahs. However, these approaches are consistent with the rigour of full-time institutions only because its objective is to produce religious leaders or Muslim professionals. For young students attending lessons for three hours a week, the social and cultural context in which they live cannot be ignored. While the recitation and memorisation of Qur'anic verses and prayers remain an important feature in aLIVE, to focus on theology, dogmas, and rituals independent of the daily lives of students living in a globalised and multicultural world, would likely be ineffective in inculcating religious knowledge and practices.

The importance of supporting teachers' training cannot be understated given the drastic changes to the curriculum. To ensure teachers are well-trained and prepared to deliver the lessons, Muis developed a more structured training programme, which included training in pedagogy, student development, classroom management and assessment, and acquiring teaching qualifications. Mosque madrasah teachers' close involvement during the pilot programme was key to the successful implementation of aLIVE in its early years. Teachers familiarised themselves with the new approach of teaching Islam to the young through bi-weekly pre- and post-implementation meetings. The regular feedback and discussions were crucial in refining the details of the aLIVE materials and approach, especially for "Teens" aLIVE.

Acknowledging the discomfort teachers and parents have with the new medium of instruction, Muis also initiated training programmes for teachers to improve their proficiency in English. A course on how to conduct Islamic education in English was also developed, in which teachers are given tips and guidance on how to translate Arabic terms into easy English. These courses were held in the early years of aLIVE and went on until 2010. By then, a younger workforce in the teachers emerged. Graduates of the full-time madrasahs and the alumni of aLIVE came into the teaching force as teaching assistants to the main teachers. These groups of teachers, though lacking in experience, were proficient in English. It was then that English courses for teachers were no longer needed, as teachers grew more comfortable with English as the medium of instruction. Teachers were also given the flexibility to conduct lessons in Malay if all the students in the class are comfortable (Muis, 2007). The teacher development courses were then focused on enhancing pedagogical skills of teachers. Today, English is more accepted as the medium of instruction for Islamic education, not just in the aLIVE programmes, but also in programmes provided by other providers.

Apart from teacher training, continuous engagements with parents to encourage participation in students' Islamic learning was also introduced through various efforts. A key finding in the aLIVE validation exercise, especially in "Teens" aLIVE, is that parents were not aware of the progress of students, and were unclear on how the activities would impact the students. An orientation session for parents and students were thus held at the beginning of a semester to familiarise parents to the objectives, curriculum, and structure of the aLIVE programme. To keep parents updated with students' progress in class, programme administrators and teachers would hold parent–teacher conferences once every six months. Additionally, Muis also improved the home activity booklets for "Kids" and "Tweens" levels which students brought home, to include more information about what was taught in class. This includes the list of verses and prayers that were taught, so as to assist parents support their children's learning at home.

The aLIVE programme requires the support and engagement with various stakeholder aside from parents, teachers, and students. The key highlight to achieve this was through the Mosque Madrasah Convention (MMC) 2007, which involved the Mosque Management Board (MMB) members, Muslim youths and students, religious leaders, private Islamic education providers, and educationists. Altogether, 735 members of the community were consulted on the philosophy and objective of the aLIVE curriculum, and the subsequent implementation process at all mosque madrasahs. Although this proved successful in building consensus and raising support for the aLIVE curriculum among stakeholders within the sector, engagement with parents and students needed to continue throughout the semesters. Public education efforts such as "aLIVE Day" and "aLIVE Fest" were intensified following the MMC to bring greater awareness of the programme to the public.

Ultimately, revamping the mosque madrasah was aimed at encouraging more young children to learn about Islam in a more meaningful way. In an effort to increase participation in structured Islamic education, 70 private Islamic education providers collaborated to increase the number of spaces[11] for both younger and adult students under the programme Private Islamic Education Network (PIENet) (Jangarodin, 2012). The curriculum provided by these various education providers vary: from lectures dealing with traditional Islamic subjects to those more experiential in nature. They catered to the diversity of needs and preferences of students' learning styles. The diversity in structured Islamic education is indeed a valuable asset that should continue to bloom to meet various needs of students and adult learners.

Future Challenges for Part-time Islamic Education

Today, even more youth-friendly structured Islamic education programmes have risen to respond to changes among youths' learning preferences. More use English as the medium of instruction, and incorporate technology such as video learning through live YouTube lessons or short online courses. Lessons held in trendy cafes would also invite youths who are more comfortable with such a unique setup (Diman, 2016). Such innovative approaches, while still grounded on Islamic tradition, respond to both market development and young learners' needs to provide even better Islamic learning. However, in the same way that the aLIVE programme has responded to changes in the past, how can the Islamic education sector respond to the new waves of challenges?

The role of religious teachers in Islamic education for the young in the future may be increasingly challenging. In an effort to ensure that the curriculum content remains relevant and current, they would have to be able to quickly respond to issues and concerns raised by youths. As part of the aLIVE curriculum, students are indeed strongly encouraged to ask and discuss difficult questions relevant to their everyday lives. While social media and the abundance of diverse information and opinions have been a challenge for

---

[11] Both mosque madrasahs and providers under PIENet worked together to meet the target of increasing 50 percent student enrolment.

quite some time already, the diversity of opinions will only grow as the socio-political space continues to grow and become more complex. Teachers will have to be equipped to navigate through sensitive issues that may polarise discussions, such as intra-faith issues and minority rights.

The diversity and wide accessibility to Islamic knowledge may also prove a challenge for Islamic education curriculum content providers. Given the global climate of religious radicalisation and extremism through the internet and Islamic educators who lack credibility, there may be a need for Muis to have a broader oversight of the curriculum content provided by private Islamic education providers. The extent to which Muis regulates the curriculum content of other Islamic education providers may be a point of contention in the future. A strong working relationship between Muis and Islamic education providers, including home-based religious classes, would be crucial in handling the challenge of ensuring credible religious content.

References

Abu Bakar, M. (2011). Kids aL.I.V.E. Research Report. *Muis*.

Abu Ghuddah, A. F. (2003). *Prophet Muhammad: The teacher and his teaching method-ologies*. (Mahomedy, M, Trans). Zam Zam Publishers, Karachi.

Atan, R. (1998, July 12). Sesuaikan pendidikan madrasah. *Berita Harian*.

Berita Harian (2002, March 10). Tingkatkan madrasah sepenuh masa bagi tangani cabaran akan dating. *Berita Harian*.

Chew, P. (2014). Coming to grips with modernisation: The Teens aL.I.V.E. programme and the teaching of Sadaqah (giving of alms). In Buang, S. and Chew, P. (Eds.), *Muslim Education in the 21st Century: Asian perspectives* (pp. 142–161). London: Routledge.

Diman, H. (2016, June 23). Pusat pembelajaran agama ala kafe. *Berita Harian*.

Jangarodin, S. (2012, August 6). Jaringan bagi menarik golongan muda pada pendidi-kan Islam. *Berita Harian*.

Marranci, G. (2009). Teens aLIVE Evaluative Report of Year 4. *Muis*.

Muis (2007). Mosque Madrasah Convention. *Muis*.

Muis (2008). Kids a.L.I.V.E. Programme: A Conceptual Curriculum Framework. Youth Education Strategic Unit, Islamic Religious Council of Singapore. Nooraman, I. (2003). Assessing religious instructions of mosque madrasah in Singapore. Muis.

Tan, C. and Abbas, D. (2009). The 'Teach Less, Learn More' initiative in Singapore: New pedagogies for Islamic Religious Schools?, *KEDI Journal of Educational Policy*, 6(1), pp. 25–29.

Annex A

Name of Scholar	Institution	Review Component
1 Sheikh Ali Abdel Baqi	Islamic Research Academy, University of Al-Azhar	Conceptual Framework and Islamic Religious Content
2 Professor Sidek Baba	Institute of Education, International Islamic University Malaysia	Programme Design, Islamic Religious Content and Pedagogy
3 Dr Johdi Salleh		
4 A/P Gabriele Marranci	National University of Singapore (Sociology)	Impact of Teens aLIVE on the students
5 A/P Phyllis Chew	National Institute of Education, Singapore	aLIVE's Pedagogy (as part her ongoing NIE-research)

Part 3

Managing Assets and Services

7

MOSQUES IN SINGAPORE: MANAGING EXPECTATIONS AND THE FUTURE AHEAD

Mohamad Helmy Mohd Isa

When the Prophet Muhammad arrived in Medina (after his emigration from Mecca), the first move he made was to build the Quba Mosque. This story resonates with many Muslims, so much so that the significance of the institution of the mosque and the social functions it serves, are built into their psyche. As such, many Muslims feel that it is unacceptable to tear down any mosque.

The future of old mosques was put into question during the early years of Singapore's independence in 1965. There was an urgent need for land to be freed, to make way for urban development needs, and religious spaces too were affected. Should mosques — many of which were built from land endowments — be demolished to make way for development? This chapter highlights how Muis worked closely with the government and other stakeholders in ensuring the institution of the mosque evolved with changing times as Singapore prospered. The challenge was to convince the community that the concept of the mosque must move with time, and that the government played a role in facilitating the community's religious and spiritual interests, despite it being a secular government. The first section of this chapter will demonstrate, how Muis was tasked to work with relevant agencies and volunteers within and beyond the Muslim community to ensure the sustainability of mosques during those early years.

The second section of this chapter will then explore the policy experience behind managing mosques beyond its physical construction. This entails an exploration of how Muis has tried to optimise the physical structure of mosques by supporting it with manpower, programmes and structures so that mosques can fulfil their socio-religious and developmental purpose. The final section of this chapter will consider the challenges mosques face in meeting the myriad of expectations emanating from various stakeholders. These stakeholders have differing views on what constitute the value and function of the mosque. To be sure, the various engagement platforms which Muis has developed over the years are meant to provide Muis, the mosque fraternity, the community, the government, and all other players in the mosque's ever-expanding ecosystem with the space to assess needs and co-create solutions to meet those needs. In the long run, this iterative engagement process will help converge divergent expectations and renew the community's traditional and deeply entrenched expectations for the mosque. Such engagement will ensure that mosques remain sustainable and relevant.

Constructing and Sustaining a Place for Worship

To make way for the establishment of HDB towns, the government had to acquire various sites, including mosque sites. The very first challenge for Muis was to ensure that the primary function of the mosque as a place of worship is sustained, given this government move. For that reason, numerous mosques had to be demolished, much to the dismay and concern of the Muslim community. Muis understood the need to replace the demolished mosques, and that its task during that period of transition was to raise funds to build new mosques. However, fundraising was a serious problem in the early years. Mosque committee members and volunteers had to organise house-to-house visits to solicit funds from villagers in order to build new mosques (Green, 2007). This arrangement, while effective in a village set-up, was not sustainable once new satellite towns were established. The cost of building mosques became a lot higher, simply because they could no longer be built like in the past with cheaper materials such as zinc and wood.

Despite all the fundraising efforts, Muis did not manage to build any new mosques in any satellite town (Green, 2007). This led Muis to approach the government for a solution. In its 1973 annual report, Muis stated that the government should refrain from acquiring mosque sites, and if there were no other options, it should provide alternative sites so that new mosques can be built to replace those demolished (Hussain, 2012, p. 75). To this, the government responded that such a suggestion was not feasible because if made equally available to all religious groups, this would entail having to replace 11 mosque sites and 172 temple sites (Hussain, 2012, p. 76).

Nevertheless, the government and then prime minister Mr Lee Kuan Yew understood the uncertainties felt by the Muslim community: they had to transition into a new living set-up in high-rise flats; and to face with new responsibilities such as paying rents, utility bills, and conservancy charges, all of which required financial capacity, which the community did not possess. Therefore, the government saw the need to balance the community's desire for the mosque institutions to be retained, and not to compromise its standing as a secular country.[1]

To this end, the government was able to extend two solutions so that mosques can co-exist with its new environment in new HDB towns. One way was to exempt the mosque building committee from being subjected to a tender process when buying land to build a mosque. This move led to the lowering of the land purchase[2] (Mattar, 1986). In every HDB town, the government would make land available, and the community would then have to raise funds to finance the new mosques (Green, 2007, p. 45). In addition, the government also proposed a solution that would facilitate fundraising for mosque building. Therein lies the impetus for the establishment of the Mosque Building Fund (MBF) (Karim, 1990, p. 16).

The MBF was established in August 1975 after the Administration of Muslim Law Act (AMLA) was amended. MBF refers to an automatic deduction

---

[1] The late Minister Mentor, Mr Lee Kuan Yew, who was prime minister during the early years of mosque building, explained that he 'had to find a solution which did not involve the government in building religious places of worship. If the government gets involved in building temples and churches, it's an impossible position. Because we want to hold ourselves as a secular government' (Green, 2007, p. 44).

[2] Typically, in a tender process, the cost of the land will be set at the price valuated by the chief valuer.

mechanism that allows $0.50 to be deducted from each Muslim worker's monthly CPF contribution with the right to opt out (Green, 2007, p. 45). The MBF was a crucial tool put in place to efficiently pool community resources in order to ensure the building and sustainability of mosque structures. This is evidenced by the fact that, within the span of four years between 1977 to 1981, six new mosques were built across six new HDB towns.[3]

Even though the MBF scheme was able to build a new generation of mosques in HDB towns, Muis soon realised that mosque-building and its necessary financial and building requirements were evolving, along with the demographic realities of its congregants. The first generation of mosques built via MBF could not keep up with the growing number of congregants 10 to 15 after years they were built. It became clear that more mosques were needed to accommodate not only the growing population of congregants but also its changing profile. By 2011, it became clear that the upgrading of old mosques was necessary.

However, the rising cost of land and building cost added further strain in the effort to ensure sufficient financial reserves. At the time when the first phase of mosques were built (1976–1980), the average land cost per mosque was estimated to be $282,500 and the average building cost per mosque was estimated at $1,345,830. By the time the fourth phase of mosques were built (2006–2010), the average land cost per mosque has risen to $3,635,000 while the average building cost per mosque rose to $8,000,000 (Green, 2007, p. 130). The exponential increase in the cost of sustaining mosque's space for worship increased the pressure on Muis and the community to pool the necessary resources to continue mosque-building and, later on, mosque-upgrading.[4] This necessitated the review of the rate of MBF contribution. To date, the rate of contribution of every worker to MBF has been revised four times. In fact, as seen in Table 1, in 1995, the revision in rates was no longer flat but differentiated according to the income range of the Muslim worker.

Aside from the coordination of sufficient financial reserves, an additional challenge for Muis during its early experience of mosque-building was that it lacked the necessary expertise to design and build the physical structure of a

---

[3] Between 1977–1981, six mosques were built, namely, Muhajirin Mosque (1977), Mujahidin Mosque (1977), Assyakirin Mosque (1978), An-Nur Mosque (1980), Al-Ansar Mosque (1981), Al-Muttaqin Mosque (1981).

[4] The MBF policy was revised in 2009 to include mosque upgrading.

Table 1: **Rates of contribution for Mosque Building Fund/Mosque Building Mendaki Fund from 1975**

Monthly Total Wages	1975	1977	1984	1991	1995	2005	2009	2016
$1,000 and below	$0.50	$1.00	$1.50	$2.00	$2.00	$2.00	$2.00	$2.00
$1,001–$2,000	$0.50	$1.00	$1.50	$2.00	$3.00	$3.00	$3.50	$3.50
$2,001–$3,000	$0.50	$1.00	$1.50	$2.00	$3.00	$4.00	$5.00	$5.50
$3,001–$4,000	$0.50	$1.00	$1.50	$2.00	$5.00	$8.50	$12.50	$13.50
$4,001 and above/ $4001–$8000 (as of 2009)	$0.50	$1.00	$1.50	$2.00	$5.00	$11.00	$16.00	$19.00
$8000 and above (as of 2009)							$16.00	$21.50

modern mosque. In this regard, Muis was able to leverage the expertise of the Housing Development Board (HDB) and later, the Technical Advisory Panel (TAP)[5] (Tong, 1999) to assist the mosque-building committees in developing mosque designs and eventually facilitating its construction. The choice to team up with HDB was because it was overseeing the construction of houses in the new HDB towns, and therefore, it was deemed well-positioned to advise how mosques could fit into the larger housing plans. This is reflective of Muis' aspiration to have mosques fit well into Singapore's housing landscape.

The sum of the mosque-building and upgrading experience highlights the importance of Muis' relationship with several key partners. In pooling the necessary resources in terms of finances and expertise, Muis' efforts were predicated firstly, on the support of the government for the community's aspiration for the mosque in the new urban set-up of post-independence Singapore and, secondly, by leveraging the necessary expertise which might not have been present within the community. Thirdly, Muis' efforts were also centred on the support and the value that the community placed on the mosque. Much literature have pointed to the lack of trust of the community for Muis in its earlier years of establishment (Green, 2007). This distrust

---

[5] The Technical Advisory Panel (TAP) was a panel that comprises experts from within the community whose primary task was to translate user requirements between the mosque building committee and the architects and those responsible for the physical construction of the mosque (Green, 2007, p. 60).

stemmed largely from the belief that Muis existed as an agent of the state rather than as a representative of the Muslim community. Despite the climate of distrust, the community leveraged the platform and concessions provided by the state and facilitated by Muis to realise its aspirations for mosque-building in these early years. This was only likely to be possible given the value and reverence that the community has placed on the mosque and its primary function as a place of worship.

The MBF experience has also brought about a "sense of collective ownership of the new mosques" (Sukaimi, 1982, p. 9). The community has vested interest in the success of the mosque arising from a "greater collective concern and accountability for the success of the mosque building programme" (Sukaimi, 1982, p. 9). By this time, the community's sense of what accounts for a successful mosque has evolved beyond simply building the mosque's physical structure. What constitutes a successful mosque includes the performance of the "people who manage it, or the congregation members, or both, the managers and the members" (Sukaimi, 1982, p. 5), on top of its "activities and programmes, the participation and involvement of the Muslims in these activities" (Sukaimi, 1982, p. 5). All these requirements point to the need for mosque to fulfil a different dimension to its purpose, namely, its mission in the socio-religious development of the mosque.

Sustaining Mosque's Socio-Religious and Developmental Mission

The socio-religious development mission of the mosque cannot be said to be the exclusive by-product of the community's evolved, modern expectations for the mosque. Historically, mosques in the region have functioned as social hubs, even in the traditional set-ups (such as in the villages or kampong mosques and *suraus*). Mosques remain the sites on which village communities meet and discuss ways to improve their welfare (Markasan, 2005, p. 184). Even as the community moved out of the village set-up and into communities of high-rise flats, this social mission remained (Markasan, 2005, p. 190). Where mosques existed, the Muslim community within the vicinity of the mosque will leverage mosque space to spur its social mission. The mosque committee, or the Lembaga Pentadbir Masjid, with the support of the community, will establish a welfare office, or a Jabatan Kebajikan, to oversee the welfare of its community (Markasan, 2005, p. 190). This underscored the expectations of the community when it came to the socio-religious and developmental function of the mosque.

Despite these expanding expectations, the conditions in the first generation of MBF mosques highlighted some of the challenges in realising the community's aspirations in this regard. Firstly, it was difficult for mosques to sustain a consistent and constant delivery of programmes, be it for Islamic learning or other forms of community development, because they faced a strain in manpower as the administration of the first generation of MBF mosques were run by mosque volunteers. While mosques in the earlier years had employed some administrative staff to oversee the daily function and operations at the mosques, the mosques were still highly dependent on volunteers to deliver services and programmes. The scope of work undertaken by volunteers at the mosques in the 1980s and 1990s would range from fundraising, organising family events and religious lectures (*syarahan*) for the congregants, and to the scheduling of the *khatib* for Friday prayers. Mosque volunteers, many of whom were teachers, were also responsible for the development of the curriculum and examination papers of the part-time religious schools, or madrasahs, at mosques.[6] During this period, each mosque management board was headed by a chairperson whose role was to provide leadership in the organisation and administration of mosques. Even with only a handful of salaried staff at mosques, MBF mosques during this period were able to function on the manpower of volunteers. This was a considerable feat given the scope of work undertaken. The role of volunteers at the mosque cannot be understated as being crucial to its sustainability, considering the serious financial constraints the community faced in building the mosques.

Despite its successes, it became apparent that voluntary manpower was no longer sufficient to meet the demands facing the mosques. There was insufficient consistent manpower to support activities and leadership that would enable mosques to fulfil its socio-religious and developmental mission, such as computer courses, fundraising for the less fortunate, or even organising programmes for rehabilitated drug offenders (Karim, 1990, p. 47). In addition to this, the demography of volunteers at the mosque was also shifting. In its initial years, much of the regular volunteers were made up of teachers whose work schedule permitted the expenditure of a reasonable number of hours per day managing the daily affairs at the mosque. By the

---

[6] Part-time religious school was made available weekly at mosques, usually during weekends, to cater to the religious education of Muslim children and youth who attend secular schools over the week.

late 1980s, the profile of Muslim professionals were shifting, whereby one's work hours are quite likely to stretch to the end of the day, therefore making voluntary work at the mosques a difficult commitment to make.

Without a systemised management of manpower and accountable leadership at the mosque, important tasks such as governance and accounting were compromised. It was even surfaced in the 1980s that accounting at the mosque did experience incidents of lapses (*Berita Harian*, 1980). This has highlighted the need for proper training of mosque manpower to ensure the integrity and governance of mosque as an institution (*Berita Harian*, 1980).

The community's expectations with regards to services and programmes at the mosques were no longer able to be fully supported by a largely volunteer-based manpower at the mosque. These were often highlighted by the community through letters published in the newspapers, altogether underscoring some of the community's unfulfilled expectations in the early years of mosque-building with regards to the socio-religious and developmental mission of the mosque.

Mosques did not have sufficient resources to finance programmes and activities that were able to fulfil its social developmental mission fully. In the 1980s, during the formative years of Singapore's baby-boomers, there was a call among Muslims parents for more Muslim preschools, and some mosques stepped forward to try to provide this service. As a result of the lack of regulation over the type of activities, programmes, and services offered, mosques had the flexibility to respond to the needs of its congregants freely. While this may seem favourable, given the limitations in resources at mosques, when certain mosques focused on expanding its social developmental mission, they may end up doing so at the expense of the core function of the mosque, as a place for religious learning. This was clearly highlighted by Muis in 1989, when it was found that a number of mosques were running courses such as IT programmes but were then unable to run Islamic education programmes (*The Straits Times*, 1989) which were fundamental to the core function of the mosque. Subsequently, mosques were reminded not to lose focus on providing Islamic learning above and beyond other types of courses that are less fundamental to the core function of the mosque (*Berita Harian*, 1989). This not only highlighted the need for better optimisation of mosque resources, but also the need for a structure that allows mosques across Singapore to strategise a way to prioritise and optimise mosque resources better.

To rectify this situation, Muis understood that to fully optimise the community's investment in the construction of mosques, manpower, structure and programmes supporting the mosques must be equally invested in and developed.

Manpower

Introduced in the early 2000s, the Professional Executive Leadership (PEL) scheme was meant to strengthen mosque leadership, management, and governorship. Through the PEL scheme, Muis would recruit and appoint experienced mosque leaders and competent professionals as the Executive Chairman of the Mosque Management Board (MMB).[7] Although both the Executive Chairman and MMBs are appointed by Muis, the introduction of a salaried Mosque Executive Chairman (MEC) signalled a shift in the management of mosques as the MEC is directly responsible for the overall management and operations of the mosque and reports to the Muis Director overseeing the Mosque sector. With the implementation of the Mosque Cluster System in 2008, the MECs report to the General Manager (GM) of the cluster. The MEC works closely with the MMDs, who now play the role of board of governors.[8] The PEL scheme was implemented incrementally over many years at MBF mosques and a few other selected mosques who could afford it.

Further initiatives were introduced at mosques to support the socio-developmental mission of the mosque. To support social development services and programmes for low-income families and *zakat* recipients, Social Development Officers (SDO) were introduced in 2008 at mosques to administer primarily, info-referral services. Although Muis plays a big role in institutionalising regulation and standards in the administration and hiring process at the mosque sector, this pursuit is being heavily supported by the community through mosque funds. Even though the GMs and the EMC office are salaried through Muis, personnel such as the MECs and the SDOs are being partly salaried through mosque funds. This underscores the interwoven

---

[7] MMBs are volunteers appointed by Muis to lead and manage mosque operations and services.
[8] Refer to p. 141 for an explanation of the role of the GM of an Enhanced Mosque Cluster who is a senior Muis officer.

roles that Muis, the mosque sector, and the community play in providing the resources and structures needed to develop the mosque sector as a whole.

Even with the implementation of policies that placed salaried full-time staff at mosques, Muis recognises that mosques are still heavily dependent on the role of volunteers in supporting many of its activities. Among those who were disgruntled by the implementation of a full-time mosque executive chairman were segments of the community who felt that the contributions of mosque volunteers to these schemes were not being fully appreciated, and that these new schemes were ways for Muis to do away with volunteers at the mosque altogether, including those who had served as volunteer leaders at the mosques for a very long time (Jimin, 2010). Among mosque volunteers who were most suspicious of this initiative were the MMB members. Many of them felt that the implementation of the MEC as part of the larger PEL scheme was a plan to reduce their roles at the mosques and over time, making the MMBs irrelevant.

In fact, the implementation of the PEL scheme over time was meant to move the role of the voluntary MMB from mosque administration and operations into the domain of leadership, planning, and governance by putting in place a structured process of appointments approved by Muis. The appointment of volunteer mosque board members is meant to be as rigorous as hiring a full-time employed staff, which encompasses screenings and interview sessions. Selected individuals are then made to undergo training, providing them with an overview of their leadership roles and expected personal conduct as an MMB member. The implementation of these measures enabled mosques to ensure that the voluntary MMB at mosques are fully equipped with the skills necessary to provide leadership in operating a mosque while being plugged into the overall strategy of mosques across Singapore as a sector. For the community and mosque fraternity to understand and accept the rationale behind this initiative, Muis has had to continually ensure them that the implementation of the PEL and initiatives such as the EMC scheme is meant to evolve the role of the voluntary MMBs and not to deplete it into obsolescence.

The professionalisation of the mosque sector also seeks to upgrade the role of non-MMB volunteers as well. While volunteers at the mosque in the past would take on *ad hoc* tasks such as providing logistical support during events or cleaning the vicinity of the mosque or even preparing food for mosque events, these tasks are unrelated to their personal or professional skills and not related to a larger outcome. Part of the objective of professionalising the mosque as a sector is to grow the scope of work of the volunteers beyond these basic tasks. In the past, volunteers delving in welfare work at the mosques may, for instance, bring packet food to the doors of a low-income neighbourhood. However, now with the Befrienders Scheme,[9] the same volunteer would have been given some level of proper training on how to engage effectively with families and individuals living in the low-income neighbourhoods. Another example is in the performance of the annual *korban* during the yearly *Eidul Adha*. In the past, volunteers may freely volunteer to take on roles during the sacrificial ritual. Now, with the implementation of the new *korban* regime overseen by the Jawatankuasa Korban Masjid Singapura (JKMS), all volunteers must go through proper training, for instance, in the logistical set-up for the site for sacrifice, preparing the tools used for the sacrifice, and even in how to handle the animals prior to and during the sacrifice. In summary, the training and professionalisation of mosque volunteers serves to optimise the impact and the quality of the volunteer work itself.

Structure

To further strengthen the interwoven structures that bind Muis, the mosque, and the community in developing the mosque sector, the Enhanced Mosque Cluster (EMC) was introduced. Under this structure, mosques were segmented into six clusters of between eight to 20 mosques. Each cluster has an office comprising a General Manager (GM) and two managers, who are all Muis staff. The EMC office will oversee, among other things, the focused and smooth implementation of sector-wide policies based on closed consultation with Muis and the community on the ground. The structure of the EMC by virtue of its connectedness to both Muis and the community on the ground enables smoother sector-wide planning, coordination, and implementation

---

[9] The Befrienders Scheme is a volunteer-based social befriending service for Muis' long-term (LT) financial assistance beneficiaries (e.g., the aged, chronically ill, disabled etc.) The volunteers or "Befrienders" provide invaluable services to beneficiaries such as providing companionship, offering emotional support and developing their self-confidence through regular home visits. Muis has developed a comprehensive Befrienders Management Framework to enhance the quality of intervention and ensure active participation of Befrienders. This framework includes strategies for recruitment, induction and orientation, training and deployment, as well as appreciation and recognition of Befrienders' services.

across all mosques. For instance, it allows mosque personnel to better communicate the needs of the ground to Muis while, at the same time, also enables mosque personnel to communicate sector-wide changes and aspirations to the mosque fraternity and the community. The communication of needs and the coordination of solutions to meet these needs are also structurally supported by the EMC through the Mosque Convention. The Mosque Convention is an engagement platform held in 2005 and 2011 for the mosque fraternity, the community, and Muis to collectively plan and coordinate the development of the mosque sector for the coming years.

Programme

With the proper employment of mosque personnel to deal with administration and operations and the EMC structure, mosques are better able to assess and respond to the developmental needs of the community. For instance, during the Mosque Convention 2005, the mosque fraternity, Muis, and the community came to a consensus after assessing the community's needs that Islamic Education at mosque must be able to address the social challenges shaped by global drivers such as globalisation and modernisation. To serve this purpose, the aLIVE Islamic education programme was implemented at all mosques. The structure at mosques and its connectedness to Muis' structural support meant that mosques were better able to facilitate the delivery of aLIVE programmes at mosques.[10] Thus, Muis is able to provide accessible support through teacher training and providing a fully developed curriculum ready for delivery at mosques. This ensures that mosques are in a stronger position to effectively fulfil its religious development mission. Beyond Islamic education, mosques have expanded the range of programmes to include community outreach, social development as well as a conduit for national agencies to deliver public education programmes on various issues like healthy lifestyle, financial planning, etc.

Positioning Mosques within the National Landscape

In this modern ecosystem, mosques have moved from existing within and serving "homogenous ethnic communities" and are re-organised and

---

[10] The Learning Islamic Values Everyday (aLIVE) programme is an part-time Islamic education programme offered in mosques. See Chapter 6 on Rethinking Islamic Education for the Young, for more information.

interwoven into "heterogeneous, multi-ethnic communities" (Tong, 1999, p. 89). In this new cosmopolitan context, mosques have to deal with the diversity and divergences in expectations of not just their congregants, but also that of the government, other Muslim non-congregants, as well as non-Muslims within the vicinity. As the mosque-demolition experience mentioned earlier demonstrates, divergences between the expectations of the Muslim community and the government have occurred with regards to the treatment of old mosques. While the government's expectations have been for mosques to be interwoven into the new urban development plans, the Muslim community's expectations have been that mosques should not be demolished. This highlights the "tension between [the expectations of] the state with its particular set of values [as determined by] 'pragmatism', 'rational planning', 'efficient' use of land'" (Kong, 1993, p. 346) and the expectations of the Muslim community, which may have been determined by religious values of reverence or other "alternative values such as historical significance" (Kong, 1993, p. 346).

The same divergences have also occurred between the Muslim community's and the state's expectations for the mosque in other instances, such as the regulation of mosques' call to prayer, or *azan*. Before independence, mosques' *azan*. was "exclusive to Islamic rural communities" (Tong, 1999, p. 89). However, with the heterogeneous urban setting, the soundscape of the mosque is being cohabited by non-Muslims as well. To accommodate this shared space, a new regulation was introduced in 1974 to "re-direct the loudspeakers of the mosques inwards" (Tong, 1999, p. 89). The community's adverse reactions to this move indicated tensions arising from differences in expectations between the regulating entity (the state) and the Muslim community, with regards to not just the physical space but also the sound space of the mosque (Tong, 1999, p. 89). Both the episodes of mosque demolition and *azan* regulation demonstrated that the mosque-building experience in Singapore has been about interweaving religious life into the urban, cosmopolitan and multicultural setup of modern Singapore.

However, expectations for the mosque have gone beyond simply where or how mosques should exist physically in the national physical landscape. Divergent expectations now occur in relation to how a mosque should be run. So far, the chapter has examined the rationale behind Muis' implementation of policies across mosques as a sector, such as the PEL, and structures, such as the EMC, as a way to optimise community's investment into the mosque and its socio-religious developmental mission. However, the community's reactions at the onset of these policy and structure implementations highlight the divergence in expectations between different segments of the Muslim community. While some segments of the community welcomed the introduction of the MEC scheme for instance, others perceived this scheme with suspicion and distrust. Some have voiced grievances in the local newspapers that if such a scheme was to be made compulsory through Muis' regulatory authority, MECs should be placed fully under Muis' payroll.

Similar grievances could also be seen in the implementation of the EMC structure. As described earlier, through the EMC structure, all mosques are grouped into clusters, with each cluster being under the supervision of a GM. The GMs are part of Muis' payroll and human resource. Similar to the experience of the MEC scheme, this policy was also met with distrust from a small segment of the Muslim community, who viewed this move as yet another ploy on the part of Muis to exploit mosque resources for Muis' agenda.

At various occasions, Muis has engaged the public on their perspective on the issue, explaining that the implementation of the MEC scheme which entails training mosque staff and implementing administrative and governance policies at mosques is meant to optimise (rather than exploit) mosques' assets (*Berita Harian*, 2010) while meeting the community's expectations of the mosque.

However, from the perspective of policy-making, it is important for Muis to recognise that at the core of such divergent expectations are different understandings of whose aspirations and needs mosques should prioritise. While those who oppose the scheme might consider that mosque resources should be channeled to benefit only those within the mosque, those who were supportive agreed with the need to optimise mosque resources for the wider community beyond just the mosque. For instance, when the aspiration to make mosques open and friendly was articulated at the Mosque Convention 2005, the mosque fraternity, the participating segments of the Muslim community, and Muis came to a consensus through multiple engagements, that mosques should be run as 'constituency mosques', which serve beyond just their congregation by reaching out and touching every member of the community within the constituency' (Muis, 2005, p. 21). This aspiration also encompassed being open to all segments of this constituency including families, the youth, and the migrant Muslim community.[11] While segments of the community warmly welcomed this aspiration, others were not as keen. This could be observed from the negative reactions to, for instance, the presence of youth activities[12] at the mosque or the presence of women in mosque leadership.[13] Such divergences reflect the differing values of a diverse Muslim community in how they viewed the mosque.

Muis' engagement with the mosque fraternity and community through the EMC and through engagement platforms over the years, such as the mosque seminars and conventions, are meant to provide a solution to this tension in the long run, by allowing various stakeholders to envision common values which the mosque can espouse. These structures and platforms are meant to give Muis, the mosque fraternity, and the community a chance to assess the current needs of the community together and to co-create solutions and opportunities to address those needs. Since the value of the institution lies in the need and purpose which it serves, co-identifying those needs and co-creating solutions to those needs, in time, will help to update the value of the mosque to a larger "in-group", therefore sustaining its relevance and utility to its contemporary ecosystem.

The importance of these engagement platforms will only continue to grow as expectations begin to rise along with the diversity of the mosque ecosystem and the mosque's role as a social node further widens. Mosques have been frequently approached to partner with numerous national and grounds-up initiatives to reach out to the community. These initiatives can range from health initiatives to educate the community on healthy living and eating to green movements that educate the community on ways to save the environment. Beyond reaching out to the community, the mosque has also begun to model some of these initiatives. For instance, as part of the national movement to

[11] See (*Berita Harian*, 2008) for excerpt of Muis President Haji Mohammad Alami Musa's speech delivered at Appointment of Lembaga Pentadbiran Masjid (LPM) in 2008.
[12] Some community members have made suggestions in newspaper forums on ways to attract the youth to the mosques through sports (*Berita Harian*, 2006) or theatre while others have expressed discomfort in doing such activities in mosques.
[13] Some segments of the community have called for the greater participation and role of women in mosque leadership which other segments of the community disagree with.

encourage healthy living, mosques have made the step to consciously incorporate more healthy options as part of the menu at mosque events. Other examples are the green initiatives being modelled at various mosques through their campaign to save water, by educating mosque-goers on how to perform their ablution while being economical with water consumption. The trend of more mosques going into these initiatives highlights the inadvertent widening of mosque policies, from simply ensuring the sustainability of their relevance and value to the Muslim community to ensuring their sustained relevance and value to the larger ecosystem in which they exist.

Mosques' and Muis' focus in the mosque conventions exemplifies this widening scope in mosque policy-making. In response to the changes affecting the Singapore Muslim community which include globalisation, modernity and key demographic shifts, the mosque no longer serve only the Muslim community, even though it still remains as the mosque's main constituents. The joint committee of the mosque convention, which encompassed mosque and Muis officials as well as members of the Muslim community, jointly agreed the need for the mosque to "assist [in disseminating] a set of attributes that would shape the identity of Singapore Muslims who would also identify themselves as contributing Muslims to global humanity" (Mosque Convention, 2005). To meet this objective, the joint committee recommended strategies for mosques to "keep [its] *Jemaah* (congregation) updated and sensitive to current realities and challenges" (Mosque Convention, 2005). On top of that, it also recommended the pursuit of "social bonding projects and humanitarian aids to anyone in need — regardless of race or religion" (Mosque Convention, 2005). Such aspirations underscore a widening of the social value of mosques from a node that seeks to serve only the Muslim community, to a more inclusive node that is relevant to the larger ecology of diverse community and societal interests.

The Future of Policy-making at Mosques

This chapter has highlighted that as the social fabric of the community and the larger Singaporean society becomes more complex in its composition in terms of identity, circumstance and sensitivity, the expectations of the constituency as a whole for the mosque is far from singular. For instance, what entails a mosque fit for spiritual fulfilment may differ between a senior citizen and a youth. Similarly, what constitutes a mosque with a meaningful social value may differ between a Singaporean Muslim and a

Muslim migrant worker. Mosques as a sector has tried to encompass these differing needs and, in the process, has tried to fit mosques into every individual's notion of home. This can be seen in the myriad of examples highlighted in this chapter of how Muis has worked with mosques to deliver services that go beyond their primary functions to better serve the needs of their congregation and larger ecosystem. However, the question as to whether mosques will be able to sustain its accommodation to this growing multiplicity of expectations is something that future policy makers must take into serious consideration.

References

Berita Harian. (1980, June 23). Kira2 masjid banyak yg tidak lengkap. *Berita Harian*. Retrieved from NewspaperSG.

Berita Harian. (1980, March 31). Muis timbang sistem selaras wang masjid2. *Berita Harian*. Retrieved from NewspaperSG.

Berita Harian. (1989, September 15). Kegiatan masjid: Muis luas peranan. *Berita Harian*. Retrieved from NewspaperSG.

Berita Harian. (1989, October 9). Muis minta masjid luas kelas agama. *Berita Harian*. Retrieved from NewspaperSG.

Berita Harian. (1992, April 18). Laras diberi peranan lebih luas. *Berita Harian*. Retrieved from NewspaperSG.

Berita Harian. (2006, June 17). Kaji langkah masjid tayang siaran piala dunia untuk tarik belia. *Berita Harian*. Retrieved from NewspaperSG.

Berita Harian. (2008, March 10). Cabaran Pertingkat 'mesrakan' masjid. *Berita Harian*. Retrieved from NewspaperSG.

Berita Harian. (2010, April 24). Latar Belakang MEC. *Berita Harian*. Retrieved from NewspaperSG.

Berita Harian. (2011, September 30). Peranan penting Muslimah menyokong masjid. *Berita Harian*. Retrieved from NewspaperSG.

Berita Harian. (2011, October 1). Tidak elok wanita pimpin masjid. *Berita Harian*. Retrieved from NewspaperSG.

de Haan, J. F., Ferguson, B. C., Adamowicz, R. C., Johnstone, P., Brown, R. R., and Wong, T. H. (2014). The needs of society: A new understanding of transitions, sustainability and liveability. *Technological Forecasting and Social Change* (85), pp. 121–132.

Green, A. (2007). *Continuing the Legacy: 30 Years of the Mosque Building Fund in Singapore*. Singapore: Majlis Ugama Islam Singapura.

Hussain, S. Z. (2012). *Keeping the Faith: Syed Isa Semait Mufti of Singapore 1972–2010*. Singapore: Straits Times Press.

Jimin, M. H. (2010, April 10). Jangan lupa yang lama berkhidmat. *Berita Harian*. Retrieved from NewspaperSG.

Karim, Z. A. (1990). Kepelbagaian Peranan Masjid di Singapura. Singapore: Jabatan Pengajian Melayu University Nasional Singapura.

Kong, L. (1993). Negotiating conceptions of 'sacred space'. *Transactions of the Institute of British Geographers,* 18(3), pp. 342–358.

Lee, T. S. (1999). Technology and the Production of Islamic Space: The Call to Prayer in Singapore. *Ethnomusicology,* 43(1), pp. 86–100.

Markasan, S. (2005). Surau masjid dan madrasah sebahagian daripada identiti bangsa melayu singapura. In S. Markasan, *Bangsa Melayu Singapura Dalam Transformasi Budayanya*, pp. 183–196. Singapore.

Mattar, A. (1986). *New-Generation Mosques in Singapore and their Activities.* Singapore: Majlis Ugama Islam Singapura.

Muis. (1992). *Annual Report 1992.* Singapore: Muis.

Muis. (2005). *Mosque Convention 2005: Remodelling Mosques.* Singapore: Muis.

Sukaimi, M.H. (1982). *Dynamic Function of Mosques: The Singapore Experience.* Singapore: Majlis Ugama Islam Singapura.

Tan, E.K. (2007). Norming "Moderation" in an "Iconic Target": Public Policy and the Regulation of Religious Anxieties in Singapore. *Terrorism and Political Violence,* 19(4), pp. 443–462.

The Straits Times. (1989, September 12). Mosques told not to run courses, schools. *The Straits Times.* Retrieved from NewspaperSG.

The Straits Times. (1989, September 26). 'Use new mosques mainly for prayer'. *The Straits Times.* Retrieved from NewspaperSG.

The Straits Times. (2011, September 26). Wanted: More female mosque leaders. *The Straits Times.* Retrieved from NewspaperSG.

Tong, S. L. (1999). Technology and the Production of Islamic Space: The Call to Prayer in Singapore. *Ethnomusicology,* 43(1), pp. 86–100.

8

DOING THINGS DIFFERENTLY: *ZAKAT* AND SOCIAL DEVELOPMENT IN SINGAPORE

Zulfadhli Ghazali

The giving of alms, also known as *zakat*, bears an emotive significance for Muslims around the world. As one of the pillars of Islam, the literal meaning of *zakat* is purification, whereby one "purifies" one's wealth by giving a portion of the wealth to the needy. It is seen as an important step to redistributing one's wealth for the purposes of spreading help and social justice. In the Muslim psyche, it fulfils both a spiritual and a social calling that is inseparable from one's identity as a Muslim, hence, the elevation of this form of giving as a mandatory obligation of the faith itself.

Traditionally, *zakat* in Singapore was managed at a personal level, often entailing the direct transfer of *zakat* from the payee to the beneficiary or through an appointed administrator (*amil*) who collected and disbursed *zakat* on behalf of the payee. The latter was often informally organised at the village or community level through a community-appointed or recognised *amil*. The absence of any overseeing, legally bound authority meant that there were often cases of *zakat* not being responsibly collected and properly distributed. This worried a handful of community leaders that the true purpose of *zakat* had been short-changed by the lack of proper organisation and regulation (Select Committee, 1966, p. 38). The purpose of this chapter is firstly, to trace the context and process of establishing a proper system of *zakat* management and administration in the context of Singapore's transition into a newly independent nation run by a secular government. Second, this chapter will seek to explain the role of Muis in this transition and in the modernisation of Singapore's *zakat* administration.

The second segment of this chapter will explore the motivation for Muis' move to integrate social development into the management of *zakat*. This entails the application of social development thinking and implementation of social development programmes to *zakat* financial assistance (FA) beneficiaries. It also involves the mapping of *zakat* FA onto the larger landscape of social assistance available country-wide which allows *zakat* FA beneficiaries to access a slew of national assistance with greater ease. The chapter will conclude by discussing the implications of this shift in Muis *zakat* management's focus in the face of rising social inequality in Singapore.

The Institutionalisation of *Zakat* in Singapore

Prior to Muis' role in *zakat* administration, it was mainly paid, collected, and disbursed informally. An individual who wished to contribute would do so either by making a direct transfer to a beneficiary or through a representative, or *amil*, who collected and disbursed the contribution to the needy on behalf of the individual. In this traditional arrangement, the *amil* was someone appointed or recognised by a community of people as a trusted representative to administer *zakat* on behalf of a group of people.

This absence of an overseeing legal entity meant that *zakat* collection and disbursement in traditional pre-independent Singapore faced its share of problems. As reported by community leaders in the select committee hearing of 1955, there were observed incidents whereby "collection was not done properly as the rate fixed by the Majlis Ulama was not followed and the money collected was not used as it was intended" (Select Committee, 1966, p. 38). This, to early Muslim community leaders in Singapore, meant that the true purpose and meaning of *zakat* in the upliftment of Muslims were not fully realised.

Zakat regulation under a legal entity was incepted when Singapore was at the crossroads of its independence. This critical juncture brought to light the need to formalise the legal and proper administration of key institutions, including *zakat*, through the passing of a bill. With the passing of the 1966 Administration of Muslim Law Bill, a number of provisions were created to ensure that *zakat* in Singapore would be better protected from various dysfunctions, therefore, enabling it to better fulfil its religious and social purpose. These provisions among other things ensured that *zakat* would be solely collected and disbursed by a Majlis Ugama, and no other entity. The rationale behind this move was to ensure that there was a single entity that would be made responsible and accountable for the proper administration of *zakat* in Singapore.

It was apparent from the amendments proposed by the community leaders that the socioeconomic upliftment of the Muslim community was a key concern for them when it came to *zakat*. For instance, one representative cautioned that enforcing of a clause that made non-payment of *zakat* punishable by law might run counter to the spirit of social justice that underpins *zakat* (Select Committee, 1966). Another instance of concern towards the maintenance of the spirit of social justice in *zakat* was the amendments proposed to ensure that the amount paid for *zakat* was deductible from an individual's taxable income (Select Committee, 1966). These instances of expressed concern of the early community leaders exemplified the importance of fulfilling the spirit of social justice that underpinned *zakat*. This concern on maintaining spirit of social justice remains a recurring concern as Muis further modernises *zakat* management in Singapore.

Modernisation of *Zakat* Management in Singapore

The primary objective of Muis' modernisation of *zakat* management is the establishment of accountability and transparency in the administration of *zakat*. To this end, Muis has significantly invested in the centralised professional appointment of *amils*. As mentioned earlier, the lack of regulation on the appointment of *amils* has caused certain dysfunctions in the *zakat* management, such as the improper *zakat* collection and distribution to its entitled beneficiaries. The centralised appointment of *amils* ensures that individuals licensed to collect *zakat* are equipped with the necessary literacy and resources to facilitate proper record-keeping. For instance, some *amils* were replaced as they were not able to write in Romanised letters and therefore unable to prepare the necessary paperwork to properly track accounts. Certain living areas which had multiple *amils* due to the different groups insisting on having their own *amils* to manage their *zakat*. Some of these *amils* had to be replaced or removed. Other *amils* were also replaced because they refused to conduct *zakat* collection at mosques and insisted on doing so at home (Muis, 1971). Centralising the appointment of *amils* also provided Muis with the terms and conditions governing *amil* appointments. These were the necessary steps Muis had to take as part of its move to professionalise *amils* and in ensuring that they are qualified, have the necessary skills, and are in good financial standing to receive public monies on behalf of Muis.

The centralisation of *zakat* management through Muis also allowed the community to be better apprised of the progress of *zakat* collection and its positive value to the beneficiaries. For instance, with the advent of mass media and communication, Muis leveraged these means to strengthen its transparency. Muis' annual reports containing financial information pertaining to the collection and disbursement of *zakat* began to be made publicly available via the internet. Television commercials, documentaries, short films, and social media channels were also subsequently adopted to raise awareness of how *zakat* has made a difference to the lives of some of its beneficiaries.

Modernising the *zakat* system by creating ease of access to *zakat* services (for both contributors and beneficiaries) was also important in optimising *zakat* collection and disbursement in a shorter span of time. For the contributors, earlier on in its history, Muis relied solely on cash transactions with manual receipts performed over the counter at the mosques and at Muis headquarters. Muis finally made the move to computerise receipting systems and re-engineer its processes for more efficient *zakat* collection. Muis rapidly expanded its collection channels to include AXS, Nets, internet payments, internet banking, mobile payments, and even tele-polls. These payment channels have paved the way for *zakat* payers to fulfil their *zakat* obligations with better ease and efficiency. These structures have also facilitated smoother collection of *zakat* from a growing pool of contributors, as the local Muslim community becomes more affluent and therefore, more able to make greater contributions to *zakat*.

To facilitate the ease of access to *zakat* services for potential beneficiaries, Muis has had to devise a way in which it could easily identify the profile and the volume of beneficiaries that it should serve. The first step to this was the establishment of a system to register beneficiaries in need of financial assistance (*Berita Harian*, 1971). This was to address a common issue with the *zakat* system prior to the establishment of AMLA and Muis, whereby *amils* were not able to properly disburse *zakat* to as many deserving beneficiaries.

Beneficiaries' ease of access to *zakat* was further facilitated later as Muis began to decentralise *zakat* services and functions at the community level. This decentralisation first materialised in the late 1990s, when Muis received funding from then Ministry of Community Development (MCD) to set up satellite *zakat* disbursement centres based at mosques — termed as Family Development Centres (FDCs). Beneficiaries could access *zakat* FA at the various FDCs at mosques as opposed to coming down to Muis headquarters. This new operating model for *zakat* disbursement was a welcomed development for Muis and the community. It provided some reprieve for the handful of officers who were handling impossibly high caseloads of about 300 cases per person. More importantly, for the beneficiary, *zakat* FA was more accessible for them and the application process was considerably sped up because of the additional manpower. The FDCs managed to add value to the typically transactional engagements that Muis had with the *zakat* beneficiaries through the introduction of support programmes. This signalled the state's recognition of Muis and mosques as significant links to the national social safety net. This was an important milestone for Muis in locating itself in the national grid. The FDC model was short-lived, however, as the centres were closed when the grants from MCD were discontinued.

Despite the short-lived experience of the FDCs at mosques,[1] Muis learnt the importance and value of providing decentralised *zakat* services and bringing *zakat* closer to the ground, and it became Muis' goal to scale up to the FDC model in order to reach out to the *zakat* beneficiaries more effectively. Finally, in 2008, Muis introduced the Enhanced Mosque Cluster (EMC) system, where the *zakat* disbursement function was devolved to 29 mosques. Under the EMC, mosques took over the social assistance function previously centred at Muis headquarters and directly disbursed financial aid from *zakat* funds to the needy within their respective communities. This was similar to

---

[1] In 2004, the FDC model was discontinued and *zakat* disbursement was once again centralised at Muis.

the Community Development Councils (CDCs) when they took over the financial assistance schemes from then MCD. Mosques would also collaborate with other agencies to come up with specific programmes and customise services according to local needs, to help the low income and disadvantaged families.

This was another significant milestone in Muis' management of *zakat* disbursement. The strategy was to complement the CDCs' services in administering ComCare and other welfare programmes. With the same service boundaries, the mosques can work more effectively with the CDCs in streamlining welfare services and programmes (Ibrahim, 2008). This was an attempt for Muis to weave its social development function closer to the national framework. Of significance to the de-centralisation process was Muis' partnership with the mosques in carrying out the *zakat* disbursement function. This public (Muis)–people (mosque) sector collaboration allowed Muis to provide better care to the *zakat* beneficiaries through the shared resources. Also, the role of the mosques in this new operating model was critical to the transition process of de-centralising. The mosques were very supportive in not only providing resources but also in taking on the responsibility of caring for the *zakat* beneficiaries staying within the locality.

Limitations of *Zakat*

While much improvements have been made to the *zakat* system in Singapore with documented evidence of the positive impact on the life of some beneficiaries, it is important to consider the implication of this proven effectiveness in the larger scheme of the Singapore's national social assistance. Muis' role in the socioeconomic upliftment of the Muslim community is characteristic of Singapore's model of ethnic-based or community-based self-help, where members of a particular community are responsible for the mobility and upliftment of its members. It is very evident from its early history till the present that *zakat* in Singapore fulfils this expectation well. However, as literature on poverty and inequality in Singapore has rightfully pointed out, this model has brought on some 'mixed results' (Donaldson *et al.*, 2015, p. 39). While this model has done a lot in supporting the needs of community members, it begs the question whether it can make a real difference in encouraging mobility and equality, not just within the community, but across all communities nationally (Donaldson *et al.*, 2015, p. 39). For instance, if *zakat*

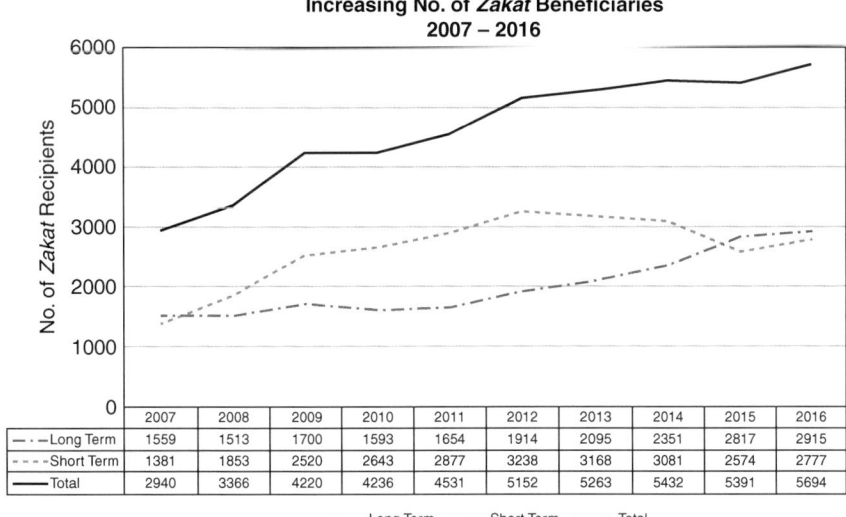

Increasing No. of *Zakat* Beneficiaries
2007 – 2016

	2007	2008	2009	2010	2011	2012	2013	2014	2015	2016
— · —Long Term	1559	1513	1700	1593	1654	1914	2095	2351	2817	2915
- - - -Short Term	1381	1853	2520	2643	2877	3238	3168	3081	2574	2777
—— Total	2940	3366	4220	4236	4531	5152	5263	5432	5391	5694

— · — Long Term   - - - - Short Term   —— Total

Figure 1:   Number of *zakat* beneficiaries (2007–2016)

and its quantum (which is comparatively smaller than the quantum provided by national assistance) remains the primary assistance that the Muslim poor depends on, in the long run, more Muslim needy are short-changing themselves from the available resources and assistance available nationally for all Singaporean needy.

Yet, taking this reality into consideration, it is also not possible for Singaporean Muslims to discontinue *zakat* FA, and rely solely on the assistance and resources available nationally through sources such as Comcare. The expectations which the community and the government hold for *zakat* remains high. For instance, for some segments of the community, there was always a perception that *zakat* was not doing enough to help the poor, as evidenced by various postings on Facebook, through feedback channels, and even mainstream media. This is evidence that the community's expectations for *zakat* to do more for its poor have not reduced and has in fact further increased over the years.

In addition to community's expectations, the government has signalled some level of reliance on Muis' *zakat* system as well in reaching out to the Muslim community in its development efforts as seen from the EMC experience. Since the launch of the EMCs in 2008, national agencies and VWOs readily referred Muslim cases to Muis for assistance and follow-up. Before the establishment of the EMCs, Muis averaged a total of around 3,000 cases annually. By the year 2016, Muis handled around 5,000 cases annually, an increase of almost 70 percent.

In addition to the rising expectations and reliance on *zakat*, it is also not realistic for *zakat* to ever relinquish all responsibilities in uplifting the community, as it still possesses a sacred and symbolic significance that remains central to the tenets of the Muslim faith.

Therefore, for Muis, the challenge therein is to optimise the *zakat* dollar in creating as much meaningful impact in the economic upliftment of Muslim low-income families and to also improve their social mobility in comparison to national standards. This challenge requires a shift in the manner in which *zakat* is managed. It has to move beyond just disbursing *zakat* to incorporate a more holistic social development regime which promotes self-reliance and seamlessly connect Muis FA into the national social assistance scheme.

Incorporating Social Development and Connecting with National Social Assistance

The incorporation of social development in Singapore's *zakat* management entails instilling certain disciplines in providing assistance to beneficiaries (DSW, 1978) primarily in terms of planning. Here, planning refers to "a set of tasks, within an organisational, inter-organisational, social problem, or social service arena, involving community organisation and administration" (DSW, 1978, p. 225), and these tasks often "focus on particular programmes [and] programme development" (DSW, 1978, p. 226).

Programmes

The incorporation of social development into the *zakat* disbursement approach with stronger adoption of the planning discipline was materialised when the mandatory support programmes were implemented for all *zakat* FA beneficiaries in 2009. These support programmes aim to improve beneficiaries' knowledge on life skills through religious and spiritual development. While there are many different types of programmes on life skills organised by other agencies and VWOs, Muis is careful not to duplicate the efforts and instead, work closely with the mosques to design unique life skills programmes which are contextualised to spiritual development. Grants were awarded to those mosques to design and implement these support programmes for the *zakat* beneficiaries.

Further, Muis also administers a family support programme — the Empowerment Partnership Scheme (EPS) — which aims to bring selected families out of the *zakat* assistance cycle. The EPS is a two-year programme that looks into the multiple needs of the family, and provides intervention plans that include training for the parents' career progression personal financial management, Islamic learning, parenting skills, and enrichment classes for children. The EPS is an investment in the development and growth of the family, with the hope that they would be able to be financially empowered and independent from *zakat* assistance. Unlike before, the incorporation of social development (SD) principles ensures that the programmes are able to equip *zakat* beneficiaries with the necessary skills and knowledge to be more resilient and socially mobile.

Controls and Structures

An important aspect in the planning of Muis' social development is having frequent reviews of the structures and programmes in order to meet the social development objectives and controls of the regulating entity (DSW, 1978, p. 226). This is especially pertinent. With greater awareness of Muis' work, there were growing concerns from the state and community about the nature of Muis' controls within its systems and processes. Therefore a more holistic and robust governance system had to be put in place, to ensure that *zakat* FA programmes and structures are able to meet their social development objectives. To this end, Muis together with the mosques introduced a system of reporting and review of the social development policies and processes on the ground. Every mosque that oversees the disbursement of *zakat* FA and the running of core support programmes is made to regularly report on the progress of these programmes to Muis. Social development programmes, such as the mandatory support programmes and the EPS, also undergo frequent internal reviews, where feedback is collated from both service providers and clients, and is then used by Muis to improve the next programme cycle. These improvements have materialised in changes to the design of the programmes and the systems and processes in the mosque social development services. These additional planning tasks are new elements in Muis' management of *zakat* which were absent in the earlier years.

Capabilities Development

Another essential aspect to meet Muis' social development objectives is ensuring that Muis *zakat* service providers are equipped with the necessary capabilities and professionalism and are informed by the social work and social development expertise and their relevant communities of practice. To do this, Muis had to ensure that it maintains the level of professionalism of other agencies in the social service sector. This includes training officers at mosques who oversee *zakat* services and ensuring that they undergo a basic level of training in social work. This is especially pertinent given the fact that most social development officers at mosques have not been trained in social work. This impeded their ability to provide quality social development services to beneficiaries. For instance, a frequent complaint aimed at *zakat* officers at mosques before was their perceived insensitivity in handling beneficiaries' non-financial needs. Beyond delivering the monetary assistance to beneficiaries, *zakat* officers may not go the extra mile to enquire or assist with the beneficiaries' other pressing needs. With some basic level of social work training, *zakat* officers, now referred to as Social Development Officers (SDOs), are better equipped to assess the needs of beneficiaries and refer them to the relevant sources of assistance within the network of national social assistance beyond *zakat* FA. Over time, SDOs at mosques are able to take other social work functions, such as case conferences, case management, intervention plans, and monitoring of beneficiaries' cases. Through these functions, *zakat* is in a better position to achieve its social development objective to "meet human social needs" (DSW, 1978, p. 223).

Connecting with National Social Assistance

With the incorporation of the social development dimension within Muis *zakat* management, *zakat*'s relevance in the scheme of social assistance of Muslim beneficiaries has further grown. Other social assistance agencies are also more aware of Muis' role in delivering social assistance, with more of *zakat* SDOs' referrals of their beneficiaries to other agencies. Despite the awareness, uncertainty still persisted among other social assistance agencies with regards to Muis' and *zakat's* role in the larger scheme of social assistance for Muslim beneficiaries. For instance, *zakat* SDOs and Muis headquarters received a high number of referrals from other social assistance agencies, for any Muslim family seeking assistance, regardless of the nature of assistance required. This went against Muis' original intent of linking its *zakat* beneficiaries to national sources of assistance and social capital. This highlighted the urgent need to engage the social service providers comprising national agencies and VWOs so that they understand Muis' role and the types of assistance that Muis could offer. Figure 2 (adapted from the Ministry of Social and Family Development (MSF)) illustrates where Muis' social development services are located within the social service landscape.

The primary messaging when engaging with the larger network of social agencies is that *zakat* can only complement the national assistance. For low-income families to access a greater chance for self-reliance, mobility, and equality, the national assistance must be their primary source of assistance.

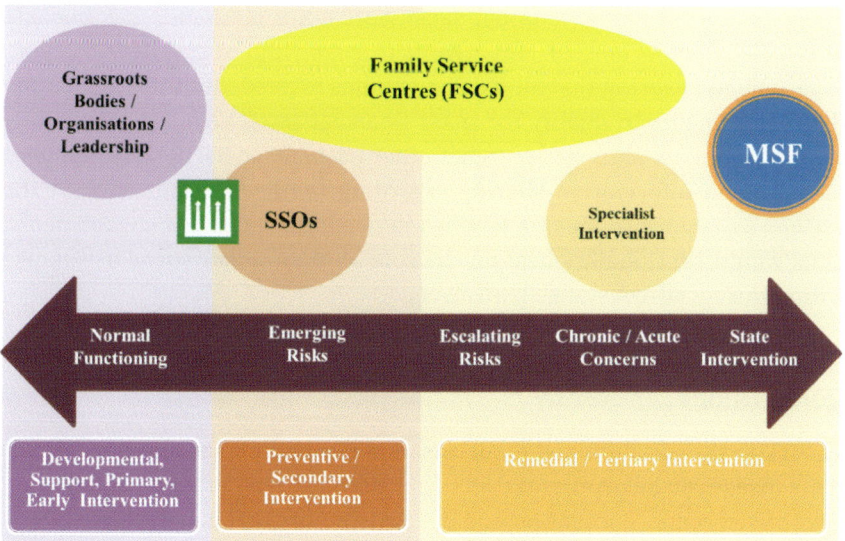

Figure 2:   Muis Social Development Services within the Scheme of National Assistance

As Figure 2 has shown, the nature of Muis' social development role is between that of a Social Service Office (SSO) and a grassroots organisation. The scope of its intervention is limited to beneficiary families that are functioning normally, with some early signs of emerging risks which do not require extensive specialist intervention. For instance, even though Muis is able to provide a quantum of *zakat* financial assistance and some developmental support programmes to a beneficiary family with a per capita income (PCI) that is below $350, it is unable to help a family whose PCI is above $350 but is ridden with overwhelming debt. The nature and the scope of assistance required by the second family goes beyond a financial handout, and religious and spiritual developmental support programmes provided by Muis. In fact, this family may require a specialised debt management programme or some other type of specialist intervention. In this situation, Muis may be the family's first touch point and assess the family's needs and assistance required. However, Muis may not be the family's primary source of help. Therefore, it is important for Muis to position itself in the larger social assistance landscape as an important touch point for Muslim families in need and, at the same time, be an effective link between beneficiary families and the available array of national assistance and intervention.

Being connected to the national social assistance landscape has become increasingly important to Muis' work in *zakat* and social development, especially in ensuring that all Muslim families in need, despite not meeting the requirements to qualify for *zakat* financial assistance, are adequately assisted. To date, Muis has engaged other national social service agencies for data and information sharing regarding the level of outreach of the various assistance to Muslim families in need. During those engagements, Muis would continually question the role of Muis' *zakat* social assistance within the social assistance landscape.

Doing Things Differently

The institutionalisation and modernisation of *zakat* management as well as the subsequent incorporation of social development practices into *zakat* have raised some concerns among the contributors and beneficiaries. These concerns relate to the fear that the mechanisms put in place to systemise *zakat* collection and disbursement may end up short-changing or not fulfilling the symbolic meaning of *zakat* as a form of assistance that should be made readily available for all needy Muslims. This is a common concern directed at the eligibility requirement of *zakat* FA beneficiaries, which technically only allows families with PCI below $350 to receive *zakat* FA. Some segments of the community feel that it is not right for Muis to turn away any Muslim family in need, regardless of their eligibility or PCI. Another mechanism which incurred the displeasure of some segments of the community is the utilisation of *zakat* to pay for the professionalisation and employment of Muis officers overseeing the management of *zakat*.

These concerns highlight the potency of the religious–symbolic value and the expectations of the community with regards to the social justice mission of *zakat* itself, and are rooted in society's general expectations towards any form of assistance and social welfare, not just *zakat*. Even in Western democracies run by secular governments, social welfare has commonly been understood as being grounded in "the religious doctrine of charity", "the power of the sovereign to protect or enhance the health, safety, and morals of the community", and, "the legal doctrine of individual rights" (Leiby, 1985, p. 323). In totality, society views social welfare as something that is firstly, a moral and religious obligation; secondly, provided for by the state; and lastly, an inalienable right of the individual. These three moral foundations of social welfare mirror the expectations of the Muslim community, and can explain why segments of the community may react negatively to individuals being turned down for assistance due to certain bureaucratic measures.

Evidently, society as a whole must be further socialised to the idea that these bureaucratic measures and other forms of innovations in policies that govern social assistance and welfare are shaped for specific developmental objectives, be it of *zakat* or any other social welfare levers as a whole. At the same time, Muis must strike a balance between meeting these specific social developmental objectives and fulfilling the religious symbolic value of *zakat* as an inalienable right of the Muslim *fakir* (poor) regardless of how "poor" is being defined. To this end, Muis has exercised flexibility in providing one-off cash or voucher assistance to meet the beneficiaries' most pressing daily needs, regardless of whether the said beneficiary meets the requirements for Muis *zakat* FA. In the process, it has also begun playing the role of linking up all families and individuals who pass through Muis *zakat* system to the relevant assistance beyond Muis and *zakat*. In doing so, Muis' management of *zakat* has spanned beyond the provisions encapsulated in AMLA and the early Muslim community leaders' vision of *zakat*'s role in the upliftment of Singaporean Muslims.

The Future of Assistance

Local literature on the rising complexity and volume of human needs in Singapore seems to point to the urgency for the providers of assistance and social welfare to innovate and maximise capital beyond monetary assistance, in order to meet these needs. The story of Muis' *zakat* modernisation and eventual interweaving into the national social service landscape highlights two important policy lessons. These developments highlight the importance of looking deeper into the needs of the beneficiaries, beyond simply disbursing financial handouts. It also highlights the importance of optimising the impact of a single *zakat* dollar through non-monetary means.

The future of assistance in Singapore is looking towards seeking non-monetary forms of help that would create a greater impact on the lives of the needy. The government has signalled the need to further strengthen the social safety net by "utilising the strengths of the community, private sector and the government" (Tan and Ng, n.d., p. 3). This signal has now been taken up by various social assistance organisations that are looking into implementing, for instance, the Asset-Based Community Development Model, to firstly identify the assets that reside in a particular community, and then creating and leveraging on the social capital within this community by "involving [entities and individuals with] ample social connections to mobilise the community to address the needs" (Tan and Ng, n.d., p. 9) through the community's participation and active citizenry. With these streams of assets and capital, the community will work to improve the economic development of the target group within the community. Despite the hopeful tone of these nascent initiatives in the social service sector, the question remains as to whether the community is ready and willing to explore new ideas developed by experts in the field of social mobility, social work, and social development to optimise financial handouts and create a greater chance for self-reliance and mobility. Moving forward, organisations, including Muis, must develop a way to further familiarise the community to the need to expand their role in helping the needy beyond providing financial support and through active citizenry.

References

Berita Harian. (1971, October 21). Sa-ramai 16,000 fakir miskin sudah berdaftar. *Berita Harian*. Retrieved from NewspaperSG.

Berita Harian. (1971, November 19). Lantekan amil: MUIS jelaskan. *Berita Harian*. Retrieved from NewspaperSG.

Donaldson, J. A., Smith, C. J., Mudaliar, S., Kadir, M. M., and Lam, K. (2015). *A Handbook on Inequality, Poverty and Unmet Social Needs in Singapore*. Singapore: Lien Centre for Social Innovations.

DSW, I. A. (1978). Social Development and Social Work. Administration in Social Work, pp. 221–233.

Green, A. (2009). Honouring the Past, Shaping the Future: The Muis Story. Singapore: Islamic Religious Council of Singapore.

Ibrahim, Y. (2008, March 5). Minister-in-Charge of Muslim Affairs MCYS Committee of Supply Sitting. *Speech Singapore*. Singapore. Retrieved from: http://www.nas.gov.sg/archivesonline/data/pdfdoc/20080306998.pdf.

Lee, H. L. (2009, July 11). *Muis 40th Anniversary Celebrations*. Retrieved from: http://www.pmo.gov.sg/newsroom/speech-mr-lee-hsien-loong-prime-ministermuis-40th-anniversary-celebrations-11-july-2009.

Leiby, J. (1985). Moral Foundations of Social Welfare and Social Work: A Historical View. *Social Work*, pp. 323–330.

Lim, X. (2007). *Security with Self-Reliance: The Argument for the Singapore Model*. CSC. Retrieved from: https://www.cscollege.gov.sg/knowledge/ethos/issue%203%20oct%202007/pages/Security-with-Self-Reliance-The-Argument-for-the-Singapore-Model.aspx.

Ong, K. (2010, June 8). *Singapore's Social Policies: Vision Accomplishment and Challenges*. Singapore. Retrieved from: https://lkyspp.nus.edu.sg/ips/wp-content/uploads/sites/2/2013/06/sp_oky_The-Centre-for-Social-Development-Asia-Conference_080610-1.pdf.

Philip, G., and Sheila, F. (2006). The Role of Religion and Spirituality in Social Work Practice. *The British Journal of Social Work*, 36(4), pp. 617–637.

Report of the Select Committee on the Administration of Muslim Law Bill, Parl. 3. (1966, May 31).

Rippin, A. (2005). *Muslims: Their Religious Beliefs and Practices*. London: Routledge.

Tan, J., and Ng, K. (n.d.). *Strengthening the Social and Cultural Well-Being of the Elderly Population: A Review of the Working Model of COMNET Befriending Service Based on the Asset-Based Community Development (ABCD) Model*. Retrieved from amkfsc.org.sg

Tan, K. P. (2007). *Renaissance Singapore? Economy, Culture and Politics*. Singapore: NUS Press.

9

ENHANCING COMMUNITY
ASSETS: SUSTAINING THE
WAKAF LEGACY
ENHANCING COMMUNITY
ASSETS: SUSTAINING THE
WAKAF LEGACY
Masagoes Muhammad Isyak

Introduction

A row of dilapidated shop houses and an old bakery lay in the heart of the Katong district. Vacant since 2003, the iconic Katong Bakery and Confectionary, also known as the Red House Bakery, was once known for its famous Swiss rolls and curry puffs. The bakery and the commercial properties alongside it were deemed structurally unsafe and were forced to close. Situated along East Coast Road, these properties were bequeathed by a philanthropist named Sheriffa Zain Mohamed Alsagoff as a *wakaf* in 1957, with the noble intention of using the rental proceeds to fund an outdoor dispensary providing free medicine to the poor. The properties however had subsequently fallen into a state of disrepair due to the lack of funds to perform renovations by the trustees. Although the *wakaf* was managed by trustees who were descendants of Madam Sheriffa Zain, the overall duty of care, as provided for by section 58 of the Administration of Muslim Law Act (AMLA), still lies with Muis.

Elsewhere, two kampong houses stay tenanted,[1] as if locked in time, on a plot of land in the prestigious and prime area of District 10, Bukit Timah. Situated alongside good class bungalows and other private properties, the tenants of these kampong houses were paying rents that were not even enough to pay for the property taxes. Located at Jalan Haji Alias, the land was bequeathed as a *wakaf* in 1905 with Al-Huda Mosque as the sole beneficiary. As with Wakaf Sheriffa Zain, Wakaf Al-Huda was not able to keep up with the rapid pace of property development set by its neighbours. Unable to reinvent itself, its rental income becomes depressed further.

How does Muis manage society's expectations about land endowments and the state's position about land development? The harshest critics within the community lamented that Muis' poor financial management of the *wakaf* had led to its state of disrepair and potential obsolescence, while the more forgiving criticised Muis' expertise, or lack thereof, in managing properties. In extreme cases, testators' descendants would allege mismanagement by Muis, and would attempt to oust Muis in favour of themselves as trustees in the civil courts (Syed Abbas bin Mohamed Alsagoff and Islamic Religious Council of Singapore, 2009).

On the other hand, Singapore's relentless post-independence urban redevelopment and housing programme necessitated the implementation of government land acquisitions, including that of *wakaf* land. Some of the affected *wakaf* properties were left with the acquisition's cash proceeds as their remaining capital and little else. Such cash needed to be invested into capital guaranteed or secured investments, such as other freehold properties, but the *wakaf* simply could not afford to do so. The capital thus remained unutilised, and being non-income generating, the *wakaf* did not serve their purpose of benefiting those they were intended for. Furthermore, statutory and audit requirements would make these *wakaf* incur expenses that they had no means to pay for other than by depleting its capital, which, if allowed to continue protractedly, would result in nullifying the *wakaf* eventually.

This chapter aims to firstly, discuss Muis' deliberate approach to revitalise the institution of *wakaf* in Singapore in response to its challenges and

---

[1] A traditional village house predominantly built for housing purposes before public housing in the form of HDB flats in Singapore was made available; usually constructed out of wood and with a zinc or *attap* roof.

opportunities; secondly, the various financing schemes developed to achieve a favourable outcome for stakeholders and the wider community and society in general; and lastly, highlight the policy lessons that can be gleaned from such experience.

Financing *Wakaf* Development Projects

Muis, in its earlier years of administering *wakaf*, found itself as the custodian of *wakaf* properties when AMLA handed over the responsibility of managing the *wakaf* previously handled by the trustees. Muis had then focused on maintaining the status quo, which was to keep the properties tenanted and to disburse the monies to the rightful beneficiaries. Save for the occasional *ad hoc* repairs, little thought had been given to the regular and systematic upkeep, maintenance, and development of the properties, as Muis itself was only just beginning to build capacity in property development through its mosque projects with the Housing Development Board (Muis, 2009). The financing required for revitalising *wakaf* properties also proved to be a challenge, as many of these properties comprised pre-war shophouses that required major renovation works beyond what the *wakaf* could afford.

The fact that the global *wakaf* environment was no better where "even the best *waqf* buildings, with tremendous commercial potential, are not getting basic repairs and maintenance." (Abdul Hassan and Mohammad Abdus Samad, 2010) brought little comfort to Muis' early leaders. Subsequently, Mr Ridzwan Haji Dzafir (former Muis President) and Ustaz Kamil Suhaimi (former Muis Council Member) initiated a closer look at the properties (Muis, 2009), which brought about a resolve within Muis to improve the *wakaf* situation in Singapore.

The economic conundrum for *wakaf* is that all income derived from its properties must be disbursed to its beneficiaries, such as the mosques, madrasahs, poor relatives, and other segments of the community. Expenses incurred in administering the *wakaf* were strictly controlled with the aim of maximising returns for the beneficiaries. The Control of Rent Act enacted in 1953 and in effect until 2001, further created financial challenges for the *wakaf*, as extensive repair works required to maintain the property often exceeded the income received. As a result, any extensive property rectification works needed had to be postponed, in most cases, indefinitely. In 1985, Muis' immediate concern was the development of properties situated at Duku Road, Changi

Road, and Gentle Road belonging to Wakaf Jabbar, Wakaf Kassim, and Wakaf Abdul Hamid respectively. The Ministry of National Development issued notices to clear all temporary structures on these properties to make them either presentable, or alternatively, prepare them for redevelopment, failing which, these properties would be seized and acquired. The *wakaf* had no source of funding and the deadline given then was June 1988.

Lacking professional expertise in property development, Muis then formed the Wakaf Development Committee in 1985 where 12 professionals who included lawyers, architects, representatives from trust companies, trustees, and businessmen volunteered their time and expertise to rigorously find a solution for these properties (*Berita Harian*, 1985). This committee first mooted the idea of using *baitulmal* funds to finance *wakaf* property development.[2] *Baitulmal*, whose purpose is for the general benefit of the Muslim community, would serve as an internal funding mechanism, without the need for bank loans or other external funding sources.

First Foray into Property Development

A joint venture or partnership approach (Abdul Karim, 2010) was undertaken between the various *wakaf* and *baitulmal*, such that *baitulmal* would finance these *wakaf* with a cash advance. The *wakaf* would then repay *baitulmal* progressively or through a shareholding of the redeveloped property. Through this approach and subsequent extensions in deadlines, the *wakaf* property at Duku Road was transformed, in 1990, into four units of terrace residential housing, which increased its annual rental income from a mere $68 to $36,000 (Muis, 1990). Similarly, in 1991, the *wakaf* property at Changi Road, which originally housed an old mosque and some dilapidated shophouses, were replaced with a much bigger mosque (Kassim Mosque), a commercial complex (Wisma Indah), and 20 units of maisonettes (Telok Indah) in 1991. The land at Gentle Road, on the other hand, was deemed too small and oddly shaped to be developed, and was turned into a park instead (*Berita Minggu*, 1987). However, this would be revisited in later years.

While largely successful, these initial developments were not without their challenges. Some tenants who had grown fond of their premises, or had an

---

[2] *Baitulmal* refers to the General Endowment Fund managed by Muis.

existing customer base, were reluctant or had adamantly refused to leave the property to allow it to be redeveloped. This required significant engagements between Muis and the tenants; and in some cases, an offer to compensate them for their losses (Abdul Karim, 2010).

In 1990, a property department was also created in Muis to handle *wakaf* development matters and to build relevant internal expertise within Muis. The use of *baitulmal* funds, the Wakaf Development Committee's professional inputs and the oversight by Muis' property development paved the way for Muis to undertake multiple redevelopment projects such as those at Mayo Street, Dunlop Street, North Bridge Road, Kandahar Street, and several others. As a result of these *wakaf* development projects, their annual rental income was increased from S$198,000 in 1990 to S$3,341,000 in 2000, a quantum leap indeed.

Asset Migration

Despite *baitulmal*'s entry as a financier for *wakaf* development projects and the resultant improved yields, several other *wakaf* faced possible dissolution. These *wakaf* were those affected by Singapore's urban renewal plan and whose lands had been acquired through the Land Acquisition Act. Such *wakaf* were compensated in cash by the government but were, individually, unable to purchase a replacement property of good quality using the cash proceeds. The cash therefore became the *wakaf*'s sole residual asset or capital.

To avoid unnecessary risk to the *wakaf*, the capital remained uninvested in any financial instrument and was therefore non-income generating. The larger problem, however, was that the mandatory statutory audit expenses associated with the *wakaf* still needed to be paid and the only way for this was to deduct from the capital. This effectively meant that the *wakaf* was being whittled away bit by bit, and eventually, into oblivion.

The challenge presented to Muis then was to find an investment option that could benefit these "cash *wakaf*". One such option considered was to invest in a *Syariah*-compliant equity on the Singapore Stock Exchange. This idea however, was quickly dropped as it failed the litmus test of being both capital-guaranteed nd low-risk. Furthermore, *Syariah*-compliant equities in Singapore were non-existent then.

The thinking process and research behind the investment in equities did not go wasted, however. It led Muis to conceptualise idea of creating a Real Estate Investment Trust (REIT)[3] structure for *wakaf*. A REIT structure was appealing as the underlying asset for investors are properties. It is also "...comparable to a mutual fund and allows both small and large investors to acquire ownership in real estate ventures..." (Investopedia, n.d.). The high cost of property ownership can therefore be shared among multiple investors, or in this case, multiple *wakaf*. The cash available in all of these acquired properties could thus be pooled together to purchase one or more good quality properties. These properties could then be rented out with the proceeds being shared among the various *wakaf* depending on its equity share in the property.

The idea of a REIT was further developed within Muis. Muis' Property Department made a controversial proposal of disposing *wakaf* properties that were poor-performing and in unfavourable locations; the proceeds of which would then be pooled together with the cash *wakaf* to purchase a better property in an asset migration exercise. However, there was controversy surrounding the classical religious understanding that *wakaf* properties are perpetual in nature and cannot be sold or transferred. Muis' Property Department however clarified that the underlying intent was not the sale *per se*, but to ensure that these low-yielding *wakaf* were improved for the sake of its beneficiaries. In 1999, the Fatwa Committee's opinion was sought to resolve, once and for all, the question of the permissibility of asset migration (*Istibdal*) for *wakaf* properties. The Fatwa Committee deliberated and eventually issued a *fatwa* in favour of allowing asset migration on the grounds that such migration did not short-change the *wakaf*, and on the condition that the testator's intention and named beneficiaries were not modified. This *fatwa* was indeed a major pioneering milestone for *wakaf* development in Singapore.

With the religious position thus clarified, Muis then further consulted *Syariah* advisors, legal firms, property consultants, and banks to determine a suitable property for acquisition, and to derive a working *Syariah*-compliant structure for multiple *wakaf* to have joint ownership of this property. Based on these consultations, a six-storey commercial building at 11 Beach Road was identified for purchase by using the sale proceeds of 27 *wakaf* properties

---

[3] REIT is a type of secrutiy that invests in real estate and is often traded on the stock exchange. Investors participate in the REIT and become partial owners of the property. Investors typically receive high yields to their investments.

including contributions from unutilised cash *wakaf*. A *sukuk musyarakah*[4] structure — the first of its kind in Singapore[5] — was also formulated to partially finance the property purchase in 2001.

Through this initiative, three key challenges at that time were addressed, namely: i) the need to reinvest cash *wakaf* into a *Syariah*-compliant investment instrument, ii) to consolidate and relocate poor performing *wakaf* properties to a better-quality property, and iii) to generate higher income for beneficiaries of these *wakaf*.

However, having the benefit of hindsight and several years of having 11 Beach Road in the *wakaf* portfolio, a shortcoming of this model became evident, particularly during periods of property market correction. Having multiple *wakaf* concentrated in a single property creates a wider impact on all the individual *wakaf* when the property is not tenanted or when a tenant defaults on its rent. Conversely, a diversified portfolio of properties, where each *wakaf* holds its own real estate, will be self-compensating in impact. For this reason, tenancy movements at 11 Beach Road must be monitored very closely and needs to be actively marketed whenever a vacancy arises.

Corporatising Warees

Apart from the purchase of 11 Beach Road, the year 2001 also saw the lifting of the Control of Rent Act. For the first time in Muis' history of administering *wakaf*, property rental rates could be determined by market forces. Up until then, Muis' Property Department handled the various *wakaf* property related functions directly. The scope of work included project management, tenancy matters, property development, and facilities management. With the lifting of rent control, rental rates and tenancy matters became highly dynamic in nature and required an increase in agility, speed and creativity in keeping properties tenanted.

---

[4] *Sukuk Musyarakah* functions like a *Syariah*-compliant commercial bond that is asset backed where investors will subscribe to the bond and get a fixed return. The *sukuk musyarakah* by Muis carried a sovereign rating and was fully subscribed.

[5] Muis received international recognition for the sukuk issuance and was awarded the Sheikh Mohammed bin Rashid Al Makhtoum Islamic Finance Award, Dubai in 2006 for this innovation.

In line with the government's approach of corporatising some of its functions then, Muis commissioned Ernst and Young to study and propose possible Muis functions which could be corporatised. Not surprisingly, *wakaf* property management and the Property Department were identified.

Muis' management saw the benefit in corporatising its Property Department as it would allow the entity to react in a commercially agile manner for property matters while segregating regulatory functions in Muis. The possibility of outsourcing the function to property management companies instead of corporatising was also considered. However, a key consideration was that mosques also required property maintenance and development services, and it was deemed to be more efficient for these services to be housed in a single corporate entity to oversee both *wakaf* and mosque properties. In 2002, Warees Investments Pte Ltd was incorporated as a Muis subsidiary. Warees' business model was centred on mosque and *wakaf* development, maintenance, and *wakaf* tenancy. They would charge project management fees as their income and recycle it back as a financing resource for future *wakaf* development projects, thus making Warees a social enterprise for the *wakaf* institution in many ways.

Enhancing *Wakaf* Properties: The Next Phase

The changing landscape of the commercial rental market — *sans* rent control — was viewed as providing more opportunities to maximise rental yields on *wakaf* properties. The catch was that other property owners who owned large and modern commercial buildings were now incentivised to gain better rentals, and had started to aggressively market their properties and redeveloping them to attract tenants. This had the potential to comparatively depress the rental rates of *wakaf* properties which were far simpler in their facilities as they comprised primarily old shophouses. *Wakaf* properties therefore had to be enhanced to compete with the industry, failing which, the income to be generated from them and resultant disbursements to the *wakaf*'s beneficiaries would be affected.

These developments drove Warees to rethink the *wakaf* portfolio strategy as its first order of business. A list of properties was identified by Warees in 2001, and categorised for the second wave of property development, asset migration, or basic upgrading. With Muis' approval, the plan was set in motion. Similar to the earlier developments, joint venture schemes were devised to mitigate risks for the *wakaf* and to provide the necessary funding, this time with Warees being the joint venture partner. The Gentle Road property mentioned earlier, for example, was previously deemed to be too small and irregular shaped for development. However, through Warees, Muis was now able to tap on a larger pool of professionals in the commercial sector and managed to redevelop the vacant land into a three-storey semi-detached house. This redevelopment had effectively allowed for annual disbursements of S$30,000, to the beneficiary Abdul Hamid Kampung Pasiran Mosque, where there was initially none.

Other notable redevelopment projects embarked through such a joint venture approach were for Wakaf YAL Saif Charity Trust and Wakaf Raja Siti Kraeng. For the former, five dilapidated bungalow houses at Chancery Lane were redeveloped into a 34-unit cluster housing known as "The Chancery Residences" in 2005. The latter were shophouses along North Bridge Road that were refurbished and have since appreciated by about twice the original value.

More recently in 2015, Warees had entered into a joint venture development with Wakaf Al-Huda. Nestled in Singapore's prime District 10, the *wakaf* comprised a mosque in urgent need of redevelopment and a vacant land that was occupied by two kampong houses. The lessons in the earlier years of *wakaf* management and government land acquisition were hard-learned, and Muis is constantly concerned about properties that may be acquired should it remain unattended to. Nevertheless, one of the key considerations prior to embarking on any redevelopment project is to ensure that tenants' needs are being addressed. The first stage of the Wakaf Al-Huda project thus involved actively engaging the tenants of the kampong houses to relocate. Alternative housing arrangements were sourced and offered to the tenants, and ample time was also given for them to do so. It was only after the kampong houses were vacated did any plans for redevelopment proceed thereafter.

The *wakaf* land has since completed its redevelopment in 2017. Where two kampong houses and a dilapidated mosque were, now stands six new luxury semi-detached strata units. The mosque, being part of the *wakaf*, has also been redeveloped with an increase in capacity from 200 to 250, a new women's prayer section, and a new wing for an administration office and meeting rooms.

It is also important to creatively look for investors within the community and its institutions to finance *wakaf* development projects as opposed to relying on *baitulmal*, Warees or other sources of external funding. Through such an arrangement, development projects can be undertaken to mutually benefit *wakaf* and the community. One example of such a funding structure was in the development of the Red House project mentioned earlier in the chapter. In 2014, Warees implemented an initiative where Muslim institutions such as mosques and madrasahs were given the opportunity to invest their surplus funds in *wakaf* development projects and, in return, would receive an annual sum in the form of a *hibah*.[6] Known as the "Institutional Investment Initiative" (3I), this particular joint-financing structure was used for the redevelopment of Wakaf Sheriffa Zain, or more prominently known as the Red House project.

Five mosques — An-Nur, Al-Mukminin, Darul Ghufran, Haji Muhammad Salleh (Palmer Road) and Assyakirin — had invested S$5 million collectively in surplus funds to support the redevelopment of the Red House. In return, the mosques received an annual 2.1 percent of their investment amount as a *hibah*. This was a beneficial arrangement for all parties, where mosque investors were able to place their reserves in a *Syariah*-compliant instrument while enjoying returns that are higher than conventional fixed deposits. On the other hand, the *wakaf* was able to be redeveloped using those funds as a cash advance. Completed in 2016, the dilapidated Red House and its five adjacent shophouses have now been transformed into a 42-residential unit condominium and five retail shops. The Red House bakery has also been reinstated with a new tenant in a bid to retain its heritage.

Policy Lessons

Financing *wakaf* development projects continues to be a challenge today. As with all properties, regular upkeep, maintenance, and upgrading is required for it to remain structurally sound and in a tenantable condition. Ideally, the rectification works should occur incrementally every year and the costs are offset by the income generated by the rental of the properties. However, property maintenance needs often come unexpectedly and fall outside of property maintenance schedules. A leaking roof, sudden breakdowns of

---

[6] *Hibah* is a gift of any kind to a beneficiary. In Islamic banking, a *hibah* in cash is given to investors or deposit account holders as a way to share profits and give returns to their investments.

air-conditioners, building material obsolescence, and new safety requirements are just some of the issues that may arise requiring urgent rectification and funding.

Clearly, *baitulmal* and Warees' resources as joint venture partners or financiers are finite. Furthermore, the funding requirements of *wakaf* and the community need to be approached in a balanced manner. Careful cost discipline and cash flow management is a pre-requisite for any project undertaken jointly by *baitulmal* and Warees. As such, *wakaf* projects cannot all take place at the same time; or even in rapid succession. In some cases, these redevelopment projects have to be prioritised and may face extended delays before being implemented.

A key learning point from Muis' experience in administering *wakaf* is to approach its administration creatively and in an explorative manner. Engaging partners, specialists, and industry practitioners was also crucial in developing expertise in *wakaf*-related matters. From the earlier days of the Wakaf Development Committee, a wealth of knowledge was derived from the members, not just in financing but also in property development strategies. This evolved to the corporatisation and professionalisation of Warees, where experienced industry practitioners were recruited and, in other cases, professional consultants engaged to build internal expertise. Looking outwards to external capital markets has also allowed Muis to consider alternative structures such as the REIT structure to unlock the potential of cash *wakaf* assets and maximise the value of poor performing properties.

Conclusion

While *baitulmal*, Warees, and institutional financing have allowed many *wakaf* to be rejuvenated, these developments come with repayment periods that can sometimes stretch beyond 10 years. Although the income of these redeveloped *wakaf* has increased manifold, repayments still have a significant impact on the disbursements to the beneficiaries of the *wakaf*. One might argue that obtaining financing and its subsequent repayments are necessary in any property development venture, and that the benefit comes from the return on investment in the medium- to long-term. However, unlike other property ventures, *wakaf* income is, for the most part, distributed in its entirety to the beneficiaries. The *wakaf* thus has little in the way of surpluses for its future planning. Compounding this is the real possibility that a *wakaf* property will be in need of redevelopment again immediately after a long period of repayment. Muis will once again look outwards for ideas for a more sustainable source of funding for *wakaf.*

The notion of having a sinking fund was frequently considered as this was commonly practised by other property owners.[7] Through a sinking fund, a *wakaf* could then deliberately set aside a portion of their annual income and accumulate funds for future development projects. This would then minimise the need for other sources of financing, and allow the *wakaf* to be financially sustainable. However, the provision of a sinking fund was not allowed for in AMLA.

Through many discussions with the relevant authorities, Muis sought to amend AMLA to allow for a sinking fund for *wakaf.* It was only in 2017 that a public consultation was issued to obtain feedback from the larger community on the possibility of legislating a sinking fund. Through consultations with law practitioners, financial advisors, trustees, and members of parliament, the provision of a sinking fund for *wakaf* was approved and legislated into the AMLA. Although the benefits of implementing this sinking fund can only be realised in the years to come, the institution of *wakaf* has been strengthened through this legislation, and is now in a better position for the future.

Today, the landscape surrounding *wakaf* properties continues to evolve. In a portfolio that comprises more than 140 properties, it is important to evaluate the needs of each methodically. The complexity and urgency of each *wakaf* and its associated properties will constantly require prioritisation against financing and manpower resources within Muis. The rental market is also in constant flux. The retail sector for example is undergoing change due to the proliferation of online shopping while Singapore is undergoing massive land restructuring with key ports being relocated from its existing premises and new heartland neighbourhoods being built. These developments will have an overall impact on *wakaf* properties. Muis' administration of *wakaf* will therefore have to maintain a culture of constantly seeking creative solutions and repositioning *wakaf* to remain relevant to prepare itself for the next 50 years of *wakaf* development.

---

[7] In real estate, a sinking fund is a sum of money which is set aside by the property owners to cover any major work or unexpected emergency which is needed on the property in the future.

References

Abdul Karim, S. (2010). *Contemporary Shari'ah structuring for the Development and Management of Waqf Assets in Singapore.* (Doctoral dissertation). Retrieved from Durham University website: http://etheses.dur.ac.uk/778/

Berita Harian (1985, May 23). 12 profesional anggotai j-kuasa kecil wakaf. *Berita Harian*. Retrieved from NewspaperSG.

Berita Minggu (1987, March 8). Tanah Wakaf Dibangunkan? *Berita Harian*. Retrieved from NewspaperSG.

Investopedia (n.d.) *Real Estate Investment Trust (REIT)*. Retrieved from https://investopedia.com/terms/r/reit.asp.

Muis Annual Report (2009). *Muis*.

10

HAJ ASPIRATIONS: A 'HYBRID' OF PUBLIC AND PRIVATE MODELS FOR SINGAPORE

Abdul Rahim Saleh

Introduction

In November 1975, as thousands of hopeful *haj* pilgrims depart from Paya Lebar Airport to make their way to the Holy Land in Jeddah, some 300 prospective Singaporean *haj* pilgrims were left stranded at the airport as *haj* operators failed to secure air passage for them. In September 1978, despite having paid thousands of dollars for travel and accommodation services, 81 prospective *haj* pilgrims were left disappointed as the managing director of a trading firm fled the country with $125,000 of misappropriated funds (Speech by Ahmad Mattar, 1978). In 1990, yet again, more than 200 prospective *haj* pilgrims were left stranded at the airport because the respective travel agents failed to secure their flights and accommodation.[1] These incidents highlight not only the importance of the authorities' role in regulating the *haj* sector, but also the growing operational challenges of *haj* management in the face of a changing global landscape.

---

[1] These incidents, though infrequent in Singapore, are not uncommon in *haj* management around the world. In 1984, more than 200 Malaysian pilgrims were stranded at the Malaysian *haj* office and were sent home soon after, while 20 Indonesian pilgrims were stranded in Mecca without visas, betrayed by their former *haj* travel agents.

Today, more than two million Muslims gather in Mecca, Saudi Arabia annually to perform *haj* from the 8th to 13th Zulhijjah, the last month of the Islamic calendar. Organising the logistics for such an operation is a massive exercise requiring cooperation and coordination between the *haj* authorities in Saudi Arabia and the respective counterparts of the pilgrims' originating countries. Part of the strategy in managing a fast-growing international crowd is to liaise with only one authorised official organisation for each country. In Singapore, Muis is appointed for such a role. However, with Singapore being a secular state, it begs the question whether the community should be governed by a centralised system of *haj* management provided by the government, or allow *haj* management to be open to the free market with minimal state intervention.

This chapter will firstly situate the context within which Muis approaches the regulation of *haj* services to ensure a smooth and successful *haj* over the years. It examines the pressures faced by Singapore's *haj* management to meet expectations from two fronts: Saudi policies and consumers' expectation. It also explains the dynamics between Muis, private *haj* operators, and the Saudi government in ensuring that these expectations are met despite evolving challenges, such as pilgrim safety, the rising costs of *haj*, and the limited *haj* quota. Through a study of the unique dynamics between the three industry players, this chapter seeks to highlight useful insights for future *haj* policy deliberations.

Background

The history of *haj* industry in Singapore can be traced to the late 19th century, where over 10,000 Muslims from around the Southeast Asian region gathered in Singapore annually to set sail to Mecca via pilgrim ships (*kapal haji*). As a pilgrim hub, the *haj* industry in Singapore during the colonial period thrived. It involved pilgrim *sheikhs* or brokers arranging and escorting pilgrims to Mecca through private shipping agencies which were largely owned by the Arabs, British, and Dutch companies. Pilgrims were then handed over to pilgrim guides in Mecca, who would then act as service providers arranging for lodging, food, and pilgrims' travel needs. Most pilgrims were retirees and aged, having spent their life savings to make the journey to Mecca in an effort to fulfil the fifth pillar of Islam.[2] While the *haj* is

---

[2] The five pillars of Islam refer to the five basic mandatory tenets the declaration of faith, performing five daily prayers, giving *zakat* (tithe), fasting in the month of Ramadan, and performing the *haj* if they are physically and financially able to do so.

a deeply personal and spiritual journey, the pilgrim's experience is nonetheless shaped by the business aspects of *haj*.

Historically, pilgrimages performed by any religion might be intertwined with some form of commercial venture as any form of movement of peoples would generate significant commercial returns for businesses (Miller, 2006). Given the competitive and commercial nature of the *haj* industry, elderly prospective pilgrims were vulnerable to exploitation by pilgrim brokers or guides. Globally, pilgrim guides were reportedly notorious for their tendency to take advantage of pilgrims by lying about costs and other businesses in the pilgrim trade.[3] In Singapore, the extent of regulation and protection for pilgrims was the enactment of the Ordinance to Provide for the Regulation and Control of Pilgrim Passenger Brokers in 1906, empowering the police chief to issue licences to brokers. By 1926, pilgrims were required to undergo compulsory medical checkup as well as attain a pilgrim pass (*pas haji*), which ensured that pilgrims had return tickets. Although this put in place some control over the *haj* industry, no one organisation or governing body was given the responsibility or legal rights to regulate and centralise *haj* activities. The challenge of coordination was even bigger in the 1970s, as the number of Singaporean *haj* pilgrims rose.

As steamships were phased out and air passage became the safer, faster, and the preferred travel option by the mid-1970s, the *haj* became increasingly accessible to Muslims around the world. By 1982, the number of pilgrims arriving in Mecca surged to more than one million for the first time. With more than 2.5 million people in Mecca, the *haj* infrastructure was severely overstretched, and pilgrims' safety became a serious risk. Tragic incidents of stampedes resulting in deaths, and the spread of illnesses in such close quarters were some of the main issues that the authorities needed to tackle (Green, 2006). In Southeast Asia, the growth in demand was manifested in the tightening competition within the *haj* industry, and reports of *haj* travel agents in the region swindling pilgrims of their money.

In 1984, the Saudi *haj* authorities set up the Establishment of the Mutawwif of South-East Asian Pilgrims (Muassasah) to take over the responsibility of individual *sheikhs* in managing pilgrims. With the establishment of Muassasah, the Saudi authorities required a reciprocal official body of the country to be responsible for their pilgrims. Muis was recognised by the

---

[3] For examples on the exploitation of Malay pilgrims by pilgrim brokers in 1896, see Ismail, K. (1987).

Saudi government to be the sole authority on *haj* matters as it was already vested with the power to administer *haj* under the Merchant Shipping Act, already in existence under the British colonial rule. The Act has since been repealed when the pilgrims ceased using sea passage. Muis then invoked its powers under AMLA in 1968, when pilgrims began making their journey by air, and in regulating the provision of goods and services for *haj*. Henceforth, all *haj* visa applications have to be submitted through Muis. Similarly, all notices and directives on *haj* are channelled via Muis.

Haj Provision Models Around the World

The lack of stringency in *haj* regulation, as shown above, highlighted a serious need for Muis to take on a larger role as a statutory board to regulate the sector. However, the extent of Muis' intervention was an issue Muslim leaders contended with in Muis' early years (Buang, Abbas and Simon, 1984). Generally, *haj* management around the world is either left to the private market or under the jurisdiction of the public sector. Providing *haj* as a government service would entail not only the provision of administrative and management services, funded by taxation, but also in some cases, leveraging economies of scale to provide subsidised standard *haj* packages. The government would thus act as both a regulator and a price stabiliser. A *laissez-faire* approach, conversely, would entail minimal government regulation as the free market sets the price, and private *haj* operators deal directly with the Saudi *haj* authorities and embassy for quota negotiations and visa applications.

In other countries such as Australia and the United Kingdom, *haj* services are organised through a number of *haj* groups, private travel agents, or tour operators who deal directly with the Saudi authorities, embassy, and the affiliated service providers in Saudi Arabia. Unlike Singapore, these countries do not have a centralised religious authority to administer *haj* for the community. Each tour operator has to negotiate on behalf of their pilgrims individually for *haj* visa applications (Abdat, 2008). In the UK, support for pilgrims' safety is provided by the Foreign and Commonwealth Office (FCO). To combat malpractices and deviance by *haj* agents, the FCO, in conjunction with other government departments, helps to raise awareness on pilgrims' consumer rights with respect to *haj* packages and guidance on *haj* travel (Williams, 2008). Their biggest challenge is the limited *haj* visas issued to them as the quota system imposed is on a travel company or agent basis.

On the other hand, for countries with majority-Muslim populations, having *haj* management as a public provision is considered necessary. For example, Indonesia is accountable for more than 200,000 pilgrims annually. Managing and coordinating such a large volume of pilgrims would require a high level of coordination with Saudi *haj* authorities, an effort that can most effectively be undertaken by a government body. There may also be a need for these countries to negotiate large numbers of *haj* quota with the Saudi government — something that can only be done between sovereign states, not private operators. A defining characteristic of this government-regulated model is also the provision of affordable and subsidised standard *haj* packages by the government. These can either be funded by taxation or through an investment banking scheme such as the Tabung Haji in Malaysia.[4] Alternatively, premium *haj* packages offering better accommodation and transport services are provided by private *haj* providers.

The main advantage of the government-regulated model, as used in Muslim-majority countries, is that the government is able to provide a check and balance to the competitive commercial *haj* industry. If left completely to the private market, overpricing, market malpractices, non-compliances, and incorrect teachings on *haj* rituals can occur, which can cause serious repercussions for pilgrims. Although Muslims are a minority in Singapore, there is still a substantial number of Muslims who can still benefit from greater regulation and services of the *haj* industry. Furthermore, providing standard and subsidised *haj* packages can alleviate the financial burden of the increasing costs of *haj*, especially for countries with a rural population who may find *haj* services too costly.

However, centralising the entire *haj* management and service provision may not be suitable in Singapore's context. Historically, *haj* management was a flourishing sector run by private operators — *haj sheikhs* and general sales agents. These private operators have the business expertise in running *haj*

---

[4] The Malaysian government's Lembaga Tabung Haji (LTH) — the Pilgrim Fund- is an Islamic banking and investment system set up in 1962 to aid the Malaysian rural population in saving up for *haj*. In the past, most Muslims were wary of placing their savings in non-Islamic banks as complicity in interest (*riba*) which is considered unpermissible (*haram*). The LTH system, however, accepts deposits and makes investment in a manner approved by the Islamic law. Tabung Haji is a good example how a specialised financial institution can work successfully in accordance with the Islamic principles.

services, including coordinating transport, accommodation, and administration. Muis did not have such expertise, especially in its early years. Furthermore, in line with the Singapore government's policy for the private sector to provide goods and services to the public, Muis too has left it to the private sector to provide direct services to the pilgrims. A competitive and business-oriented industry can offer better services to pilgrims, including better travel and accommodation arrangements.

Haj Management in Singapore

Singapore's model of *haj* management is one that relies on the strong collaboration and cooperation between Muis as a statutory board and the private sector, through the Association of Muslim Travel Agents, Singapore (AMTAS). Instead of pilgrim brokers, travel agents today are licensed to provide outbound and inbound travel services, and are appointed by Muis to manage the pilgrims (Amin, 2008). AMTAS is a non-governmental organisation (NGO) representing the General Sales Agents (GSAs), formed in June 1996 to promote and safeguard the common interest of its members (AMTAS Constitution). In the report by the Pilgrimage Review Committee (PRC),[5] the PRC recommended that activities or tasks that were operational in nature could be delegated based on the rules and guidelines stipulated by Muis. An "organisation" should be identified or created to manage the non-regulatory and operational functions and services of *haj*. An AMTAS representative informed the PRC that AMTAS was willing to manage gradually certain non-core but essential operational *haj* functions from Muis, and would send their staff to Muis for study attachment. In view of this, the PRC recommended that Muis delegate certain operational functions and services of *haj*, albeit in stages, to AMTAS when it is constitutionally and operationally ready. AMTAS would act on the advice, rules, and regulations to be agreed upon by AMTAS and Muis. The PRC thought that AMTAS is the appropriate organisation as there is no other organisation having the experience dealing on *haj* matters (Pilgrimage Review Committee, 1998).

As a statutory board, Muis functions both as a *haj* regulator and facilitator to safeguard the interest and welfare of the Singaporean pilgrims from before

---

[5] The committee was formed by Muis on 9 March 1998 to review the present *haj* procedures and recommend procedures which can be performed by other agencies.

they leave for *haj* and while they are in the Holy Land. Firstly, this involves administering the registration of *haj* pilgrims and managing the *haj* quota allocation. In regulating *haj* services, Muis ensures the robustness and resilience of the Singapore *haj* management system.

Secondly, Muis also functions as an administrator and regulator of the *haj* industry. Over the years, Muis has developed a unique system of calling for tenders for *haj* sevices. It provides a bankers/insurance guarantee to ensure compliance with the requirements for good service delivery. There is also a system of demerit points imposed if services are not rendered as promised, or if there are lapses and unsatisfactory services (Ibrahim, 2008). The *haj* package offers are evaluated by Muis Pilgrimage Committee comprising Muis Council members and respected members of the local Muslim community (Amin, 2008). In preparing for *haj*, the prospective pilgrims are guided by their *mutawwif* on the *haj manasik* or rituals, while the GSAs advise them on matters pertaining to their stay, lodgings, and movements during the *haj* (Amin, 2008). As the *haj* regulator, Muis works closely with AMTAS to ensure that the GSAs deliver a high standard of services to pilgrims in terms of their travel, accommodation, welfare, and services in the Holy Land (Ibrahim, 2008).

Thirdly, it involves the provision of medical services. At every *haj* season, Muis assigns about a 20-member delegation from the Singapore Pilgrims' Affairs Office (SPAO) to ensure the well-being of Singaporean pilgrims through providing medical and welfare services provided in the Holy Land. The delegation includes Muis officials, doctors, nurses, and assistant pilgrim officers. The SPAO also works closely with AMTAS and the GSAs to deal with the *maktabs*,[6] and the relevant Saudi *haj* authorities on the arrangements for services to pilgrims and other pilgrims' welfare such as arranging for admission to hospitals for further treatment, searching for missing pilgrims as well as making the necessary arrangements in the event of any death (Amin, 2008).

---

[6] *Maktab* is literally interpreted as the office or place that regulates the affairs of *haj*. *Maktab* is assigned to divide the group of pilgrims in every Muassasah. Each Muassasah is divided into several *Maktabs*. Every *Maktab* usually takes care of about 2,000–3,000 pilgrims. *Maktab* also manages the distributuion of lots in Arafah and Mina, including taking care of accommodation and storing documents such as pilgrims' passports. *Maktab* offices are scattered in various places in the cities of Mecca and Medina.

Given that Muis has powers to regulate *haj* under AMLA, and that it falls under the official requirements by the Saudi *haj* authorities, it is not feasible for AMTAS to manage all core administrative and functions (Pilgrimage Review Committee, 1998). AMTAS not only forges goodwill among its members in providing *haj* and *umrah* services,[7] it also acts as a link between suppliers, Saudi government agencies, and Muis. The many collaborations between AMTAS and Muis have helped to build efficient communication and coordination in the execution of tasks and dissemination of information for the GSAs who manage Singaporean *haj* pilgrims annually (Amin, 2008). The Haj Rules, introduced in 1999, empowers Muis to regulate the GSAs in providing goods and services for *haj*. In this way, both the service providers and the pilgrims are aware of their rights and obligations. Muis as the *haj* authority will therefore continue to be guided by these overarching principles to act in fairness and in the best interest of all parties concerned, including both the pilgrims and GSAs.

Contemporary Challenges

Today's contemporary *haj* challenges have evolved significantly compared to those during Singapore's early years. Although the issue of non-compliance and fraud in *haj* management is absent today, Muis' role in administering and managing the pilgrims' welfare has expanded. There is now a greater need to ensure that *haj* package prices remain affordable, and that the official *haj* quota can meet the demand of a growing Muslim population. Most Singaporean Muslims today are familiar with the difficulty in securing a place to perform *haj*. Since 2012, the Saudi authorities imposed a reduction in quota for domestic and foreign pilgrims due to the major development and upgrading projects near the Holy Mosque in Mecca. However, Singapore was not affected by the quota reduction as the quota assigned to Singapore is a small number (800 places) as compared to other larger Muslim-majority countries (Muis, 2017). In 2017, the Saudi Haj Ministry reinstated the official *haj* quota to all countries. In general, the prospective Singaporean pilgrim is expected to wait up to 34 years in the queue for the *haj* quota. Although priority is given to first-time pilgrims, many may be anxious that they will not be able to fulfil their religious obligations despite having the financial means to do so. Singaporean *haj* providers also have to contend with the issue of escalating *haj* prices, and

---

[7] *Umrah* is a minor pilgrimage that can be performed at any time of the year except during the *haj* season.

consumers' high expectations of quality *haj* services. These challenges stem firstly from the modern realities of both the management of *haj* in Saudi Arabia and a changing demography of Singaporean *haj* pilgrims.

A significant turning point in *haj* management around the world is the rapid global surge of demand for *haj* pilgrimage. To ensure the safety of pilgrims, the Saudi government took on a multi-billion-dollar infrastructural expansion of Jabbal Omar in Mecca. Modern facilities now cater to the comfort,[8] safety, and welfare of pilgrims. However, pending completion, the new and high-rise hotels, coupled with a higher demand for accommodation in Mecca, have resulted in escalating prices of *haj* package services, including transportation and accommodation. Although the *haj* has always been an expensive affair, the price hikes, coupled with economic slowdown and structural unemployment in the early 2000s, were a cause of concern among Singaporean Muslims. Relative to the subsidised costs in countries like Malaysia and Indonesia for standard *haj* packages, there was thus a need for Muis and GSAs to ensure that the *haj* remained affordable.

In order to manage the rapid growth of pilgrims, more stringency in the Saudi Haj Ministry's quota management was needed to keep the number of pilgrims at a manageable level, and this has been done in consultation with different countries. The *haj* quota given to all countries is capped at 0.1 percent of its Muslim population. Singapore's official quota has always been 680 which does not meet the demands of Singapore's Muslim population. However, on 5 February 2017, the Saudi *haj* authorities eventually increased Singapore's *haj* quota to 800 places. To mitigate the limited number of places, annually between 1996 and 2011, the Minister-in-charge of Muslim Affairs would make an official request to the Saudi *haj* authorities and would eventually, receive additional *haj* places. Getting the additional *haj* places however, came with more issues which added more pressure to the *haj* management process.

The experiences of the *haj* seasons in 2008 and 2009 showed the need to anticipate and better manage uncertainties and other challenges in Muis' management and administration of *haj*. These uncertainties include late approvals for additional *haj* places, a possible reduction in the number of

---

[8] Some examples of the modern facilities in place include the Jamarat bridge in Mina, automated umbrellas around the Prophet's Mosque, special shuttle train service between Arafah and Mina, expanded Mataf area surrounding the Holy *Kaabah* and Mas'aa between Safa and Marwa, travelators inside new tunnels from Mina to Jamarat.

additional places, the possibility of GSAs' failing to secure pilgrims' accommodation notwithstanding bookings made, and even the escalation of *haj* cost. Muis would need sufficient time to inform successful pilgrims to select their *haj* packages, submit the pilgrims' passports for the application for *haj* visas, and arrange for medical support services for pilgrims. In their planning for *haj*, the GSAs would need to make advance bookings and payments to the service providers for the pilgrims' accommodation and other arrangements (e.g., transportation, support services, and other logistical needs). The GSAs would depend very much on the progressive payment made by their pilgrims, which, in turn, is contingent on whether they would get the additional *haj* places.

The above efforts taken to manage the crowd during the *haj* has ultimately resulted in the reduction of supply of *haj* places. Yet, at the same time, the demand for *haj* from the Singapore Muslim community is also growing. The early 1990s marked a boom in Singapore's economy, creating a growing middle class who could afford performing the *haj* at a younger age. A survey Muis conducted in 2005 on 1,285 prospective pilgrims showed that a large majority of the respondents preferred and were prepared to pay for a four- or five-star accommodation, while most wanted shorter travel time from the hotel to the Holy *Kaabah*. For the services at Arafah and Mina, 65 percent preferred VIP services, which include special services and better tents in Arafah with buffet-type meals (Muis–AMTAS Workgroup, 2005). This shift in expectations reflects the evolving needs and expectations of an increasingly affluent Muslim society.

Mitigating Contemporary Challenges

The effective *haj* management in Singapore depends on, among other factors, the strong relationship between Muis and the private sector, represented by AMTAS. One of the challenges that this partnership seeks to address is the rise of *haj* prices. In 2005, Muis and AMTAS formed a workgroup to study *haj* trends and recommend strategies to alleviate some of the challenges. To keep *haj* prices affordable, the workgroup recommended the following strategies: (i) reduce the GSAs' operating costs through mergers or forming a consortium and employing more local personnel (i.e., the Saudis); (ii) shorten the pilgrims' period of stay in Medina (iii) offer a shorter period of *haj* package; (iv) lease a building in Mecca for Singaporean pilgrims; (v) accommodate pilgrims in Aziziyah and Shisha instead of Mecca during the entire *haj* season; and (vi) consider a *haj* savings scheme (similar to the

Tabung Haji concept in Malaysia) when the *haj* package prices reach an unaffordable level. Firstly, the GSAs arranged for pilgrims to stay at an interim accommodation apartment in Aziziyah and Shisha, a neighbourhood of Mecca during the peak period, that is from 4th to 13th *Zulhijjah*. Secondly, AMTAS chose a Basic service rather than a VIP service for Muassasah services in Arafah and Mina to reduce cost. Thirdly, the GSAs helped to reduce their operating costs and offered a shorter period *haj* package. Finally, the GSAs offered three types of packages: economy, standard, deluxe, as well as a backpacker's package. These strategies helped to control *haj* prices, ensuring that quality services remained affordable.

The Singapore government and Muis have also forged a cordial and good working relationship with the Saudi Haj Ministry and *haj* agencies, including the Royal Embassy of Saudi Arabia in Singapore. The Embassy provides timely guidelines for *haj* visa applications and requirements to Muis for dissemination to the Muslim public and AMTAS. In Saudi Arabia, the Singapore Consulate in Jeddah works closely with the relevant Saudi authorities to assist the SPAO on the application of permits required for the *haj* operations such as bringing in medical supplies and setting up medical clinics as well as vehicle permits and passes to enter the *haj* airport terminal (Amin, 2008). The Saudi Haj authorities have indicated that Singapore has a good *haj* administration model, its pilgrims were organised, and were provided with good medical and welfare services (Ibrahim, 2008). These examples highlight the importance of the three-way partnership between Muis, AMTAS, and the Saudi government in ensuring the effective management of *haj* pilgrims both in Singapore and Saudi Arabia.

The Future of *Haj*

The sustainability and effectiveness of the *haj* management sector in Singapore, as this chapter has argued, is dependent on the strong relations between the two governments — Singapore, as represented by Muis as a statutory board, and Saudi Arabia — and between Muis and private *haj* service providers. As the *haj* landscape continues to evolve in today's rapid, globalised world, it is important and timely for Muis, supported by AMTAS, to plan ahead and study the changing trends and profiles of *haj* pilgrims to ensure operational readiness in addressing future *haj* challenges.[9]

---

[9] The demographics of *haj* pilgrims are shown in Annex B.

With Singapore's ageing population, there may be more elderly pilgrims registering in the advanced *haj* registration system. As it is, in 2016, 14 percent of pilgrims were more than 65 years of age. The implications are two-fold: there may be a longer waiting time for elderly pilgrims, and there may be a need to increase or strategise medical services. The *haj* registration system works on a first-come, first-served basis, with priority given to first-time pilgrims. This system may be disadvantageous to elderly pilgrims who were unable to register earlier on and may thus miss out on the opportunity to perform the *haj*. The Singapore *haj* contingent needs a good mix of younger and older pilgrims in every *haj* season so that the younger pilgrims can lend support to the older pilgrims in need. There may also be a need to increase medical support for elderly pilgrims who may be vulnerable to falling ill during the pilgrimage. Medical support for pilgrims today are on three fronts: i) medical support at Muis' clinics, which then refers pilgrims to Saudi hospitals; ii) the Emergency Medical Assistance (EMA), managed by AMTAS, which allows them to visit private medical centres; and iii) free medical services by the Saudi government. Increasing medical support may result in the increase of *haj* package prices, therefore placing pressure on pilgrims.

Other than medical support, other factors such as infrastructural developments in the Holy Land and airline prices may drive cost and prices of *haj* packages. The price of a *haj* package varies according to the travel itinerary, duration of stay in the Holy Land, and type and location of accommodation (Amin, 2008). It is imperative for Muis, the Muis Pilgrimage Committee and AMTAS to closely monitor and study the rising trends, and generate creative ideas and solutions to stabilise the rising *haj* package prices. In Singapore, there are two organisations which have offered a savings fund scheme for *haj* or *umrah*. Pergas (Singapore Islamic Scholars and Religious Teachers' Association) started a good initiative for their members to set aside savings for *haj* or *umrah*. However, it was not sustainable as the members who subscribed were very small. Maybank Singapore has offered the Muslim community its Syariah-compliant savings product to the Muslim community launched in June 2011.[10] These strategies may need to be reviewed in time to come.

---

[10] The idea to form the Tabung Haji concept in Singapore is not new. In 1972, Muslim leaders had announced their intent to form Tabung Haji as announced by the first Muis President, Haji Ismail Aziz (*Berita Harian*, 1972). Jamiyah too had a similar plan to form Tabung Haji, to resolve the difficulties faced by *haj* pilgrims travelling by ships, as announced by its Acting General Secretary, Mr Abdullah Musa (*Berita Harian*, 1972) However, Muis' plans to set up Tabung Haji did not materialise due to poor response from the Muslim community (*Berita Harian*, 1972).

The *haj* is an important spiritual event that is a part of Muslims' religious identity. Even though it occurs only annually within a month, it is a massive global event that has implications on international relations, the economy, and pilgrims' personal safety. Thus, the coordinated efforts between Muis, the Saudi government, and the private sector, will continue to be important for the future of *haj*.

References

Abdat, N. (2008), *Haj Services: An Australian Viewpoint, Singapore International Haj Seminar.* Singapore: Muis. pp. 4–6.

Abimanyu, A. (2013, June 10). Progress and Challenges of Indonesian Haj Management. *The Jakarta Post.* Retrieved from: http://www.thejakartapost.com/amp/news/2013/06/10/progress-and-challenges-indonesian-haj-management.html.

Administration of Muslim Law Act (AMLA) and Administration of Muslim Law (Haj) Rules 1999.

Amin, A. H. (2008), *Singapore Haj Management Systems, Singapore International Haj Seminar — Sharing Amongst Muslim Minority Countries.* Singapore. Majlis Ugama Islam Singapura (Muis). pp. 1–3, 5–8, 10–13.

Berita Harian (1984, July 5). Ramai alu2 saranan tubuhkan Danamis. *Berita Harian.* Retrieved from NewspaperSG.

Berita Harian (1972, March 7). Muis ranchang Tabong Haji. *Berita Harian.* Retrieved from NewspaperSG.

Berita Harian (1972, March 17). Tabong Haji Jamiyah di-ura2 dulu. *Berita Harian.* Retrieved from NewspaperSG.

Berita Harian (1973, May 18). Urusan haji: Inisiatif terbaru Muis. *Berita Harian.* Retrieved from NewspaperSG.

Buang, Z., Abbas, D., Simon, M. (1984, July 3). Tabung untuk tunaikan Haji, *Berita Harian,* p. 1.

Changes to the Administration of Muslim Law Act (Haj Rules), 2010, p. 5.

Constitution of the Association of Muslim Travel Agents, Singapore, AMTAS, p. 1.

Green, A. (2006), *Our Journey: 30 years of Haj Services in Singapore.* Singapore. Muis. pp. 50–51.

Ibrahim, Y. (2008). Speech by Dr. Yaacob Ibrahim, Minister for the Environment and Water Resources and Minister-in-Charge of Muslim Affairs, *Singapore International Haj Seminar.* Singapore on 2008, May 17. Muis. pp. 5–6.

Ismail, K. (1987). The *haj* and Singapore: a historical and biographical study of its effects. Academic Exercise, National University of Singapore.

Mattar, A. (1978). Speech by Dr. Ahmad Mattar, Acting Minister for Social Affairs, 10th Anniversary Celebrations of the Muslim Welfare Association, Toa Payoh, Singapore on 1978, November 25. pp 2–3.

Muis (2015, May 12). Authorised Travel Agents and Approved Packages for *Haj* 1436H/2015, *Muis*.

Muis–AMTAS Workgroup (2005, October 28), Study on *Haj* Market Trends and Package Prices, pp. 5–8.

Muis' Pilgrimage Review Committee (1998, May 25), *Review on the Present Haj Services — Report and Recommendations*, pp. 5–8.

Miller, M. B. (2006). *Pilgrims' Progress: The Business of the Hajj*. Past and Present, Number 191, pp. 189–228.

Roots.sg. (2015). Bussorah Street (Former Kampong Kaji). Retrieved from: https://roots.sg/Content/Places/landmarks/kampong-glam-heritage-trail-one-kampong-glam/bussorah-street-former-kampong-kaji.

Williams, J. (2008, May 17), *UK Haj Support Services, Singapore International Haj Seminar*. Singapore: Muis. pp. 7–8.

Annex A

Key Milestones in *Haj* Services by Muis (1970–2018)

S/N	Date/Year	Key Events	Remarks
1	1970	Muis establishes Pilgrimage Committee	
2	November 1975	Some 300 pilgrims without flights at Paya Lebar Airport; Ministry of Social Affairs and Muis work to resolve the matter	
3	1979	First medical team of two nursing officers dispatched by Muis	
4	1981	First doctor sent by Muis	
5	1982	Medical team enlarged to two doctors, including nursing officers	
6	1984	Muassasah system established (Establishment of the Mutawwif of South-East Asian Pilgrims) June 1984: Under Muassasah system, pilgrim guides in Saudi Arabia must submit visa applications through Muis	Saudi authorities request Muis to register all Singapore pilgrims Saudi Embassy in Singapore will only deal with Muis on *haj* matters
7	1990	More than 200 pilgrims stranded because of failure of Tanorm Travel	
8	1991	Muis introduces GSA system From 1991, Muis has all records of pilgrims going on *haj*	Travel Agents replacing *Syeikh Haji*
9	1995	Muis introduces registration schemes to accommodate quotas	Priority for those over 55 years old

(*Continued*)

(Continued)

S/N	Date/Year	Key Events	Remarks
10	1996	Haj Registration System for extended family	
11	July 1997	*Haj* registration on first-come, first-served basis	
12	15 September 1997	Muis Advanced Haj Registration System implemented	Individual applicant allowed to register five years in advance
13	27 September 1999	AMLA amended	All travel agents need a licence from Muis before they can manage the *haj* All *Mutawwifs* to be registered with Muis
14	2001	Online Haj Registration System implemented	
15	2002	Consortium of General Sales Agents implemented	GSAs with less than 20 pilgrims to form a consortium with one lead agent
16	2004	Muis outsourcing to AMTAS	For non-core but essential operational functions
17	2004	First Muis Post *Haj* Seminar	To obtain feedback from stakeholders to further improve *haj* services
18	2004	Muis opens Mina Command Post	To increase security and supervision of Singapore pilgrims at Mina
19	2005	ISO certification awarded	For *haj* quality management system
20	2006	Muis extends its medical services to about 200 Australian pilgrims	There is no official Haj mission to accompany Australian pilgrims
21	17 May 2008	Muis organises first Singapore International Haj Seminar	For sharing among Muslim minority countries
22	Oct 2010	AMLA amended	Amendments of Haj Rules on registration, deferment, cancellation and refunds

(Continued)

(Continued)

S/N	Date/Year	Key Events	Remarks
23	15 March 2013	Muis Haj Registration System revised	Time out period of 10 years for repeaters
24	5 February 2017	Singapore's *Haj* quota revised from 680 to 800 after Minister's request was approved by Saudi authorities	Singapore's quota set at 0.1 percent of the Muslim population
25	25 January 2018	Singapore *Haj* quota revised from 800 to 900	

Source: Green, A. (2006), *Our Journey: 30 years of Haj Services in Singapore*. Singapore. Muis. pp. 50–51.

Annex B

Demographics of *Haj* 1437H / 2016 Singaporean Pilgrims

Age Group	Male	Female	Total
Below 12	0	0	0
12 to 20+	3	1	4
21 to 29+	7	3	10
30 to 39+	15	13	28
40 to 44+	15	18	33
45 to 49+	25	48	73
50 to 54+	38	72	110
55 to 59+	77	118	195
60 to 65	85	91	176
Above 65	55	49	104
Total	320	413	733

Source: Muis Haj Services Strategic Unit.

Annex C

Muis Approved *Haj* Packages (2012–2017)						
Haj	**2012**	**2013**	**2014**	**2015**	**2016**	**2017**
Lowest Package Prices (*)						
Official *haj* quota	680	680	680	680	680	800
Price includes EMA	$6,190	$8,105	$7,295	$6,795	$7,190	$6,215
No. of days/Rate per day	14 ($442/ day)	19 ($427/ day)	23 ($317/ day)	16 ($425/ day)	15 ($479/ day)	10 ($622/ day)
Convert to 14 days (rate per day x 14 days)	$6,190	$5,978	$4,438	$5,950	$6,706	$8,708
Type of accommodation (double/triple/quad room) in Mecca and Medina/No. of star rating	Quad 4-star	Quad 4-star	Quad 4-star	Quad 4-star	Quad 4-star	Quad 4-star
Pre-*Haj* accommodation	Aziziyah	Shisha	Shisha	Shisha	Shisha	Shisha
Highest Package Prices (*)						
Official *Haj* quota	680	680	680	680	680	800
Price includes EMA	$13,650	$13,650	$13,650	$14,335	$18,092	$18,632
No. of days/Rate per day	30 ($455/ day)	30 ($455/ day)	30 ($455/ day)	31 ($462/ day)	31 ($584/ day)	30 ($621/ day)
Convert to 30 days (rate per day x 30 days)	$13,650	$13,650	$13,650	$13,860	$17,520	$18,632
Type of accommodation (double/triple/ quad room) in Mecca and Medina/No. of star rating	Double 5-star	Double 5-star	Double 5-star	Quad 5-star	Double 5-star	Double 5-star

(Continued)

(Continued)

Haj	2012	2013	2014	2015	2016	2017
Pre- and Post-Haj accommodation (peak season from 4th to 8th Zulhijjah and from 13th to 25th Zulhijjah)	Shisha	Mecca	Mecca	Mecca	Mecca	Mecca
Airfare	$2.2k to $2.6k (SQ/SV)	$2.2k to $2.6k (SQ/SV)	$2.2k to $2.6k (SQ/SV)	$2.2k to $2.6k (SQ/SV)	$1.8k to $2.5k (TR/SV)	$1.8k to $2.5k (TR/SV)

(*) Package price excludes airfare and prevailing taxes.
SQ: Singapore Airlines.
SV: Saudia Airlines.
TR: Scoot.

11

MANAGING DEMAND GROWTH FOR *HALAL* FOOD

Dewi Hartaty Suratty

"Mr Speaker, Sir, the changes the amendment makes to Muis are indeed welcome. The move to empower Muis to regulate *halal* certification...reflects the need to better manage changing expectations within the community. Many food outlets in Singapore have recognised the growing Muslim market and have turned *halal* in order to attract this market. Muis' new role in the regulation of *halal* certification should reassure the Muslim community that outlets with *halal* certification are *halal* throughout their operations."

Dr Yaacob Ibrahim, Parliamentary Debate, 30 June 1998

One of the first requests to Muis for *halal* assurance and certification was made in 1978, when anxieties arose regarding the authenticity of *halal* labels by product manufacturers and abuse of *halal* claims on a noodle product containing pork. Muis also received requests from beverage manufacturer Yeo Hiap Seng for Muis' endorsement of its exports to the Middle East. By 1981, Muis had given 100 companies *halal* certificates. However, the 1990s saw several companies misusing the *halal* label. These were evident in local news headlines, such as "Syarikat gunakan label *halal* tanpa izin"[1] (Mohtar, 1992) and "Rise in number of complaints against authenticity of *halal* food imported and sold here" (1994).

A significant turning point in the *halal* food industry in Singapore was the amendment of the Administration of Muslim Law Act (AMLA) in 1999 to strengthen Muis' statutory powers to issue *halal* certificates. Since its introduction, the demand for *halal* certification has grown by five-fold each decade. To date, more than 50,000 product types and 4,000 food establishments are certified *halal*, making Singapore the world's top *halal* destination among non-Muslim countries (Wong, 2016). While these trends are reflective of Singapore's growth in the food industry, they are also driven by developments in the global *halal* food industry.

The *halal* food industry, both locally and globally, has transformed in the past 40 years. This transformation is driven not only by globalisation, technological, and economic growth, but also by significant developments in the global Muslim population. The burgeoning global food industry firstly raises concerns on the integrity of *halal* food within the global supply chain. As sources of ingredients and food components within the supply chain grow increasingly complex, it has become much harder for consumers to determine the permissibility of food products. This anxiety was also partly fuelled by the increasing Muslim religious practice in the 1980s and 1990s during the revivalist period, when the practice of Islam became more closely tied to Muslim identity. This chapter will firstly delve into these key drivers of Muis' entrance into the *halal* market through not only the certification process, but the preventive measures taken to alleviate the misuse of *halal* labels.

Today, the concern has evolved from the uncertainty of *halal* certification, to the extreme usage of *halal* labelling, particularly for non-food items such as supermarket trolleys, carbon dioxide, household detergents, and personal care products (Arshad and Leong, 2016). This phenomenon raises two key issues: i) Muslims practising religion beyond what is expected of the primary religious requirements; and ii) traders commercialising religion and *halal* by promoting what Muslims should use and consume. In highlighting the evolution of the *halal* industry in Singapore, and the subsequent growth of the global *halal* market and its impact on Muslims, this chapter will argue that while the provision of *halal* certification is necessary in today's context,

---

[1] English translation: "Company used *halal* label without permission."

collaborative efforts between Muslim consumers, authorities and businesses are important to effectively manage the demand for *halal* growth.

Understanding *Halal* Food

Islam urges Muslims to eat food that is *halal*, which linguistically means "permitted" in Arabic. The antonym of *halal* is *haram*. According to Al-Qaradawi (2001), the first principle pertaining to the lawful and prohibited is that the things which Allah has created, and the benefits derived from them are essentially for humankind's use, and hence are permissible. In Islam, the sphere of things prohibited is very small, while that of things permissible is extremely vast. Salman al-Farsi once reported that when Prophet Muhammad was asked about animal fat, cheese, and fur, he replied: "The lawful is that which Allah has made lawful in His Book and the prohibited is that which He has prohibited in His Book, and that concerning which He is silent He has permitted as a favour to you".[2] The latter part of this quote serves to highlight that most foods fall under the latter category. Food that is prohibited in Islam is those derived or mixed with the following (Hussaini, 1993):

- Meat of dead animals (carrion)
- Swine including all its products and by-products
- Flowing or congealed blood
- Food immolated unto idols
- Intoxicants
- Carnivorous animals with fangs, such as lions, dogs, wolves, or tigers
- Birds with sharp claws (birds of prey), such as falcons, eagles, owls, or vultures
- Land animals such as frogs or snakes

Apart from *halal*, Muslims are also ordained to ensure that the food they eat is good and wholesome. This is clearly mentioned in the Qur'anic verse: "And eat of what Allah has provided for you, which is lawful and good. And fear Allah, in whom you are believers" Qur'an, 5: 88. Wholesomeness takes into consideration the nature and processing of food to ensure that the end product is safe, clean, and of good quality (Turcsik, 2001; Nakyinsige *et al.*, 2012; Tieman *et al.*, 2012;

---

[2] Hadith (Prophet's Tradition) narrated by At-Tirmidhi and Ibn Majah.

Omar *et al.*, 2013). Therefore, in determining whether a product such as meat sausage is *halal*, one has to ensure that it is derived from *halal*-slaughtered animals and that it is free from diseases, manufactured in a clean environment, and free from direct contact with any *haram* items.

Halal Food Verification

Halal is a credence quality attribute which can hardly be evaluated or ascertained by an individual consumer even upon or after consuming the food (Darby and Karni, 1973). The *halal* food chain begins from the farm to the table. *Halal* encompasses origin, species, production system, and the food processing method. All these characteristics are not visible and cannot be verified by the consumer during the pre-purchase stage. With the advent of science and technology, determining the *halal* authenticity of a food product through analytical techniques can be made possible. For instance, quantifying the alcohol content of a beverage can be done using gas chromatography, while the presence of pork, lard or blood plasma can be detected through polymerase chain reaction, Fourier transform infrared spectroscopy, and enzyme-linked immunosorbent assay techniques (Nakyinsige *et al.*, 2012; Van der Spiegel *et al.*, 2012). Unfortunately, laboratory testing has its limitations. Many processing aids are at levels below those that traditional testing can detect (Al-Mazeedi *et al.*, 2013). Processing aids refer to substances that are added during the processing of food but are removed before it is packaged. These include lubricants used on equipment and agents that help in peeling fruits or vegetables, some of which may not be *halal* as they contain lard or tallow. Besides being costly and time-consuming, analytical testing is also not a full proof verification method as it is unable to determine whether meat is derived from a Muslim-slaughtered procedure, this being a critical *halal* criterion, for instance.

Product labels provide a good source of information for consumers on the ingredients that are used in food. In Singapore, the frequency of using food labels is high among supermarket shoppers (Vijaykumar *et al.*, 2013). With thousands of ingredients and additives used in the food industry, many of which are labelled in confusing e-codes (e.g., E322, E471, E476) or chemical names (e.g., Methyl *p*-hydroxybenzoate, Isobutyl cinnamate, Xanthan gum), determining the *halal* status of a food product is no easy feat for the layman. Furthermore, not all compounds used in food processing are labelled. Most processing aids are not required to appear on product's ingredient label, as they are not meant to be part of the final product's ingredients (Codex Alimentarius, 2001). The lack of understanding and information on how a product is manufactured just by reading the food labels give rise to doubt and avoidance by Muslims who choose to stay clear for fear of committing a *haram* act.

Halal Certification

Muslim consumers rely on the *halal* certificate or certification mark as a symbol of assurance that a product is *halal*. Riaz and Chaudry (2004, p. 170) define *halal* certification as a "document issued by an Islamic organisation certifying that the products listed on it meet Islamic dietary guidelines". The literature has shown that *halal*-certified products create greater assurance for Muslims (Mohamed *et al.*, 2008; Rezai *et al.*, 2012). This is due to the rigorous checks conducted by an independent auditor involving the following processes:

- Submission of new/renewal application by the company;
- Review of the application by an independent *halal* certification body, especially the type of product/service and its ingredients used;
- Audit of premises — this includes interview of personnel, review of workflow, review of the production/kitchen equipment, inspection of ingredients, verification of documents, assess for possible cross-mixing and product-testing. For a slaughterhouse, inspection involves the review of holding areas, method of stunning, actual slaying, pre- and post-slaughter handling, etc.;
- Approval of application; and
- Issuance of *halal* certificate/certification mark.

Compared to product labels, the *halal* mark is a more straightforward means of ascertaining permissibility of food compared to reading the long, complex ingredient list on product labels. It also provides ease in the minds of consumers, who may be inundated by different opinions on the interpretation of *halal* among *mazhabs* (Islamic schools of legal thought) and Islamic organisations worldwide. For instance, food products that have undergone *istihalah*[3] such as vinegar, gelatin, industrial alcohol, and '*tapai*'[4] are classified as *halal* by one group of scholars including Maliki, al-Syawkani, Hanafi, and

---

[3] *Istihalah* refers to complete transformation of physical and chemical nature of a substance, which results in another product having no physicochemical resemblance to the original material.

[4] *Tapai'* is a traditional fermented food and a rice wine found throughout much of East and Southeast Asia.

Ibn Hazm al-Zahiri, if both natural and synthetic (i.e., with human intervention) transformation are involved (Jahangir *et al.*, 2016). On the other hand, the second group of scholars (Hanbali and Syafi'i) accept such food products if they undergo natural transformation only. Other differences of opinion on *halal* food include the allowable limit of ethanol in food flavourings, permissibility of mechanical slaughtering, and animal stunning. The *halal* logo allows one to identify the organisation that certifies a product, thus enabling an individual to choose only a product that is endorsed by a certifier that subscribes to the same *mazhab* or one that is known to hold similar beliefs.

Drivers of Demand for *Halal* Certification

Despite originating from a Muslim-minority country, the Muis *halal* certification is recognised in key markets such as Brunei, Indonesia, Malaysia, and the Gulf Cooperation Council (GCC) through the MABIMS,[5] and GCC-Singapore Free Trade Agreements. The Muis *halal* certification programme has gone through four phases of evolution: The Beginning (1978 to 1989); Building Foundation (1990 to 1999); Coping with Demand (2000 to 2009); and Sustaining Growth (2010 onwards).[6]

The *halal* landscape in Singapore has undergone significant change over the years. While *halal* certification is not mandatory, the number of certificates issued over the years have increased from just 100 in early 1980s to more than 50,000 in 2017. The surge in *halal* demand is related to three key factors — namely the globalisation of food systems, the increase in religious consciousness and the growth potential of the *halal* industry. In the next segment, I will explain these driving forces as well as Muis' efforts to manage the burgeoning market through two strategic objectives: i) to facilitate demand for *halal* certification; and ii) to strengthen compliance within the *halal* industry. These are demonstrated through various legislative, systems and structural changes made by Muis.

Globalisation of Food Systems

The phenomenon of globalisation has a major impact on food systems around the world. Globalisation here refers to the reduction in barriers to

---

[5] MABIMS stands for the Unofficial Meeting of Religious Affairs Ministers of Brunei, Indonesia, Malaysia and Singapore.

[6] Refer to Annex A for the key milestones of Muis *halal* certification.

the cross-border movement of foods, services, and capital; an increased flow of commodities, technologies, information, financial capital, modes of distribution and marketing; and, to a certain extent, migration of peoples and labour (Shetty, 2003). Food systems along the food chain are changing, from production and processing to retail and marketing, resulting in greater availability and diversity of food. Many of these changes are closely associated with modernisation, increasing incomes, market liberalisation, and foreign direct investment.

The globalisation of food systems presents both opportunities and challenges for the *halal* industry in Singapore. Through the globalised food supply chain, Singapore is able to overcome its limited land space for farming and fishing by importing 90 percent of food consumed in the country, both *halal* and non-*halal* (Agri-food and Veterinary Authority of Singapore, 2015). It also results in enhanced access to thousands of food and ingredients because of changing prices, production practices and trade. It is not uncommon for a Singapore-made food product, for instance, to contain dozens of ingredients from various manufacturers in different countries such as Malaysia, Thailand, USA, and France.

Questions have been raised on the integrity of *halal* food as it passes through the supply chain. With multiple sources of raw materials, will the risk of "contamination" with *haram* ingredients be higher? Given the inter-connectedness of the food supply chain, is it possible to trace to the actual ingredient or supplier where the "contamination" takes place? In 2011, it was reported that porcine DNA was found in a popular butter product, even though it was certified *halal* by three Islamic bodies in Australia, Indonesia, and New Zealand (Yeo, 2011). In 2014, a similar issue was detected in Malaysia, this time on Cadbury Chocolates (Yong, 2014). As a country that operates an open economy system, the risks of globalisation are real. Singapore has been vulnerable to doubtful products even though they are labelled *halal* (*The Straits Times*, 1994). Furthermore, in the absence of an international *halal* accreditation framework, the credibility of some *halal* certificates remains questionable.

As early as the 1990s, Muis began establishing networks with foreign *halal* certification bodies (FHCBs) to better understand the organisations that endorse foreign raw materials used in Muis-certified products and food establishments, as well as to determine that the *halal* standards adopted by them were aligned to that in Muis. Subsequently, a framework was institutionalised to recognise FHCBs that comply with terms and conditions imposed by Muis before higher risk imported ingredients such as meat, meat-based items, and flavours can be used by Muis-certified companies in Singapore. To date, more than 70 FHCBs worldwide are recognised by Muis. At the government level, Muis enters into multilateral cooperation through the ASEAN Working Group on Halal Food,[7] and MABIMS Special Technical Committee on Halal Development.[8] These platforms promote cooperation, exchange of information, and harmonisation of standards. This is a strategic move by Muis to ensure that it remains connected and recognised by other FHCBs in neighbouring countries such as Malaysia and Indonesia, being Singapore's key trading partners (Department of Statistics Singapore, 2017).

As the global demand for *halal* food grew, Muis began receiving requests for *halal* certification from overseas companies. These were generally businesses that operate in countries where a *halal* certification framework was absent or relatively unknown. Additionally, many of them were attracted by Muis, being one of the world's pioneers in *halal* certification, as well as Singapore's reputation and branding in terms of credibility, transparency, efficiency, and effectiveness. In 2006, Muis incubated a *halal* international function within a division of Warees Investments Pte Ltd, a wholly-owned subsidiary of Muis. The objectives were to provide *halal* certification overseas and sharing of expertise with the eventual hope of positive spin-offs for Singapore and the Muslim community. In September 2014, the division was corporatised as Warees Halal Limited, a not-for-profit public company limited by guarantee. As a standalone company, Warees Halal is able to have a specialised management board to provide value-added strategic direction on *halal* matters and corporate governance, in addition to allowing for

---

[7] To address the issues on *halal* food, an ASEAN Working Group on Halal Food was established in 2000. This Working Group is made up of 10 ASEAN member states namely Brunei Darussalam, Cambodia, Indonesia, Lao PDR, Malaysia, Myanmar, the Philippines, Singapore, Thailand, and Vietnam. The Working Group has the mandate to promote cooperation, exchange of information, and harmonisation of ASEAN *halal* Food sector regulation and policies as well as to conduct reviews of the processing and marketing of *halal* food in the ASEAN region. Among the activities which have been conducted and implemented by the Working Group are: registration and compilation of *halal* Food additives, capacity building programme of *halal* food activities (i.e., trainings for *halal* Inspectors, *halal* food auditors, and laboratory analysts), and implementation of ASEAN Guidelines on Halal Food for both intra- and extra-ASEAN trade.

[8] The MABIMS Special Technical Committee on Halal Development was formed in 2012. It comprises *halal* certification bodies in MABIMS member countries — Brunei, Indonesia, Malaysia, and Singapore. The terms of reference of the Committee include forging close working relationship, discussing *halal* technical matters, sharing information and research findings, and establishing a *halal* coordination protocol to facilitate development of the *halal* industry.

clearer business focus to ensure efficiency and effectiveness. To date, Warees Halal has trained and certified companies and organisations in various countries such as Korea, China, Japan, Belgium, and Italy.

Increasing Religious Consciousness

The primary impetus for Muis' *halal* certification is the strong rise in demand from the Singapore Muslim population who is concerned about the permissibility of food products. Reports on the use of *halal* claims by non-Muslim businesses and misuse of *halal* logo on an instant noodle product containing pork emerged in the 1970s (Salleh, 1977; *The Straits Times*, 1978). As mentioned above, Muis came under intense public pressure to ensure that *halal*-labelled products are indeed suitable for Muslim consumption. Despite the introduction of *halal* certification in 1978, the food industry continued to be plagued with *halal* scandals in the 1990s. Negative headlines hit the news — "Syarikat gunakan label halal tanpa izin" and "Rise in number of complaints against authenticity of *halal* food imported and sold here". There were also reports of non-compliance among *halal*-certified companies (*The Straits Times*, 1992; Hamzah, 1994).

Such public reactions became more observable during the period of growing Muslim religious fervour in the 1970s triggered by the stronger demand for Islamisation throughout the world, including the Southeast Asia (Lapidus, 1997). This demand for Islamisation was largely driven by the emergence of Islamic revivalist movements. Key factors which fueled the rise of these movements were the defeat of the Arab states in the 1967 war with Israel, the failure of many development programmes of these post-colonial states, and the Iranian revolution. More Muslims began to return to Islamic traditions and to the fundamentals of their faith by adhering to the norms of proper religious practice — especially prayer, avoidance of alcohol, and modesty. In fact, literature has shown that there is a positive correlation between religiosity and attitude towards *halal* food (Mukhtar and Mohsin Butt, 2012). For someone who professes Islam as his religion, consuming *halal* food is more than just fulfilling a religious obligation. Muslims believe that whatever they consume becomes part of them, and has an effect not only on his physical body, but also on his spiritual self. By consuming only what is *halal* and good, a good Muslim is showing his gratitude towards Allah for all the blessings Allah has given.

It is against this backdrop that a legislative change was made to AMLA in 1999 to address growing concerns on the integrity of *halal*-labelled food in

Singapore (Official Reports of Parliamentary Debate, 1998). The amendment enabled Muis as the Islamic authority in Singapore to regulate the holders of its certificates and prosecute those who display *halal* certificates or use the Muis *halal* mark without approval. The Act was further amended in 2008, during an expanding global food industry and Singapore's exports to the Middle East, enabling Muis to deal with *halal*-related offences in a more efficient and cost-effective manner through a composition (fine), instead of having to initiate court proceedings. Singapore's status as one of the few countries with a regulation that backs its *halal* sector is one of the key reasons behind the recognition of Muis' *halal* certification.

Apart from enforcing AMLA, Muis continued to take proactive measures to strengthen *halal* compliance in the food industry. In 2008, it implemented what is believed to be the world's first Halal Quality Management System, or HalMQ. Beyond ensuring that the product ingredients are *halal*, HalMQ attempts to establish a good *halal* system within Muis-certified companies by requiring that they form a *halal* team, monitor and document the preparation of *halal* products, as well as conduct an internal audit. HalMQ has provided companies a 10-step[9] systematic and preventive approach to *halal* management similar to international standards such as ISO and HACCP.[10] The introduction of HalMQ not only raises the industry's *halal* compliance and provides assurance to local and foreign consumers, it also creates a competitive advantage for Singapore companies.

Growth Potential of the Halal Industry

Th global *halal* market has grown to a phenomenal US$ 1.2 trillion in 2015, higher than that of China's and US' markets (Thomson Reuters, 2016). It is expected to expand further to US$ 1.9 trillion by 2021, corresponding to the increase in Muslim population. The *halal* food market is deemed to be one of the fastest-growing segments in the world, not only in predominant Muslim

---

[9] 10 principles of HalMQ: (1) Establish the *halal* team; (2) Define the product/nature of business; (3) Construct and verify flow chart; (4) Identify *halal* threats and their control measures; (5) Determine *halal* Assurance Points (HAPs), their allowable limits and prescribed practices; (6) Establish monitoring system for each HAP; (7) Establish corrective actions for each HAP; (8) Establish documentation and record-keeping system; (9) Verify the *halal* system; (10) Review the *halal* system.

[10] HACCP stands for Hazard Analysis Critical Control Point. It is a management system in which food safety is addressed through the analysis and control of biological, chemical and physical hazards from raw material production, procurement and handling to manufacturing, distribution, and consumption of the finished product.

regions, but in non-Muslim economies as well (Ghaus, 2014). This trend is partly contributed by the increasing Muslim middle class worldwide. In Singapore, the Muslim community's median household income — a key measure of economic progress — grew by 3.6 percent annually between 2000 and 2010, with median monthly household incomes rising from $2,709 to $3,844 during that period (Association of Muslim Professionals, 2012). Characterised by larger disposable incomes and affluence, the growing middle class spends more on eating out, experience and quality (Yong, 2017). Most Singaporeans dine out at least once a month, mainly at hawker stalls and restaurants/cafes (Weber Shandwick, 2014). Convenience and more nutritious food have come on strongly as these middle-income earners purchase ready-to-eat meals and healthier product options from supermarkets as well as and patronise eateries serving up quick grabs for the busy individuals. As awareness of the economic potential of the Muslim market grows, driven by the bigger middle class population, more companies including global multi-nationals such as Nestle, PepsiCo, and Cargill have jumped onto the *halal* bandwagon. For these companies, going *halal* is a strategic move to further establish their market position, expand their market share, and win over Muslim consumers who contribute to 16.6 percent of the global expenditure on food (Thomson Reuters, 2016).

Muis *halal* certification has evolved to certify various products and establishments within the value chain, corresponding to the changing Singaporean Muslim lifestyle. The products that Muis certified were simpler (e.g., ketchup, instant noodles) in the earlier years. Subsequently, this expanded into more value-added ones, such as health supplements and convenient healthy food, catering to the health conscious and busy professionals. Demand for Muis to certify '*halal*' corners within supermarkets has also grown, as Muslims seek out products that are not only *halal*, but of good quality too. Apart from products, Muis certifies food and beverage (F&B) services, which constitute more than 65 percent of the *halal*-certified premises in Singapore. The types of F&B services certified *halal* by Muis have evolved through the years, from food stalls to fast-food chain restaurants to hotel kitchens and hipster cafes. To manage the increasing demand from companies of various nature of business, Muis needed a strategy to effectively manage the voluminous applications without compromising on quality. This led to the introduction of the Muis eHalal System in 2007 to automate both front- and back-end processing of *halal* applications, and the outsourcing of its audit/inspection functions to Warees Halal Limited. The intent of the outsourcing was to allow Muis to focus on regulatory and standards development. As a company, Warees is more agile in ensuring the availability of adequate manpower to respond to market growth and demands. Muis also obtained ISO/IEC 17065 accreditation in January 2018 — a testimony that its *halal* processes and management systems conform to international standards for certification bodies.

As the *halal* value chain in Singapore becomes more diverse with the emergence of producers, supermarket operators, food preparation kitchens, and eating establishments that are certified *halal*, so do the supporting activities. One of the actors that play a significant role in the development of Singapore's *halal* industry are private consultants or consultancy firms. More companies rely on professional services to help attain Muis' *halal* certification, maintain an effective *halal* quality management system and advise on strategies to penetrate the Muslim market. This is one way how food companies overcome their day-to-day operational issues and manpower crunch within the food sector. Muis worked with Enterprise Singapore, formerly known as SPRING Singapore[11] and the Singapore Business Advisors and Consultants Council (SBACC)[12] to introduce a certification scheme for *halal* consultants in 2011. Under this scheme, prospective consultants are required to undergo training and assessment by Muis before they can be certified by SBACC and entitled to Enterprise Singapore's funding. This initiative was launched with the policy intent of facilitating demand for *halal* certificates while ensuring compliance within the *halal* industry.

Emerging Challenges

While the provision of *halal* certification has brought both social and economic benefits to Singapore, *halal* certification poses two emerging

---

[11] Enterprise Singapore was formed on April 1, 2018 following a union of International Enterprise Singapore and SPRING Singapore. Enterprise Singapore is the government agency championing enterprise development. It works with companies to build capabilities, innovate, and internationalise. It also supports the growth of Singapore as a hub for global trading and startups. As the national standards and accreditation body, Enterprise Singapore builds trust in Singapore's products and services through quality and standards.

[12] The Singapore Business Advisors and Consultants Council (SBACC) is an independent not-for-profit organisation that is supported and recognised by government agencies. SBACC governs the activities and certification of Practising Management Consultants. SBACC was formerly known as the Practising Management Consultants Certification Board.

issues, namely i) over-reliance on *halal* certification; and ii) proliferation of fake *halal* news.

Over-reliance on Halal Certification

One observation arising from the growing demand for *halal* assurance is the seemingly over-reliance on *halal* certification as the only means of discerning what is "*halal*". Some time in 2005, Muis received a long-distance call from a Singaporean Muslim on a work trip in Rome and was in a supermarket there. He asked whether an energy bar product was *halal* as it was not affixed with a *halal* logo. Although the ingredients were stated on the product and could have been used as reference to discern its *halal* status, it was evident that the caller was only comfortable after the validation from Muis itself. While it can be argued that such behaviour only stems from a need to be careful and sure, it is symptomatic of an over-reliance on the *halal* certification. A religious outlook survey of the Singapore Muslim Community conducted by Muis in 2011 revealed that 62.3 percent of the respondents disagreed or strongly disagreed with the notion that they were willing to consume food without the *halal* logo even if they considered the food is *halal*. According to Marranci (2012: 96), "many Muslims in Singapore unquestioningly follow certain *halal* practices as defined by unwritten (and unofficial) practices and *halal* logo, instead of applying acquired Islamic knowledge available on the subject". He added that younger generations are becoming so used to the green *halal* logo that they are not able, for instance, to implement strategies used by Muslims living in western countries which are still within the realm of Islamic orthodoxy. Arshad and Leong (2016) reported on the increasing trend of "*halal* extremism" as Muslim consumers are found to demand that even non-food items such as household and personal care products be certified *halal*. This raises the issue of whether some Muslims are practising the religion beyond what is expected of the primary religious requirements and traders are commercialising religion and *halal* by promoting what Muslims should use and consume.

The *halal* status of food remains unchanged with or without *halal* certification. There has been perception that a product without the *halal* logo is unsuitable for Muslim consumption. This is not true. *Halal* certification is voluntary in most countries, including Singapore. A product that bears the *halal* logo implies that the company has submitted an application to the *halal* authority or Islamic body in the country and complies with its requirements. Without the logo, it simply means that the company has not applied or does not fulfil the certification requirement, whether religious, technical or administrative in nature. Most foods are permissible for Muslims except those that are prohibited in the Qur'an and Hadith (prophetic sayings). To insist on *halal* certification for every product, especially if it exists in the natural state (e.g., spices, vegetables, carbon dioxide) and involves minimal processing (e.g., ice, steamed fish), is therefore unnecessary.

Relying solely on *halal* certification stems from the lack of knowledge that magnifies the fear of contamination and creates confusion regarding the limits of *halal* permissibility (Marranci, 2012). It impedes the ability for one to adapt in the absence of a *halal* logo on a food packaging or a certificate displayed at a food establishment especially in Muslim-minority countries. There is a need for Muslims to adjust according to the contextual circumstance and make informed decision on the *halal* status of a food or drink prior to consumption. Such behaviour is what Muis desires for the community: to 'hold strongly to Islamic principles while adapting itself to changing context' (Majlis Ugama Islam Singapura, 2006). To adapt does not suggest that each Muslim will forsake Islamic values and principles; rather, it means that one is able to thrive in all circumstances while living according to the religion.

Proliferation of Fake "Halal" News

The world is undergoing an era of democratisation of knowledge where the acquisition and spread of information occurs among the common people, not just the privileged few. Public libraries and modern digital technology such as the internet has made it possible through the open access of information to the masses. The advent of social media such as Facebook, Instagram, and Twitter has further democratised information. Social media is a group of internet-based applications that allows the creation and exchange of User Generated Content in a participatory and collaborative fashion (Kaplan and Haenlein, 2010). Today, 50 percent of the global population are internet users and 34 percent are active mobile social media users (Hootsuite, 2017). Singapore doubles this as 70 percent of its population are active users on-the-go due to having its average fixed internet connection speed close to three times the global average (Tan, 2017).

Unfortunately, the internet has been used to amplify fake news. This happens due to unrelieved anxieties and uncertainties to make sense of a stressful and nebulous situation by theorising one's own and through others when no acceptable information is available (Rosnow *et al.*, 1986). *Halal* is not spared from the proliferation of misinformation via the internet. In 2007, chaos erupted in the *halal* cyberspace when a picture of "*halal*" pork, supposedly certified by Muis, was circulated online. In 2013, claims emerged that the Muslim Judicial Council of South Africa had withdrawn McDonald's *halal* certificate due to traces of pork fat in its sauces. In 2017, Magnum ice-cream, which is certified *halal*, was rumoured to contain E471 derived from pork. These are just some of the internet claims found to be untrue.

The spread of fake news, particularly through the media systems, can be problematic. According to Lewandowsky *et al.* (2012), people are generally geared towards the acceptance of new information rather than towards scepticism, especially when they confirm the person's pre-existing attitude, regardless of whether the information is true or otherwise. The research further concludes that misinformation is more difficult to debunk as it becomes widespread and popularly held. Fake news relating to *halal*-certified food cast doubt on the credibility of the *halal* certification regime. They also create *waswas* (sense of doubt) among consumers who would then shun the product which then affects businesses and their established brands. From a religious perspective, the act of spreading falsehood is considered to be more sinful than killing and thus has to be avoided.[13]

Conclusion

The demand for *halal* certification has grown in Singapore since 1978. This is primarily driven by globalisation of food systems, increasing religiosity, and the burgeoning *halal* industry. As an Islamic body charged with the sole responsibility to issue *halal* certificates in Singapore, Muis has made efforts to manage the burgeoning market by facilitating demand for *halal* food and strengthening compliance within the industry through legislative, systems, and structural changes. Unfortunately, *halal* certification has its unintended consequences including consumer over-reliance on the *halal* mark and the proliferation of fake '*halal*' news.

Effective management of demand for *halal* food involves a tripartite arrangement: Muslim consumers, *halal* authorities, and businesses. Greater consumer involvement, referring to the time, thought, energy, and other resources people devote to the purchase process is necessary for Muslims to

---

[13] Qur'an, 2: 217.

make informed *halal* food decisions (George and Edward, 2009). In fact, Muslims are advised to always read the product labels, with and without a *halal* logo, to ensure that the ingredients are good and wholesome for the human body. In the absence of a *halal* mark or certificate, consumers must adapt and decide for themselves the permissibility of food based on other alternative information such as the food labels and company/product information from credible websites. *Halal* authorities such as Muis must balance their roles in response to the burgeoning market. It is not only to meet the certification demands of the industry, but importantly, they have a religious obligation and fiduciary duty to ensure high standards of compliance to maintain trust and confidence in the *halal* system. Authorities also have a role to play in educating the public on *halal* to help them make informed food choices. They must keep up with the times by leveraging on new technology such as the social media to lend a credible voice in the space of democratised *halal*-related information. Muis has found its outreach efforts through its Twitter account, @halalsg, to be extremely effective in combating fake news online and educating the public in a timely manner. For *halal* businesses, complying with certification requirements is not just for commercial purpose but a social accountability towards the Muslim community whom they serve. This tripartite arrangement, involving consumers, authorities, and businesses is crucial to effectively manage the growing demand for *halal* food in Singapore.

References

Agri-food and Veterinary Authority of Singapore (2015). The Food We Eat. Retrieved from http://www.ava.gov.sg/explore-by-sections/food/singapore-food-supply/the-food-we-eat.

Al-Mazeedi, H., Regenstein, J., and Riaz, M. (2013). The issue of undeclared ingredients in *halal* and kosher food production: a focus on processing aids. *Comprehensive Reviews in Food Science and Food Safety*, 12(2), pp. 228–233.

Al-Qaradawi, Y. (2001). The Lawful and the Prohibited in Islam (K. al-Hilbawi, M. Siddiqi and S. Shukri, Trans.). *Cairo: Al-Falah Foundation for Translation, Publication and Distribution*.

Arshad, A. and Leong, T. (2016, June 14). Rising trend of *halal* labelling generates concern. *The Straits Times*, p. A12.

Association of Muslim Professionals (2012). Publications. Retrieved from http://www.amp.org.sg/publications/

Codex Alimentarius (2001). Codex general standard for the labelling of pre-packaged food. Retrieved from http://www.fao.org/docrep/005/Y2770E/y2770e02.htm

Darby, M. and Karni, E. (1973). Free competition and the optimal amount of fraud. *Journal of Law and Economics*, 16, pp. 67–88.

Department of Statistics Singapore (2017). Singapore in Figures 2017. Retrieved from https://www.singstat.gov.sg/docs/default-source/default-document library/publications/publications_and_papers/reference/sif2017.pdf.

George, B. P. and Edward, M. (2009). Cognitive dissonance and purchase involvement in the consumer behavior context. *IUP Journal of Marketing Management*, 8(3/4), p. 7.

Ghaus, F. (2014, June 3). Drivers of the dynamic *halal* market. Retrieved from http://www.apfoodonline.com/index.php/features/item/334-drivers-of-the-dynamic-*halal*-market

Hamzah, N. (1994, March 29). Muis tarik balik sijil *halal* firma penyembelih ayam. *Berita Harian*, p. 1.

Hootsuite (2017). New Research Reveals Global Social Media Use Increased by 21 Percent in 2016. Retrieved from https://hootsuite.com/en-sg/newsroom/press-releases/digital-in-2017-report.

Hussaini, M. M. (1993). *Islamic dietary concepts and practices*. The Islamic Food and Nutrition Council of America.

Jahangir, M., Mehmood, Z., Bashir, Q., Mehboob, F., and Ali, K. (2016). *Halal* status of ingredients after physicochemical alteration (Istihalah). *Trends in Food Science and Technology*, 47, pp. 78–81.

Kaplan, A. M. and Haenlein, M. (2010). Users of the world, unite! The challenges and opportunities of Social Media. *Business Horizons*, 53(1), pp. 59–68.

Lapidus, I. (1997). Islamic Revival and Modernity: The Contemporary Movements and the Historical Paradigms. *Journal of the Economic and Social History of the Orient*, 40(4), pp. 444–460.

Lewandowsky, S., Ecker, U. K., Seifert, C. M., Schwarz, N., and Cook, J. (2012). Misinformation and its correction: Continued influence and successful debiasing. *Psychological Science in the Public Interest*, 13(3), pp. 106–131.

Majlis Ugama Islam Singapura (2006). Risalah for Building a Singapore Muslim Community of Excellence. Retrieved from http://www.muis.gov.sg/officeofthemufti/documents/Risalah-eng-lr.pdf.

Marranci, G. (2012). Defensive or offensive dining? *Halal* dining practices among Malay Muslim Singaporeans and their effects on integration. *The Australian Journal of Anthropology*, 23(1), pp. 84–100.

Mohamed, Z., Rezai, G., Shamsudin, M. N., and Eddie Chiew, F. C. (2008). *Halal* logo and consumers' confidence: What are the important factors. *Economic and Technology Management Review*, 3(1), pp. 37–45.

Mohtar, J. (1992, August 4). Syarikat gunakan label *halal* tanpa izin. *Berita Harian*, p. Back.

Mukhtar, A. and Mohsin Butt, M. (2012). Intention to choose *halal* products: the role of religiosity. *Journal of Islamic Marketing*, 3(2), pp. 108–120.

Nakyinsige, K., Che Man, Y., and Sazili, A.Q. (2012) *Halal* authenticity issues in meat and meat products. *Meat Science*, 91, pp. 207–214.

Official Reports of Parliamentary Debates (Hansard), Vol. 69, 1998, June 30.

Omar, E. N., Jaafar, H. S., and Osman, M. R. (2013). Halalan Toyyiban Supply Chain of the Food Industry. *Journal of Emerging Economies and Islamic Research (JEEIR)*, 1(3).

Rezai, G., Mohamed, Z. A., and Shamsudin, M. N. (2012). Assessment of consumers' confidence on *halal* labelled manufactured food in Malaysia. *Pertanika Journal of Social Sciences and Humanities*, 20(1), pp. 33–42.

Riaz, M.N. and Chaudry, M.M. (2003). *Halal Food Production*. CRC press.

Rosnow, R. L., Yost, J. H., and Esposito, J. L. (1986). Belief in rumor and likelihood of rumor transmission. *Language and Communication*, 6(3), pp. 189–194.

Salleh, Z. (1977, September 4). Penyembelih ayam di pasar akan diberi surat tauliah Muis. *Berita Harian*, p. 2.

Shetty, P. (2003). Impact of globalisation on food and agriculture from the farm to the plate. In *Workshop on Impacts of Globalization on Agricultural Production and Marketing with Focus on Food Quality, Tokyo (Japan), 22–24 January 2003*. Japan FAO Association.

Tan, A. (2017). 7 in 10 Singaporeans use social media on mobile, double global average: survey. Retrieved from http://www.businesstimes.com.sg/consumer/7-in-10-singaporeans-use-social-media-on-mobile-double-global-average-survey.

The Straits Times (1978, March 23). Deceptive '*halal*' label: Council will press for prosecution. *The Straits Times*, p. 9.

The Straits Times (1992, October 21). First Restaurant to Lose *Halal* Certificate. *The Straits Times*, p. 24.

The Straits Times (1994, August 26). Rise in number of complaints against authenticity of *Halal* food imported and sold here. *The Straits Times*, p. 31.

Thomson Reuters (2016). State of the global Islamic economic report 2016/2017.

Tieman, M., Van der Vorst J.G.A.J., and Ghazali, M.C. (2012). Principles in *halal* supply chain management. *Journal of Islamic Marketing*, 3(3), pp. 217–243.

Turcsik, R. (2001). Kosher and *halal*: more than just product. *Supermarket Business*, 56(11), p. 81.

van der Spiegel, M., van der Fels-Klerx, H., Sterrenburg, P., van Ruth, S., Scholtens-Toma, I., and Kok, E. (2012). *Halal* assurance in food supply chains: Verification of *halal* certificates using audits and laboratory analysis. *Trends in Food Science and Technology*, 27(2), pp. 109–119.

Vijaykumar, S., Lwin, M. O., Chao, J., and Au, C. (2013). Determinants of food label use among supermarket shoppers: a Singaporean perspective. *Journal of Nutrition Education and Behavior*, 45(3), pp. 204–212.

Weber Shandwick (2014). Food Forward Trends Report 2014 (Singapore). Retrieved from http://webershandwick.asia/wp-content/uploads/2014/04/FF-SINGAPORE-16April.pdf.

Wong, S. (2016, March 23). Singapore remains top Muslim-friendly destination among non-Muslim countries. Retrieved from http://www.straitstimes.com/singapore/singapore-remains-top-muslim-friendly-destination-among-non-muslim-countries.

Yeo, C. (2011, August 4). Golden Churn butter confirmed to contain pig DNA, says Daud. Retrieved from https://www.thestar.com.my/news/community/2011/08/04/golden-churn-butter-confirmed-to-contain-pig-dna-says-daud/.

Yong S. (2017, May 12). The pillars of growth for 2013. Retrieved from http://www.apfoodonline.com/index.php/features/item/75-the-pillars-of-growth-for-2013.

Yong, Y. N. (2014, June 3). Cadbury chocs free of pork, says Malaysia's Islamic Authority. *The Straits Times*, p. A7.

ANNEX A: KEY MILESTONES OF MUIS *HALAL* CERTIFICATION

The Beginning (1978 — 1989)

- Introduced Muis *halal* certification services
- Began issuing *halal* certificates for products, eating establishments and slaughterhouses

Building Foundation (1990 — 1999)

- Introduced the Muis *halal* certification mark
- Began issuing *halal* certificates for poultry abattoirs, imported meat and food preparation areas (catering and supermarkets)
- Amended the Administration of Muslim Law Act (AMLA) to govern *halal* certification in Singapore
- Joined the ASEAN Working Group on Halal Food (AWGHF)

Coping with Demand (2000 — 2009)

- Obtained ISO 9001 certification, in compliance with international standard for quality management system
- Developed Singapore Muis Halal Standards
- Began issuing *halal* certificates for storage facilities, whole plant and non-food products
- Formed Warees Halal division within Warees Investments Pte Ltd to issue *halal* certificates to foreign companies
- Launched the Muis eHalal System, which automates both front- and back-end processing of *halal* applications
- Published the Singapore Halal Directory, in hardcopy and online versions
- Introduced the Singapore Muis Halal Quality Management System (HalMQ), a set of systems-based *halal* certification requirements to enhance industry compliance
- Attained *halal* recognition through the Gulf Cooperation Council — Singapore Free Trade Agreement (GSFTA)

Sustaining Growth (2010 onwards)

- Joined the MABIMS Special Technical Committee on Halal Development

- Imposed *halal* training and assessment as a mandatory requirement for certified companies
- Partnered Singapore Business Advisors & Consultants Council (SBACC) and Enterprise Singapore to certify *halal* consultants
- Corporatised Warees Halal as a not-for profit company limited by guarantee
- Leveraged social media (@halalsg) for *halal* public education
- Attained ISO 17065 certification, in compliance with international requirements for bodies certifying products, processes and services

12

SEEKING THE MEANING OF SACRIFICE: EVOLUTION OF *KORBAN* IN SINGAPORE

Sakdun Sardi

Korban is the slaughter of livestock as an act of worship by Muslims carried out on *Eidul Adha,* also known as *Hari Raya Haji,* or during the three days after it. Goats, sheep, camels, cows, and cattle are livestock normally used for *korban.* There is no difference between a *korban* slaughter and the normal method of slaughtering of livestock, except in the intention of the person performing the slaughter. As an act of worship, the animal used for *korban* must be in good health and free from any disability or handicap. *Korban* is also more than just a personal act of worship. The meat of the slaughtered animal is normally divided into three parts: one-third for the poor and needy, one-third for relatives and friends, and the remaining portion for the person performing the *korban.* In Singapore, mosques offering *korban* services distribute *korban* meat to poor and needy families, as well as to transient workers who are not able to celebrate *Eidul Adha* with their families in their home countries. Due to the limited number of imported sheep for *korban* in Singapore, many local Muslims perform *korban* overseas and, at the same time, provide relief to the sufferings of some of the disadvantaged Muslim communities in other parts of the world.

On 30 May 2011, an Australian investigative journalism/current affairs documentary television programme, *Four Corners*, revealed a shocking exposé of the cruelty inflicted on Australian cattle exported to slaughterhouses of Indonesia. The programme showed video footages taken by the television station's team, and separately by animal activists across a range of slaughterhouses in Indonesia. These footages showed cattle being subjected to a range of horrifying acts of brutality, mainly due to the inability of workmen at these slaughterhouses to handle the cattle inside the processing plants. Cattles smashed their heads repeatedly on concrete floor as they struggle against ropes, and took minutes to die in agony after repeated and clumsy cuts to the throat. In some cases, the cattle were also subjected to horrifying cruelty such as kicking, hitting, eye-gouging, and tail breaking as workers try to force the cattle to go into the slaughter boxes.

This exposure caused major public outrage and soon resulted in the suspension of all livestock exports to Indonesia (*The Straits Times*, 2011). Subsequently, the Australian Government commissioned an independent review to look into issues of livestock export trade and animal welfare for livestock exports. On 29 July 2011, delegates from the Austalian Government, including its First Secretary of the Australian High Commission in Singapore, visited the Islamic Religious Council of Singapore (Muis) to inform about the pending implementation of new rules governing the export of Australian livestock worldwide. Australian livestock is exported to Singapore only for the purpose of the annual *korban*. On 21 October 2011, the Australian Government announced its new regulatory framework — the Exporter Supply Chain Assurance System (ESCAS) — for livestock exports to improve the welfare of exported Australian livestock. Under the new regulatory framework, Australian exporters seeking a permit to export livestock will need to show that the animals are handled in accordance with the World Organisation for Animal Health (OIE) animal welfare guidelines, right from the farm in Australia and up to the point of slaughter. The exporters will have to ensure that there is control of the animal movement within the supply chain, the animals can be tracked and accounted for throughout the supply chain and independent audits are carried out to ensure compliance with these new requirements.

Korban operations carried out at mosques and Malay/Muslim organisations (MMOs) were generally *gotong-royong* events,[1] where volunteers assist in the handling, slaughtering, and processing of meat without proper training in the various procedures other than basic food hygiene standards regularly emphasised by the Agri-Food and Veterinary Authority of Singapore (AVA). Methods and equipment used were often improvised and improved over the years without any comparison to industry standards used in abattoirs or any real consideration to international standards for animal welfare. Even though volunteers at the mosques and MMOs are aware of the Islamic religious injuction to be kind to animals, most do not know exactly how to do so, such as in areas of animal handling and slaughtering techniques. However, as *korban* is carried out only once a year, not much attention was given on these matters until the review of livestock exports by the Australian Government which threatened the import of Australian livestock to Singapore.

There are essentially two parts to the challenge faced by Muis in ensuring *korban* continued to be performed in Singapore. First is to ensure the supply of livestock. Under the law, livestock may only be imported from AVA-approved countries which have been assessed to be able to meet the standards for public health, food safety, as well as animal health and welfare. One of the key requirements is freedom from Hand, Foot and Mouth Disease (HFMD), as well as other major diseases of importance to public and animal health in the exporting country. Muis works very closely with AVA and the livestock importer to ensure supply of livestock for *korban*. Second is to meet the OIE requirements for animal welfare when handling the *korban* animals. Under the ESCAS regulatory framework, this involved subjecting our religious rituals to external audits by international auditors engaged by the Australian livestock exporter. This was unprecedented and could potentially lead to a clash between the need for the Singapore Muslims community to continue with their traditional method of performing their religious rituals, and the need to comply with the Australian livestock export regulations. This requires the collaborative efforts involving government agencies (Muis and AVA), the private sector (livestock exporter from source country, local livestock importer, and the airport operator), the community (management

---

[1] "Etymologically, the phrase *"gotong-royong"* comes from Javanese, *"gotong"* meaning foster and *"royong"* meaning together. *Gotong-royong* as a concept has two meanings: respective capacity, towards completion of a task for public/common interest. As a spirit: the attitude of mutual cooperation or assistance." (Rasheed and Saat, 2016).

of *korban* centres at mosques and MMOs and their volunteers) as well as members of the public performing the *korban*. It involves setting clear policies and procedures to meet the evolving new challenge, engagement of all stakeholders for their support, and ensuring compliance with the policies and procedures while safeguarding the local food security. Evidently, the way the *korban* has evolved in Singapore is an example of a progressive and adaptive religious outlook which leverages technical and industrial expertise. This ensures the fulfilment of contemporary requirements in animal welfare and food safety as well as operational meticulousness and efficiency while keeping alive the spirit of *gotong-royong* in performing religious rituals.

This chapter will first cover major milestones in *korban* implementation in Singapore. Second, it will cover the new *korban* operation regime implemented by Muis to ensure that the Muslim community would be able to continue to perform *korban* in Singapore following the implementation of the ESCAS by the Australian Government. Third, it will cover the criticism on *korban* in Singapore. The chapter will conclude by discussing future challenges in *korban* operations in Singapore and how they may evolve in future.

Major Milestones In *Korban* Implementation

Prior to the formation of Muis in 1968, there was no central management of *korban* in Singapore. *Korban* services, covering supply of animal, slaughtering, skinning, butchering, and waste disposal, were offered by mosques and MMOs to meet the demand of the local Muslim community. The annual event was also a source of income for the mosques and MMOs. With the formation of Muis, *korban* continued to be managed individually by mosques and MMOs. When the supply of local livestock ceased to exist following the phasing out of farmland in the 1960s, there were a few suppliers offering imported livestock imported for *korban* in Singapore. There was no standardisation on the price of animals as the purchase of livestock was left to individual mosques and MMOs. In the 1970s and 1980s, there were calls from the Muslim community for better central procurement of *korban* animals and to ensure consistency in prices and service delivery standards (Mohd Don, 1977). Due to different prices offered and occasional contractual issues faced with livestock suppliers, there were also suggestions for Muis to coordinate or organise the annual *korban* in Singapore (*Berita Harian*, 1980). At that time, Muis understood very well the difficulties involved in managing *korban* operations, and preferred that mosques and MMOs offering *korban* services continue to manage their own operations and procure livestock from their preferred supplier. Muis' stand then was that it would not want to take on new responsibilities unless it could discharge them satisfactorily. It also would not want to bear the brunt of public displeasure should there be any disruptions to the supply of livestock or when the prices of livestock went up, which were beyond the control of Muis. However, as the Islamic religious authority in Singapore, Muis was expected to play an active role in ensuring the supply of livestock for the annual *korban*.

Involvement of Muis in *korban* started in 1988 when it took legal actions against a businessman for the failure to deliver animals to three mosques and a madrasah (Hussain, 1989). To achieve better control on the supply and prices of animals, Muis worked with a few mosques to centrally manage the procurement of livestock in 1993. When Muis first started managing the central procurement, only eight out of about 40 mosques offering *korban* services at that time joined Muis in the open tender exercise. Over the years, more mosques were persuaded by the benefits of central management and, in 1996, the number of participating mosques grew to 33 mosques. However, the confidence in Muis was marred the following year in 1997, when the contractor appointed by Muis failed to deliver 3,424 sheep and 20 cows for *korban* at 35 mosques (Ismail and Ismail, 1997; Nadarajah and Ting, 1997). The Korban Review Committee formed to review, evaluate, and recommend the appropriate improvements for future *korban* found that the main reason for the debacle was the contractor's failure to provide for the necessary transportation for the delivery of livestock from Australia to Singapore. Muis was also blamed for awarding the contract to the lowest bidder without any consideration to its financial standing and track record, and failing to monitor the various stages of the contract until it was too late.[2] The findings of the Korban Review Committee provided valuable lessons for Muis and further strengthened the processes in sourcing of livestock for *korban*. Following the review, the Singapore Mosques Korban Committee (JKMS) comprising mosque representatives was formed to undertake the procurement of livestock for *korban*. The involvement of mosque representatives provided JKMS with the expertise required in relevant fields such as contract

---

[2] Report on the Review of the Procurement System for Livestock for the Korban Project submitted by the Korban Review Committee on 10 June 1997.

management, shipping and logistics. Under the management of JKMS, *korban* was conducted smoothly from 1998 to 2004.

In 2005, there was a major delay in the arrival of 4,500 sheep purchased by JKMS in Australia, which resulted in *korban* taking place two days after *Eidul Adha* but within the permissible period for the ritual. A Panel of Inquiry was formed to determine the causes of the delay and make appropriate recommendations. Two major changes were made to the management of *korban* in Singapore, namely, the privatisation of the supply of livestock in 2007, and the use of air freight for the transportation of livestock from Australia to Singapore instead of sea freight in 2009. Privatisation of *korban* involved the appointment of an Approved Korban Vendor (AKV) through open tender for the supply of livestock to participating mosques for *korban*. Under the sales agreement, *korban* participants purchase animals directly from the AKV, while Muis/JKMS ensure that all terms and conditions of the contract are properly managed. Participating mosques provide the facilities for the conduct of the ritual slaughter and facilitate the distribution of meat to the needy. When air freight was used in 2009, the time taken to deliver livestock from Australia was reduced from several days to several hours. This provided more certainty to the delivery schedule of livestock in Singapore. At that time, it appeared that Muis had finally developed and implemented a robust system for the supply of livestock for the annual *korban*, with good control over procurement processes, clear contractual obligations and responsibilities of all parties involved and mode of transportation that would guarantee timely delivery of livestock.

However, the implementation of ESCAS in 2012 posed a big challenge for our mosques in meeting the required animal welfare standards. Muis/JKMS worked with the mosques, the AKV, and the AVA to conduct a total review of *korban* operations, developed the required standard operating procedures (SOPs), conducted training sessions for personnel, and carried out the mandatory ESCAS compliance audits prior to the effective implementation date of ESCAS regulations for Singapore on 1 September 2012. The intensive collaborative efforts of various parties and government agencies paid off when the import of Australian livestock was finally approved in time for *korban* on 26 October 2012. However, the number of mosques and MMOs offering *korban* services were reduced drastically from 51 in 2011 to only 18 in 2012, and correspondingly, the total number of animals imported was reduced by about 54 percent from 5,476 in 2011 to 2,500 in 2012. Even with the implementation of ESCAS, there were growing calls by animal rights advocates in Australia for a total ban on livestock exports. Therefore, an inter-agency Korban Review Committee comprising officers from Muis, MCCY, and AVA was formed in December 2012 to explore the possibility of alternative sources of livestock in the event of supply disruption from Australia. As a result, Muis imported 500 lambs from Canada as a trial for *korban* at five mosques in addition to the 2,000 Australian sheep imported by the AKV in 2013. With the successful trial importation of lambs from Canada, the AKV was required to provide livestock from two sources. From 2014 to 2016, the AKV provided lambs from Ireland in addition to the supply of sheep from Australia. The supply from an alternative source allowed for an increase in the number of mosques offering *korban* services to 26 mosques, and the total supply of livestock for *korban* at mosques increased to 3,700 animals. Even though the livestock from Ireland is not subjected to ESCAS requirements, all mosques and MMOs in Singapore adopted the same planning and operational standards to ensure that proper animal welfare and food hygiene standards are observed at all centres during *korban* operations.

On 2 October 2014, Singapore experienced its first case of high mortality since imports of livestock were made via air freight in 2009. A total of 174 out of 2,200 sheep died upon arrival in Singapore from Perth, Australia due to heat stress caused by disruption of temperature in a section of the aircraft. On 10 September 2016, Singapore was struck with another case of high mortality when a total of 121 out of 1,700 lambs from Shannon, Ireland, died of heat stroke upon arrival in Singapore. Subsequently, Muis carried out a review and decided that from 2017, the appointed AKV would no longer be required to supply livestock from alternative sources. The reasons for this decision were that the risks of supply disruption from Australia are much less now compared to 2012 when ESCAS was first implemented. Any supply disruption due to the failure to meet ESCAS requirements is low because of consistently good audit performance reports for participating mosques over the last five years, which have led to Australian authorities allowing more mosques to be ESCAS-approved *korban* centres. With the successful implementation of ESCAS worldwide over the years, the Australian authorities take immediate action against their livestock exporters for any serious breach of ESCAS requirements, including revocation of export permits. In summary, the key developments in the implementation of *korban* in Singapore are as follows:

Year	Key Developments
1993	Muis took the lead by heading an internal committee with representations from mosques to centrally manage the procurement of livestock for the annual *korban*.
1998	Muis no longer sources for livestock. Mosques carried out their own procurement of livestock through the Singapore Mosques Korban Committee (JKMS) comprising mosque representatives. Muis assigned an *ex officio* in JKMS and also provided guidelines on tender specifications.
2007	Privatisation of the supply of livestock for *korban*, i.e., the appointment of Approved Korban Vendor (AKV) through open tender. Revised terms and conditions of contract. Sale of *korban* animal is between *korban* participant and AKV.
2009	Delivery of livestock to Singapore via airfreight instead of sea vessel.
2012	Implementation of the new Korban Operation Regime to meet ESCAS requirements.
2013	Muis imported 500 lambs from Canada as a trial for secondary source of livestock for *korban*.
2014	AKV required to provide livestock from secondary source. Irish lambs were offered to *korban* participants from 2014 to 2016.
2017	Muis decided to revert to single source of livestock for *korban* due to inherent high risk of transporting livestock over very long distance.

New Korban Operation Regime

To determine whether *korban* operations in Singapore were able to meet ESCAS requirements, AVA carried out a comprehensive survey during the *Eidul Adha* period from 2 to 7 November 2011. The survey involved 47 mosques, four MMOs and four livestock importers with a total of 5,476 animals (3,316 sheep and 2,160 goats). It covered every stage from the transportation of animals from airport to mosques/MMOs, and the entire *korban* operations. Based on their observations, AVA concluded that *korban* practices generally deviated from OIE guidelines on animal welfare, and that the standard of organisation and management of *korban* could be improved. It was clear to Muis/JKMS that there was an urgent need for a total revamp in the way *korban* was planned and conducted at the mosques in Singapore.

This was not only to meet animal welfare and food hygiene requirements, but also to comply with Islamic teachings on compassion in handling and slaughtering of livestock. More importantly, to ensure that all slaughtermen tasked to perform the sacrificial slaughters were able to carry out the correct slaughter technique required by the *Syariah*. Hence, JKMS in consultation with AVA, developed the new Korban Operation Regime that would prepare the mosques/MMOs for ESCAS audits. Under the new operation regime, JKMS developed SOPs that specify the requirements on planning for *korban* process flows, manpower requirements, and layouts of facilities to ensure good management and organisation of *korban* operations; training on OIE guidelines on animal welfare and training on specific areas for animal handlers, slaughterers, skinners, and butchers; and supervisory functions to ensure compliance to animal welfare, safety, and food hygiene standards. Manpower requirements for *korban* continued to be provided largely by volunteers at mosques and MMOs, and this cost is not included in the price of animal sold to *korban* participants. Administrative and utility costs are also excluded from the price as *korban* is considered as a service offered by the mosques to the community. However, actual operational costs incurred, such as costs of equipment, setting up of *korban* facilities, and other ancillary costs, are included in the price of *korban* animal. Under the new regime, JKMS would fix the annual mosque operational cost in consultation with participating mosques based on the average cost incurred per animal by all mosques offering *korban* services in the previous year. To facilitate the implementation of the new Korban Operation Regime, each participating mosque must appoint a Korban Operation Manager (KOM) to undertake the entire planning and operation at the mosques. KOMs are required to attend special training sessions conducted by JKMS. After completing the training sessions, KOMs are required to plan and develop their own local SOPs, organise their operations team, and ensure that team members undergo specific training sessions by JKMS/AVA. Under the new procedures, only mosques that have adopted and met the requirements of the new operation regime will be supported by Muis for AVA's approval of slaughter licences for *korban*. AVA required mosques/MMOs to submit the layout plan of facility where the animal holding area and slaughter process would take place, training records of personnel involved, and SOPs for transporting, handling, holding, and slaughter of animals. AVA also provided SOPs for animal inspection and emergency management to ensure proper care are given to the animals including injured animals.

To ensure compliance with the new operational standards, AVA/JKMS would make site inspections at mosques prior to *Eidul Adha* to ensure that the facilities and equipment meet animal welfare and food hygiene requirements. For example, facilities are free from protrusions and other objects that can cause injury to animals, are clean, and in good working order. Design of facilities considers protecting animals from extreme weather and provides good ventilation. Failure to comply with these requirements may result in AVA not issuing or cancelling the permit for slaughter at the mosque. The number of livestock allocated to each mosque is also controlled. KOM must demonstrate through a time and motion study that the facilities, available manpower, and the intended *korban* operation hours are able to manage the number of livestock requested by the mosque. This provided better control on work schedules and resulted in better levels of service delivery, in terms of timely slaughter and collection of meat by *korban* participants.

Under OIE guidelines, livestock must be loaded and transported in a calm and efficient manner to avoid pain and injury, and to minimise the risk of adverse animal health and welfare outcomes. Ramps are designed to minimise animals slipping or falling which can cause distress or injury to animals. The race is clear of any obstruction, protrusion, and sharp edges that could hamper the movement of animals or injure the animals. The floor of the race must not be wet or slippery. There is a specific space requirement for each animal kept in holding pen. The holding pen should be designed to facilitate natural movement of animals, prevention or minimisation of injury and stress to animals, shelter from sun and rain, and have proper ventilation. Troughs for feed and water are located for easy access by all animals, and are placed such as to avoid faecal contamination of feed and water. A catchment pen (big enough to accommodate three to five animals at any one time) must be constructed at the entrance to the holding pen to facilitate catching of animals for delivery to the slaughter area. It is no longer acceptable for animal handlers to chase after sheep in the holding pen and wrestle them to the ground to bring the sheep to the slaughter point. Proper handling technique must be employed to minimise stress to animals.

Slaughtering of animals is the biggest challenge faced in *korban* operations. The slaughter area must be totally shielded from public view and other animals, and facilitates calm and effective slaughtering process. All slaughtering process must be carried out on custom-made slaughter platforms to enable the animal to be securely restrained without undue stress and pain. The slaughter platforms must be kept clean between slaughters. Only trained appointed slaughterers are allowed to slaughter animals. The knife is one of the most important equipment in *korban*. Suitable knives must be used for different job of slaughtering, removing heads and hooves, skinning and evisceration, and butchering. For slaughtering, the length of the knife blade must be at least twice the width of the neck of the animal being slaughtered. Animals placed on the slaughter platform must be held securely, particularly the head and neck to facilitate sticking, before cutting the throat. Any movement may result in a poor cut, bad bleeding, slow loss of consciousness, and pain to the animal. The slaughter must result in a cut that severe the trachea, oesophagus, both carotid arteries, and both jugular veins of the neck without cutting the spinal cord. The knife must be razor sharp to ensure a swift and smooth cut across the throat behind the jaw and to ensure immediate and maximum gush of blood. Poor bleeding causes slow loss of consciousness and reduces meat quality. Therefore, in the new Korban Operation Regime, the sharpening of knives is an important activity that must be carried out at a designated area by properly trained personnel.

During the 2012 *korban* operations, six ESCAS auditors carried out performance audits at the mosques and MMOs as required under the Australian regulatory framework. Failure to meet ESCAS audit requirements may affect future applications for export of livestock to that supply chain. Representatives from the Australian livestock exporter were also present to observe the *korban* operations and provide guidance on animal handling and slaughter where necessary. In addition, a total of 50 AVA officers were attached to the 16 mosques and two MMOs throughout the *korban* operations, from the delivery stage up to the slaughter of the last sheep. At the closing meeting, the auditors noted that the *korban* operations met the ESCAS requirements, with minor issues which were immediately rectified. Overall, there were good procedures and processes in place, and high levels of hygiene were observed. AVA officers deployed to the mosques and MMOs agreed that there had been significant improvements to the *korban* operations carried out, and noted the strict observance of the new operational requirements by all involved. With the implementation of ESCAS and AVA's revised regulatory requirements for importation and slaughter of livestock for *korban* in Singapore, the price of *korban* animals sold to the public is standardised. Moreover, there is stricter control on the import of livestock to Singapore and for *korban* and, as a result, the AKV appointed by Muis is the sole livestock importer. In January 2015, the Australian Authorities published an ESCAS Report to provide details of what had and had not worked in ESCAS. The reported stated that the short development time and immediate implementation has resulted in a system that is clunky, rigid, and complex, at times. It was an administratively burdensome regulatory arrangement for both government and industry. Despite these shortcomings, the system has been effective in delivering improved animal welfare outcomes. In the document, Singapore was reported to have no allegations of non-compliance with ESCAS requirements. For the Singapore Muslim community, the implementation of ESCAS provided the impetus to review *korban* operations, ensure kindness and compassion towards *korban* animals, ensure proper planning and management of *korban* operations, and require all *korban* workers to be properly trained to perform their specific tasks before every *korban* season.

Criticisms on *Korban* in Singapore

With its vision of a gracious Muslim community of excellence that inspires and radiates blessings to all, a section of the community expects Muis to be involved in every aspect of the community's religious life. With its limited resources and huge areas of responsibilities, Muis will have to decide how much it should get involved in any particular aspect of the community's religious life. For the annual *korban*, the involvement of Muis has evolved from total non-involvement in the 1980s, to animal supplier in the 1990s, to its current regulatory role covering religious regulations relating to *korban*, appointment of vendor for the supply of livestock to the community, as well as to ensure compliance with statutory regulations with respect to importing and slaughtering of livestock. In performing this role, Muis employs the resources available at mosques to ensure that the Singapore Muslim community will be able to perform the annual *korban* in Singapore. As expected, there are criticisms and suggestions on the management of *korban* in Singapore. The first criticism is on the source of livestock supply. There are those who are of the view that it is the responsibility of Muis to ensure that there will always be adequate livestock for *korban* in Singapore. To this end, there have been proposals from the community for JKMS and Muis to form joint ventures with livestock farms in Malaysia, Indonesia, or other parts of the region (A. Rahman, 2012). Another suggestion is for Muis to work with the local Muslim business community to develop its own livestock farm for *korban* in Singapore (Syed Agil, 2012). This way, Singapore will no longer rely on Australia as the supplier of livestock for the annual *korban*. Such a business venture has its risks, and even if such a farm can produce animals for *korban*, the unit cost of the animal would not be as low as one would think compared to livestock from Australia where there are economies of scale from a huge livestock industry. Setting up a farm only for the livestock for the annual *korban* would not make a viable business plan. According to statistics from Meat and Livestock Australia, Malaysia imported a total of 25,283 cattle, 57,928 sheep, and 32,235 goats from Australia between April 2016 and March 2017. These figures illustrate that Malaysia is importing livestock from Australia even though Malaysia has its own livestock industry. The reason for this could be the competitive price offered by the Australians compared to local farms. Another factor could be the shortage of supply from local farms to meet demands. With many pressing issues facing the Singapore Muslim community that require immediate attention, it would not be tenable for Muis to allocate its limited resources to livestock farming business. Even if it does, there is no guarantee that Muis will provide a more sustainable source of livestock at a lower price than that of Australia. The second criticism is the issue of the price of animal for *korban*. Since the 1980s, there has always been some expectation from the Muslim community for Muis to reign over the price of animal slaughtered for *korban*. In 1981, there were unhappiness over the 20 percent increase in the price of sheep for *korban* from between $190 and $240 per animal in 1980, to between $240 and $280 per animal that year (*Berita Harian*, 1981). Throughout the 2000s, the price of *korban* animals continued to rise in tandem with the cost of living in Singapore and the costs of other goods and services. One of the biggest increase was in 2010, when the price of sheep increased by 28 percent from $292 in 2010 to $375. The price of sheep increased further in 2011 by another 18 percent from the previous year to $443.50 (Hasim, 2011). Between 2011 and 2016, the price of sheep has remained stable at an average of about two percent increase per year. The price of sheep in 2016 was $490. JKMS/Muis does not charge for their work or recover any costs incurred in managing the annual *korban* operations. The price of *korban* to the public is the sum of the price offered by the AKV through open tender and the mosque operation cost. Even though the price of sheep has remained stable over the last five years, JKMS/Muis has little control over the price of sheep as the appointment of AKV is made via open tender.

To keep prices low, JKMS/Muis has taken two steps. The first step is to specify the number of animals in the tender that would correspond to a full load of aircraft. This would ensure the lowest unit cost per animal for airfreight, which makes up a large portion of the cost of logistics. The second step is working with participating mosques to keep operation costs low and absorb overheads, such as the use of facilities and utility charges, as *korban* operation is a service to the community. Every year, the mosque operating cost is determined by taking the average cost incurred by all participating mosques in the previous year. This will encourage mosques to learn from each other and continue to keep operation costs low. However, there is no guarantee that the price will remain stable in the future, as livestock for *korban* in Singapore are imported, which means that the price of an animal includes the costs for logistics, operation costs, and other overheads. The third issue is with the new Korban Operation Regime implemented in 2012 to meet the ESCAS requirements. The new regime imposes strict procedures for the slaughter of animals, including having non-Muslims (AVA officers) stationed at the slaughter points to observe the Islamic religious rituals. There were criticisms against Muis in social media, alleging that by having to comply with ESCAS requirements, Muis is conceding that the way Muslims in Singapore has been conducting their slaughter rituals is not proper, or therefore not valid (*sah*), in the religious context. Others were not satisfied that Muis chose to comply with the Australian regulations and subjected mosques to ESCAS audits, instead of looking for alternative source of livestock from other countries. The President of Muis rejected these allegations, and explained that the requirements of ESCAS were similar to Islamic teachings on how we should treat the animals with compassion. He added that the same operation regime would be implemented even if we were to import livestock from another source not regulated by the ESCAS (Razali, 2012). The new operation regime also requires strict operational requirements in the handling and holding of animals. This has reduced the number of participating mosques which, in turn, has reduced the number of *korban* performed in Singapore. Singapore is probably the only metropolitan city in the world where slaughtering of livestock is allowed outside proper slaughterhouses or abattoirs. In the ESCAS report issued by the Australian Government in January 2015, Singapore was mentioned as the only exceptional case where temporary slaughter facilities, instead of abattoirs, are approved each year for the export of Australian livestock. While exceptions have been made by the authorities to allow for the annual slaughter of livestock at mosques and MMOs for *korban,* JKMS/Muis must ensure that all *korban* centres have sufficient space and proper facilities.

When JKMS conducted the review of *korban* prior to the implementation of ESCAS in 2012, many mosques were found to be unsuitable for *korban* operations, due to lack of space and their very close proximity to residential buildings. With rapid urban development, many of the current approved mosque *korban* centres may face difficulty when existing empty plots of land next to the mosques which are utilised for *korban* become unavailable in future. Thus, it may be expected that future *korban* in Singapore can only be maintained at the current scale or possibly, reduced further. This should not dampen the spirit of *korban* as there are increasingly more service providers providing for the community more options for overseas *korban*.

Conclusion

This chapter describes the evolution of *korban* operations in Singapore, covering the supply of livestock and the way animals are handled for *korban*. Although Muis was initially reluctant to get involved in *korban*, it eventually grew more involved. Muis had to learn quickly from setbacks and weaknesses, and implemented policies and procedures to avoid similar problems from recurring. Muis also has to work closely with the community and other government agencies to ensure successful implementation of *korban* policies. Over the years, Muis has strengthened control over procurement processes, developed clear contractual obligations and responsibilities of all parties involved, and identified the mode of transportation that would guarantee timely delivery of livestock. Muis successfully achieved in getting *korban* centres to implement new operational procedures to improve animal welfare and food hygiene standards. This was done through the introduction of specific requirements on *korban* operation areas, training of personnel, and performance of tasks such as handling and slaughtering of animals. Even though today's annual *korban* is conducted in a more regulated manner, the intent is to sustain the spirit of *gotong-royong* at the mosques and MMOs offering *korban* services to the community. More commitment is now expected of *korban* volunteers. They are not only required to turn up during the rituals, but are also required to undergo training sessions prior to *Eidul Adha*, to ensure that they are sufficiently competent to perform their tasks. Planning and management of *korban* operations are also more challenging, as Singapore becomes more densely populated with most mosques being located very close to residential buildings. While Muslims perform their *korban*, they must also ensure that other residents are not inconvenienced. Such adjustments which Muslims have to make, demonstrate the true spirit of sacrifice (*korban*) that is embodied in the annual *korban* ritual which will spur greater improvements in future.

Australia will continue to be Singapore's primary source of sheep for the annual *korban* for many years to come. This is because Australia is one of the biggest livestock exporters in the world with a mature livestock export industry. Australia is also the nearest to Singapore compared to the other AVA-approved countries (Canada, France, Ireland, New Zealand, and USA) for import of livestock to Singapore. Indonesia and Malaysia are also importing livestock from Australia to meet local demands. According to the Australia's Department of Agriculture and Water Resources, livestock (cattle, goats, and sheep) exported to Indonesia and Malaysia in 2016 were 616,194 and 148,384 animals respectively. Therefore, the price of animals for *korban* in Singapore will continue to be much higher than the price of the animals at the farms in Australia or the price of *korban* in neighbouring countries using local sheep or goats. The high price of *korban* livestock in Singapore is due to the high cost of transporting livestock from the farm in Australia to the *korban* centres in Singapore, as well as the operational costs at these centres. Muis will continue to ensure that there is a supply of livestock for the annual *korban* in Singapore, and obtain the best price for through the open tender process to meet the needs of the Singapore Muslim community.

References

A. Rahman, M. N. (2012, September 29). Cari sumber lain haiwan korban. *Berita Harian*, p. 29.

Berita Harian (1980, October 22). Muis disaran selaras kegiatan2 korban. *Berita Harian*, p. 3.

Berita Harian (1981, September 8). Harga kambing untuk korban naik 20%?. *Berita Harian*, p. 3.

Hasim, H. (2011, September 29). Ramai terkejut, gesa JKMS kawal harga bekalan. *Berita Harian*, p. 2.

Hussain, R. (1989, April 21). Gagal bekalkan daging korban: Lelaki diarah bayar $75,945. *Berita Harian*, p. 18.

Ismail, N. and Ismail, H. (1997, April 15). *Kambing, lembu korban terkandas. Berita Harian*, p. 1.

Mohd Don, A. (1977, November 22). Selaraskan harga: Muis boleh main peranan. *Berita Harian*, p. 8.

Nadarajah, I. and Ting S. L. (1997, April 16). 35 mosques forced to cancel ritual. *The Straits Times*, p. 3.

Rasheed Z.A. and Saat, N., *Majulah! 50 Years of Malay/Muslim Community in Singapore* (World Scientific Publishing Company Pte Ltd, 2016), p. 49.

Razali, N. A. (2012, November 5). Alami perjelas isu peraturan penyembelihan korban. *Berita Harian,* p. 3.

Syed Agil, S. G. (2012, October 6). Muslim Singapura upaya bina ladang haiwan korban. *Berita Harian*, p. 22.

The Straits Times (2011, June 9). Australia halts cattle export to Indonesia. *The Straits Times*, p. A29.

Part 4

Beyond the Singapore Muslim Community

13

INTERNATIONAL NETWORKING: BRINGING THE WORLD TO MUIS
Asri Aziz

Introduction

Muis was created with very specific functions and roles — to advise the government on matters relating to the Muslim religion in Singapore, and to administer specific matters relating to Muslim life in Singapore, such as the management of *haj*, mosques, Muslim religious schools, *zakat*, and endowments. Like all other statutory boards in Singapore, Muis has a very local focus. However, as will be seen, Muis' activities have gone beyond Singapore's borders, in a series of engagements which may be loosely called "international networking". This appears to go beyond its primary mission. The question becomes especially important given the fact that, despite being a statutory board, Muis' resources and revenue streams largely are derived from Muslim community assets such as *zakat* and *wakaf*. This chapter examines the triggers and motivations behind Muis' conscious decision to deploy efforts and (limited) resources on international networking, despite its primary local focus.

International networks traditionally refer to inter-connected systems which are able to communicate with each other. International networking, in the context of agencies, refers to the ability to establish links with each other and to work together without losing their independence (Learn and develop through networking, n.d.). For example, UNESCO sees value in cross-cultural comparisons of how values and ethics can be taught (UNESCO, 2017). In the context of Muis, it refers to the cultivation of relationships, whether with individuals, institutions, or even communities overseas. One overarching principle is that the expansion of resources on these networking efforts must result in some level of benefit. This benefit, however, need not necessarily be immediate or tangible, but will certainly eventually accrue to Muis and/or the Muslim community, and to the nation as well.

As mentioned, Muis is both a community and a state institution, tasked with representing and managing the interests of the Muslim community. Thus, it is well-placed to perform the role of a cultural bridge for all of Singapore's dealings with the outside world, especially in any interaction which involves any segment of the Muslim community or stakeholders. The following highlights Muis' efforts in fostering ties with organisations, institutions, and officials from the region and beyond.

Regional Networks

Since independence, Singapore has been a red dot in a sea of green. It is an anomaly, being a Muslim-minority state surrounded by two Muslim-majority giants, Indonesia and Malaysia, as well as Brunei. However, the history of the region meant that Singapore was well-placed to maintain good relations with her Muslim neighbours. There were existing regional networks formed out of commonalities of language, race, religion, and kinship, throughout Southeast Asia, particularly in Malaysia and Indonesia.

In the 20th century, Singapore was a hub for Islamic education in the region. Throughout the 1960s to 1980s, Madrasah Aljunied Al-Islamiah provided the nascent Islamic scholastic and intellectual incubation for many senior Islamic scholars from Malaysia and Brunei. Madrasah Aljunied graduates went on to become religious teachers back in their home countries (Madrasah Aljunied Al-Islamiah, 2016). This would lay the foundation for networking and collaboration with Muis' regional counterparts, in various Islamic institutions such as the state religious councils in Malaysia, and the Ministry of Religious Affairs and other religious institutions in Brunei. To this day, because of Madrasah Aljunied, many of Muis' senior officers as well senior *asatizah* in Singapore have close personal relationships with many senior appointment holders in many Ministries and religious institutions in Malaysia and Brunei. These personal networks also translated into professional networks as well.

Muis is well-placed to perform the role of cultural bridge for Singapore's relations and engagement with Muslim communities and authorities in the region. The clearest manifestation of this may be seen in Muis' membership in the Unofficial Meeting of the Religious Affairs Ministers of Brunei, Indonesia and Malaysia, more commonly referred to as MABIMS.[1] In the beginning, the idea of MABIM as a platform for regional collaboration for Muslim communities in Southeast Asia did not include Singapore, because the other three countries were the Muslim-majority countries in the region. However, thanks to the close personal bonds forged with the regional Muslim religious leadership because of the Madrasah Aljunied connection mentioned earlier, MABIM was open to include Singapore. There was an implicit recognition of Singapore as being part of the regional diaspora, despite the Muslim community being only a minority in secular Singapore.[2]

The admission of Singapore (through Muis) into MABIMS meant that Muis had to devote commensurate resources to ensure it could participate as an equal member in this regional collaboration with the three Muslim-majority countries — Brunei, an Islamic monarchy; Indonesia, which has the biggest Muslim population in the world; and Malaysia, which has always projected itself as a leading Muslim nation within the Organisation of Islamic Conference (OIC). This meant a commitment from management to these engagements, as well as allowing resources to be deployed, for planning as well as participation at various levels of MABIMS activities. It would have been entirely possible for Singapore to merely remain a passenger in this grouping. However, that would have meant not tapping more fully into the potential mutual benefits accruing from greater regional collaboration.

---

[1] MABIMS was officially formed on 7 August 1989 as a platform for religious ministers from Brunei, Indonesia and Malaysia to examine the issues facing the Muslim World (National Archives of Singapore, n.d.).

[2] In the first few years, Singapore attended MABIM meetings only as an observer, until its membership was cemented (and MABIM became MABIMS) in 1994 (Hanief, 1994).

From being a mere observer in the beginning, Muis became a full-fledged member of MABIMS and, indeed, has taken a very active role in this collaborative platform. In 2008, Singapore, led by then Muis President Haji Mohammad Alami Musa, spearheaded a review of MABIMS' strategic direction and consolidated MABIMS' existing sub-committees into eight focused areas of collaboration. The two initiatives coordinated by Singapore — the projection of the MABIMS ethos beyond MABIMS, as well as MABIMS Youth Leadership Development — were well-received, and spawned two projects which were among MABIMS' first co-creation initiatives in its history — the MABIMS Youth Bus Expedition, as well as the first MABIMS Humanitarian Project in Cambodia. Muis' forward thinking approaches to *fatwa* development, mustering current and future issues such as science, technology and bioethics, were very well-received by its peers among the MABIMS countries. This thought leadership continued in 2015, as Singapore again played an active role in the most recent MABIMS strategic review — spearheading collaborative efforts in sharing approaches to maintaining social cohesion in the face of increasing diversity — one of the biggest challenges facing the global Muslim community today.

In MABIMS, one finds a manifestation of international networking in the immediate region, through the cultivation of personal, institutional, and professional relationships which positively impact Singapore's interactions with the three countries, beyond MABIMS' official parameters itself, and supplementing diplomatic and consular relations by the Ministry of Foreign Affairs. Muis has indeed expanded its mission beyond its original local focus. For example, in the spirit of MABIMS, Muis is able to look into the welfare of Singaporean students studying in Muslim schools in Malaysia, Indonesia, and Brunei. Singaporean *halal* businesses are able to export their products into MABIMS countries without much difficulty, thanks to a mutual recognition of *halal* certification standards. Singapore is also kept closely abreast of developments in Muslim family law which may have inter-jurisdictional impact. When sensitive issues crop up in the region, the various MABIMS Senior Officers are able to comfortably share perspectives and exchange information, where necessary.

One welcome benefit to Singapore's relations with the region comes from one of the outcomes of this regional collaboration: the improvement in Singapore's image in the region, regarding the treatment and management of the Muslim community in Singapore. Muis is seen as an example of how the state respects the Muslim community. MABIMS fostered many interactions with religious leaders, and facilitated many learning journeys by institutions from districts, provinces and states in Indonesia and Malaysia to Singapore. It is not an exaggeration to say that, thanks to MABIMS, many popular myths about the alleged 'mistreatment' of the minority Muslim community in Singapore are corrected. One such popular myth was that the Singapore government had 'torn' down mosques and did not allow new ones to be built. This was a myth created because many places of worship, including mosques, had to be demolished as rural Singapore made way for industrialisation in the 1970s. However, Muis is able to neutralise this myth by referring to the state-facilitated Mosque Building Fund, which made possible the building of modern mosques in every new housing estates. Indeed, Muis is often able to turn such myths on its head, thereby assuring its regional visitors. For example, Terengganu, one of the staunchest Muslim states in Malaysia, sent some 2,000 of its officers to observe how Singapore manages its mosques (Dhuha, 2006).

Having developed internal capabilities to network at the regional level through MABIMS, Muis began expanding its reach by participating in the Regional Islamic Da'wah Council of Southeast Asia and the Pacific (RISEAP), an umbrella body for Islamic organisations in the region. The Muis model of managing Muslim religious affairs and its capabilities in managing key aspects of Muslim religious life drew earnest interest from RISEAP's Muslim-minority communities who were looking for possible solutions relevant to their own situations. This resulted in a Memorandum of Understanding between the Muis Academy and RISEAP for Muis to share its model with RISEAP members. This led to the PRISM (Programme for RISEAP Members) programme, which had its inaugural run in 2016, with delegates from Hong Kong, Sri Lanka, the Philippines, Thailand, Korea, and Malaysia undergoing workshops sharing Muis' best practices in *zakat* and mosque management. Extending from this programme, Muis officers subsequently visited Taiwan to assist in mosque design for the Muslim community there.

Expanding mission

The fulfilment of the role of "cultural bridge" and the broadening of Muis' mission to include international networking quickly expanded beyond the countries in MABIMS in the region. We can see in these regional collaborations how Muis is able to serve Singapore's interests. It should be noted that these engagements do not happen overnight. Muis was only able to pursue these engagements because it made the conscious decision to devote attention and dedicated resources to international networking — resources which ordinarily would have been devoted to its "local" mission.

Muis began to institutionalise knowledge management in this area, and built up relationships with other agencies in other ministries, as well as diplomatic missions in Singapore. Muis approached international networking with twin objectives — to build and strengthen networks which could bring additional benefit and resources to the Singapore Muslim community, and to add to the Singapore brand, thus manifesting the narrative of the Singapore Muslim Identity as a contributing member of Singapore society.

Muis began supporting Singapore's relations (Muslim and national) with other parts of the Muslim world, namely the Middle East. Muis facilitates the well-being of Singaporean Muslims performing the *haj* in Saudi Arabia as well as pursuing tertiary Islamic education in the Middle East and North African region.

At a national level, Muis' *halal* certification standards became a part of the Free Trade Agreement (FTA) signed by Singapore with the Gulf Cooperation Council (Hussain, 2008). This is a clear recognition by the state that the Muis model of managing Muslim affairs had acquired enough rigour and quality to be accepted as part of the Singapore brand. This is a higher level of public sector capability, leading Muis to have combined engagements with outward facing public agencies such as the Ministry of Trade and Industry, in addition to the Ministry of Foreign Affairs. Earlier, Muis also directly and indirectly supported Singapore's bilateral engagements with various Middle Eastern countries as Singapore was courting the region as part of the Asia-Middle East Dialogue (AMED).

Positive Models

In addition, Muis continues to add to the public relations value which the state can leverage by showcasing the religious institutions of the Singapore Muslim community (such as mosques) to visitors to Singapore with whom the state has had various foreign policy and economic engagements. For example, Muis is an important stop for parliamentarians from Muslim countries who are in Singapore engaging with their Singaporean counterparts. The Harmony Centre is also a frequent stop in the learning journey of foreign civil servants who are undergoing training at Singapore's Civil Service College or who are guests of the Singapore government. In this case, the Singapore public sector capability being showcased is Singapore's approach to managing diversity and maintaining social cohesion in the context of a secular state and multi religious society.

Singapore, having a minority Muslim community with positive relations with the (secular) state, a unique Singapore Muslim Identity suited for its context, and an efficacious way of managing socio-religious life, became a potential model for countries looking for a way for Muslim communities to coexist within the modern nation state. The successful showcasing of the Singapore model of administering its minority Muslim population would also raise the prestige of the Singapore Government. In 2017, the Harmony Centre welcomed His Royal Highness, Charles, the Prince of Wales (Seow, 2017). This example, as well as the collaboration with the minority-Muslim communities in the Regional Islamic Da'wah Council of Southeast Asia and the Pacific (RISEAP), coming from non-Muslim countries such as Australia, New Zealand, Japan, Korea, and Sri Lanka, is a clear indication of Muis' value to the state, and how far Muis' international networking missioning has developed (*The Straits Times*, 2016).

Indeed, Muis' international networks have long gone beyond the region. Beyond Southeast Asia and the Middle East and North Africa (MENA) region, Muis also began cultivating relationships with diplomatic missions in Singapore whose countries also have significant Muslim communities and institutions. In part, this allowed Muis to showcase its model to those countries too. However, international events soon provided another catalyst for this expansion of networks.

Silver Linings

The September 11 attacks became an important milestone for Muis. Extremist terrorism sharpened the potential for adversity for the Singapore Muslim community, as it tainted the image of Islam and threw a shadow of suspicion over the community. However, it also brought a silver lining and facilitated a widening of Muis' overseas network.

Post-9/11, in the wake of global events which precipitated a growing divide between the Middle East and the West (particularly the US and the UK), Middle Eastern countries were considering alternative areas of investment for their funds. The Singapore government, which had long been venturing overseas, was demonstrating increasing interest in developing relationships and business links with the Middle East. The successful administration of Muslim affairs in Singapore (through Muis) enhanced the credibility of the Singapore government in their outreach to majority Muslim countries. This would help their efforts to develop relationships and reach out to their markets. Muis and the Singapore Muslim community could serve as a cultural bridge to facilitate this — and it did, as mentioned before in the example of the GCC-S FTA and Asia-Middle East Dialogue (AMED).

Beyond economics, there arose a quest for a more 'moderate' version of Islam, as opposed to the radical and violent version peddled by Al-Qaeda. Suddenly, Southeast Asia's "smiling face of Islam" become a sought after version of mainstream Islam. While this term is often taken to refer to Indonesian Islam, Singapore has become a potential model for a 'moderate' Islam, particularly because it had a minority Muslim community who was able to integrate into Singapore's multi-religious society and secular state.

In the wake of this interest in models which could assuage the climate of fear caused by the threat of Al-Qaeda, international networking engagements flowed both ways, with Muis reaching out to its networks to learn, as well as offering its own experiences to interested visitors. Muis officers visited London and Spain, two countries with immediate experience in dealing with terror attacks. In addition, Muis received new visitors from Europe, such as France and Germany, who were interested in looking at how Singapore was administering the socio-religious affairs of Muslims. Muis also strengthened her existing networks with the UK, the US, Canada, and Australia, within the same ambit of the projection of a 'moderate' Islam and best practices in administering religious life in multi-cultural societies. These increased engagements yielded many benefits for the Singapore Muslim community.

For example, the increased networking with the US yielded a collaboration between Muis and the Connecticut-based Hartford Seminary, which has allowed Muis officers and Muslim interfaith practitioners to undergo training at the Seminary (Hussain, 2006). Many of these interfaith practitioners are from the Harmony Centre, which, as mentioned previously, has itself become a landmark institution in Singapore, receiving many visitors from overseas who are keen to learn from Singapore's model of maintaining interfaith harmony and social cohesion.

Through the networking with the UK, Muis was able to bring in scholars and prominent Muslims, including the current Mayor of London Sadiq Khan, who was in Singapore in 2006 as part of a delegation brought in by the Foreign and Commonwealth Office, and had engagements with the local community as well as policy-makers (Kwek, 2006).

Shaping Discourse

As a result of the renewed interest in 'moderate' Islam brought about by 9/11, Muis embarked on a new policy which capitalised on its international networks in a structured manner, as a deliberate strategy to glean additional resources and enhance its local programmes and activities. By this time, Muis already had an *ad hoc* network of contacts and collaborative partners, particularly in the areas of Islamic education and contacts with Muslim bodies around the world. The next logical step would be to cement existing ties and build new ones in a strategic, cohesive, and structured manner. It was also a time where the networks could be used to shape discourse in Singapore.

Muis used its networks to bring in distinguished scholars from all around the world. Why was this important? Muis saw the value of these scholars to articulate positions which needed to be made to policy-makers and non-Muslims — in particular, to reassure them about 'moderate' Islam. The primary vehicle for this is the Muis Distinguished Visitor Programme (DVP). The DVP was a product of Muis' international networking with Egypt as part of its support for Singapore's outreach to the Middle East in general. The DVP is designed to widen and deepen progressive discourses through engagement sessions, discussions, and lectures delivered by eminent Muslim statesmen, intellectual leaders, and thinkers of international standing to discuss contemporary issues on Islam and Muslims.

The DVP received support from the Singapore Press Holdings Foundation, whose patron was Singapore's seventh President Dr Tony Tan, who had been involved in the engagements with Egypt together with Muis. Distinguished Visitors were also accorded courtesy calls with the President and Prime Minister of Singapore, as well as engagements with ministers, interfaith and community leaders, in addition to engagements with the Muslim community. The late Grand Imam of Al-Azhar, Shaikh Muhammad Sayyid Tantawi, became the first Muis Distinguished Visitor in 2006 (*The Straits Times*, 2006).

The DVP is important because through it, Muis was able to project important narratives articulated by prominent international Muslims to both Muslims and non-Muslims in Singapore. It also served as validation for Singapore's approach in administering Muslim affairs. Other luminaries since then have included renowned historian Karen Armstrong, the former Archbishop of Canterbury Rowan Williams and Shaikh Abdallah bin Bayyah.

Other than its distinguished visitors, Muis has also brought in many other prominent scholars to speak on and present a wide range of perspectives, such as Olivier Roy, Giles Keppel, Hamza Yusuf, and Tariq Ramadan. Muis developed a network of progressive individuals and agencies who could serve as resources for the Singapore Muslim community, and moved towards more structured and focused engagements for specific target segments. For example, it was important to balance the over-emphasis on security and terrorism among policy-makers, which often led to a de-emphasis on the need to pursue a much-needed reformist and development agenda for the Muslim world.

Muis built relationships with progressive scholars in various fields in order to enrich the discourse as well as make resources available to the Muslim community. Hence, in 2008, Muis organised a conference specifically titled "Revisiting the Development Agenda in Southeast Asia". Muis also held an international conference on *wakaf* in 2006, as well as an international conference on Muslims in Multicultural Societies in 2009. In all of these conferences, Muis took care to include engagements with policy-makers and political office holders, so that the international scholars invited could share their perspectives and shape the discourse at a time when there was so much anxiety about the future trajectory of global Islam.

Recent Developments

International networking has become embedded into Muis workstreams. This can be seen in how Muis units are consistently receiving visitors from overseas who are keen to learn from Singapore,[3] and conduct learning journeys overseas to look at models to adopt, as well as international articulators for specific discourses.

Muis continues to engage in specific collaborations via MABIMS, which are now tailored to existing functions, such as the management of inter- and intra-faith diversity. Muis also continues to strengthen functions designed to specifically serve community segments overseas. For example, the Student Resource Development Secretariat (SRDS), which looks after the welfare of Singaporean students pursuing tertiary Islamic education overseas, has now been consolidated into the Student Career and Welfare Office (SCWO), with more Student Liaison Officers (SLOs) and a twin emphasis on both the MENA region as well as Southeast Asia. The Rahmatan Lil Alamin Foundation (RLAF) has channelled the humanitarian ethos of the Singapore Muslim community in the form of aid to victims of humanitarian crises all around the world since 2004.

Muis also continues to record markers of recognition for its model of administering religious life. Singapore's Halal Quality Management System (HalMQ) was adopted by TFK Corporation (Singapore Airlines Terminal Services (SATS) Subsidiary) to achieve *halal* certification for Tokyo's Narita Airport in 2014 (*The Straits Times*, 2014). Singapore's model of madrasah education has been adopted by several madrasahs in Indonesia. Visitors from Malaysia intent on learning how Singapore manages its mosques have become a regular part of the landscape. Interestingly, Brunei has adopted a very similar model to the Mosque Building Fund, first via voluntary contributions, and since 2017, through a compulsory monthly contribution scheme, to fund and build new mosques.

The network Muis has built over the years is also proving invaluable in another initiative being undertaken by Muis — the exploration of models for a local Islamic College. Muis has visited educational institutions in Egypt, Jordan, Turkey, the UK, the US, and Canada to look at viable models which it could eventually incorporate into its own version.

---

[3] Singapore mosques host an average of three delegations per month from overseas who come to see how mosques are run in Singapore and to get a snapshot of Muslim life. Singapore mosque officers from Muis also regularly present the Singapore experience of managing mosques at state-level conferences in Malaysia. Other divisions in Muis regularly participate in overseas conferences in their respective domains, e.g., *zakat* and *wakaf* management, presenting papers as well as learning from the experience of others.

The Way Forward

The primary outcome of Muis' regional collaborations and international networking is the accruing of benefits and resources for the community. Some of the benefits have been very tangible and clear, such as increased *haj* quotas, the export of *halal* products, scholarship opportunities, and access to scholars and discourses which help enrich the perspectives of the Singapore Muslim community, as mentioned throughout this chapter.

Other benefits are subtler. As Singapore's model for administering Muslim religious affairs accentuates, it naturally gains attention and recognition from overseas. This increases the mindshare for both Muis as well as Singapore abroad. In addition, Muis continues to play a role as a cultural bridge to support Singapore's relations abroad, both in the region and in economic quarters such as in the Middle East. This reinforces the value of Muis to the state and national society within which the Muslim community is an intrinsic part of.

However, these indirect benefits come at a cost. Every resource deployed in the pursuit of international networking is a resource which could have been deployed in what is arguably Muis' primary mission: the optimisation of the provision and administration of the community's socio-religious life and the strengthening of local religious institutions. Given that Muis is largely self-funded, with most of its assets contributed by the Muslim community, there is an implicit expectation that those resources, and Muis' efforts, be channelled directly to the community. In such a scenario, the only way Muis can justify its collaborative pursuit of the national interest through international networking is by making such initiatives be resourced from national, and not community coffers or if there are visibly enhanced benefits accruing to the community.

This idea of expectations is even stronger in the age of social media. Critics of Muis abound on social media, often alleging that not enough is being done to assist the poor and needy. Other popular negative narratives are that Muis serves the government interest first, ahead of the community, and that Muis is too "progressive" (read: "liberal", non-traditionalist) for the community, bringing in too many 'liberal' scholars.[4] Too aggressive a pursuit of

---

[4] Critics of Muis actually formed two Facebook interest groups: Singapore Muslims for an Independent Muis and Singapore Muslims Against Liberal Islam. Most recently (independently of these two pages), there was online criticism of Muis' visit to educational institutions in the US, as part of its search for models for the Singapore Islamic College. The critics pointed to the existence of a similar model already developed and implemented in Malaysia.

international networking may reinforce these negative narratives. Muis' dabbling in international humanitarian relief efforts may also have an unintended effect, as it raises expectations for involvement in more Muslim humanitarian crises, such as in Myanmar and Palestine.

This does not mean that Muis must reduce its international networking. On the contrary, globalisation and the rapid pace of change in the world and impact on all things local mean that it is even more vital for Muis to continue applying its international networking framework, and maintaining its efforts to bring benefit to the community, or mitigate negative trends from impacting the community. So many examples exist, as pointed out elsewhere in the book — how animal rights movements in Australia may impact the *korban* ritual in Singapore, for example, and how the lack of a clear authority impedes the full ratification of a Free Trade Agreement in certain countries. This may well necessitate the enhancement of dedicated resources to the existing international networking unit, which will not only maintain existing relationships and networks, but also scan the horizon for global developments which may impact the Singapore Muslim community.

Such an enhanced unit will have to draw on the current institutional knowledge available, but also incorporate analyses of current events and trends which may open opportunities and mitigate challenges for Singapore and the Muslim community. For example, will the new trend of low-tech, lone-wolf terror attacks around the globe, coupled with more cases of self-radicalisation in Singapore, increase Islamophobia and affect the social fabric of Singapore? Will the trend of foreign preachers on social media (some of whom appear innocuous but have been banned by Singapore) lead to less reliance on local religious authority (and hence, less relevance for Muis' existence)?

It is argued that the inter-connectedness of today's world, and its resulting impact on Singapore and the Singapore Muslim community, justifies the dedication of commensurate resources for the upscaling of Muis' current capabilities into a more capable and effective unit. Muis can no longer limit itself and its mission to activities within its shores. It must develop the intelligence to identify tendencies and trends, understand their potential impact, and not only make adjustments in terms of relationships and networks overseas, but even adjustments to the local context where necessary. No country and no community can afford to ignore the world.

Reference

Background of MABIMS (n.d.). Retrieved from National Archives of Singapore website: http://www.nas.gov.sg/archivesonline/data/pdfdoc/20170725002/Mabims%20Background.pdf.

Hanief, J. (1994, August 4). Singapura rasmi anggota Mabims. *Berita Harian*. Retrieved from NewspaperSG.

Hussain, Z. (2006, September 26). Muis in US tie-up to boost faith dialogue. *The Straits Times*. Retrieved from NewspaperSG.

Hussain, Z. (2008, December 16). Singapore, Gulf states sign landmark trade pact. *The Straits Times*. Retrieved from NewspaperSG.

International networking (2017). Retrieved from United Nations Educational, Scientific and Cultural Organization (UNESCO) website: http://www.unesco.org/new/en/social-and-human-sciences/themes/bioethics/ethics-education-programme/activities/international-networking/

Kwek, K. (2006, July 20). UK Muslim Leaders learn from Singapore's religious balance. *The Straits Times*. Retrieved from NewspaperSG.

Learn and develop through networking (n.d.). Retrieved from: https://www.nibusinessinfo.co.uk/content/advantages-international-networking.

Madrasah Aljunied Al-Islamiah A Tradition of Excellence Forging into the Future (2016). Retrieved from Madrasah Aljunied Al-Islamiah website: http://www.aljunied.edu.sg/about-us3/historical.

Seow, J. (2017, October 31). Britain's Prince Charles attends interfaith dialogue with religious leaders and young people. *The Straits Times*. Retrieved from: https://www.straitstimes.com/singapore/britains-prince-charles-attends-interfaith-dialogue-with-religious-leaders-and-young.

The Straits Times (2006, May 24). Egypt's eminent Muslim leader here on 3-day visit. *The Straits Times*. Retrieved from NewspaperSG.

The Straits Times (2014, September 25). TFK Corporation. *The Straits Times*. Retrieved from NewspaperSG.

The Straits Times (2016, May 31). Muis Academy signs partnership to train Muslim organisations in the region. *The Straits Times*. Retrieved from: http://www.straitstimes.com/singapore/MUIS-academy-signs-partnership-to-train-muslim-organisations-in-the-region.

14

SPIRIT OF BLESSINGS TO ALL: MUIS' CONTRIBUTION TO SOCIAL COHESION

Zalman Putra Ahmad Ali and Zainul Abidin Ibrahim

Introduction

The importance of social trust has always been foremost within the community not only for pragmatic reasons of survival, but it is also within the Islamic tradition. Muslims have been enjoined in the Qur'an to understand other communities and cultures so that they could learn from one another.[1] It is also embedded in the spirit of *rahmatan lil alamin* (blessings to all), which calls upon Muslims to bring goodness to everyone.[2] From the past until the present, the community has manifested this spirit through various efforts. Nevertheless, such efforts had been hampered by other circumstances which have projected Muslims in a negative light.

As early as the 1980s, the government was concerned how Singapore's social cohesion could be undermined through what it saw as an apparent heightened religious fervour among the local religious communities. This led to the introduction of the Maintenance of Religious Harmony Act, which came into effect

---

[1] Qur'an, 49: 13.
[2] Qur'an, 21: 107.

in March 1992. For the Muslim community, the concern on the issue of heightened religiosity, which could be traced to the rising trend of global Islamic resurgence in the 1970s and 1980s, became conflated with issues of national integration and loyalty to the country (Tan, 2004). Growing religious consciousness was perceived to be making Muslims isolate themselves from the mainstream. The community's shared history and cultural ties with the rest of the Muslim-dominated region, as well as close religious ties to the *ummah* or global community of Muslims, triggered questions on the community's ability to give its full loyalty to Singapore. This became further entrenched after 9/11, when terrorists attacked the World Trade Centre and the Pentagon in the United States. This was followed by the arrests in December 2001 of 15 local members of the Jemaah Islamiyah who were detained under the Internal Security Act (ISA) for their plans to bomb American and Western targets in Singapore. The perception that has emerged is that terrorism and aggression is inextricably linked to Islam, and that Islam is the cause of violence and terror. This episode has put Islam and Muslims in the spotlight, and there was serious concern on the impact of the level of social trust within the wider Singapore society.

This chapter will highlight the community's intrinsic spirit of inclusiveness, which was evident in earlier efforts to forge social trust whether institutionally through the formation of the Inter Religious Organisation (IRO) during the colonial period or efforts through individuals like the second Mufti of Singapore, Syed Isa Semait, and Habib Syed Hassan Al-Attas, *Imam* of the Ba'alwie mosque. This conviction to build a harmonious and socially cohesive society was pivotal in Muis' support for the Maintenance of Religious Harmony Act in the 1990s and the post-9/11 efforts, through the forging of the Singapore Muslim identity and the creation of new institutions like the Harmony Centre and the Rahmatan Lil Alamin Foundation (RLAF). Important lessons can be drawn from how Muis reconnected the extrinsic national imperative to build social cohesion to the community's intrinsic religious ethos of inclusiveness underlying the concept of *rahmatan lil alamin* (blessings to all). This has shaped the way Islam is understood and expressed in the religious life of Singapore Muslims and transformed the way religious institutions are managed. It has become the core inclusive message to nurture confident Singapore Muslims who are religiously devout and socially engaged with other communities in promoting good in the society and nation.

Community's Intrinsic Spirit of Inclusiveness

Inter-Religious Organisation (IRO)

Throughout the colonial period, the different ethnic communities have generally lived harmoniously, engaging in their daily business and interacting with one another while under the British plan of "divide-and-rule", where each community had their own distinct roles and were living in separate enclaves (Nasir *et al.*, 2009). Each community had its own social structure and was thus more inwardly focused on the interests of their respective communities. For the Muslim community, a key Muslim organisation which emerged early in the 20th century was the All-Malaya Muslim Missionary Society, or Jamiyah, formed in 1932, on the initiative of Maulana Muhammad Abdul Aleem Siddiqui, an eminent Muslim missionary, who arrived in Singapore in 1928 from Meerut, India. Jamiyah played a significant role not only in providing religious and welfare services and broadening the community's understanding of Islam, but also promoted understanding between different religious communities (Haikal and Yahaya, 1996).

The need for inter-community understanding became even more critical during the immediate post-World War II period, where there was political upheaval and uncertainty amid growing anti-colonial sentiments and independence movements across the colonised world. Maulana Muhammad Abdul Aleem Siddiqui again was pivotal when he initiated the idea of a board of religious leaders to work together on common issues of concern and spread good virtues in society (Lai, 2008). The idea of inter-religious solidarity had the support of religious and political leaders in Malaya, which eventually led to the formation of the Inter-Religious Organisation (IRO) in 1949.[3] The IRO aimed to inculcate the spirit of friendship and cooperation among the leaders and followers of different religions for the good of mankind, and give mutual respect, assistance, and protection among the adherents of different religions. It became the main platform for the various religious leaders to engage each other and work together, sometimes on contentious issues between them. It also ran education programmes which discussed religions and religion-related issues. The IRO played an important

---

[3] Originally named the Inter-Religious Organisation of Singapore and Johor Bahru, it was renamed the Inter-Religious Organisation of Singapore in 1961.

role in the weeks after the Maria Hertogh riots in the 1950s to reduce the tensions and initiate the reconciliation process (Aljunied, 2000),[4] originally a custody dispute between two families which gradually evolved into a serious ethnic and religious conflict due to the mishandling and exploitation of a religious issue by political or social groups.

Since the beginning and until the present time, Jamiyah Singapore has been at the forefront representing the Muslim community in the IRO. Then Jamiyah Singapore President, Dato Syed Ibrahim Omar Alsagoff, was among the founding members of IRO and, through him, Jamiyah was consistently supportive of IRO in the provision of premises, facilities, and manpower for key IRO activities (Lai, 2008). This strong and active support was continued by subsequent generations of president and staff, including Haji Abu Bakar Maidin, who became IRO President in 2003–2004. Another prominent Muslim leader who was active in IRO was Dr Ahmad Mohamed Ibrahim, Singapore's Attorney General (1965–1967) who drafted the IRO constitution, and was also responsible for the legislation of the Administration of Muslim Law Act (AMLA) which gave birth to Muis in 1968. The active involvement of Jamiyah and those prominent individuals in driving IRO reflected the spirit of inclusiveness and commitment to religious harmony and social cohesion, which was evident long before Singapore became an independent nation.

Individual Efforts: Mufti Syed Isa Semait and Habib Syed Hassan Al-Attas

A similar spirit was also evident through two other prominent individuals who were also central in manifesting the ethos of *rahmatan lil alamin*. First is the second Mufti, Syed Isa Mohd Semait, who also played an active role in IRO.[5] It was through Dato Syed Ibrahim Omar Alsagoff that Mufti Syed Isa became first exposed to the IRO (Hussain, 2012). Prior to becoming Mufti, during his youth, he had a stint at the Iraqi Consulate where Dato Syed Ibrahim Omar Alsagoff was the honorary consul. It was there that he first read the reports and magazines of the IRO, and became attracted to its mission. Three years after his appointment as the Mufti of Singapore, Syed Isa became a council member of the IRO in 1975, and was subsequently

---

[4] The Maria Hertogh riots occurred in Singapore between 11 and 13 December 1950 over the custody lawsuit of Maria Hertogh, which left 18 people dead and 173 injured.

[5] Syed Isa Mohd Semait was the second Mufti of Singapore from 1972 to 2010.

made a life member of the group. Through Mufti's work at IRO, Muis was able to build close links with the other religious leaders. By 1993, when Syed Isa became the President of IRO, he already had a rich experience in resolving controversial issues privately in a calm and objective manner with other religious leaders whom he regarded as close friends.

Another prominent individual who has been active in promoting social cohesion and inter-religious harmony is Habib Syed Hassan Al-Attas, the *Imam* of Ba'alwie Mosque. Habib Hassan continued the good work of his late father, Habib Syed Muhammad Bin Syed Salim Al-Attas, who founded the Ba'alwie Mosque, and became its first *Imam* in 1952. Since its opening, the mosque has been a pioneer in interfaith work through the way it has been very open and welcoming to people of all faiths. Habib Hassan has designated a space in the mosque where he displays his family's collection of ancient Islamic artefacts and copies of the Qur'an and other holy scriptures. Over the years, Habib Hassan has hosted various religious, community, and grassroots groups, not only to share aspects about Islam, but also to forge close links and build friendships (Tay, 2009). His hospitable approach has inspired others including other mosques to follow suit by welcoming other communities for meals during Ramadan or festive seasons. For his work, Habib Hassan received an award from the IRO in 2015, recognising his contribution to interfaith efforts (Mahbob, 2013).

The above examples have demonstrated that the community's involvement in promoting social cohesion is not merely to comply to national imperatives for social cohesion. The early activism of Jamiyah and prominent individuals like Syed Ibrahim Omar Alsagoff, Haji Abu Bakar Maidin, Mufti Syed Isa Mohd Semait, and Habib Syed Hassan Al-Attas reflected the natural and organic inclination to be committed to social cohesion. It has been driven by the spirit of inclusiveness that is inherent in the Islamic tradition.

However, through the influence of certain religious ideas, small segments in the community became inclined to keep themselves from involving with the larger society as a way of ensuring that their religious belief and practice remains pure and uncorrupted. Such exclusivist orientation became a concern that it could undermine social cohesion. Subsequently, through geopolitical developments in the Middle East, particularly the Afghan-Russian war, the exclusivist strand spawned into a more virulent violent strand, which eventually grew to become the perpetrators of global terrorism.

Commitment to Religious Harmony and Social Cohesion

Maintenance of Religious Harmony Act

In the 1980s, heightened religious fervour was observed across all religions (Government of Singapore, 1989). The government became concerned that greater conviction in exclusive beliefs could increase the possibility of friction and misunderstanding among the different religious groups which could inflame passions, kindle violence, and jeopardise Singapore's good record of religious harmony. This led to the introduction of the Maintenance of Religious Harmony Act 1990. It came into effect in March 1992, and not only provided for the maintenance of religious harmony, but also for the establishment of a Presidential Council for Religious Harmony, headed by the President of Singapore. The Council was to be a consultative body, to moderate relations between the various religious groups in Singapore, and to advise the government on how to deal with sensitive religious issues in the country. The government would now be able to take action against any religious group which violated the Act by serving restraining orders on religious leaders and members of any religious group who threaten Singapore's religious harmony in words or actions, and conduct political and subversive activities under the guise of religion.

During the consultation process on the Maintenance of Religious Harmony Bill in 1990, Muis was among the many organisations and individuals who submitted their views and ideas on the Bill. In its written submission to the Select Committee on the Maintenance of Religious Harmony Bill, Muis highlighted that it sought the views of 11 Muslim organisations, and received representation from one Muslim organisation (Government of Singapore, 1990). All of whom accepted the Bill in principle, with reservations on certain provisions. A key concern was whether the Bill might prevent Muis from performing its functions as stipulated in AMLA, such as formulating *fatwa* rulings which might be deemed political, especially if the rules conflict with government policy. This was reiterated by Mufti Syed Isa during the Select Committee Hearing on 20 September 1990. Haji Mohd Muzammil, a Muis Council member who was part of the Muis delegation, illustrated with the example of abortion, where the Fatwa Committee had decided as prohibited in Islam but was allowed by the government. In this instance, the Mufti highlighted that the scope of Muis' efforts would be to advise the community through education but without resorting to a public campaign to pressure the government to take a particular action which could result in disharmony and unhappiness.

The Committee assured the Muis delegation that the Bill would not affect Muis' statutory powers, and Muis was in a position to raise any concerns if there was any government policy which might affect the Muslim community. Nevertheless, a controversy which arose during and after the proceedings was the apparent contradiction to Muis' support for the Bill, with respect to the notion that in Islam, there is no separation between religion and politics. This was a key point raised by Mr Chiam See Tong, a member of the Select Committee, who highlighted that by supporting the Bill, Mufti Syed Isa had given up his right to speak up against the government if it was in the wrong. This was also echoed by Mr Juffrie Mahmood, the Vice-Chairman of Singapore Democratic Party, in a separate session during the hearing. He felt that the Mufti had not given a true representation of Islam that politics is an integral part of Islam (Government of Singapore, 1990).

Mufti Syed Isa remained steadfast with Muis' position to support the Bill, despite the objection by some segments of the community. Several weeks after the hearing, the Mufti clarified Muis' position in an interview to the local Malay media (*Berita Minggu*, 1990). Mufti Syed Isa emphasised that that there was no contradiction between Islamic principles and the new law, which was necessary to preserve the peace in Singapore's multi-religious society. While there is no separation of religion and politics in Islam, the religion also forbade a person to use religion for political objectives or to mix religion and politics for personal gain. He added that the faith did not condone the use of the religion to incite people to create chaos which might result in violence. Nevertheless, it did not mean that people could not speak up to register their disagreement in matters which affect their religion through proper channels in a respectful way.

Muis' response to the entire controversy surrounding the Bill demonstrated its clarity in putting the agenda of religious harmony and social cohesion as a top priority. Muis clearly understood that the intent of the Bill was not to prevent the freedom to practise religion, but to safeguard against practices which could create a climate of religious disharmony in Singapore. Recognising Singapore's multi-religious context, Muis espouses living one's faith without incurring displeasure, by modelling good behaviour and practice instead of aggressive salesman-type or provocative approaches.

9/11 and JI Arrests

The government's fears and concerns towards the uncertain trajectory of growing religiosity among Muslims became further entrenched after 9/11, when terrorists attacked the World Trade Centre and the Pentagon in the US. Just a few months later in December 2001, 15 local members of the Jemaah Islamiyah (JI) were detained under the ISA for their plans to bomb US and Western targets in Singapore. This was the beginning of even more terrorist incidents which had significantly transformed the global security landscape even until the present time.

The perception that has emerged is that terrorism and aggression is inextricably linked to Islam, and that Islam is the cause of violence and terror. In short, the teachings of Islam can be interpreted for aggression and violence. It created an atmosphere of suspicion and distrust, and raised questions on whether Muslims are becoming more susceptible to radicalisation. The government was prompt in addressing those divisive misgivings and suspicions between fellow Singaporeans (*The Straits Times*, 2001). It highlighted that the vast majority of Singaporean Muslims are moderate, tolerant, and law-abiding, and do not support the actions of the Muslim militants. It quickly dispelled any concern that increasing religiosity would equate to supporting violence and terrorism. Similarly, Muis as well as the Muslim community and religious leaders came out strongly and unequivocally to condemn the 9/11 attacks and JI (*The Straits Times*, 2001). It was further emphasised that JI members were a small and isolated group of misguided Muslims with no support from the community.

In the heightened post-9/11 environment, the government was concerned that the social fabric, while strong, may not withstand the impact of a terrorist attack, and insecurity can easily be expressed through hatred and violence, and justified on religious grounds. The attack resurfaced concerns relating to the community's identity and its impact on social cohesion. It has inevitably caused the Singaporean Malay/Muslims to feel the fear of being ostracised as they may be blamed for events that took place outside Singapore.

The government proceeded to enhance measures to strengthen social cohesion and religious harmony (Tan, 2008). Inter-Racial Confidence Circles (IRCC) and Harmony Circles were formed at community levels, schools, and workplaces to promote better inter-racial and inter-religious understanding between the different communities, and provide a platform for confidence-building among the different communities, as a basis for developing deeper friendships and trust over time. The rationale is that regular interactions will build up inter-racial and inter-religious rapport, and also provide opportunities for all parties to immediately address racial and religious problems on the ground. A Code on Religious Harmony became a framework to guide all religious groups, and helped to crystallise the consensus of Singaporeans of all races and religions about how each community should conduct themselves as they pursue their respective religious beliefs in multiracial Singapore.

In the immediate aftermath of the 9/11 episode, Muis and the community responded and took ownership by organising a series of talks to various groups on the basics of Islam. Many mosques also opened their premises for non-Muslim visitors to find out more about Islamic practices. A group of *asatizah* came together voluntarily and formed the Religious Rehabilitation Group (RRG), which was launched in April 2003, to rehabilitate detained JI members and their families through counselling. RRG has since broadened its scope to include public education, to correct misinterpretations of Islamic concepts and dispel extremist ideologies, as well as counselling for troubled individuals. Such efforts were necessary to challenge the extremist narratives and prevent them from dominating the community's religious discourse. It was important for the Muslim community to articulate an Islam that is relevant and compatible to Singapore's context, one that supports social cohesion and ultimately loyal to Singapore.

Muis' Post-9/11 Efforts in Building Social Cohesion

The September 11 attacks and the subsequent series of global terrorist attacks by Al-Qaeda in the name of Islam provided an important reflection point for Muis and the community to make sense of the implications for Islam in Singapore. Instead of merely turning inwards, Muis opted to analyse the issue from a broader view, particularly in how social transformation in modern societies has impacted religion and its role in such societies. This helped in clarifying how Muis should respond, not reactively, but proactively with a longer term view of the role of religion in the context of a continuously changing modern society. This led to three inter-connected points of focus:

i) positing the positive role of religion in society; ii) forging a Singapore Muslim identity; and iii) driving the interfaith agenda.

Positing the Positive Role of Religion in Society

The challenge of 9/11 was not viewed merely as a problem within Islam. It was located within the broader discourse on the global rise of fundamentalisms across all religions. Major works on this has pointed to common characteristics observed in virtually all faith traditions as a reaction to the process of social change which has caused the marginalisation of religion in modern life (Almond *et al.*, 2003). Instead of taking a destructive or divisive path as represented by the violent extremist and isolationist strands, religious traditions should opt for a positive and constructive approach by drawing from their respective philosophical, moral, and spiritual teachings. They can help to soften the severe abrasions on individuals and communities caused by social transformations. Through such common alleviating experiences, religious leaders and faith communities would then focus on working together towards the common good rather than be preoccupied with minor self-accentuated differences.

This constructive role is already embodied in some of the good examples of how progressive social and religious actors have succeeded in undertaking reform and renewal in contemporary post-independent Southeast Asian societies (Alatas, 2009). Religion which is not only rooted in its tradition but supports the progressive development of the wider society through the quality of the people and institutions. These ideas were the core issues discussed in a series of conferences[6] and seminars organised by Muis between 2005 and 2009, as well as publications which provided the intellectual framework to develop a contextualised understanding of Muslim identity and build stronger interfaith relations with other communities.

Forging the Singapore Muslim Identity

Inspired by how globally Muslims, especially in Western plural societies, are grappling with issues of identity, this led to the reaffirmation of a set of attributes and values which came to be known as the Singapore Muslim

---

[6] Muis organised several conferences and seminars with the following themes: Globalisation and Religious Resurgence Conference (2005), Religion in Industrial Society (2006), Muslim Reform in Southeast Asia (2007), Revisiting the Development Agenda in Southeast Asia (2008) and Muslims in Multicultural Societies (2009).

Identity (SMI) (Musa, 2016). Fundamentally, it is about having a contextualised understanding of Islam, and is driven by the ethos that Islam is a blessing not only to Muslims but also to all humanity. This has always been within the Islamic tradition. Nevertheless, the SMI narrative was a call to manifest it in the way we live Islam in Singapore.

Muis saw it as a deeper appreciation of Islam's inclusive tradition and living Islam without having a sense of contradiction or discomfort in a secular state and plural society. This required Muslims not to be fixated on the idea that they are perpetually under siege, but one who is confident and able to adapt. It therefore challenges the thinking among certain segments of Muslims who claim that it is not possible or that it is difficult for Muslims to practise Islam in Singapore.

A series of consultations with various stakeholders (including community and religious leaders) were held in 2004 to build a consensus on the SMI 10 desired attributes. The meaning and essence of the SMI 10 desired attributes were distilled into a public document — *Risalah* — for wider dissemination (Majlis Ugama Islam Singapura, 2006). This became the guiding narrative for sermons, mosque lectures, and forums, and messaging during major festivals (e.g., Ramadan, Zikral Hijrah and other events). Prominent Islamic scholars and Muslim thinkers were invited to aid Muis' content development work and articulate the SMI narrative to a wider audience. The 10 desired attributes were subsequently reduced to five RICAP values — Religious Resilient, Inclusive, Contributive, Adaptive and Progressive, to facilitate better messaging.

To ensure effective infusion of the SMI values and streamlining of content across various platforms, the Master Content Framework (MCF) was developed. The MCF provided a deeper conceptual understanding of the RICAP with reference to the key principles and messages of primary Islamic sources — the Qur'an and Prophet's life, and complemented with appreciation of the i) socio-historical development and evolution of religious ideas over the long period of Islamic history; and ii) the contemporary and modern intellectual thoughts on the evolving social norms and current realities. This ensured that critical issues of the day were discussed in the various learning platforms instead of being limited to the learning of basic Islamic beliefs and practices. Specific content gaps in the learning platforms were addressed by incorporating topics such as Islam in a Secular State, Impact of Globalisation on Religious Life, Criticality in Islamic Thought and Practice, and Rise of

Exclusivism. Such content was customised for delivery through more directed learning platforms, such as the Adult Islamic Learning (ADIL) and aLIVE programmes for the young, as well as discursive platforms offered by the Muis Academy in capacity-building of religious elites and, more recently, in the professional development of *asatizah* through the Asatizah Recognition Scheme Continuous Professional Education (ARS-CPE).The SMI formed the underlying ethos and narrative deployed by Muis as a means to orientate the community towards a progressive and contextualised understanding of Islam to the lived realities of Singapore's multicultural society and secular state. The SMI values were not only disseminated and cascaded through tangible initiatives and platforms, but also underpin the progressive transformation of key institutions like the mosque and madrasah, in the design of policies, programme and curriculum. For example, mosques adopt an inclusive outlook through their community, family, and youth-friendly programmes, as well as position themselves as key nodes within the national grid. The redesign of the Joint Madrasah System curriculum to incorporate greater contemporary application of traditional religious concepts reflects the forward-looking orientation driven by the SMI values.

Driving the interfaith agenda

Muis has earlier responded in the aftermath of 9/11 by sharing with various groups on the basic information on Islam. While this helped to address certain misconceptions, the low intensity of such sessions did not facilitate the building of closer bonds with other religious communities. It was during a visit to the UK to learn on how British society coped after the events of 7/7[7] that it reaffirmed the value of interfaith engagement. Through meetings with apex religious leaders from the Three Faiths Forum in the UK,[8] the Muis delegation gained insights on how strong interfaith bonds have strengthened the resilience of British society, especially in the aftermath of a terror attack. This provided the impetus for Muis to take a more proactive role in driving the interfaith agenda through two key initiatives — the Harmony Centre and the Rahmatan lil Alamin Foundation (RLAF).

---

[7]The 7 July 2005 London bombings were a series of coordinated terrorist suicide attacks in London, United Kingdom, which targeted commuters travelling on the city's public transport system during the morning rush hour.

[8] The Three Faiths Forum is one of the UK's leading interfaith organisations established in 1997 in London by Sir Sigmund Sternberg, the Reverend Marcus Braybrooke and Sheikh Zaki Badawi.

The formation of the Harmony Centre in 2006 became the centrepiece of Muis' interfaith agenda. Although it was originally conceived to be a centre to promote correct understanding of Islam, the interfaith dimension was later incorporated as an integral part of the centre's objective. According to Haji Mohammad Alami Musa, President of Muis since 2004, it was a "policy response" to the JI plot to attack the local targets (Musa, 2017). He highlighted that the idea to focus on the "interreligious engagement agenda" was drawn from study findings, which "showed that the interaction and active engagement amongst leaders of the various religions could contribute significantly to conflict prevention and peace-building." The Harmony Centre was considered as breaking new ground. It is possibly the only such centre housed in a place of worship, and not only presents the core of teachings of Islam but also beliefs and practices of other faith traditions. During the initial years of its formation, this was done very subtly through hidden pull-outs. However, when the centre's exhibits were refreshed in 2011, the information was made more visible, as there was greater acceptance from the community on the value of sharing such information to not only help understand other faith traditions but also to showcase Singapore's model of religious harmony (Ahmad, 2016). Muis' commitment to the interfaith agenda as a means to strengthen social cohesion is palpable from the comprehensive approach that it has undertaken. The Harmony Centre was not just running *ad hoc* activities, but it works within a framework which covers capacity-building, engagement, and learning.

Through the connection with a visiting American Muslim professor, the late Professor Ibrahim Abu Rabi', in 2005, Muis was able to establish links with a renowned interfaith institution in the US, the Hartford Seminary. Through a Memorandum of Understanding with the Hartford Seminary in 2007, Muis was able to continuously send its officers and *asatizah* to attend interfaith development programmes such as the Building Abrahamic Partnership programme at Hartford Seminary. Correspondingly, Hartford Seminary faculty members were also invited to Singapore to conduct interfaith training. There was mutual learning between the Hartford Seminary and the Harmony Centre through those exchanges which have enriched the respective institutions.

The Harmony Centre became better resourced to uplift its programme offerings, particularly in the areas of engagement and learning. When the former Archbishop of Canterbury, Rowan Williams, came to Singapore in

2007 to organise his flagship Christian–Muslim Building Bridges programme, Muis saw the value of the model of close engagement between Christian and Muslim religious leaders through mutual learning and discovery. This led to Muis customising a local version of the Building Bridges Programme through collaboration with the National Council of Churches of Singapore (NCCS) in 2011. Scholars from both sides engaged in the topic of "Religious Tradition and Authority in the Postmodern World", which culminated in a seminar. It was a key milestone as this was the first time that both faith traditions engaged in deep dialogue and learn from each other. The programme was subsequently continued with the Buddhist community through collaborations with the Singapore Buddhist Federation in 2014, on the topic of "Human Suffering, Spiritual Renewal and Common Action." Following the close relationships established, classes which offered deeper learning on Christianity and Buddhism were also conducted by the Harmony Centre, and received strong participation.

Beyond the deeper engagement, learning platforms for the wider community, particularly the young, were also intensified. In 2011, the Harmony Centre started the flagship Maulana Muhammad Abdul Aleem Siddiqui Memorial Lecture to feature apex religious leaders who could address a wider interfaith audience instead of their own usual flock. Dr Mohamed Fatris Bakaram, who just took office as the new Mufti that year, became the first religious leader to present his thoughts to a wider Singapore audience. This was also an important milestone for religious discourse in Singapore, where matters on religion could now be discussed not only within the confines of particular religious communities. Mufti Dr Mohamed Fatris, and many successive apex religious leaders who spoke, had to respond to respectful yet challenging questions from the curious and critical youthful audience. This took interfaith engagement in Singapore to a new level, beyond the usual niceties and "Religion 101" sessions.

Since its inception 10 years ago, the Harmony Centre continues to enjoy good flow of visitors. In 2016, there were more than 7,000 local and overseas visitors. They came from all segments — schools, grassroots organisations, faith communities, uniformed groups, as well as dignitaries and guests of the different government agencies. It has also been able to secure a positive image for Singapore and the Singaporean Muslim community, as the work of the centre received coverage in the region and beyond. It had been invited to share its experience in countries such as Malaysia, Indonesia, China, Australia, Japan, Spain, Qatar, and Russia. Some countries experiencing the challenges of religious diversity, such as Sri Lanka, were attracted to the Harmony Centre model, and considered establishing a similar centre.

While the Harmony Centre contributed to the interfaith agenda largely at the ideational level, the establishment of the Rahmatan Lil Alamin (RLA) Foundation manifested the interfaith agenda through deeds and collective action to serve fellow humanity regardless of race or religion. The RLA Foundation was formed in 2009 to promote blessings to all. It initially started through the community's generosity in contributing to special mosque fund collections for overseas disaster relief. At that time, Mercy Relief, a local humanitarian agency established by Perdaus, was already in existence. Although Mercy Relief started as a Muslim community initiative, it eventually evolved as a national humanitarian organisation. Muis felt that the community has to be more visibly involved to project the values of *rahmatan lil alamin*. Thus, RLAF was launched, and it expanded its role beyond just special mosque fund collection to becoming a grant maker to support overseas and local humanitarian projects. Additionally, the "blessings to all" ethos became a movement driven by the Enhanced Mosque Clusters through the annual RLA month. This was delivered through various activities like the Food-for-All and Blood Donation Drive, as well as other projects throughout the year, such as soup kitchens and beach cleaning, to embody the spirit of caring within the Muslim community. These were done in collaboration with Community Development Councils (CDCs), grassroots bodies, and other VWOs, with the involvement of the wider Singapore society, regardless of race or religion.

Despite the positive impact of Muis' response to the post-9/11 environment through the above efforts, there were voices which viewed them as government agenda in reaction to the security challenge. In other words, the religious harmony that has been forged was viewed as artificial and not sustainable, as it was thought to be driven top-down. Within the Muslim community, initial participation from among the *asatizah* fraternity was also low. A key factor was that they did not view the interfaith agenda as something which is intrinsic within the Islamic tradition. This became a learning opportunity for Muis to educate the community that it is an integral part of the Islamic tradition.

"Blessings to All": Community Narrative to Build Social Cohesion

For Muis alone to be at the forefront to drive the interfaith agenda to build social cohesion, it would not be effective and sustainable. From the onset, it recognised that getting community support would be a challenge, due to the perception that interfaith events are merely theatrics to project that the different communities are living harmoniously. Thus, Muis saw the need for the community to have greater ownership. To do this, it has to be intrinsically motivated with a deeper internalisation of its value and importance. Thus, Muis initiated a plan, which began with reframing the interfaith narrative that shaped the curation of new exhibits and displays at the Harmony Centre. The learning journey begins with a deeper exposure and insight into the idea of interfaith within the Islamic tradition — from the primary sources, the Prophet's historical life, and key examples in Islamic history. This helped to broaden the scope of the Muslim community's concern beyond just within the Ummah, but towards the wider humanity. This is the thrust of the "blessings to all" ethos. Muslims do not just care for fellow Muslims, but instead strive for the common good for the benefit of the wider society. With the inculcation of such values, the community will not be fixated with the concern that this is a government agenda. Instead, it takes it upon itself to be proactive and drive the transformation. Similar, to how Mufti Syed Isa, Haji Abu Bakar Maidin, and Habib Syed Hassan Al-Attas took it upon themselves to build bridges with other communities in the early years after Singapore's independence.

Using this narrative, the Harmony Centre also intentionally facilitated the early participation of *asatizah* by targeting the pre-university madrasah students. The early exposure on the importance of the interfaith agenda, particularly in the context of Singapore's plural society, has built a wider pool of *asatizah* who are now more confident and comfortable in engaging people of other faiths. They do not just discuss about Islam, but also wider concerns of how religious communities could collaboratively work towards a common good for the nation and society. This has facilitated authentic appreciation of interfaith relations and the forging of humanistic bonds across communities and cultures.

Conclusion

Social cohesion remains an important part of Singapore's lived reality as it has significant impact on Singapore's survival and prosperity as a nation comprising diverse communities. Due to the complex challenges of terrorism and growing exclusivism and extremism globally and regionally, Muis has progressively embraced a more expanded role in promoting greater social cohesion through its religious messaging as well as policies and programmes. Thus, Muis' focus is no longer merely to manage the community's religious concerns but in the process, contribute also to the well-being of the nation.

For the Muslim community, the existing structures would help to better prepare for a more complex future where there will be greater diversity beyond the usual inter- and intra-faith diversity. The "blessings to all" ethos will remain relevant as the community deals with diversity across social class, generational differences, orientations, and lifestyles. As society evolves, change is inevitable, and there has to be the continuous effort to adapt and renew the bonds of trust as new generations and new issues emerge.

The community's response towards 9/11 and JI has driven efforts to institutionalise measures which have proven to be critical and useful, especially at the present time, as we face the threat of ISIS in the region. The need to educate the larger society about Islam and Muslims will need to be refreshed. In the world of fake news and misinformation, correct information has become even more critical. Through the narratives for over more than a decade, there is greater consciousness and awareness on the need to build strong social trust. More young people are coming forward to contribute through various ground-up initiatives, such as the Roses of Peace, CommaCon, MCollective, Movement for Affirmation of Pluralism and Ask Me Anything. With access to such networks of like-minded groups, Muis will be able to build a broader alliance which can project a stronger voice of reason, moderation, and toleration, critical in strengthening social cohesion and religious harmony.

References

Ahmad, R. (2016, June 21). Small Singapore Muslim community plays big role in religious harmony. *The Star Online*. Retrieved from: https://www.thestar.com.my/news/nation/2016/06/21/singapore-muslims-play-big-role-in-promoting-religious-harmony.

Alatas, S. F. (ed.) (2009). *Muslim Reform in Southeast Asia: Perspectives from Malaysia, Indonesia and Singapore*. Singapore: Majlis Ugama Islam Singapura.

Aljunied, S. M. K. (2009) *Colonialism, Violence and Muslims in Southeast Asia — The Maria Hertogh Controversy and its aftermath*. Oxford, UK: Routledge.

Almond, G. A., Appleby, R. S. and Sivan E. (2003). *Strong Religion: The Rise of Fundamentalisms Around the World.* Chicago: University of Chicago Press.

Government of Singapore (1989). *Maintenance of Religious Harmony White Paper.* Cmd. 21 of 1989. Presented to Parliament on 26 December 1989.

Government of Singapore (1990). *Report of the Select Committee on the Maintenance of Religious Harmony Bill [Bill No. 14/90]* Parl. 7 of 1990. Presented to Parliament on 29 October 1990.

Haikal, H. and Yahaya, A. G. (1996). Muslim Organisations in Singapore: An Historical Overview. *Islamic Studies*, 35(4), pp. 435–447.

Hussain, S. Z. (2012). *Keeping the Faith — Syed Isa Semait, Mufti of Singapore 1972–2010.* Singapore: Straits Times Press.

Lai, A. E. (2008). The Inter-Religious Organisation of Singapore. In A.E. Lai (Ed.) *Religious Diversity in Singapore* (pp. 605–641) Singapore: ISEAS.

Majlis Ugama Islam Singapura (2006). *Risalah for Building a Singapore Muslim Community of Excellence (Second Edition).* Retrieved from Muis website: http://www.muis.gov.sg/-/media/Files/OOM/Resources/Risalah-eng-lr.pdf.

Musa, M. A. (2016). Living as Faithful Muslims in Secular Singapore. In Zainul Abidin Rasheed and Norshahril Saat (Ed.) *Majulah! 50 Years of Malay/Muslim Community in Singapore.* (pp. 225–238) Singapore: World Scientific.

Musa, M. A. (2017). Personal Interview.

Mahbob, N. A. (2015, May 13). Habib Hassan terima Anugerah IRO. *Berita Harian.* Retrieved from: http://www.beritaharian.sg/setempat/habib-hassan-terima-anugerah-iro.

Nasir, K. M. Pereira, A. A. and Turner, B. S. (2009). *Muslims in Singapore: Piety, politics and policies.* London and New York: Routledge.

Tan, E. K. B. (2004) "We, the Citizens of Singapore...": Multiethnicity, its Evolution and its Aberrations". In A. E. Lai (Ed.) *Beyond Rituals and Riots — Ethnic Pluralism and Social Cohesion in Singapore* (pp. 65–97). Singapore: Marshall Cavendish.

Tan, E. K. B. (2008). In A. E. Lai (Ed.) "Keeping God in Place — The Management of Religion in Singapore." *Religious Diversity in Singapore* (pp. 55–82). Singapore: ISEAS.

Tay, D. (2009, September 13). Getting to know and love Our Muslim Neighbour. *The Catholic News*, 59(19). Retrieved from: http://catholicnews.sg/index.php?option=com_content&view=article&id=3226&lang=en.

Annex A

The 10 Desired Attributes of a Muslim Community of Excellence

1. Holds strongly to Islamic principles while adapting itself to changing context
2. Morally and spiritually strong to be on top of the challenges of modern society
3. Progressive, practices Islam beyond forms/rituals and rides the modernisation wave
4. Appreciates Islamic civilisation and history, and has a good understanding of contemporary issues
5. Appreciates other civilisations and is confident in interacting and learning from other communities
6. Believes that good Muslims are also good citizens
7. Well-adjusted as contributing members of a multi-religious society and secular state
8. Be a blessing to all and promotes universal principles and values
9. Is inclusive and practices pluralism, without contradicting Islam
10. Be a model and inspiration to all

Conclusion

DIVERSITY AND DISRUPTION: CHARTING NEW PATHWAYS FOR THE FUTURE

Albakri Ahmad and Zalman Putra Ahmad Ali

Our society is changing, and so is the Muslim community. The new generation of Singaporeans are more exposed to new ideas and influences, and more confident in expressing views and debating issues... Muis has been quietly managing the diversity within the Singapore Muslim community. There are different sects and ethnic groups, including among new migrants who follow different schools of Islam. Unity within the community is vital. This is one aspect of Muis' work which the public may not be conscious about. Singapore has attracted international attention and admiration because of the way our different communities live in harmony in a turbulent world. Muis can share its model of self-administering Islamic affairs with Muslim communities in other countries.

Prime Minister Lee Hsien Loong's Interview with *Berita Harian*, 11 July 2009 (Prime Minister's Office, 2009)

For the last 50 years, Muis has progressed in tandem with Singapore's development as a nation. The introduction of AMLA in 1968 has provided a legal framework that facilitated the practice of Islam in a plural and secular state, as the community adjusted to the transformative effects of modernisation. Nevertheless, as the chapters in this book have demonstrated, legal dimension alone was not adequate in driving societal change. Ultimately, multiple factors have driven this change, with trust among the different stakeholders — state, society, and international counterparts — being the most crucial one. Forging trust did not happen overnight: it took several decades of deliberate efforts to engage various segments of the community and address the community's unmet religious needs, before the community gradually grew to appreciate that Muis had the community's interests at heart. The factor of leadership was also significant. Muis leadership in the past comprised individuals who were well-connected with ground sentiments. With Muis surpassing expectations, the community began to acknowledge its genuine efforts to provide quality service, to the extent that they were willing to go beyond financial contribution, by offering to work together and actively co-create with Muis. With guidance from visionary and sincere leaders, this accumulation of trust, funds, and talent over the years has propelled the community forward towards excellence, as it simultaneously navigated different phases of change.

Several episodes in the course of Muis' history were triggered by the evolving external environment. At certain critical junctures, the community would encounter new issues which demanded a rethinking of its earlier positions and assumptions. A case in point was discussed in Chapter 3 on "Contextualisation and Modernisation: Islamic Thought through *Fatwas* in Singapore" by Dr Nazirudin Nasir on the need to consider new jurisprudential frameworks to interpreting religious text. This had led to the most recent fatwas on organ donation and inheritance. The community's support has enabled Muis to be confident in exploring new solutions and pathways. For instance, Islamic education is an area which has to continuously evolve in order to effectively engage with successive new generations of young Muslims. Unlike in the past, not only are they exposed to different ideas, they also experience new ways of learning. In the same vein, religious scholars and teachers are expected to keep up by having a broader knowledge mastery and skillset to deal with contemporary issues. In turn, this raises expectations on the quality of madrasah education and the development of future religious leadership. This pattern of evolution also applies to other domains such as mosque management, *halal* certification, and others. This ongoing process of sensing, reviewing and transforming has become very important in an ever-changing, volatile, and uncertain world, so that Muis and the community can remain dynamic and thrive in the future.

The next 50 years will be virtually no different as this process continues. However, the pace of change will be faster, and the challenges faced will be more complex. How will some of these challenges impact the Muslim community? To be sure, Singapore will undergo demographic transformation, a more contested political landscape, changing economic landscape, disruptions due to the digital revolution, and emergence of new social fault lines. Certain key guiding principles and policy considerations will continue to be relevant in dealing with the more complex emerging issues. Still, certain issues may require a fundamental rethinking of earlier assumptions in order to find new answers and solutions.

Reaping the Benefits of Current Structures

Despite the good progress and significant achievements that have been made by Muis for the last 50 years, there are voices which remained dissatisfied with the way Islam is managed in Singapore. A common critique is what they view as the state's disproportionate regulation of Islam in Singapore compared to other religious groups and faith communities. (Nasir, 2017).

Such a view tends to reinforce the perception that the state feels threatened by Islam, and any attempt to regulate by the state is viewed from this lens. However, it disregards the fact that, as highlighted by Dr Norshahril Saat in the book's Introduction, the government of the day has to serve the interest of all citizens, regardless of race or religion, which include Muslims as well. It is in the interest of all citizens that the state adopts a strong position in safeguarding public order, social cohesion, and religious harmony. It is incorrect to say that only Muslim religious practices are regulated, as state laws such as the Maintenance of Religious Harmony Act and the Sedition Act have been used against people from various faith communities for offending other faiths including Muslims. There have also been past cases of religious leaders from other faith communities who have also been warned by the state, such as in the case of Senior Pastor Rony Tan of Lighthouse Evangelism Independent Church, who denigrated Buddhism in 2010 (*Reuters*, 2010).

As shown in Chapter 1 on AMLA by Alfian Yasrif Kuchit, the present regulatory structure is a colonial legacy, and has mirrored certain aspects of the way Islam has been administered in the region in countries such as Malaysia and Brunei. It has been integral to Singapore's social compact since the country's independence, by virtue of it being a product of numerous debates which involved both the contribution of Muslim and non-Muslim elites.

Most importantly, over the years, the community has benefited from the current structure which facilitated key religious practices through legal provisions for *zakat, haj, halal, wakaf,* madrasah education, Islamic education, mosque building, and Muslim marriages. Additionally, the community's assets have grown significantly facilitated by state-sanctioned mechanisms such as the MBMF (through compulsory CPF deductions). The scheme has contributed to further enhancement and expansion of various religious development initiatives. The Muslim community has often leveraged Muis' position as a statutory board to reap certain benefits and concessions that have been central to Muslim religious life in Singapore. This can be seen, for instance, in the purchase of State Land allocated for purpose of mosque building set at the underlying market value, and the role of the Minister-in-charge of Muslim Affairs and Muis in maintaining a positive relationship with the authorities in Saudi Arabia in securing the *haj* quota for Singaporean Muslims every year. Even till now, members of the community have highlighted in traditional and social media the need for Muis to play a more central role in various matters, such as the regulation of religious life, for instance, the control of deviant teachings or assurance of the *halal* certification of *halal*-certified eating establishments. Thus, there is more compelling evidence to demonstrate that regulation is accepted as a central part of Muslim religious life in Singapore to meet the community's unique needs which differ from other faith communities.

Regardless of whichever position one holds regarding state regulation of religion, everyone has benefited from Singapore's state of religious harmony, which is acknowledged by the majority of the people in Singapore as being high (Neo, 2014). In this regard, Muis has been a key contributor, not only through its programmes, but through its overall guidance and leadership, which has ensured that the community is united and not divisive, and made Muslims conscious of how to live Islam in a uniquely different environment, compared to other Muslims in the region and other parts of the world.

The community's distrust towards Muis during the early years of Muis' formation has changed. Today, the community has shown stronger support and greater confidence to Muis for its work to uplift the community. This can be seen from the continuous growth in *zakat* collection, as well as findings from the Muis Public Perception Survey in 2016 which reflected the community's high level of trust for Muis' leadership (Islamic Religious Council of Singapore, 2016).[1]

---

[1] The findings found that three in four Muslims are very appreciative of its work; 82 percent of the respondents "Trust Muis for developing the Muslim community", and 83 percent of the respondents "Trust Muis in disbursing *Zakat.*"

Internationally, these achievements have not gone unnoticed with Singapore being increasingly recognised as a reference point in the management of Islamic affairs of Muslim minorities. For example, through PRISM, a collaboration between Muis and the Regional Islamic Da'wah Council of Southeast Asia and the Pacific (RISEAP), Muslim minority communities have come to Singapore to learn about Muis' approach in mosque management, *zakat* collection and disbursement and *halal* certification (*The Straits Times*, 2016). With Muis attaining the Singapore Quality Class (Star) award for Organisational Excellence in 2013 and 2017, it gives further assurance to these countries of the credibility and integrity of Muis' organisational processes. Singapore also attained high ratings on *halal*-travel websites, such as Crescentrating.com, for its large array of quality and trusted *halal*-friendly accommodations and restaurants for the *halal*-conscious Muslim traveler (Cheow, 2017). Indirectly, Muis has also contributed to Singapore's tourism and economy. This reflects the outcome of mutual facilitation between Muis and the state that can be leveraged further so that more benefit can be gained by both the community and nation.

Future Challenges

Singapore will also inevitably undergo significant change due to the effects of driving forces which are beyond its control. Global economies are becoming more volatile, and the high acceleration of technological change will profoundly impact the way one works, lives, and interacts with one another. Prime Minister Lee Hsien Loong has identified three critical challenges: i) economy, ii) population, and iii) identity which will impact Singapore in the next 50 years (Ng, 2015). Each of these challenges may differ in terms of level of criticality across different time horizons. Nonetheless, Singapore will be faced with the dilemma of sustaining an employable population to continuously drive economic growth while simultaneously, having to reinvigorate a sense of identity and nationhood as a consequence of the changing social compact. This is due to the need to import fresh labour in response to low fertility rates and ageing population. These challenges facing Singapore will certainly impact the Muslim community which would require Muis' response.

Changing Economic Landscape

The Singapore economy is undergoing a major transformation into becoming a mature economy that delivers a high rate of homegrown innovations. Simultaneously, it also has to cope with the changes brought about by the opportunities and disruptions of automation, machine learning, and artificial intelligence. These new technologies have made certain jobs in some sectors such as manufacturing and services redundant while, at the same time, created opportunities for the innovation of new businesses. Both big and small countries are intensely leveraging on these technologies to enable them to compete in the global market. To thrive in this global competition, Singapore also has charted its own economic pathway to create new engines of growth through a combination of innovation, enterprise and internationalisation (Public Service Division, 2017).

Being a small and open economy, Singapore is highly dependent on global markets. The prolonged depressed oil prices since 2014, the economic slowdown in the US, China, and Japan, and the political and economic changes in Europe with Brexit,[2] and the impact of the Trump administration's policies are contributing to the dampening of global trade growth, which has negative effects on Singapore's economic growth (Chia, 2016). This is further aggravated by the growing backlash against globalisation which has driven many nations to increasingly adopt protectionist measures. China's shift towards greater insourcing has also caused a decline in demand for imports including those from Singapore (Chia, 2016).

Nevertheless, there are other opportunities which are potential growth sectors, particularly in the region in countries such as the Philippines, Vietnam, and Indonesia that are doing well. Growth sectors would include healthcare, infocomm technology, and precision engineering, as well as the rise of the middle-class and urbanisation in Asia, which will increase demand for finance, hub services, logistics, as well as urban solutions (Chia, 2016).

The more educated and upwardly mobile in the community may be able to leverage the new opportunities in the region which will boost the growth of the Malay/Muslim middle class. This growth would also shape the community's tastes, preferences, and lifestyles which would, in turn, expand the differentiated demand for religious services such as customised Islamic learning, spiritual retreats, premium *haj* packages, to name a few. The growth in upper middle class will also yield opportunities for Muis to tap on their

---

[2] Brexit is the prospective withdrawal of the UK from the European Union. In a referendum on 23 June 2016, 51.9 percent of the participating UK electorate voted to leave the EU.

resources and networks for greater benefit to the wider community, in particular the lower income group. Existing processes and new activities to engage and relate these well-endowed segments of the community towards a targeted set of socio-religious objectives will need to be reviewed and curated. However, the disruptions would most likely pose a significant challenge for the community especially, that a high proportion of the community is within the lower income group with qualifications which limit them to low-skilled employment. Thus, there will be greater expectation for Muis to disburse more *zakat* and to provide additional assistance to support those people and their families who are affected by retrenchments or having difficulty finding employment. In addition to support those displaced by the economic restructuring, there are also requests for Muis to close the religious services and attendant amenities gap for the special needs and persons with disabilities. Increasingly, the predicament of the special needs children and challenged adults are featured in the media and the Muslim public expects Muis to attend to their religious needs. This new demands will correspondingly require additional resources and new capabilities for Muis to respond accordingly.

Ageing Population

Economic growth is also impacted by the size of the working-age population. Despite various government incentives like the Baby Bonus scheme,[3] childcare subsidies, and flexible working hours, Singapore's persistent low fertility rates have not made significant increases, due to the reality of the demands of Singapore's modern society and high cost of living. It has become increasingly challenging for married couples to have many children. Moreover, with more women in the workforce, many have chosen singlehood or postponed starting a family, in order to pay more attention towards career advancement (Yong, 2016). These circumstances have paved the way for Singapore's rapidly ageing workforce and population. A United Overseas Bank (UOB) report has highlighted that 2018 marks the "Singapore's demographic time bomb" (*The Straits Times*, 2017) or a turning point where the population segment of 65 years and above will match those 15 years and below for the first time. According to experts, this would have implications on taxes, immigration rules, and social services.

---

[3] The Baby Bonus scheme, which was introduced on 1 April 2001, supports parents' decision to have more children by helping to lighten the financial costs of raising children. The scheme consists of two components — a cash gift and a Child Development Account.

To mitigate the challenge of an ageing workforce and increase labour supply, the government may need to ease immigration restrictions. However, this would have to be calibrated to minimise the risk of jeopardising the support of the local populace if the hiring of foreigners would mean greater competition for jobs, property, and education. The outcome of the General Elections in 2011 was a key learning point of how the "local-foreigner" divide could have serious repercussions on local politics (Tay, 2015). Nevertheless, it is inevitable that the need to supplement the shrinking working-age population with immigrant labour will become a perennial agenda which has to be addressed.

Relative to the other communities, the Malay/Muslim community will be more youthful because of a larger proportion of young people (due to higher birth rates). Nonetheless, in the longer term, this would change as declining birth rates in the community would also mean that it would experience ageing. For the community, an ageing population may result in greater demand for caregiving, especially for the elderly who are chronically ill. The current high incidence of chronic illness within the Malay/Muslim community may have serious repercussions with respect to the challenge of caregiving (Khalik, 2014). Resources in the households might become stretched with higher demands for caregiving, as families struggle to balance with other demands, especially those from low-income households and large families with young children. This will be further compounded when these families have their aged parents living with them. Sandwiched between having to meet the basic needs of their young children, on the one hand, and the care and resources required by their aged parents who are chronically ill on the other, these families will require all the institutional and community support they need to keep going. The profile of the Malay/Muslim elderly would also change, comprising a larger segment of those who are more educated. Mosques would need to adjust its programmes and facilities including assistive technologies to accommodate a more active senior citizenry with higher aspirations to contribute more in their twilight years. It therefore presents an opportunity for the mosques to tap on the expertise of seniors who have a range of skills and experience to offer.

Maintaining a Sense of Identity

The significant injection of immigrant labour would immensely transform Singapore's ethnic, cultural and possibly, religious make up. This is already evident in recent years, and the government has introduced various measures to facilitate the integration of new Singapore citizens and foreigners. At the same time, Singaporeans had begun adapting to the changing everyday lived experiences as they go to work, school, and play. With the growing diversity, there will be expectation to ensure that there is cultural coherence and a sense of national identity.

In a more globalised world, it will also be a norm for many Singaporeans to venture abroad, which may affect their rootedness to Singapore. The sense of being Singaporean may be lost as individuals find more meaning and sense of belonging in other parts of the world in embracing new cultures. Another threat to the sense of identity is when the society becomes more fractious, preferring to keep to their own exclusive identities. Without any motivation or purpose to come together as one people, the default will be a tendency to keep apart and being comfortable in our respective comfort zones whether it is race, religion, social class, or interest. The weak connections across different groups will cause a depletion in social capital and may be detrimental especially in times of crisis.

Thus, it is important to perpetually rekindle a sense of pride of being Singaporean, as it is anticipated that nothing will stay constant as Singapore adjusts to the ever-changing external environment and maintains coherence in a volatile and uncertain world. The loss of a sense of identity could cause the eventual demise of Singapore as a nation and society.

The community has been able to adjust well with the increasing number of foreign and migrant Muslims in Singapore. In the last few years, Muis has taken steps to connect with the new Muslim groups through efforts via selected mosques to integrate them with the local Muslim community. Muis has also worked with the other national agencies to ensure that the socio-religious needs of the Muslim transient workers such as the Bangladeshi workers and Indonesian domestic helpers are catered to. Nevertheless, it is expected that the new residents from other ethnic and religious groups would not be familiar with the local Malay/Muslim community's beliefs and practices. This would present new opportunities for the community to continue to promote better understanding of the Malay culture and Islam. The corresponding challenge is to understand their religious needs and to manage their different expectations of Muis as a religious authority.

Impact on the Community's Socio-Religious Life

Singapore's transformation would also affect the religious life of the community. Former Minister-in-Charge of Muslim Affairs, Dr Yaacob Ibrahim identified two key challenges: "diversity and disruption", which he felt could impact the way the community navigates itself into the future (Ibrahim, 2015). With the pervasiveness of social media, migration as well as global and regional developments, the community has a wide access to a plethora of ideas which are of diverse religious beliefs and thinking. Similarly, religious teachers are also exposed to various sources through their training in different parts of the world and not only limited to traditional institutions like the Al-Azhar University.[4] Their religious milieu would not just be what they learn in class but the entire living experience, including the socio-political tensions and the contestation of religious ideas that they are immersed in. This has changed what used to be an almost homogenous complexion of religious life among Sunni Muslims in Singapore. The dominant traditionalist strand of Islamic practice broadly identified with the Syafi'i school of law and the Asy'ari school of theology, is now coexisting with other schools of legal thought, such as the Hanbalis, Malikis, and Hanafis, as newer migrant Muslim communities settle in Singapore.

Such changes are not limited to only the Sunni community. Minority groups like the Shia[5] community would also have their own internal dynamics, as they would also have to contend with a growing community, in particular, a younger generation finding their space and making sense of their religious identity. Being in that shared space with others would mean that it is inevitable that the

---

[4] Al-Azhar University is a university based in Cairo, Egypt, which is the oldest and most prestigious in traditional Sunni Islam. The majority of Singapore's religious elites obtained their undergraduate degree in traditional Islamic Sciences from the university, which recognises the pre-university curricula offered by the madrasahs in Singapore. Annually, about 50 students enrol their studies at Al-Azhar University.

[5] Shias first arrived in Singapore from British India in the early 20th century. They were mainly Persians and ethnic Indians and were largely from the Ismaili Dawoodi Bohra and Twelver variants of Shi'ism. They have been an integral part of the local Muslim community and contributed in various community-building efforts. Following the Iranian Revolution in 1979, a small group of Malay Sunnis embraced the Twelver variant of Shi'ism. This latter community has since grown to become the largest segment of the Shias in Singapore represented by organisations, such as the Jaafari Muslim Association of Singapore and the Muslim Youth Assembly (HBI). Muis has issued a *fatwa* ruling on 24 August 1988 that Shias are unequivocally within the fold Islam with the exception of the extreme (*al-ghulah*) among them who adopt certain practices or hold certain beliefs considered as heretical.

private religious practice will intersect with the public space shared with the majority Sunnis. Thus, the differences which have always existed have become more apparent as they can now be vividly seen, heard, and felt. In fact, the diversity of religious piety and expression is no longer limited to matters of rituals and theology, but extending to socio-political interests and ideas.

However, diversity alone is not the challenge. Historically, the community has embraced people of various ethnicities and schools of Islamic legal thought into its fold. They have worked together for the betterment of the community without accentuating their differences. The problem arises when the competition for spaces and mindshare has become divisive as each group claims to be the most authentic, and indoctrinates the community to believe that the group holds the only truth while the rest are wrong. This would then trigger a counter-reaction and if left unchecked, will degenerate into mutual demonisation. Before the advent of social media, this would have been dealt with quietly through engagement with individuals who profess such ideas or lead certain groups. However, with mobile access to the internet, these contesting ideas have become widespread, and facilitated the growth of organic groups which pursue their own narrow interests or causes. This would make it more difficult for the community to preserve cohesion between groups. While there are isolated calls for a clearer religious position and policy stand on who are considered to be in the fold of Islam, its motivation is both binary in outlook and divisive. Furthermore, it will impact on trust in religious authority, and will affect Muis' long-term capability to provide effective religious leadership for the community.

Diversity is also not limited to the emergence of new religious groups. Disruption caused by significant social shifts in society has not only raised new questions about our religious norms and practices, but also what it means to be a Muslim in Singapore. Recent demographic trends have shown that inter-ethnic marriages are more prevalent among Muslims (Philomin, 2014). The socio-cultural practices that intertwined Malay and Islam may become eroded, as families find new markers of religious identity not defined by their ethnicity. However, the growing inflow of Muslim migrants would add further to this cultural richness but potentially cause diminishing dominance of the Malay tradition if the Malay population does not grow.

Family structures also may evolve with the changing roles of women. With better education and more women in the workforce, certain assumptions about the typical family or the household may no longer hold. This is especially so when women take a prominent role in family decisions. Today, there is already greater visibility of women's groups assertively challenging some of the existing religious norms which they view as impinging on the rights of women to greater equality. For example, in the report by Musawah for the 68th CEDAW Session (Musawah, 2017),[6] the group has called for comprehensive reform of the AMLA to grant equal spousal rights and responsibilities in marriage, including equal rights for women to enter into marriage without permission of male guardian, equal rights to divorce, and the prohibition of polygamy. These recommendations are supported by strong justification based on compelling evidence from religious practices globally as well as views from experts and scholars.

While such contestation of religious ideas may become more prevalent in the future as segments in the community find new sources of authority to grapple with the disruption, it also presents opportunities for religious institutions and leaders to develop ideas, rulings and policies to shape a constructive and progressive narrative. Besides demography and changing family structure, new social faultlines may also be created by the changing social norms of the larger society. A key issue which has become a point of friction for several years is the growing presence and acceptance of the LGBT community.[7] It has become a matter of public attention especially with the global acceptance of same sex marriages in many countries. There is a growing anxiety among conservative groups including Muslims on the impact of the LGBT community on the prevailing notion of the family. Episodes such as the calls for the repeal of Section 377A of the Penal Code,[8] and the Health Promotion Board's frequently asked questions

---

[6] Musawah is a global movement for equality and justice in the Muslim family. It was launched in February 2009 in Malaysia attended by more than 250 women and men from some 50 countries from around the globe comprising NGOs, activists, scholars, legal practitioners, policy-makers, and grassroots women and men.

[7] LGBT is a loosely defined grouping of lesbian, gay, bisexual and transgender and LGBT-supportive people, organisations and subcultures, united by a common culture and social movements.

[8] The government's decision in 2007 to retain Section 377A of the Penal Code which criminalises sex between mutually consenting adult men sparked strong protest from the LGBT community and supporters. An open letter was sent to the prime minister and online petition site, Repeal377a.com was set up (Ling, 2010).

(FAQ)[9] on sexuality, as well as annual events such as the Pink Dot SG[10] have triggered a counter reaction from segments of the Christian and Muslim communities, which led to the Wear White movement. Such confrontational positioning between opposing groups is frowned upon by the government, as it could cause a divide in society and affect cohesion (Lai, 2017).

Thus, how should the community respond to this dual challenge of diversity and disruption? A reasonable approach would be to shun intolerance, opt for moderation, and be inclusive. However, in practice, it would also have its own set of implications and trade-offs, which include losing the trust and support of some segments of the community which in turn would impede progress in certain areas. Moving forward, what role would Muis play in such a complex environment?

Charting New Paths

Former Head of Civil Service, Peter Ho called for Singapore to shape its own future by continuously reinventing itself (Yong, 2017). Muis has no other choice but also to reinvent itself in order to respond to massive changes that are coming. Nevertheless, certain key principles had put Muis in good stead for the last 50 years and would still be of relevance for the next 50 years.

Haji Abdul Razak Maricar, the Chief Executive of Muis since 2013, distilled three salient principles that have been at the heart of Muis' developmental ethos which should continue into the future (Maricar, 2016). These principles are: i) shaping a progressive religious outlook; ii) forging trust and confidence; and iii) investing in assets to drive change.

---

[9] The Health Promotion Board released a series of questions and answers about homosexuality on its website, which led to polarised reactions from Singaporeans. While the LGBT community welcomed the move, others who opposed the move felt that HPB was normalising homosexuality (Tan, 2014).

[10] Pink Dot SG is an annual event which started in 2009 in support of the LGBT community in Singapore. Since 2014, it drew strong reaction from Muslim and Christian religious groups in Singapore. In 2014, the Wear White campaign was initiated by some Muslims to promote traditional Islamic values when the Pink Dot SG 2014 coincided with the start of the Muslim month of Ramadan. The Faith Community Baptist Church and the LoveSingapore network of churches also called for their members to dress in white which they continued in 2016 (Lee, 2016).

Muis has to always take a future-oriented outlook while drawing on lessons from the past. This would mean not to be too fixated to always find precedence from the past or recycling old and existing models, but having the courage to imagine and create the future. New circumstances may demand the need to develop and innovate new solutions that have never been considered before. That spirit was evident in how Muis has responded to some of the policy challenges highlighted in the earlier chapters.

As highlighted earlier, diversity brings with it both challenges and opportunities. Hence, the need to build trust will continue to be an integral part of Muis' focus. Increase in expectations for good governance will drive Muis to strengthen its policies, systems, and processes to match public sector requirements and greater scrutiny. Better governance and controls will result in greater public trust. However, how the trust can be earned and forged may change as Muis deals with a new generation of Muslims who may have different expectations of Muis. Thus, trust may not necessarily come from being a strong and effective religious authority but possibly, through a sense of solidarity or being a strong supporter or facilitator. This emerging generation may prefer to take greater ownership of deciding and initiating change. Thus, a more appropriate arrangement for certain circumstances would be for Muis to allow for more spaces where the community can organically develop and take a more proactive role. Furthermore, an effective use of social media and the ability to harness its potential may extend Muis' reach to this emerging generation and amplify positive online and physical engagements. In other words, Muis may choose to focus in areas where its value is needed most and co-create with individuals and informal groups for greater impact.

Muis has been able to meet the socio-religious needs of the Muslim community mainly through the availability of resources and that has allowed it to progressively do more for the community. *Zakat* was initially the primary source. However, over the years, Muis has developed new revenue stream from MBMF, *wakaf, baitulmal*, and various investments which cumulatively have expanded Muis' resources to hire more and better talent. The improvements in the quality of services have contributed to further injection of funds and talent, as the community has full confidence that Muis is able to deliver. However, there is a limit. With an ageing population, sources of *zakat* may be reduced, and there may be a need for increased spending to support those under long-term *zakat* assistance.

Thus, the continuous development of new revenue streams and investments in assets have to be perpetual, as the traditional sources may one day reach its limit and become depleted. Thus, for Muis to sustain its operations and thrive in the future, this becomes very critical. Muis must be very strategic, able to harness digitalisation efforts, gain connectivity with the Public Sector systems and processes, and utilise its resources optimally.

While those principles remain relevant, they may not be adequate in dealing with the future emerging challenges of diversity and disruption. Muis will have to deal with a multiplicity of voices with their respective robust arguments on what kind of religious life they want for the community. Thus, it has to start building new capabilities that would help to engage with those multiple voices, and to find ways of channelling them towards convergence and a constructive outcome.

The upcoming formation of a Singapore Islamic tertiary institution will be a good opportunity for the community to consider designing a comprehensive curriculum that would shape the religious leadership of the future (Philomin, 2016). Graduates from this institution will be exposed to both the traditional Islamic sciences and the modern social sciences, which will allow them to synthesise the best of both worlds in charting new paths that will bring the community forward. Future religious leaders must be equipped with the ability to engage on complex issues with a deep appreciation of their external environment, be it global developments, national policies, contemporary ideas, or ground sentiments. Most importantly, they are able to articulate views in a mature and effective way, not only to the community but also to a wider Singapore audience. With a more inclusive outlook, the community's religious leadership will be able to bring people together and inspire them to be good Muslims, who excel not only in their religious obligations but also in their other pursuits which contribute to the well-being of the nation and humanity.

References

Cheow, S. (2017, October 26). Singapore is the 6th most popular travel destination for Muslim millennials: study. *The Straits Times*. Retrieved from: http://www.straits-times. com/singapore/singapore-is-the-6th-most-popular-travel-destination-for-muslim-millennials-study.

Chia, Y. M. (2016, October 3). Shedding light on slowing growth: What ails Singapore's economy? *The Straits Times*. Retrieved from: http://www.straitstimes.com/business/economy/what-ails-singapores-economy.

Ibrahim, Y. (2015). Our Place in History: Journey Towards Community of Excellence. In Aaron Maniam (Ed.) *Mendaki Policy Digest 2015 SG50 Edition* (pp. 23–26). Singapore: Yayasan Mendaki.

Islamic Religious Council of Singapore (2016). *Muis Public Perception Survey 2016*. Unpublished document.

Khalik, S. (2014, December 21). Malay population the most unhealthy group in Singapore. *The Straits Times*. Retrieved from: http://www.straitstimes.com/singapore/health/malay-population-the-most-unhealthy-group-in-singapore.

Lai, L. (2017, June 28). Harassment over views on LGBT issues unacceptable. *The Straits Times*. Retrieved from: http://www.straitstimes.com/singapore/harass-ment-over-views-on-lgbt-issues-unacceptable.

Lee, R. M. (2016, May 23). 'Traditional values' wear white campaign returning on Pink Dot weekend. *Today*. Retrieved from: http://www.todayonline.com/singapore/network-churches-revives-campaign-wear-white-pink-dot-weekend.

Lim, P. L. (2010, January 31). Penal Code section 377A. *Singapore Infopedia*. Retrieved from: http://eresources.nlb.gov.sg/infopedia/articles/SIP_1639_2010-01-31.html.

The Straits Times (2016, May 31). Muis Academy signs partnership to train Muslim organisations in the region. *The Straits Times*. Retrieved from: http://www.straitstimes.com/singapore/MUIS-academy-signs-partnership-to-train-muslim-organisations-in-the-region.

Maricar, A. R. H. (2016). The Islamic Religious Council of Singapore (MUIS) Journey: Continuing the Pursuit of Excellence — Legacy from the Past. In Zainul Abidin Rasheed and Norshahril Saat (Eds.) *Majulah! 50 Years of Malay/Muslim Community in Singapore* (pp. 273–279). Singapore: World Scientific.

Musawah (2017). *Thematic Report on Article 16, Muslim Family Law and Muslim Women's Rights in Singapore* (68th CEDAW session). Retrieved from: http://www.musawah.org/sites/default/files/Singapore%20-%20Musawah%20Thematic%20Report%20for%2068th%20CEDAW.compressed.pdf.

Nasir, K. M. (2017, June 3). The Singapore Muslim community and the *Imam* issue. *The Online Citizen*. Retrieved from: https://www.theonlinecitizen.com/2017/03/06/the-singapore-muslim-community-and-the-imam-issue/.

Neo, C. C. (2014, June 18). Most in Singapore feel there is religious harmony: Study. *Today*. Retrieved from: http://www.todayonline.com/singapore/most-spore-feel-there-religious-harmony-study.

Ng, K. (2015, June 30). Singapore's 'key future challenges': Economy, population, identity. *Today*. Retrieved from: https://www.todayonline.com/singapore/econ-omy-population-identity-are-spores-key-challenges-next-50-years-pm-lee.

Philomin, L. E. (2014, July 30). Proportion of inter-ethnic marriages almost doubles. *Today*. Retrieved from: http://www.todayonline.com/singapore/proportion-inter-ethnic-marriages-almost-doubles.

Philomin, L. (2016, July 15). Singapore to consider having an Islamic college: Dr Yaacob. *Today*. Retrieved from: http://www.todayonline.com/singapore/singapore-consider-having-islamic-college-dr-yaacob.

Prime Minister's Office (2009, July 11). Prime Minister Lee Hsien Loong's Written Interview with Berita Harian. Retrieved from Prime Minister's Office website: http://www.pmo.gov.sg/newsroom/prime-minister-lee-hsien-loong's-written-interview-berita-harian.

Public Service Division (2017, October 2). Opening address by Mr Ong Ye Kung, Minister of Education (Higher Education and Skills) at the Public Service Conference 2017. Retrieved from Public Service Division website: https://www.psd.gov.sg/press-room/speeches/opening-address-by-mr-ong-ye-kung--minister-for-education-higher-education-and-skills--at-the-public-service-conference-2017.

Reuters (2010, February 10). Singapore raps evangelical pastor for ridiculing Buddhists, Taoists. *Reuters*. Retrieved from: http://blogs.reuters.com/faithworld/2010/02/10/singapore-raps-evangelical-pastor-for-ridiculing-buddhists-taoists.

Tan, V. (2014, February 28). Health Promotion Board FAQ elicits strong reactions. *Youth.sg*. Retrieved from: https://www.youth.sg/Our-Voice/Your-Take/2014/2/Health-Promotion-Board-FAQ-elicits-strong-reactions.

Tay, K. (2015, August 3). Whither the hot-button issues of the previous general election? *The Business Times*. Retrieved from: http://www.businesstimes.com.sg/government-economy/singapore-general-election/whither-the-hot-button-issues-of-the-previous-general.

The Straits Times (2017, December 6). Singapore's demographic time bomb: Number of old people will match number of young for first time next year, says UOB economist. *The Straits Times*. Retrieved from http://www.straitstimes.com/business/economy/singapore-will-reach-critical-demographic-crossroad-in-2018-says-uob-economist.

Yong, C. (2017, May 17). Peter Ho: Although small, Singapore can shape its future. *The Straits Times*. Retrieved from http://www.straitstimes.com/singapore/peter-ho-although-small-singapore-can-shape-its-future.

Yong, C. (2016, March 11). More young people in Singapore staying single. *The Straits Times*. Retrieved from http://www.straitstimes.com/singapore/more-young-people-in-singapore-staying-single.

Abdul Rahim Saleh is currently Director, Emergency Preparedness and Singapore Islamic Hub Management. He is a business and marketing graduate by training. His career started with Muis since 1987. He had leadership and pioneering roles in areas like Haj and Halal Certification. He was the first CEO of Warees Halal Limited, a public company limited by guarantee, formed to support Muis' Halal Certification functions from July 2014 to September 2017.

Albakri Ahmad is Deputy Chief Executive of Muis and Dean of Muis Academy. He joined Muis in 2000. Prior to his current appointment, he served in Office of the Mufti, Religious Education, Research and Corporate Development Units. As a member of the senior management team and working together with community partners, he is responsible for developing religious leadership and capacity building to achieve the vision of a Muslim Community of Excellence in Singapore. He holds an MSc in Systems Design and a PhD in Managerial Cybernetics. His interest areas include Islamic Education, Ethics, Interfaith Understanding, Religion and Public Policy, and Muslims in Plural Societies.

Alfian Yasrif Kuchit is currently the Senior President of the Syariah Court. He received the inaugural Muis undergraduate scholarship in 1998

293

to study at the International Islamic University, Malaysia. He graduated with a double degree in Law and Syariah and was posted to the Muis Research Development Strategic Unit in 2005. He has had secondments at the then-Ministry of Community Development, Youth and Sports (MCYS) and Ministry of Culture, Community, and Youth (MCCY). Alfian received the Fulbright Scholarship in 2008 to study at Columbia Law School, New York and graduated with a Master of Laws degree in 2009.

Asri Aziz has served in Muis since 2003. His portfolios have included human resources, organisational excellence, research and policy development and international networking. He is currently working in media relations, strategic engagements and building community resilience. Asri graduated from the National University of Singapore with a Bachelor of Arts and holds an Msc in Strategic Studies from RSIS (Nanyang Technological University). He was also awarded a Chevening Fellowship in Syariah Studies at the University of Birmingham by the Foreign and Commonwealth Office of the United Kingdom.

Azree Rahim is currently Deputy Director, Educational Policy & Systems at Muis where he is responsible for the formulation, execution and review of policies and systems relating to full-time madrasahs in Singapore. His past roles in Muis included areas covering enterprise planning and youth education. He also had stints at the Ministry of Culture, Community and Youth where he served as Assistant Director at the Youth Division and Youth Corps Singapore. Beyond his professional work, he presently serves as a member of the 15th National Youth Council and served as President of MENDAKI Club (MClub). He graduated from the

National University of Singapore with a Bachelor of Computing in Electronic Commerce (Honours) and has a Masters in Public Administration from the Lee Kuan Yew School of Public Policy.

Dewi Hartaty Suratty has more than 10 years of experience in the halal industry. She is currently Director (Asset Policy & Industry Development) overseeing the Muis halal, zakat and wakaf functions and CEO of Warees Halal Limited, a not-for-profit company within the Muis Group. Dewi has a Masters of Business Administration (With Distinction) from Hull University UK and Bachelor's Degree (Honours) in Food Science & Technology from the National University of Singapore.

Farah Mahamood Aljunied is the Director for Curriculum Planning and Development at Muis. She oversees the development and implementation of the Islamic Education Curriculum at Mosque Madrasahs (aLIVE — Learning Islamic Values Everyday), conduct and development of ADIL programmes at mosques, network of Private Islamic Education Centres as well as supervises the Mosque Based Kindergartens. In addition to that, she also supervises the development of the revised Secondary Level Islamic Studies Integrated Curriculum for the Joint Madrasah System and its execution. She was awarded the Chevening Scholarship to pursue a Masters of Science, Sociology in 2007 at the London School of Economics and Political Science (LSE) in the UK and pursued a Master's Degree in Education — Curriculum, Teaching & Learning in 2012 at the Nanyang Technological University.

Irwan Hadi Mohd Shuhaimy completed his degree in Islamic Law at Al-Azhar University in Cairo. During this period, he managed to gain ijazahs in traditional Islamic sciences from scholars such as the Grand Mufti of Egypt, Sheikh Dr Ali Jum'ah and Sheikh Ahmad Taha Rayyan. He was awarded the Chevening Scholarship to pursue Masters of Law at the School of Oriental and African Studies, University of London. He is currently the Secretary of the Fatwa Committee and a Council member of Pergas. He has served the Office of the Mufti since 2007 and is currently Deputy Director overseeing Religious Policy and Regulation in Muis.

Masagoes Muhammad Isyak is currently the Assistant Director for the Zakat and Wakaf Strategic Unit at Muis where he oversees regulatory and policy matters and works closely with Muis subsidiary, Warees Investments Pte Ltd with the objective of maximizing Wakaf income and disbursements. His team is also responsible for the collection of Zakat including public education initiatives for the community. He was previously from Muis' Enterprise Planning Strategic Unit focusing on Business Intelligence and Analytics.

Mohamad Helmy Mohd Isa is currently Director, Mosque and Community Development. He joined Muis in 2004 and has since held various positions in the areas of mosque and youth development. In 2016, Helmy received the Muis study award to pursue a Masters in Tri Sector Collaboration at the Singapore Management University. He is also a board member of the Rahmatan Lil Alamin Foundation.

Mohammad Hannan Hassan is presently Vice Dean of the Muis Academy. He completed his PhD at the Institute of Islamic Studies, McGill University, Canada, with a dissertation titled, "Islamic Legal Thought and Practices of 17th Century Aceh: Treating the Others". He received his MA in Islamic Civilisation from the International Institute of Islamic Thought and Civilisation (ISTAC), Kuala Lumpur. He holds a Bachelor of Education (Hons) First Class with Distinction from Kuwait, majoring in Arabic Language and Islamic Education.

Mohamad Khidir Abdul Rahman is presently the Assistant Director of the Youth & Community Education Strategic Unit which oversees the development of the part-time Islamic education sector that includes content development, capacity building of asatizah in the sector and outreach to the community. He joined Muis in 2007 as an executive in the Youth Education Strategic Unit. In 2011, he was appointed Head of the unit and continued the revision of the aLIVE programme and initiated new platforms of Islamic Education such as the Kids aLIVE Home Edition, the Youth aLIVE Discourse and the aLIVE Parenting Seminar. He graduated from the Islamic University of Medina (KSA) with a Bachelors in Hadith and holds an MA from Syarif Hidayatullah State Islamic University, Jakarta in Interdisciplinary Islamic Studies and a Masters in Education (Curriculum & Teaching) from Nanyang Technological University.

Nazirudin Nasir is a Senior Director of the Religious Policy and Development at Muis. He completed a doctoral degree in the comparative study of Abrahamic religions at St Cross College, University of Oxford. Prior to that, he was trained in Islamic Law at Al-Azhar University and international and comparative law at the School of Oriental and African Studies. He has published articles in the area of inter-religious dialogue and comparative religion. He is also a member of the Singapore Bioethics Advisory Committee and sits on the Panel of Community Advisors for Honour, Singapore.

Norshahril Saat is a Fellow at the ISEAS-Yusof Ishak Institute. In June 2015, he was awarded a PhD in International, Political and Strategic Studies by the Australian National University (ANU). He is a recipient of the Islamic Religious Council of Singapore (MUIS) Post-graduate Scholarship 2011. In 2015, he became the first recipient of Syed Isa Semait Scholarship (SISS). His research interests are mainly on Southeast Asian politics and contemporary Islamic thought. In 2018, he published three books: *The State, Ulama, and Islam in Malaysia and Indonesia* (Amsterdam University Press); *Tradition and Islamic Learning: Singapore Students in the Al-Azhar University* (ISEAS Publishing); and edited *Islam in Southeast Asia: Negotiating Modernity* (ISEAS Publishing). His earlier books include *Faith, Authority and the Malays: The ulama in contemporary Singapore; Majulah! 50 years of Malay/Muslim community in Singapore* (co-edited with Zainul Abidin Rasheed); *and Yusof Ishak: Singapore's First President.* His articles have recently been published in journals such as *Asian Journal of Social Science, Contemporary Islam: Dynamics of Muslim Life, Review of Indonesian and Malaysian Affairs,* and *Studia Islamika.* He has also published numerous opinion and think pieces, including those in local newspapers such as the *Straits Times, Berita Harian* and *Today*; and international newspapers such as the *Canberra Times, Bangkok Post,* and the *Jakarta Post.*

Sakdun Sardi is currently the Assistant Director (Corporate Development) of the Mosque Planning Office. His work covers the development, enforcement and review of policies on mosque governance covering Board governance, financial regulations, human resource management, religious programmes and mosque building works to ensure good governance of mosques and compliance with statutory regulations. He has served as chairman of Al-Muttaqin Mosque (2009–2011) and Al-Mawaddah Mosque (2011–2015) and the Chairman of JKMS (2013). He graduated from the National University of Singapore with a Bachelor of Science in Physics.

Yaacob Ibrahim served as the Minister-in-charge of Muslim Affairs for 16 years from 2002 to 2018. He has been a Member of Parliament since 1997 and had served in various ministerial portfolios including Community Development and Sports from 2003 to 2004, Environment and Water Resources from 2004 to 2011, Information, Communications and the Arts from 2011 to 2012 and Communications and Information from 2012 to 2018. He assumed an additional portfolio as Minister-in-charge of Cyber Security from 2015 to 2018. He graduated from the University of Singapore with an honours degree in civil engineering in 1980 and subsequently, obtained a Doctor of Philosophy from Stanford University. He returned to Singapore in 1990 and joined the National University of Singapore faculty in 1991. He received his department's teaching excellence award in 1994. He also served in the 9th Muis Council from 1992 to 1995.

Yazid Mohamed Ali joined Muis in 1998 as part of the Information Systems Unit. In 2004, as Head of the Organisational Excellence Strategic Unit, his team built the foundations for Muis' Business Excellence journey which has since seen Muis attaining the Singapore Quality Class Star, the People Developer, Innovation Class and Service Class standards. He then headed the Madrasah Policy & Planning Strategic Unit which was responsible for setting up the governance systems for the Joint Madrasah System in its formative years. He is now Assistant Director of the Strategic Policy & Planning Office which oversees the strategic planning, research and data analytics work in Muis. He graduated from the Nanyang Technological University with a Bachelors in Applied Science (Computer Technology) and holds an MBA (merit) from Bradford University.

Zainul Abidin Ibrahim is currently the Director for Strategic Communications in Muis, and holds a concurrent appointment as the Executive Director of Rahmatan lil Alamin Foundation (RLAF), an institution established by Muis to deepen the ethos of care and compassion within the community and beyond. In 2003, he joined Muis as the Head for Corporate Communications and managed Interfaith Relations and Community Engagement. His past appointments include being a current affairs broadcast journalist/producer with the then Singapore Broadcasting Corporation, Assistant Director, Corporate Communications at the Land Transport Authority, Project Manager and Trainer at the Association of Muslim Professionals and Trainer and Administrative Manager at Madrasah Aljunied. He graduated from University of Singapore in Economics and Sociology and University of California, LA (UCLA) in Broadcast Journalism and Early Childhood.

Zalman Putra Ahmad Ali is the Director, Policy & Strategy at Muis where he is responsible in supporting Muis' long-term strategic policy thinking on the future development of the Singapore Muslim community's religious life. He began his career in Muis in 1998 in the Office of the Mufti before being assigned to develop Muis' policy and research capabilities. In 2006, he was awarded the Fulbright Scholarship to pursue a Masters in Religious Studies at Hartford Seminary in

Connecticut, USA. His area of research interest is on the emerging religious orientations and ideas in the context of Singapore's cosmopolitan society. His Masters thesis was entitled 'Modern Religiosities — A Comparative Study of American Evangelicalism and the Dakwah Movement in Malaysia.'

Zulfadhli Ghazali graduated from Monash University (Australia) with a first class honours degree, majoring in Political Islam in 2006. He started his career in Muis at the Policy Development Strategic Unit. In 2012, he received the Muis' ILM scheme to study at the National University of Singapore and completed a Post-Graduate Diploma in Social Work. He is currently Manager at the Social Development Strategic Unit in Muis.

Glossary

Adat — customary law

Azan — call to prayer

Akhlaq — good character, or Moral Education — a subject taught to Muslim students at full-time and/or part-time madrasahs

Amil — *zakat* collector

Aqidah — Islamic term for any religious belief system or creed

Arafah — a mountain plain in Saudi Arabia where Muslim pilgrims gather on the ninth day of *Zulhijjah* or the Day of Arafah, as part of the *haj* ritual

Asatizah — religious teachers

Asy'ari — the foremost theological school of Sunni Islam which established an orthodox guideline based on clerical authority, founded by Abu al-Hasan al-Asy'ari (d. 936 CE)

Aziziyah — a neighbourhood of Mecca and near Jamarat in Mina

Baitulmal — the Islamic treasury or central endowment fund of a Muslim community

Darura — in Islamic legal terminology, a state of necessity on account of which one may omit doing something required by Islamic law

Dzanni — speculative

Eidul Adha — a major Islamic festival which commemorates the *Korban* and marks the end of the annual *Haj* to Mecca

Faraidh — distribution of the estate of a deceased person to his/her heirs according to Islamic law

Fardhu 'ain — acquisition of knowledge that is considered as an individual obligation that every Muslim must undertake

Fardhu kifayah — obligation to acquire certain knowledge is fulfilled if a section of the community fulfils it

Fasakh — dissolution of marriage due to any valid reason under Islamic law

Fatwa — a religious ruling to a specific question on Muslim law

Fiqh — Islamic Jurisprudence studies — a subject taught to Muslim students at full-time and/or part-time madrasahs

Fitrah — tithe collected during the fasting month of Ramadan

Ghusl — ritual washing of the whole body as prescribed by Islamic law

Hadith — tradition of Prophet Muhammad

Haj — annual pilgrimage to Mecca in the month of *Zulhijjah*

Hajjiyyat — basic needs in life that can relieve hardship and difficulty, and facilitate the normal functioning of life

Halal — permissible according to Islamic law

Hanafi — one of the four major schools of Islamic legal thought named after Imam Abu Hanifa (d. 767 CE). Followed by a significant number of Indian Muslims in Singapore

Hanbali — one of the four major schools of Islamic legal thought named after Imam Ahmad ibn Hanbal (d. 855 CE)

Haram — forbidden in Islamic law

Hibah ruqbah — conditional gift

Hisab — mathematical calculation to mark the dates of Islamic festivals

Imam — an Islamic leader, often the leader of a mosque or the person who leads prayers

Ijma' — in Islamic law, the universal and infallible agreement of either the Muslim community as a whole or Muslim scholars in particular

Ijtihad — utmost effort expended by a jurist in formulating a religious ruling which is unclear from the primary sources

Istibdal — conversion of a type of *wakaf* into another type

Istihalah — change in a substance from one form to another

Jamarat — three stone walls (formerly pillars) in the city of Mina which are pelted as a compulsory ritual of *haj* in emulation of the Prophet Ibrahim

Jemaah — congregation

Kaabah — a cube-shaped building in Mecca which Muslims face in its direction when praying.

Khalwat — a forbidden act under Islamic law where one is in excessive closeness in a secluded place with someone from the opposite gender who is not related

Korban — an Islamic religious act of ritual slaughter of animals (e.g. sheep) performed in the first three days of *Eidul Adha* in commemoration of Prophet Ibrahim's act of obedience to God's commandment to sacrifice his own son which was later replaced by a ram

Madrasah — Islamic religious school

Maktab — is literally interpreted as the office that regulates the affairs of *haj*

Maliki — one of the four schools of Islamic legal thought named after Imam Malik Ibn Anas (d. 795 CE)

Manasik — Rituals of *haj*

Mas'aa — the area between Safa and Marwa where *sai'e* takes place

Maslaha — public good or interest

Mataf — the open white area immediately around the *Kaabah* where *tawaf* takes place

Mazhab — school of Islamic legal thought

Mina — situated about 5 kilometres from the holy city of Mecca

Muassasah — establishment of the *mutawwif* of Southeast Asian pilgrims

Mutawwif — a knowledgeable person who can guide the pilgrims during *haj*

Mufti — A Muslim legal expert who is qualified to give authoritative legal opinions or *fatwas*

Nusyuz — a wife unreasonably refuses to obey the lawful wishes or commands of her husband

Nuzriah — making a vow to perform certain actions if certain conditions are met. Contextually, it refers to a vow made by someone to give part or all of his wealth before his death to another party

Qadi — judge/marriage registrar in Islam

Qur'an — the central religious text of Islam which Muslims believe to be a revelation from God

Rahmatan lil alamin — blessings to all

Riba' — usury

Safa and Marwa — two small hills located adjacent to the *Kaabah* in Masjidil Haram (the Grand Mosque) in Mecca

Sah — valid

Sai'e — one of the integral rites of *haj* and *umrah* which encompasses the ritual of walking back and forth seven times between the two small hills of Safa and Marwa in emulation of the actions of Hajar, the wife of Prophet Ibrahim

Syafi'i — one of the four schools of Islamic legal thought named after Imam Abu Abdullah Muhammad ibn Idris al-Syafi'i (d. 820 CE). Majority of Muslims in Southeast Asia including Singapore follow the Syafi'i school

Sheikh — A leader in a Muslim community or organisation

Shia — a branch of Islam which holds that Prophet Muhammad's designated successor was Ali ibn Abi Talib

Shisha — situated at the fringe of Mina and near Jamarat

Sirah — Prophetic History Education — a subject taught to Muslim students at full-time and/or part-time madrasahs

Solat — obligatory act of worship prescribed for every Muslim

Solat jenazah — prayer for the deceased Muslim

Soleh/solehah — pious

Sukuk musyarakah — bond

Sunni — main branch of Islam

Surau — a place of worship

Syariah — Islamic law

Taharah — ritual purification

Taqwa — God consciousness

Tauhid — Islamic Theology or Monotheism Studies — a subject taught to Muslim students at full-time and/or part-time madrasahs

Tauliah — accreditation

Tawaf — the ritual of performing seven circumambulations of the *Kaabah*

Ulama — collective term for Muslim scholars

Ummah — community

Umrah — a minor pilgrimage that can be performed at any time of the year except during the *haj* season

Wakaf — permanent endowment for charity

Waswas — sense of doubt

Zakat — tithe on wealth, collected annually

Zulhijjah — twelfth and final month in the Islamic calendar

Past & Present Images

Figure 1.1 The Administration of Muslim Law Bill was passed in 1966 after six years of debates. Although the bill was passed in 1966, the Administration of Muslim Law Act only came into effect in 1968. *Reprinted with permission from The Straits Times. Copyright © 2018 Singapore Press Holdings Ltd. Co. All rights reserved.*

Figure 1.2 Dr. Ahmad Mohamed Ibrahim's (then Attorney General of Singapore and drafter of the Administration of Muslim Law Act) article on the need to recognise the special context of Singapore in implementing Muslim law. *Reprinted with permission from The Straits Times. Copyright © 2018 Singapore Press Holdings Ltd. Co. All rights reserved.*

Figure 1.3 The Mohammedan and Hindu Endowment Board in the 1920s. The board had broad powers to administer and supervise Muslim and Hindu endowments. *Reprinted with permission from The Straits Times. Copyright © 2018 Singapore Press Holdings Ltd. Co. All rights reserved.*

Figure 2.1 Muis' first office premises in the Empress Place Building from 1968 to 1987, now the Asian Civilisation Museum. *Reprinted with permission from The Straits Times Copyright © 2018 Singapore Press Holdings Ltd. Co. All rights reserved.*

Figure 2.2 The Islamic Centre of Singapore, located at Braddell Road, opened in May 1988 and in operation till 2006.

Figure 2.3 Muis' building as part of the Singapore Islamic Hub, which includes Muhajirin Mosque and Madrasah Irsyad Zuhri Al-Islamiah, opened in 2009.

Figure 2.4 | Muis staff in 1986 in the old Muis office at Empress Place.

Figure 2.5 | The late Hj Buang Siraj, former Muis President (1974–1980), over-seeing Muis' work at the old Muis office at Empress Place. *Reprinted with permission from The Straits Times. Copyright © 2018 Singapore Press Holdings Ltd. Co. All rights reserved.*

Figure 2.6 Former Minister-in-charge of Muslim Affairs (1977–1993), Dr Ahmad Mattar, officiating the celebrations of Muis' 10th Anniversary in July 1978. *Reprinted with permission from The Straits Times. Copyright © 2018 Singapore Press Holdings Ltd. Co. All rights reserved.*

Figure 2.7 Former Minister-in-Charge of Muslim Affairs (2002–2018), Dr Yaacob Ibrahim, officiating the opening of Warees Investments Pte Ltd office at Beach Road in 2002, accompanied by the former Muis President (1996–2003), Haji Maarof Bin Salleh.

Figure 4.1 Then Minister-in-charge of Muslim Affairs Dr Yaacob Ibrahim engaging graduating students at the graduation ceremony of Singapore's Al-Azhar University students in Cairo, Egypt in 2014.

Figure 4.2 Asatizah from the Asatizah Youth Network attending the Workship on Counter-Narrative Constructions hosted by Google at the APAC HQ at Mapletree Business Centre in October 2017.

Figure 4.3 | An engagement session by the ARS Office with *asatizah* on the ARS Code of Ethics in 2017.

Figure 5.1 | Students from Madrasah Mahadul Irshad at its old premises in Kampong Kuari on 27 February 1972. *Reprinted with permission from Madrasah Irsyad Zuhri Al-Islamiah © 2018 Madrasah Irsyad Zuhri Al-Islamiah. All rights reserved.*

Figure 5.2 | The Madrasah Irsyad Zuhri Al-Islamiah building at the Singapore Islamic Hub, Braddell Road, which started operation in 2009. It has significantly more facilities to meet the growing demands of modern madrasah education.

Figure 5.3 | Madrasah teachers graduating in 2014 from the Specialist Diploma in Teaching and Learning, a collaboration between the National Institute of Education (NIE) and Muis.

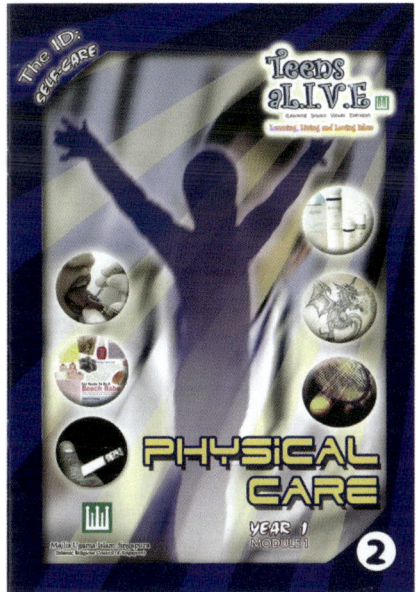
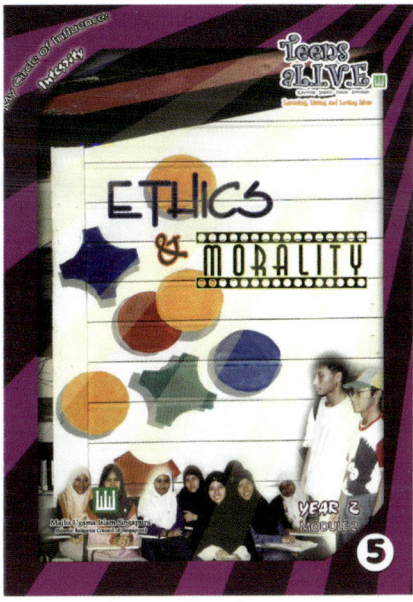

Figure 6.1 | Textbooks used in *Teens aLIVE* throughout 2004–2008, featuring topics related to contemporary realities faced by young Muslims.

Figure 6.2 | *Kids aLIVE* students learning Islam through different means: learning Arabic language through colouring and practical learning of prayer rituals.

Figure 7.1

Small *Kampong* mosques (top left) were demolished to make way for larger mosques under the Mosque Building and Mendaki Fund (MBMF) like the Mujahidin Mosque (middle left) and En-Naeem Mosque (top right), with larger prayer space capacity and better facilities, as well as running various religious programmes and services for the Singapore Muslim community. Today, more new mosques like Maarof Mosque (middle right) and Yusof Ishak Mosque (bottom left) have been built to meet the growing demand for prayer spaces. Older mosques under the MBMF like Al-Ansar Mosque (bottom right) have also been redeveloped.

Figure 7.2 | Former Muis President (1991–1996), Hj Zainul Abidin Rasheed briefing on the plans for the new Alkaff Kampong Melayu Mosque at Bedok Reservoir Road to former Minister-in-charge of Muslim Affairs (1993–2002), Mr Abdullah Tarmugi in 1994.

Figure 9.1

Revitalisation of Wakaf Haji Alias into six semi-detached strata landed units known as the Alias Villas, located along Jalan Alias off Sixth Avenue. This is to enhance the asset value of 30,450 ft of *wakaf* land parcel, bequeathed in 1905, which also houses Al-Huda Mosque. *Reprinted with permission from Warees Investments © 2018 Warees Investments. All rights reserved.*

Figure 9.2   The Red House is a *wakaf* property put in trust to Muis by Sheriffa
Zain Alsharoff Mohamed Alsagoff. The new Red House project which
began in 2012 would transform the wakaf into an Integrated Heritage
Development consisting of residential units, retail, bakery, and a her-
itage gallery by December 2018. *Reprinted with permission from
Warees Investments © 2018 Warees Investments. All rights reserved.*

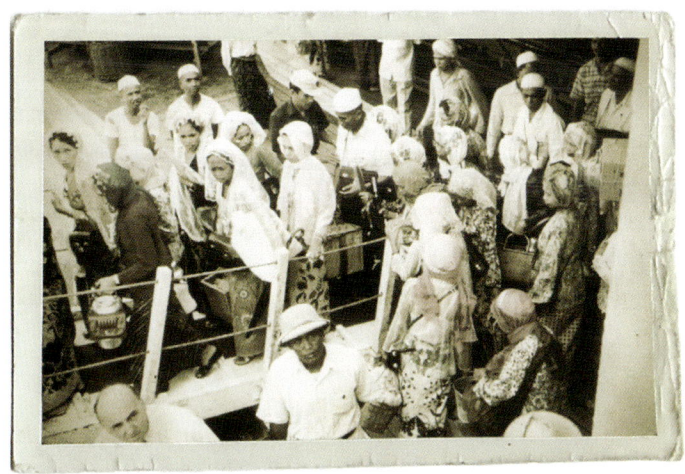

Figure 10.1 | *Haj*-goers boarding the *kapal kaji* in Singapore Tanjong Pagar Port in the 1950s. *Reprinted with permission from The Straits Times. Copyright © 2018 Singapore Press Holdings Ltd. Co. All rights reserved.*

Figure 10.2 | Then Minister-in-charge of Muslim Affairs (2002–2018), Dr Yaacob Ibrahim and Muis Chief Executive, Haji Abdul Razak Maricar, sending off pilgrims at Singapore Changi Airport in 2017.

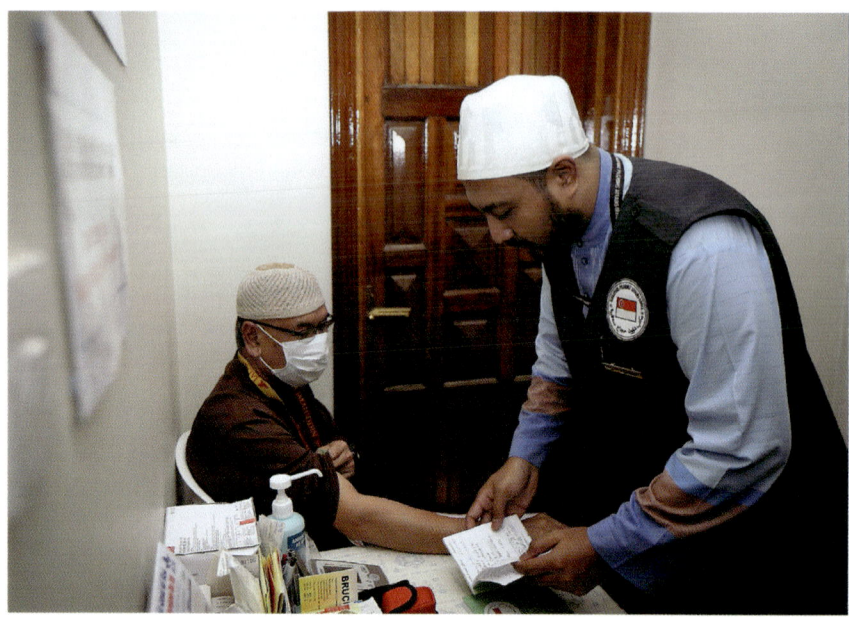

Figure 10.3 | Singapore Pilgrims' Affairs Office (SPAO) clinic in Mecca, administered by medical professionals in 2017.

Figure 13.1 | Members of the Unofficial Meeting of the Religious Affairs Ministers of Brunei, Indonesia, Malaysia and Singapore (MABIMS) at the meeting in Singapore in 2012.

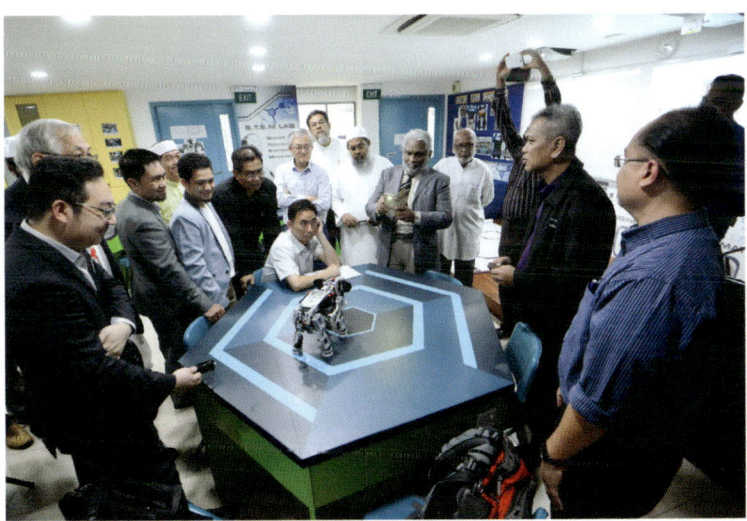

Figure 13.2 | 2016 PRISM (Programme for RISEAP Members) participants from various countries like Taiwan, Hong Kong and Australia being briefed by the Principal of Madrasah Irsyad Zuhri Al-Islamiah on the use of technology in madrasah's student learning.

Figure 13.3 | Eminent scholar Shaykh Abdallah Bin Bayyah as Muis' Distinguished Visitor in 2017, giving a lecture on *Faith, Compassion and Human Dignity*, moderated by Shaykh Hamzah Yusof.

Figure 13.4 | The Grand Shaykh of Al-Azhar, H.E. Dr Ahmad Al-Tayyeb as Muis' Distinguished Visitor in 2018, giving a lecture on *The Unifying Force of Religion*. The session was moderated by Senior Minister of State for Defence and Foreign Affairs, Dr Maliki Osman.

Figure 14.1 | Prime Minister Lee Hsien Loong and then Minister-in-charge of Muslim Affairs (2002–2018), Dr Yaacob Ibrahim at the official opening of the Harmony Centre at An-Nahdhah Mosque in 2006.

Figure 14.2 | Leaders from other faith communities learning about the new exhibits featured at the Harmony Centre.

Figure 14.3 Britain's Prince Charles visiting Harmony Centre and meeting with interfaith leaders from Singapore in October 2017.

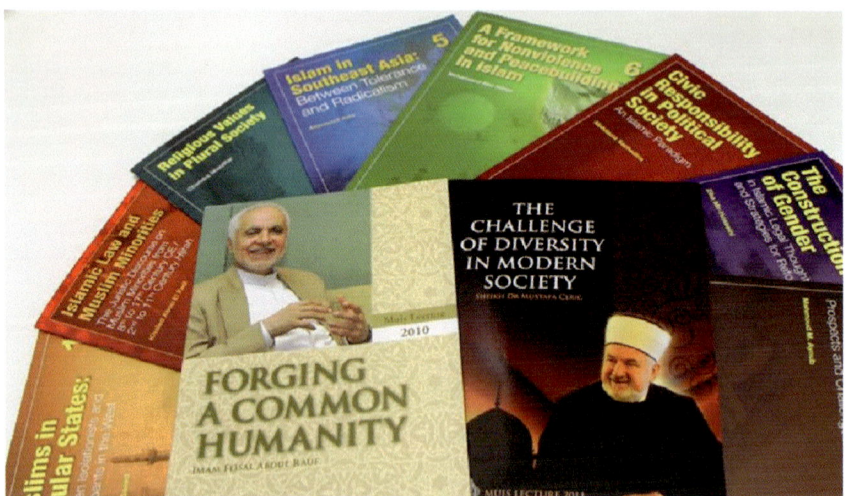

Figure 14.4 Muis publications to promote progressive understanding of Islam.

Figure 14.5 A Singaporean student in Jordan visiting and distributing supplies to Syrian refugees in Jordan, supported by the Rahmatan Lil-Alamin Foundation (RLAF) in 2017. *Reprinted with permission from Rahmatan Lil-Alamin Foundation © 2018 Rahmatan Lil-Alamin Foundation. All rights reserved.*

Figure 14.6 The RLAF team on monitoring visit to Bekaa Valley in Beirut, Lebanon in 2017 to understand education programmes for Syrian Refugees that RLAF raised funds for. *Reprinted with permission from Rahmatan Lil-Alamin Foundation © 2018 Rahmatan Lil-Alamin Foundation. All rights reserved.*

Figure 14.7   RLAF partnered with LIFE SG, a social enterprise, to empower under-privileged children regardless of race and religion through acts of giving in Ramadan, May 2018. *Reprinted with permission from Rahmatan Lil-Alamin Foundation © 2018 Rahmatan Lil-Alamin Foundation. All rights reserved.*

INDEX

9/11, 6–8, 78, 248, 249, 256, 262–264, 266, 271
@halalsg, 214, 219

Abdul Hamid Jumat, 25
Abdullah Musa, 190
Abdul Razak Maricar, 83, 287
Abu Bakar Maidin, 258, 259, 270
adat, 17
Administration of Muslim Law Act (AMLA), 1, 8, 11,
    28, 35–37, 58, 59, 76, 77, 83, 86, 93, 96, 133, 153,
    161, 165, 167, 176, 182, 186, 191, 194, 200, 207,
    208, 218, 258, 260, 275, 277, 286
Administration of Muslim Law Bill, 8, 15, 16, 24–29,
    76, 151
Administration of Muslim Law Enactment, 23
Adult Islamic Learning (ADIL), 266
Agri-Food and Veterinary Authority of Singapore
    (AVA), 223, 226–231, 234, 236
Ahmad Mohamed Ibrahim, 16, 258
Al-Azhar University, 74, 90, 96, 101–104, 107, 122,
    284
All-Malaya Muslim Missionary Society, 27
Al-Qaeda, 248, 263
al-Syawkani, 203
amil, 149–153
Amman Declaration, 85
animal welfare, 222–224, 226–230, 232, 235
APKIM, 50
Appeal Board, 21
Arafah, 185, 187–189
Armstrong, Karen, 250

asatizah, 9, 46, 50, 73–87, 96, 113, 243, 263, 266, 267, 269, 270
    Asatizah Executive Development Programme (AEDP), 79–81
    Asatizah Overseas Attachment Programme (OAP), 79
    development, 47, 50, 73, 74, 76–78, 80
    engagement, 47, 50, 82
    Muis Asatizah Immersion/ Attachment Programme (MAAP), 79
Asatizah Recognition Scheme (ARS), 9, 74, 80–86
    ARS Appeal Panel, 86
    ARS Code of Ethics, 83–85
    Asatizah Recognition Scheme Continuous Professional Education (ARS-CPE), 80, 83, 266
    Qur'anic Teachers Recognition Scheme (QTRS), 82
Ascott Limited, The, 45
ASEAN Working Group on Halal Food (AWGHF), 206, 218
Asia-Middle East Dialogue (AMED), 246, 248
Ask Me Anything, 271
Asset-Based Community Development Model, 162
asset migration, 169, 170, 172
Association of Muslim Professionals (AMP), 5
Association of Muslim Travel Agents, Singapore (AMTAS), 184–186, 188–190, 194
Asy'ari, 284
Australia, 117, 182, 194, 205, 222, 225–227, 233, 236, 247, 248, 253, 269
Australian Association for Early Childhood, 117

azan, 143
Aziziyah, 188, 189, 197

baitulmal, 24, 27, 50, 103, 168, 169, 174, 175, 288
Beach Road, 170, 171
Befrienders Scheme, 141
Bioethics Advisory Committee, 67
biomedicine, 67
Braddell, Roland, 18
Braybrooke, Marcus, 266
British, 2, 16–21, 23, 180, 182, 257, 266, 284
    Attorney General, 18, 19
    British adviser, 21, 23
    colonial authorities, 20, 25
    Crown Colony, 18
    East India Company, 17
    Executive Council, 18
    government, 2, 19
    Governor, 18–20
    Legislative Council, 18–19
    Parliament, 18
    Resident, 19
Brunei, 65, 74, 204, 206, 242–244, 251, 277
Buddhism, 268, 277
Building Abrahamic Partnership Programme, 267
Building Bridges Programme, 268
Business Excellence (BE) Framework, 42
Byrne, K.M., 24

Cambodia, 206, 244
Canada, 227, 228, 236, 248, 251
Central Provident Fund (CPF), 6, 9, 68–69, 134, 278
Chancery Lane, 173
Changi Road, 167, 168
Charter of Justice, 17
Chiam See Tong, 261
China, 207, 208, 269, 280

Christianity, 64, 268
    Christian community, 287
    Christian values, 64
Civil Service College, 38, 247
Civil Service Computerisation
    Programme (CSCP), 40
Club Heal, 50
Clustered Regularly Interspaced Short
    Palindromin Repeats (CRISPR), 67
Code on Religious Harmony, 263
ComCare, 154, 155
CommaCon, 271
Community Development Councils
    (CDCs), 154, 269
Comprehensive Islamic Religious
    Education System (CIRES), 114
Compulsory Education (CE), 7, 9, 33,
    34, 45, 90, 91, 97–99, 101, 105, 106
Control of Rent Act, 167, 171
Crescentrating.com, 279
Curriculum Development Committee
    (CDC), 77
Curriculum Development Project (CDP),
    99, 105
Cyber Ummah, 98

Darul Arqam, 50
darura, 63–65
Dawoodi Bohra, 284
Dawud Tauhidi, 117
Disraeli, Benjamin, 18
disruption, 5, 12, 277, 280–281,
    284–287, 289
diversity, 81, 85, 104, 125, 126, 143,
    244, 247, 251, 269, 271, 275,
    283–285, 287–289
Duku Road, 167, 168
Dunlop Street, 169
dzanni, 63

Edith Cowan University, 99
Egypt, 64, 249, 251, 284, 296

Eidul Adha, 141, 221, 226, 228, 230, 235
Emergency Medical Assistance (EMA),
    190
Empowerment Partnership Scheme
    (EPS), 157
English law, 17, 18
Enterprise Singapore, 210, 219
Exporter Supply ChainAssurance
    System (ESCAS), 222–224, 226–229,
    231, 232, 234, 235

fake news, 211–214, 271
Family Development Centres (FDCs),
    153
fardhu 'ain, 120
fardhu kifayah, 120
fasakh, 28
fatwa, 1, 4, 9, 23, 45, 47, 58, 170, 260,
    284
    bodies, 58, 62, 64
    CPF nomination, 69
    Fatwa Committee, 1, 24, 59–60,
        62–65, 67, 68, 70, 84, 170, 260,
        296
    fatwa making, 58, 59, 61, 62
    inheritance, 9, 62, 68, 70, 276
    joint-tenancy agreement, 69
    national *fatwa* councils, 59
    organ donation, 9, 45, 62–66, 70,
        276
fiqh, 68, 113, 117, 120
fitrah, 23–25, 27, 29, 36, 93
Fitrah Committee, 42
food labels, 202–203, 214
Foreign and Commonwealth Office
    (FCO), 102, 249
France, 205, 236, 248
Friday prayers, 19, 20

gene editing technology, 67
General Sales Agents (GSAs), 184–189,
    193, 194

Gentle Road, 168, 173
Germany, 248
Gladstone, William, 18
Goh Chok Tong, 33, 89, 97, 98
Gulf Cooperation Council — Singapore
    Free Trade Agreement (GSFTA), 204,
    218, 246, 248

Habib Syed Hassan Al-Attas, 256, 258,
    259, 270
Hazard Analysis Critical Control Point
    (HACCP), 208
haj, 4, 10, 11, 36, 179–182, 185, 186,
    191, 241, 246, 252, 278, 280
    authorities, 180–183, 186, 187, 189
    Establishment of the Mutawwif
        of South-East Asian Pilgrims
        (Muassasah), 181, 185, 189, 193
    government-regulated model, 183
    maktabs, 185
    management, 179, 180, 182–184,
        187–189
    manasik, 185
    mutawwif, 181, 185, 193, 194
    packages, 182, 183, 187–190, 197,
        280
    pilgrim guides, 180, 181, 193
    pilgrims, 11, 36, 179–181,
        183–191, 193, 194, 196
    pilgrim ships, 180–181, 190
    quota, 36, 180, 182, 183, 185–187,
        193, 195, 197, 252, 278
    registration system, 190, 194, 195
    Rules, 186, 194
    services, 11, 180, 182–187, 193
    sheikhs, 180, 181, 183
    Singapore Pilgrims' Affairs Office
        (SPAO), 42, 185, 189
hajjiyyat, 65
halal, 2, 7, 10, 11, 36, 199–214, 218,
    219, 244, 246, 251, 252, 253, 276,
    278, 279
    authorities, 201, 213, 214

certificate, 36, 199, 200, 203-205,
    208, 212-214, 218
certification, 11, 199, 200,
    203–214, 218, 244, 246, 251,
    276, 278, 279
    food industry, 200, 207–208
    Foreign *Halal* Certification Bodies
        (FHCBs), 205, 206
    halal extremism, 211
    Halal Quality Management System
        (HalMQ), 208, 218, 251
    logo, 204, 207, 211, 212, 214
    mark, 203, 208, 213, 214, 218
Hamza Yusuf, 250
Hanafi, 203, 284
Hanbali, 204, 284
haram, 183, 201–203, 205
Harmony Centre, 7, 247, 248, 256,
    266–270
Hartford Seminary, 248, 267
Hassan Salim, 74
Health Promotion Board (HPB), 286–287
hibah, 69, 174
hisab, 60
Hong Kong, 245
Housing Development Board (HDB),
    113, 132–135, 166, 167
humanitarian, 146, 244, 251, 253, 269
Human Organ Transplant Act (HOTA),
    6, 9, 62, 65–67

Ibn Hazm al-Zahiri, 204
Ibrahim Abu Rabi', 267
ijma', 65
ijtihad, 59, 61
Indian-Muslim associations, 113
Indonesia, 4, 11, 48, 100, 183, 187,
    204–206, 222, 232, 236, 242–245,
    251, 269, 280
Institutional Investment Initiative (3I),
    174
interfaith, 7, 11, 81, 85, 248–250, 259,
    264, 266–270

Internal Security Act (ISA), 256
International Baccalaureate Diploma
  Programme (IBDP), 103
International Islamic Fiqh Academy,
  65
Inter-Racial and Religious Confidence
  Circles (IRCC), 262
Inter Religious Organisation (IRO),
  256–259
intra-faith, 85, 102, 126, 251, 271
Ireland, 227, 236
Islamic college, 106, 107, 251, 252
Islamic education, 2, 39, 45, 75,
  111–126, 138, 142, 242, 246, 249,
  276, 278
    curriculum, 10, 112, 114, 116–126,
      137, 142, 266
    examinations, 113–115, 118–120
    Learning Islamic Values Everyday
      (aLIVE), 10, 44, 112, 116,
      118–127, 142, 266, 295, 297
    medium of instruction, 115, 116,
      118, 123–125
    mosque madrasah, 10, 112–121,
      123–125
    Mosque Madrasah Convention,
      124, 125
    part-time, 10, 36, 44, 77, 111–116,
      118, 119, 122, 123, 137
    pedagogies, 10, 112, 114–119,
      121–123
    Private Islamic Education Network
      (PIENet), 125
    private Islamic education
      providers, 111, 113, 119, 120,
      124, 126
    Singapore Islamic Education
      System (SIES), 116
    students, 111–115, 118–120, 122,
      125
    syllabus, 113, 114, 118, 120
    teacher, 112, 119, 120, 122, 124,
      125, 142

    youths, 112–114, 118, 120,
      124–125, 137, 268
Islamic Education Advisory Board,
  96
Islamic revivalism, 7, 8, 94
Islamisation, 207
Ismail Aziz, 190
ISO, 208, 210, 218, 219
istibdal, 170
istihalah, 203
Italy, 207

Jaafari Muslim Association of
  Singapore, 284
Jabbal Omar, 187
Jama'at Ahmadiyyah, 27
Jamarat, 187
Jamiyah, 5, 65, 113, 190, 257–259
Japan, 207, 247, 269, 280
Jeddah, 179, 189
Jemaah Islamiah (JI), 6, 7, 78, 256, 262,
  263, 267, 271
Jervois, F.D, 18
Johor-Riau Sultanate, 17
Jordan, 251
Judaism, 64
Juffrie Mahmood, 261

Kaabah, 187, 188
Kamil Suhaimi, 167
Kandahar Street, 169
Kelantan, 8, 16, 21–23, 29
    Majlis Agama Islam dan
      Isti'adat Melayu Kelantan
      (MAIK), 21–23
    State Council, 22
    Sultan, 21–23, 29
Keppel, Giles, 250
khalwat, 20
King George IV, 17
korban, 10, 11, 141, 221–236,
  253
    air freight, 226, 227

Approved Korban Vendor (AKV),
226–228, 231, 233
centres, 224, 227, 234–236
Jawatankuasa Korban Masjid
Singapura (JKMS), 141,
225–226, 228–230, 232–235
Korban Operation Manager (KOM),
229, 230
Korban Operation Regime, 224,
228, 229, 231, 234
Korban Review Committee, 225,
227
operation, 224, 225, 227, 228,
230–233, 235
overseas, 221, 235
price of animal, 233, 236
procurement, 225, 235
sea freight, 226
services, 221, 224, 225, 227,
229, 235
slaughtering, 221, 223, 224,
229–232, 234, 235
volunteers, 223, 224, 235
Korea, 207, 245, 247

Land Acquisition Act, 166, 169
Lembaga Biasiswa Kenangan Maulud
(LBKM), 75
Lee Hsien Loong, 90, 275, 279
Lee Kuan Yew, 133
Lembaga Tabung Haji (LTH), 183
LGBT, 286, 287
Lighthouse Evangelism Independent
Church, 277

MABIMS, 204, 243–245, 251
Humanitarian Project, 244
MABIMS Special Technical
Committee on Halal
Development, 206, 218
Youth Bus Expedition, 244
Youth Leadership Development,
244

madrasah, 1, 2, 7, 9, 34, 39, 43, 46–50,
76–78, 89–91, 93–100, 103, 104, 111,
122, 123, 174, 251, 266, 270
Board of Governors (BOG), 49, 100,
105
curriculum, 33, 92, 94, 97–102,
104, 266
Dana Madrasah, 96, 103
Edusave, 48, 90, 95, 106
enrolment, 91–94, 97, 101, 106
fees, 103, 104
graduates, 94, 242
Joint Committee of Madrasah
Education, 77
Joint Committee of Madrasah
(JCM), 98, 105
Joint Madrasah System (JMS), 9,
43, 44, 48, 49, 90, 91, 99–101,
105, 106, 266
Madrasah Al-Arabiah Al-Islamiah,
90, 92, 101
Madrasah Al-Iqbal Al-Islamiyyah,
92
Madrasah Al-Irsyad Al-Islamiah,
44, 48, 90–92, 97
Madrasah Aljunied Al-Islamiah,
90, 92–93, 96, 99, 101, 104–105,
242–243
Madrasah Al-Ma'arif Al-Islamiah,
90–93, 96, 99, 100
Madrasah Alsagoff Al-Arabiah,
90–92, 100
Madrasah As-Sibyan, 92
Madrasah Muhammadi, 22
Madrasah Wak Tanjong
Al-Islamiah, 90–92, 96, 100
principals, 39
Progress Fund Madrasah Assistance
Scheme (PROMAS), 104
students, 33, 48, 94, 97, 100–103,
107
teacher, 39, 48, 49, 95, 106
Magistrate's Courts, 21

Maintenance of Religious Harmony Bill, 260
Maintenance of Religious Harmony Act, 255, 256, 260, 277
Majlis, 24–30
    powers, 27, 29
    President, 25, 29
    Secretary, 29
Malay
    Malay aristocracy, 17
    Malay Peninsula, 8, 19, 21, 29
    Malay states, 20–22
    medium of instruction, 115, 116, 118, 124
    socio-economic status, 27
    vernacular school, 22
Malay/Muslim organisations (MMOs), 46, 49–51, 113, 223, 224, 226–229, 231, 234, 235
Malaysia, 3, 15, 26, 64, 74, 92, 183, 187, 189, 204–206, 232, 233, 236, 242–245, 269, 277
    Federal Constitution, 26
    Federation, 26
    Yang di-Pertuan Agong, 26
Maliki, 203, 284
maqasid, 67
Maria Hertogh riots, 258
Mas'aa, 187
Mashor Alwi, 74
maslaha, 63
Master Content Framework (MCF), 265
Mataf, 187
Maulana Muhammad Abdul Aleem Siddiqui, 257
Maulana Muhammad Abdul Aleem Siddiqui Memorial Lecture, 268
Mayo Street, 169
mazhab, 18, 67, 203, 204
MCollective, 271
Mecca, 131, 180, 181, 185, 187–189
Medina, 131, 185, 188
Mendaki, 3, 5, 76, 77, 95, 99

Mendaki Educational Congress, 95
Mendaki Religious Advisory Committee, 96
Religious Education Department, 76, 77, 96
Mercy Relief, 269
Mina, 187–189
Minister-in-charge of Muslim Affairs, 37, 76, 86, 107, 187, 278, 284
Minister of Labour and Law, 24
Ministry of Community Development (MCD), 153, 154
Ministry of Education (MOE), 33, 77, 97
Ministry of Health, 66
Ministry of National Development, 168
Ministry of Social and Family Development (MSF), 159
Ministry of Trade and Industry, 246
Mohamed Fatris Bakaram, 268
Mohammad Alami Musa, 41, 79, 244, 267
Mohammedan Advisory Board, 2, 25
Mohammedan and Hindu Endowment Board, 2, 20
Mohammedan and Hindu Endowment Ordinance, 20
Mohammedan Marriage Ordinance, 19, 20
Mohd Muzammil, 260
mosque, 2–3, 10, 19, 22–24, 27, 28, 36–41, 43, 45–50, 75, 81, 86, 111–125, 131–147, 152–154, 157, 158, 167–168, 172–174, 221, 223–235, 241, 245–246, 251, 256, 259, 263, 265, 266, 269, 276, 278, 279, 282, 283
    Abdul Hamid Kampung Pasiran Mosque, 173
    Administration of Mosque and Leadership (AMAL), 39
    Al-Ansar Mosque, 134, 174
    Al-Huda Mosque, 166
    Al-Mukminin Mosque, 174
    Al-Muttaqin Mosque, 134

An-Nur Mosque, 134, 174
Assyakirin Mosque, 134, 174
audit, 40
Ba'alwie Mosque, 259
Bencoolen Mosque, 45
building, 132–134, 136
Darul Ghufran Mosque, 174
Enhanced Mosque Cluster (EMC), 43, 44, 139–142, 144, 153, 156, 269
funds, 37
General Manager (GM), 139, 141
governance, 39
Haji Mohd Yusoff Mosque, 92
Haji Muhammad Salleh (Palmer Road) Mosque, 174
IT, 40
Kassim Mosque, 168
Mosque Building Fund (MBF), 133, 134, 136–137, 245, 251
Mosque Building and Mendaki Fund (MBMF), 3, 36, 103, 278, 288
mosque committee, 136
Mosque Convention, 48–49, 142, 144, 146
Mosque Executive Chairman (MEC), 38, 39, 48, 139, 140, 144
Mosque Management Board (MMB), 124, 139, 140
Mosque Officer Development Scheme (MODS), 39
Mosque Perception Survey, 48
Mosque Shared Services, 41
Mosque Upgrading Programme, 3
Muhajirin Mosque, 134
Mujahidin Mosque, 134
pegawai masjid, 24
Professional Executive Leadership (PEL) scheme, 139, 140, 143
properties, 174
Social Development Officers (SDO), 139, 158, 159

staff, 137, 140
Technical Advisory Panel (TAP), 135
volunteer, 137–138, 140–141
Movement for Affirmation of Pluralism, 271
Mufti, 1, 3, 22, 24, 25, 29, 37, 57–59, 65, 74, 86, 96, 256, 258, 259, 261
Muhammadiyah Association, 4, 5, 92, 105
Muis
Asatizah Network Strategic Unit, 47, 79
Audit Committee, 42
Chief Executive, 37
Distinguished Visitor Programme (DVP), 249
eHalal System, 209, 218
Empowerment Partnership Scheme, 50
Fitrah Committee, 42
governance, 40
Harmony Centre, 247
Information Systems Strategic Unit, 40
mission, 46
Mosque Strategic Unit, 40
Muis Academy, 47, 79, 245, 266
Muis Council, 37, 42, 185, 260
Office of the Mufti, 67
Pilgrimage Committee, 42, 185, 190, 193
Pilgrimage Review Committee (PRC), 184
powers, 96, 182, 186, 200, 261
President, 36, 37, 234, 267
Property Department, 170
Public Perception Survey, 50
Religious Education Department, 112
Religious Education Unit, 76, 77, 96
revenue streams, 50

services, 40
sponsorship, 39
staff, 36–38, 40, 41, 75, 141
stakeholders, 5, 6, 10, 42, 43, 47,
    51, 78, 131, 132, 242, 265, 276
statutory board, 3, 15
Student Career and Welfare Office
    (SCWO), 251
Student Resource and
    Development Secretariat (SRDS),
    79, 251
trust, 42, 52, 105, 276, 278, 285,
    287, 288
vision, 41, 78, 232
Musawah, 286
Muslim, 16, 20, 28, 57, 58, 62, 92,
    278
consumers, 200–203, 208, 209,
    211, 213, 214
converts, 24
death, 68, 70
divorce, 19, 20, 28
endowment, 20
estate, 59, 67– 69
families, 19
faraidh, 69
inheritance, 67, 68, 70
jurists, 59, 61, 64, 65, 68, 122
kidney patients, 66
law, 16, 19, 21–25, 28, 57–59, 62,
    67–69
marriage, 18–20, 28, 116, 278
middle class, 209, 280
migrant worker, 147
nation states, 58
polygamous marriage, 21
prayer times, 60
schools, 92
Shia, 284
Sunni, 284
Muslim Advisory Board, 2, 25, 26, 75
Muslim Endowment Board, 25
Muslimin Trust Fund Association, 26, 27

Muslim Judicial Council of South Africa,
    213
Muslim Welfare Association, 27
Muslim Youth Assembly (HBI), 284
Myanmar, 253

Nahdlatul Ulama (NU), 4
National Archives of Singapore, 2
National Computer Board, 40
National Council of Churches of
    Singapore (NCCS), 268
National Institute of Education (NIE),
    39, 99
national social assistance, 154
networks, 241, 242
    international, 11, 241, 246–250,
        252, 253
    progressive scholars, 250
    regional, 242, 243, 252
New Zealand, 205, 236, 247
North Bridge Road, 169, 173
nushuz, 28
nuzriah, 69

Ordinance to Provide for the Regulation
    and Control of Pilgrim Passenger
    Brokers, 181
Organisation of Islamic Conference
    (OIC), 243
Othman Wok, 28, 75, 76
Ottoman, 59
Overseas Pakistani League, 26

Palestine, 253
People's Action Party (PAP), 5
Pasuni Maulan, 74
PEACE, 50
Penal Code, 286
People's Association, 66
Perak State Council, 19
Perdaus, 77, 113, 269
Pergas (Singapore Islamic Scholars and
    Religious Teachers Association), 5,

9, 50, 75, 77–79, 80, 82–85, 98, 113, 190

Pertapis, 113

Peter Ho, 287

Philippines, 245, 280

Pink Dot SG, 287

porcine DNA, 205

Presidential Council for Religious Harmony, 260

Primary School Leaving Examinations (PSLE), 33, 49, 90, 98–100, 102
    aggregate, 91
    aggregate score, 33
    benchmark, 49, 90, 91, 99, 100

Prince of Wales, 247

Programme for RISEAP Members (PRISM), 245, 279

Prophet Muhammad, 123, 131, 201, 265

PS21, 41

Public Sector Transformation (PST), 51

Public Utilities Board, 41

Qadi, 18, 19, 21, 24

Qatar, 269

Quba Mosque, 131

Queen Victoria, 18

Qur'an, 2, 7, 64, 117, 212, 255, 259, 265

Rahmatan Lil Alamin (RLA) , 39, 269
    ethos, 39
    Foundation (RLAF), 39, 251, 256, 266
    Mosque Committee (RLAMC), 39

Rahmat Kenap, 75

Ramadan, 20, 60, 180, 259

Real Estate Investment Trust (REIT), 170, 175

Regional Islamic Da'wah Council of Southeast Asia and the Pacific (RISEAP), 245, 247, 279

Registry of Muslim Marriages (ROMM), 50

Religious Education Advisory Panel (REAP), 114

religious exclusivism, 87, 266, 271

religious radicalisation, 87, 126, 253, 262

Religious Rehabilitation Group (RRG), 263

Ridzwan Haji Dzafir, 167

risalah, 265

Rony Tan, 277

Roses of Peace, 271

Roy, Olivier, 250

Russia, 269

Sadiq Khan, 249

Safa and Marwa, 187

Saudi Arabia, 65, 180, 182, 187, 189, 193, 246

Saudi authority, 36

Sedition Act, 277

Selangor Legislative Assembly, 26

Select Committee, 8, 16, 25–29, 150, 260, 261

Syafi'i, 24, 204, 284

Shaikh Abdallah bin Bayyah, 250

Shaikh Syed Isa Mohd Semait, 74, 75, 256, 258–261, 270

Shaikh Muhammad Sayyid Tantawi, 250

Sheikh Mohammed bin Rashid Al Makhtoum Islamic Finance Award, 45, 171

Sheikh Muhammad Fadhlullah Suhaimi, 73, 92

Sheikh Omar Bamadhaj, 92

Sheikh Zaki Badawi, 266

Sheriffa Zain Mohamed Alsagoff, 165

Shipping Act, 182

Shisha, 188, 189

Sidek Saniff, 76, 77

Singapore
    ageing population, 190, 281, 282, 288
    Attorney General, 16, 26, 258

colonial government, 2
Constitution, 15
economy, 280
governance, 34, 35
government, 33
independence, 2, 5, 15–17, 92, 131, 143, 150, 270, 277
Legislative Assembly, 20, 24, 25
merger, 92
National Day Rally, 33, 89, 90
national social assistance, 43, 153–156, 158–161
Parliament, 15, 28
political leadership, 35
post-independence, 34, 73, 74, 135, 166
President, 37, 249, 260
public service, 34, 35
separation, 74
Singapore Quality Award (SQA), 42
Singapore Stock Exchange, 169
social cohesion, 11, 256, 258–263, 267, 270, 271, 277
Social Welfare Department, 25
urban renewal plan, 169
Yang di-Pertuan Negara, 24
Singapore Buddhist Federation, 268
Singapore Business Advisors and Consultants Council (SBACC), 210, 219
Singapore Muslim Identity (SMI), 7, 79, 247, 264–266
Singapore Muslim League, 26
social media, 252, 253, 284
Social Service Office (SSO), 160
South Indian Jamiathul Ulama, 27
Spain, 248, 269
Specialist Diploma in Education, 39
SPRING Singapore, 210, 219
Sri Lanka, 245, 247, 269
State Advocate General, 24, 26
Sternberg, Sigmund, 266
Straits Settlement, 17
Student Liaison Officers (SLOs), 251

sukuk musyarakah, 45, 171
Sultan Hussein Shah, 17
suraus, 22
Syariah, 170, 229
Syariah Court, 2, 20, 21, 24, 28, 50
Syed Abdillah Aljufri, 73, 75
Syed Hussein Alatas, 64
Syed Ibrahim Omar Alsagoff, 258, 259
Syed Muhammad Bin Syed Salim Al-Attas, 259
Syed Sheikh Ahmad Al-Hadi, 92

Tabung Amal Aidilftri, 50
Tabung Haji, 183, 189, 190
Taiwan, 245
Tariq Ramadan, 250
tauliah, 20
Temenggong Abdul Rahman, 17
TFK Corporation, 251
Thailand, 205, 245
Tharman Shanmugaratnam, 50
Three Faiths Forum, 266
Tok Kenali, 22
Tony Tan, 249
Turkey, 100, 251

ulama, 1, 27
Ulama Council of Indonesia (MUI), 4
ummah, 256, 270
umrah, 186, 190
United Kingdom (UK), 100, 182, 248, 249, 251, 266
United Malays National Organisation, 27
USA, 117, 205, 236, 248, 251, 280

Vietnam, 280

wakaf, 1, 2, 10, 26, 27, 44, 50, 59, 103, 165–176, 241, 250, 251, 278, 288
  beneficiaries, 167, 170–172, 175
  cash *wakaf*, 169, 171, 175
  properties, 37, 44, 59, 165–168, 170–172, 176

Property Department, 172
Red House project, 174
trustees, 165, 166, 176
Wakaf Abdul Hamid, 168
Wakaf Al-Huda, 166, 173
Wakaf Bencoolen, 45
Wakaf Development Committee, 168–169, 175
Wakaf Ilmu, 103
Wakaf Jabbar, 168
Wakaf Kassim, 168
Wakaf Sheriffa Zain, 166, 174
Wakaf Raja Siti Kraeng, 173
Wakaf YAL Saif Charity Trust, 173
Warees Halal Limited, 206, 207, 209
Warees Investments Pte Ltd, 45, 171–175, 206, 210, 218
Wear White movement, 287
Williams, Rowan, 250, 267
Wisma Indah, 168
Work Improvement Teams (WITS), 41
World Organisation for Animal Health (OIE), 222, 223, 228–230

Yaacob Ibrahim, 107, 284
Yaacob Mohamed, 25
Yeo Hiap Seng, 36, 199

zakat, 1, 10, 19, 23–27, 29, 36, 50, 81, 93, 96, 103, 104, 139, 149, 150–160, 162, 180, 241, 245, 251, 278, 279, 281, 288
    collection, 36, 93, 150–152, 160, 278, 279
    disbursement, 10, 153, 154, 156, 160
    distribution, 151
    financial assistance (FA), 39, 46, 104, 141, 153–154, 156–158, 160–161
    management, 150–152, 156, 158, 160–161, 245
    payers, 40
    recipients, 39, 43, 46, 139
    services, 152–153, 158
Zulhijjah, 180, 189, 198